Research Materials
in
South Carolina

Research Materials
in
South Carolina

A Guide

Compiled and edited for the
South Carolina State Library Board

by John Hammond Moore, Ph.D.

With the cooperation of the
South Carolina Library Association

UNIVERSITY OF SOUTH CAROLINA PRESS • 1967
Columbia, S. C.

FOREWORD

This book is another step in the State Library Board's program to improve reference service at both state and local levels and to realize a coordinated network of library service throughout the state. The listings of specialized library resources, holdings of newspapers, periodical collections, and subject collections is a first attempt in this state to produce a bibliographic tool through which the specialized reader can locate available subject material and individual periodical and newspaper titles held by all South Carolina libraries. Noteworthy are the sections dealing with the historical collections in the South Caroliniana Library at the University of South Carolina and the holdings of the South Carolina Archives Department: these two listings are the most extensive and complete published compilations of the state's official archival records as well as the state's most significant collection of historical materials.

Dr. John Hammond Moore assumed the labor of compiling the vast amount of information contained here, and he has received exemplary cooperation and help from numerous librarians in public, special, and college and university libraries throughout the state in making this book the excellent bibliographical tool that it is. *Research Materials in South Carolina* is a credit to Dr. Moore's diligence and scholarship; but it is also a source of pride for those librarians both past and present who through the years and in divers libraries over the state have collected and developed the materials listed in it.

The publication of this important study is the result of a cooperative project of the South Carolina State Library Board and of the South Carolina Library Association.

ESTELLENE P. WALKER
Director
South Carolina State Library Board

PREFACE

Much of the travel necessary to writing this book was aided by grants from Winthrop College and the South Carolina State Library Board. The State Library Board and the South Carolina Library Association have together given major aid to the publication of this survey. But because of its very nature this book is really a creation of hundreds, even thousands, of South Carolinians. Many busy editors have taken the time to complete questionnaires and return them to me; there are many people who personally guided me through comfortable old museums and sparkling new industrial plants; and scores of overworked librarians have answered scores upon scores of queries. I find it impossible to single out any individual for special praise; rather I would like to thank everyone, to express hereby my sincerest gratitude to all the many kind people who have so generously and cheerfully helped.

JOHN HAMMOND MOORE

Georgia State College
Atlanta, Georgia

November 21, 1966

CONTENTS

INTRODUCTION

Before you is the result of a one-man survey, possessing all the disadvantages as well as whatever advantages may inhere in such a work. The information contained here was gathered during the years from 1963 to 1965, and it is a first attempt to examine South Carolina's libraries, magazines, newspapers ,historical societies, and museums in a way that will quickly show what one may expect to find on the shelves or in the files of a given institution. Accuracy has been a goal but by the very nature of the task has not been fully realized: names of publications and institutions change; libraries are daily making new acquisitions. This is not, then, a complete list of all holdings; it is merely a guide, and hopefully it will help all those who wish to make use of the research materials in South Carolina.

ORGANIZATION OF THE BOOK

The material is divided into two parts; at the beginning of each of these parts will be found a list of symbols and abbreviations used in it as well as sample entries to familiarize the reader with the method of description.

Part One contains entries for both public and private libraries throughout South Carolina, information concerning files in newspaper and magazine offices, and data on the holdings of numerous historical societies, historical commissions, and museums. These entries are arranged alphabetically under the names of the towns where the various institutions are located. To aid in finding the name of a given town there are key words at the top of each page: that at the top of the left-hand page indicates the first town for which there are listings on that page; the key word at the top of the right-hand page indicates the last town for which there are discussions there.

In addition to this alphabetic list of towns and institutions in South Carolina, there is appended on pages 179–80 a short list of periodicals that are of significant importance for this state but that are published outside of it. There is also an index of subjects for Part One only; this will be found following page 332.

Part Two is a list of periodical files, serials, and continuations begun prior to 1941. (For some files begun since 1941, especially of technical journals, look under the individual library entries in Part One.) Titles are listed alphabetically. Following each title is a list of abbreviations and dates indicating all the libraries in the state that have pre-1941 files of the title and the years of each library's holdings. The system used is similar to that in the *Union List of Serials in Libraries of the United States and Canada*, published by the H. W. Wilson Company.

Nearly all libraries in the state agree on what a popular magazine is, but serials, continuations, and even some periodicals fall into a "gray" area where there is considerable confusion. Some South Carolina libraries maintain separate catalogs for such items, and some do not. Thus these pages in Part Two undoubtedly omit some listings because of the nature of files in individual libraries. However at least three of the major libraries in South Carolina—Clemson University, Winthrop College, and The Citadel—circulated guides to their periodical-serial holdings in 1964. While these guides differ in format and style, each is extremely helpful. Clemson's forty-nine-page booklet lists all titles being received as of September 1964. The Winthrop and Citadel publications specify the years covered by various collections and also cite files of many magazines no longer published.

Scholars and students interested in the files of recent magazines (1952+) should remember that the South Carolina State Library Board has an extensive collection of technical and popular publications on microfilm. These may be borrowed on interlibrary loan through local libraries in the state (see pp. 52–55).

ADDITIONAL AIDS TO RESEARCH

All too frequently the high-school student or the college undergraduate bypasses his local library in favor of a trip to Columbia, just as the graduate student and the professor tend to seek out archives in Chapel Hill, Durham, or Washington. Very often the information each is looking for can be found much, much closer to home.

As of September 1964 selected documents of the United States government were available in South Carolina at the following libraries:

Charleston	Charleston College Library
	The Citadel Library
Clemson	Clemson University Library
Columbia	South Carolina State Library
	University of South Carolina Library
Greenville	Furman University Library
Orangeburg	South Carolina State College Library
Rock Hill	Winthrop College Library

Every government publication, of course, cannot be consulted at these depositories, since each library selects the classes of publications of interest to its particular clientele.

In addition to sources such as the *South Carolina Historical Magazine, Checklist of South Carolina State Publications,* and *Proceedings of the South Carolina Historical Association* which are cited in these pages, those interested in South Carolina's past may wish to consult these publications:

David Duncan Wallace, *History of South Carolina,* 4 vols. (New York: American Historical Society, 1934): this standard history is very heavily weighted with pre-1860 material and is filled with the personal bias of Dr. Wallace, yet it is undoubtedly the best work in its field; a short, one-volume edition with a useful bibliography was published by the University of North Carolina Press in 1951 and reprinted by the University of South Carolina Press in 1961.

Ernest McPherson Lander, Jr., *A History of South Carolina, 1865–1960* (Chapel Hill: University of North Carolina Press, 1960): this is a brief but penetrating analysis of the state's last century; there is a fine selected bibliography.

Robert J. Turnbull, *Bibliography of South Carolina, 1563–1950,* 6 vols. (Charlottesville: University of Virginia Press, 1956): this is an invaluable guide to published South Carolina material.

South Carolina Bibliographies: this is a series of publications by the Historical Commission of South Carolina and the South

Carolina Archives Department from 1949 on; it includes guides to the study and reading of South Carolina history (topical and classified lists) by J. H. Easterby, a guide to articles on South Carolina literature and related subjects (1900–1955) by Hennig Cohen, and the annual *Checklist of South Carolina State Publications* (cited previously) compiled by Joan Reynolds Faunt and others since 1950.

South Carolina: A Guide to the Palmetto State (New York: Oxford University Press, 1941): this WPA guide contains material of interest to both visitor and native; and although somewhat dated, it has a good general bibliography.

George Brown Tindall, *South Carolina Negroes, 1877–1900* (Columbia: University of South Carolina Press, 1952; repr. Baton Rouge: Louisiana State University Press, 1966): this excellent study of life in this state during the late 19th century has recently been supplemented by Joel R. Williamson's *After Slavery: the Negro in South Carolina During Reconstruction, 1861–1877* (Chapel Hill: University of North Carolina Press, 1965).

Yearbooks of the City of Charleston: published by the municipal government (1880–1951), these annual reports on city life frequently contain a wealth of information in unusual appendices; a fragmentary index exists, but until a more useful guide is compiled, the full value of these volumes will not be realized.

PART ONE

Libraries, Archives, and Publishers' Files

SYMBOLS AND ABBREVIATIONS
USED IN PART ONE

( )	Incomplete file of a magazine or newspaper for the years indicated. Parentheses are also used, especially in relation to manuscript holdings, to express birth-death dates of important individuals.
+	Indicates with a library entry that the library continues to receive a publication; but with a magazine or newspaper entry, that the publication continues to publish.
A	Annual
ARP	Associate Reformed Presbyterian
CMPC	Carolina Materials Project Collection (see pp. 55–61).
CP	Current periodicals, indicates approximate number a library is receiving.
CSA	Confederate States of America
CW	Civil War
D	Daily
DAR	Daughters of the American Revolution
M	Monthly
Mann	Microfilms available from Mann Film Laboratories, Inc., Winston-Salem, N. C.
MC, mc	Microcard
MCR	Microcard reader
MFM, mfm	Microfilm
MFMR	Microfilm reader
Micro Photo	Microfilms available from Recordak Corp., Cleveland, Ohio

MRP	Microreader printer
PCE	Photocopy equipment
Q	Quarterly
R	Reference
r	Reproduced by some technique other than microfilm, microcard, or microprint; usually refers to a typed item in a manuscript collection.
re	Relative to, relating to
RW	Revolutionary War
SC	South Carolina, South Caroliniana
SCHM	*South Carolina Historical Magazine*
UDC	United Daughters of the Confederacy
US	United States
US GOVT DOC	United States Government Documents Depository
V	Volumes of Books
v	Usually refers to manuscript material which a depository classifies as a "volume."
vr	A manuscript volume reproduced by some technique other than microfilm, microcard, or microprint; usually applies to a typewritten manuscript.
W	Weekly
WPA	Works Progress Administration
WW	World War, I or II as indicated.

SAMPLE ENTRIES

Anderson Junior College Library
  V 9,000 R 600 CP 100

[This indicates a college library with 9,000 books. Six hundred of these are classified as reference material. The library is currently receiving 100 periodicals.]

Safety Journal—M 1950+

[This is a monthly publication which has files dating from 1950 at its offices.]

Barnwell People-Sentinel—W (1885–1910) 1910+
Also has files of *Edisto News* 1961+ and *Williston Way* 1961+.

[This is a weekly newspaper which has random back copies from 1885 to 1910 and a complete file from that date. At these offices one may also consult files of both the *Edisto News* and the *Williston Way* from 1961 to the present.]

Beaufort County Library
  V 30,000 R 1,000 SC 300 CP 40 MFMR PCE

[This library has approximately 30,000 books. Of these about 1,000 are reference and 300 relate specifically to South Carolina. The library is currently receiving some forty periodicals and has both a microfilm reader and photocopy equipment.]

News & Courier—D [mfm] 1873+
  Micro Photo MFMR
Also has *Daily Courier* [mfm] 1803–73 Micro Photo.

[This is a daily newspaper available on microfilm at the newspaper's offices from 1873 to the present. The film is being produced by Micro Photo and a reader can be used at the offices. Copies of the

News & Courier's predecessor are also available on microfilm by Micro Photo as indicated.]

Aiton, Thomas [44]. Abbeville, Edgefield, CW. 1839, 1861–64.

[This manuscript entry indicates 44 original items relating to Abbeville, Edgefield, and the Civil War for the dates shown.]

Eddings Family [vr]. Edisto Island genealogy. 1940.

[This is a one-volume genealogy, probably typed, and compiled in 1940.]

Fairey, F. W. (1823–95) [1,560, 14v]. Branchville, Charleston, and Orangeburg legal and business papers. 1828–91.

[According to this entry there is a substantial manuscript collection of over 1,500 original items and 14 separate volumes relating to F. W. Fairey and the areas indicated from 1828 to 1891. It is, of course, not always possible to cite birth-death dates as is done here, nor is it always advisable to cite inclusive dates for a collection. However, wherever possible such dates are shown.]

Frierson, David E. (1818–96) [271, v, 48 mfm]. Presbyterian theological notes and sermons, some material on microfilm. 1839–96.

[This collection consists of 271 original items, one volume, and 48 additional items on microfilm for the years 1839 to 1896.]

Fitzsimmons, Christopher [2v, also mfm]. Charleston letterbooks and business correspondence. 1799–1813.

[This material, consisting of two original volumes for the years indicated, may be consulted in the original form or on microfilm.]

ALPHABETIC LIST OF TOWNS AND INSTITUTIONS

ABBEVILLE

Abbeville Press & Banner—W 1930+

Files 1846+ on loan to Erskine College Library, Due West.

Abbeville Public Library
  V 3,000   R 25   CP 5

AIKEN

Aiken-Bamberg-Barnwell-Edgefield Regional Library
  V 86,785   R 3,081   SC 1,313   CP 213   MFMR   PCE   CMPC
The collection of this regional library includes (at Aiken) John Tobler's account of German-Swiss emigrants in South Carolina (1837), WPA inventories of local records, miscellaneous papers of the Aiken Historical Society, data re the Savannah River Plant, and files of the *Aiken Standard & Review* 1953+. Files of the *Barnwell People-Sentinel* 1877+ are at the Barnwell County Library. The Edgefield County Library has an unusually extensive collection re local and state history. Its holdings include *War of the Rebellion,* copies of many SC state records, and volumes from the libraries of such distinguished area families as Gary, Calhoun, Brooks, and Tillman. The John R. Abney Collection (c. 5,000v) is rich in works dealing with English, French, and American life, 1600–1900. In addition to early 19th century encyclopedias and numerous 18th-cent. histories of England, this library has *Congressional Debates, Globe, and Record* (1780–1920), *Gentleman's Magazine* 1730–1824, *Société des Antiquaires du Normandie, Mémoires,* 1824–36, and files of the *Edgefield Advertiser* 1838–73, 1917+, [mfm] 1836–1900, and of the *Edgefield Chronicle* 1890–1917.

Aiken Standard & Review—D 1930+

7

Mayfields

Estate of Colonel John A. May, Chairman of the South Carolina Confederate War Centennial Commission. An outstanding collection of memorabilia including local Indian relics, colonial and 19th-cent. artifacts, and CW items.

Savannah River Plant News—W 1953+

House organ of E. I. du Pont de Nemours & Co., Inc.

Technical Information Service Library, Savannah River Laboratory (du Pont)
  V 12,000 CP 500 MCR MFMR MRP PCE

This is a technical-reference library which, while its holdings are restricted to plant personnel and to visitors having official business with the US Atomic Energy Commission, does make its resources available through standard inter-library loan procedures. Collections include *ASM Review of Metal Literature* 1944+, *Nuclear Science Abstracts* 1948+, and *Savannah River Plant News* 1953+.

University of South Carolina, Aiken County Center Library
  V 2,000 CP 75

ALLENDALE

Allendale County Citizen—W 1947+

Also publishes *Hampton County Guardian* but keeps no back files.

Allendale County News—W 1943+

Keeps no back files.

Allendale-Hampton-Jasper Regional Library
  V 41,770 R 800 SC 150 CP 24

Library has bound copies of the *Hampton County Guardian* 1949–60.

Salkehatchie Regional Campus (U.S.C.) Library
  V 2,400 R 536 SC 20 CP 58

ANDERSON

Anderson County Courthouse, Law Library
  V 3,500

Anderson County Library
  V 59,625   R 2,529   SC 728   CP 95   MFMR   PCE
Library has a special collection of books on gardening (c. 240v)
and back files of these newspapers: *Anderson Daily Mail* [mfm]
1945–49, *Anderson Independent* [mfm] 1944+, *Anderson Intelligencer* [mfm] (1860–1916), and *Anderson Record* 1932–35.

Anderson Daily Mail—D 1899+

Anderson Free Press—W 1952+

Anderson Hospital, School of Nursing Library
  V 940   CP 15

Anderson Independent—D 1924+, [mfm] 1944+
  Micro Photo
Has random copies of the weekly *Anderson Intelligencer.*

Anderson Junior College Library
  V 9,000   R 600   CP 100

Anderson Post Office, Judge's Library
  V 1,873

National Stamp News—(issued three times per month) 1948+
Official publication of the National Philatelic Society.

Safety Journal—M 1950+
Accident prevention journal.

BAMBERG

Bamberg Herald—W 1906+
Has some copies of the *Sumter Daily Item* (1890s).

BARNWELL

Barnwell People-Sentinel—W (1885–1910) 1910+

Also has files of *Edisto News* 1961+ and *Williston Way* 1961+.

BATESBURG

Lexington County Circulating Library

V 47,300   R 1,400   SC 450   CP 40   MFMR   PCE

Collection contains considerable material re local history, minutes of Batesburg Woman's Club 1910+, the original radio script of of "Palmetto Landmarks" (1946–48), and back files of these newspapers: Batesburg *Twin-City News* 1935+, *West Columbia Journal* 1958+, and the *Lexington Dispatch News* 1949+.

Twin City News—W (1927–30) 1931+

BATH

South Carolina Voter—Q 1951+

Publication of the League of Women Voters of South Carolina.

BEAUFORT

Beaufort County Library

V 30,000   R 1,000   SC 300   CP 40   MFMR   PCE

Collection includes copies of 36 unpublished papers on area history prepared for the Beaufort Historical Society, *Beaufort Library Society Catalog (1802–62)*, copies of the SC Census of 1790 and the US Census of 1880, and back files of these newspapers: *Beaufort Gazette* 1904+, *Beaufort Republican* [mfm] 1871–74 (these reels contain random copies of the *Port Royal Commercial, Beaufort Times* 1944–45, and *Port Royal Palmetto Post* 1882–97). The library also has bound copies of the *Palmetto Post* 1895–97. Manuscript holdings include records of Beaufort College [v] 1795–1867, *Beaufort Benevolent Society* [5v] 1814–1925, Beaufort Female Seminary [2v] 1852–1935, register of St. Helena's Parish [2v] 1823–1911, journals of John Edwin Fripp (a local businessman) [2v] 1817, 1856–58, 1895–1900, and diaries of Mrs. Susan Rice [11v] 1890–1910.

Beaufort Gazette—W 1946+

United States Marine Corps Air Station Library
 V 11,000 R 250 CP 65
Library has special collections in electronics, guerrilla warfare, and naval aviation. This library cooperates closely with libraries at Parris Island and the Naval Hospital.

United States Naval Hospital Library
 V 7,000 R 3,000 CP 115
Library contains books in these three fields: general, medical, and administrative-legal. Some 60 medical journals are received and files retained 1950+.

University of South Carolina Center Library
 V 3,000 CP 25

BELTON

Belton News—W 1925+

BENNETTSVILLE

Marlboro County Public Library
 V 21,276 R 225 SC 425 CP 23
Collection includes substantial pamphlet and manuscript material re local history. Among these items are letters and papers of Frank H. Covington (1837–94); "Recording Scribe's Book," Sons of Temperance #45, Bennettsville Division (1869–81); Colonel C. W. Dudley, "History of Bennettsville" (1878); "Abstracts & Funeral Notices from the Day Book of Rev. J. A. W. Thomas" (1865–96); D. D. McColl, "Sketches of Old Marlboro" (1916); J. P. Gibson, "Resources of Marlboro County" (1902) and "A Mirror of Bennettsville & Marlboro County" (1913); and the muster rolls of Marlboro soldiers (1812–15). There is also historical data on the following churches: Beauty Spot, Great Pee Dee Presbyterian, Salem Baptist, Bethel, First Presbyterian, Brownsville Baptist, Blenheim Presbyterian, Thomas Memorial Baptist, the Pee Dee Baptist Association, and the Sunday Schools of the Methodist Church. Genealogical material re Henegan, Rogers, Reid, Kolb, Newton, and other local families

can also be found in these holdings. The library has an area scrapbook (1934+), files of material in music and gardening, and copies of these newspapers: *Pee Dee Advocate* 1928–51, *Marlboro County Herald* 1928–51, and *Marlboro County Herald-Advocate* 1951+. A collection of DAR material is housed in the Clerk of Court's Office, Marlboro County Courthouse.

Marlboro Herald-Advocate—W 1951+

Also has files of the *Marlboro County Herald* 1931–51, which merged with *Pee Dee Advocate* in 1951.

BISHOPVILLE

Lee County Messenger—W 1920+

Copies of the *Leader & Vindicator—W* 1902–20, predecessor of the *Messenger,* are at the offices of the Lee County Treasurer.

Woodward Memorial Library
   V 12,472   R 206   SC 179   CP 27

Holdings include several papers and scrapbooks on local history, a *Memoir of Rev. James Jenkins* (1842), WPA inventory of Lee County archives, and a small collection deposited by the Lee County Historical Commission.

CALHOUN FALLS

Calhoun Falls News—W (1955–61) 1961+

CAMDEN

Camden City Library
   V 20,000   R 1,500   SC 200   CP 40

Collection includes account books of Cantey & Henry of Charleston (1796–1800), minutes of the Camden Library (1915–46), Robert Mills's atlas of folio maps, *Sermons of John Tillotson* (c. 1665), and these newspapers: *Camden Chronicle* 1928–30; *National Intelligencer* (Washington, D. C.) 1811–12; and *Port Folio* (Philadelphia) 1803–5.

Camden Chronicle—W 1914+

Kershaw County Library
  V 38,382   R 510   SC 482   CP 20

Kershaw County Memorial Hospital, School of Practical Nursing
    Library
  V 580   CP 5

May Plant (Du Pont) Technical Library
  V 1,000   R 100   PCE
A technical-reference collection of company reports, research materials and notes, abstracts, and files of patents and technical correspondence. Because of the highly specialized nature of these holdings this library is not open to the public. Among the technical resources on file is the *Applied Science & Technology Index* 1953+.

May Times—M 1950+

Employee publication of the May Plant, E. I. du Pont de Nemours & Co., Inc.

CAYCE

Living In South Carolina—M 1950+

Formerly *South Carolina Electric Co-op News.*

CENTRAL

Central Wesleyan Junior College Library
  V 14,000   R 1,500   CP 170
Holdings include *Chemical Abstracts* 1961+.

CHARLESTON

Alumni News: Magazine of the Association of Citadel Men—Q
  1942+

Auxiliary News—Q 1935+

Published by the Woman's Auxiliary to the South Carolina Medical Association.

Brigadier—(semimonthly except summer) 1924+
Citadel student newspaper.

Catholic Banner—W 1953+
Official publication of the Roman Catholic Diocese of Charleston.

Charleston County Courthouse, County Bar Library
   V 1,000

Charleston County Library
   V 166,224   R 14,600   SC 2,500   CP 225   MCR   MFMR   MRP
   PCE

Holdings include WPA scrapbooks, a local clipping file, copies of early area wills and miscellaneous records (1671–1868), an index to the [*Charleston*] *News & Courier* 1931+, numerous technical guides and indexes, and files of these newspapers:

Charleston Evening Post 1941+, [mfm] 1945+
[*Charleston*] *News & Courier* 1931+, [mfm] 1945+
Folly Beachcomber (1960–61)
James Island News (1961–62)
New York Times [mfm] 1948+
North Charleston Banner 1960+
Tri-City Times 1963
West Ashley Journal 1961–64

Charleston Evening Post—D [mfm] 1894+
   Micro Photo   MFMR

Charleston Library Society
   V 72,300   CP 97   MFMR

Established in 1748, this private library has a substantial collection of reference material re life in SC, especially the Low Country. There are unusual holdings in 18th-cent. literature, history, science, and travel. Manuscript material includes miscellaneous letters, diaries, and account books. Among these are letters of John C. Calhoun [18] 1844–50, Wade Hampton III [25] 1898–1900, John Rutledge [25] 1780–82, and George Washington [8] 1789–98. Other manuscripts include the minute books of the Carolina Rifle Club [4v] 1869–91, Charleston tax records [19v] 1859–75, and copies of SC land grants [2vr] 1735–52. There are also special collections of

Huguenot material (1600–1800), data on the history of the Episcopal Church in the Charleston area, and letters of the Amory family. Library holdings contain selected US Government documents, an extensive pamphlet collection, SC almanacs (1750–1812), and an unusually fine file of original and microfilmed newspapers. Special microfilm material includes an index to the *South Carolina Gazette* 1732–38, minutes of numerous local churches [9 reels], *Charleston City Directories* (1794+) [9 reels], and *Records of the British Public Record Office Relating to South Carolina* (1663–1782) [6 reels with general index]. The Library has microfilmed and has for sale 12 reels [Micro Photo] of 18th-cent. South Carolina newspapers (1732–82):

South Carolina Gazette 1732–75
Gazette of the State of South Carolina 1777–80
South Carolina Gazette and Country Journal 1765–75
Charleston Gazette 1778–80
South Carolina Weekly Gazette 1758–64
South Carolina and American General Gazette 1764–81
Royal South Carolina Gazette 1780–82
Royal Gazette 1781–82

In cooperation with the *[Charleston] News & Courier* this library has also microfilmed and has for sale 116 reels [Micro Photo] of the *Charleston [Daily] Courier* 1803–73. The library has recently completed microfilming the *Charleston Mercury,* 1822–45 [Micro Photo]. Newspaper files (in addition to microfilm material already cited) include:

Carolina Gazette (1801–2) 1810–24 (1827–28) 1838–40
Charleston American (1916–17)
Charleston [Daily] Courier 1803–73
Charleston Daily News 1866–73
Charleston Daily Standard 1853–55
Charleston Evening Gazette (1785–86)
Charleston Evening News (1845–56)
Charleston Evening Post 1894+, [mfm] 1905–15, 1949+
Charleston Journal of Commerce (1876–78)
Charleston Mercury 1823–64 (1865–68)
Charleston Morning Post 1786–87
[Charleston] News & Courier 1873+, [mfm] 1949+
Charleston Times (1800–21)
City Gazette (1788–1833), [mfm] 1789
Columbian Herald (1784–96)
Georgetown Gazette 1798–1800, 1825–26
Investigator (1812)
Pendleton Messenger (1828–32)

15

Rambler (1843–44)
Royal Gazette (1781–82)
South Carolina and American General Gazette 1766–72, 1774–81
South Carolina Gazette 1733–57, 1758–75 (1777–1801)
South Carolina Gazette and Country Journal 1765–75
South Carolina Gazette and Public Advertiser 1784–86
South Carolina State Gazette and General Advertiser 1783–85
South Carolina Weekly Gazette 1783–84
Southern Patriot (1819–48)
Southern Standard (1852–53)
States Rights and Free Trade Evening Post 1831–34
Sun [Charleston, S. C.] (1850–51), 1887
Sunday Budget (1887–88)
Virginia Gazette [mfm] 1736–80
Weekly Ledger [Schuylkill Haven, Pa.] (1853–54)
Weekly World and Sunday Budget (1889–90)
Winyaw Intelligencer [Georgetown, S. C.] 1825, 1827, 1832–33
World [Charleston, S. C.] 1888–91
World and Sunday Budget (1888–91)
World and Sunday Budget and Weekly World 1888–89

Charleston Museum Library

V 20,000   SC 1,000   CP 100

This is primarily a staff research library specializing in art, science, and natural history. Collections include the papers of some SC naturalists; the Elephant Folio Edition of Audubon's *Birds of America* (complete) 1832–40 and Catesby's *Natural History of Carolina* 1732–38; publications of numerous scientific societies, art museums, divisions of the US government, and the Smithsonian Institution; geological surveys of several Eastern states; *War of the Rebellion;* and some 50 vols. of late 18th- and early 19th-cent. music. Museum leaflets published since 1930 include (some are now out of print): *Seasonal List of South Carolina Birds* (various editions), *History of the Charleston Museum, List of South Carolina Reptiles, Rediscovery of Squilla Negecta Gibbes, A New Grackle from Florida, Neopanope Texana Nigrodigita Rathbun, Pinnixa Lunzi Glassell and Xanthidae of the Carolinas, Notes on Callianassa Major Say, Hayden & Gragg—Jewellers of Charleston, Frogs and Toads of South Carolina, A New Amphipod of the Genus Crangonyx from South Carolina, A New Crayfish from South Carolina, The Heyward-Washington House Garden, A New Fresh-Water Amphipod from South Carolina and a New Subterranean Amphipod from Florida, Ferns of the Vicinity of Charleston, A New Amphipod of the Genus Corophium from Florida, Charleston Garden Plats, Carolina Shrimps of the Genus Eusicyonia, Building a Church on the Santee—1804–7, The Amphipod Genus Photis on the East Coast of North America, The Heyward-Washington House, Thomas Elfe—Charleston Cabinet-Maker, The Relationships and Nomenclature of the Soft-Shelled Turtles (Genus Trionyx) of the Southeastern United States.*

MANUSCRIPTS—Total holdings include 2,000 letters and papers, 1722–1930. Among the correspondents are John James Audubon [111] 1833–71; John Bachman and his family [238] 1834–1916; William Drayton [4v] 1782–86; Lewis R. Gibbes [49] 1843–85; Benjamin N. Martin, Daniel S. Martin, and their families [440] 1831–1915; Edmund Ravenel [139] 1831–61; Henry W. Ravenel [210] 1850–89; and Arthur Trezevant Wayne [872, v] 1894–1930.

Citadel Library

V 90,000   R 7,000   CP 460   MCR   MFMR   MRP   PCE   US GOVT DOC

Holdings include some 50 CW letters of Ellison Capers to his wife, a rare book room housing SC material, college records, and a memorial museum. The papers of General Mark Clark are to be deposited here. Microfilm materials include: *Charleston Courier* 1803–73, *Charleston [Daily] Courier* (1873), *[Charleston] News & Courier* 1873+, *New York Times* 1930+, Sears Roebuck & Company Catalogs (1888–89) 1892+, and *Wall Street Journal* 1944+.

Citadel Monographs—(occasionally) 1961+

Published by the faculty of the Citadel.

College of Charleston Library

V 43,000   CP 200   MFMR   PCE   US GOVT DOC

This library has unusual holdings of local newspapers [216v], a substantial file of 18th- and 19th-cent. pamphlets and almanacs, numerous folio vols. of classical literature, 19th-cent. records of the South Carolina National Bank [15v], and a collection of 19th-cent. religious works. Microfilm materials include *Records of the British Public Record Office Relating to South Carolina* (1663–1782) [6 reels with general index], 18th-cent. papers of the Society for the Propagation of the Faith [7 reels], and the 18th-cent. SC newspaper collection [12 reels]. Newspaper files not cited above include:

17

Charleston [Daily] Courier 1803–53 (1854–59)
Charleston Evening News (1849)
Charleston Mercury [and Morning Advertiser] (1822–62)
[Charleston] News & Courier [mfm] 1945+
City Gazette [and Daily Advertiser, Commercial Daily Advertiser, etc.] (1787–1833)
Columbian Herald and General Advertiser [New Daily Advertiser] (1793–96)
Investigator (1812–13)
State Gazette of South Carolina [City Gazette, South Carolina State Gazette, State Gazette and Timothy and Mason's Daily Advertiser, etc.] (1790–1802)
Southern Patriot (1826–44)
Southern Patriot and Commercial Advertiser (1815–24)
States Rights and Free Trade Evening Post 1831–33
Times 1803

College of Charleston News-Letter—(3 times per year) 1950+

Crusader—M 1962+

Publication of the Diocesan Catholic Youth Organization.

Dalcho Historical Society of the Protestant Episcopal Church in South Carolina, Library & Archives

V 1,500

This general religious library at the South Carolina Diocesan Headquarters contains publications of the Dalcho Historical Society 1953+ and numerous church records, especially of Low-Country South Carolina. This collection includes the *Historical Magazine of the Protestant Episcopal Church* 1949+, *Journals* of annual conventions of the Protestant Episcopal Church in South Carolina 1829+, and various minutes and registers of these parishes and churches: St. Matthew's, Prince Frederick-Winyah, St. Helena, St. Stephen's & St. John's-Berkeley, St. Stephen's Chapel, St. John's-Colleton, St. James Santee, Christ Church, St. Andrew's, St. Luke's of Charleston, St. Thomas & St. Dennis, Church of the Messiah-North Santee, and Claremont Parish of Stateburg.

Diocese—(five times per year) 1897+

Official publication of the Episcopal Church in South Carolina. Began publication in Sumter and at times has been a weekly.

Foreign Policy Bulletin—M 1961+

Publication of the Foreign Policy Research Institute of South Carolina.

Gateway to Charleston—M 1955+

Tourist bulletin.

Gibbes Art Gallery Library
  V 1,000   CP 11

Hanahan News—W 1959+

Huguenot Society of South Carolina
  V 600   PCE

The Society's offices have about 600 books and a substantial collection of pamphlets re Huguenot history and genealogy. Since 1889 the Society has published 69 vols. of *Transactions*. While some issues are out of print, many can be obtained at the Society's headquarters.

Inquirer—W 1963+

Medical College of South Carolina Bulletin—Q 1943+

Medical College of South Carolina Library
  V 37,000   CP 660   MFMR

Collection includes a substantial number of special reference books and periodicals. Back files of pertinent magazines can also be obtained through the Medical Library Association Exchange.

MANUSCRIPTS—The library has a few manuscripts. Among them are:

Babcock, James (1856–1922) [200, 6 feet]. Papers of superintendent of South Carolina State Hospital (1891–1914) with data on mental health, pelagra, and tuberculosis research. 1885–1920.

Davidson, William Speight McLean [v]. Notes taken by him while a student at the Medical College of South Carolina. 1840–42.

Dawson, John L. (1859–1917) [v]. Lecture notes as student at Medical College of South Carolina. 1880–81.

Minutes of Roper Hospital Board of Trustees [1,090 sheets]. Data re costs, equipment, discussions and decisions of the board members. 1856–68.

Rudisill, Hillyer, Jr. (1902–49) [285]. Personal papers and transcript of his biography of Joseph Lister. 1936–42.

News & Courier—D [mfm] 1873+
Micro Photo MFMR
Also has *Daily Courier* [mfm] 1803–73 Micro Photo.

News Post—(issued bimonthly) 1952+
House organ of *News & Courier* and *Evening Post*.

Palmettoan—A 1961+
Annual Publication of the South Carolina Federation of Colored Women's Clubs.

Poetry Society of South Carolina, Yearbook—A (1921+)

Preservation Progress—Q 1955+
Published by the Preservation Society of Charleston, Inc.

St. Francis Xavier Hospital, School of Nursing Library
V 1,660 CP 31

Scribe—(10 times per year) 1951+
Published by the Medical Society of South Carolina and the Charleston County Medical Society.

Shako—(issued three times per year) 1931+
Citadel literary publication.

South Carolina Historical Magazine—Q 1900+
Publication of the South Carolina Historical Society, formerly titled *South Carolina Historical and Genealogical Magazine*. Files can be found in many libraries throughout the state. An index is available. The society also published five volumes of papers (1857–97). Reprints of some of these are available at the offices of the magazine in the Fireproof Building.

South Carolina Historical Society
V 5,703   CP 40   MFMR   PCE

This collection, housed in the historic Fireproof Building, emphasizes Low Country Life (1680–1900), especially developments in the Charleston area. It includes 450 feet of papers, 1,446 indexed pamphlets, and the files of a large number of historical journals. The society has recently received a grant from the National Historical Publications Commission to aid in the editing of the papers of Henry Laurens. Some manuscript items have been published in the society's quarterly, the *South Carolina Historical Magazine* 1900+. See this publication (1944–47) for Helen G. McCormick's "Provisional Guide to Manuscripts in the South Carolina Historical Society." Following is a list of some of the more extensive holdings:

Adger, James [19]. Letters re travels in SC and the North, autobiographical data. 1824–55.

Aiken-Martin Papers [box]. Various papers including letters of Charles M. Bentham of San Francisco (1849). See *SCHM* (1956). Also letters of Johnson Hagood (1874) and albums, wills, and papers re Ellen D. Martin, William Aiken Martin, Robert Bentham, and Mary Ann Bentham. 1795–1935.

Aiken, Serena Daniel [v]. Album of clippings and poems re Aiken and Simons families. 1865–1919.

Allston-Pringle-Hill Papers [4,330, 63v]. Family correspondence and diaries re Gov. Robert F. W. Allston and his daughter Elizabeth Waties Allston (Mrs. John Julius Pringle). Includes letters of Jane Allston (Mrs. C. A. Hill) and Richard Allston while in France during World War I. 1812–1920.

Allston, Robert F. W. [c. 7,000, 12v]. Business records and correspondence of three generations of the Allston family. 1757–1926. See J. H. Easterby, *South Carolina Rice Plantations.*

Bacot-Huger Papers [6 feet]. A collection rich in family records; legal, social, agricultural, and political life in Charleston area; some references to national political scene; several diaries and account books. Principally papers of Daniel Huger (1779–1858), Thomas Wright Bacot (1765–1834), Thomas Wright Bacot, Jr. (1795–1851), Robert Dewar Bacot (1821–1903), and Thomas Wright Bacot III (1849–1927). 1754–1927.

Ball Papers [5v]. Personal accounts and plantation books. 1802–41.

Barnwell, Joseph W. [111 boxes, 32v]. Various papers and letterbooks (personal and professional) of a Charleston lawyer, firm of Brawley and Barnwell; also correspondence as president of the South Carolina Historical Society. 1871–1929.

Beaufort Merchant's Daybook [v]. 1785–91.

Bee, William C., Company, Charleston [100, 4v]. Correspondence and accounts including data re CW blockade-runners to England and the West Indies; also material re post-CW trade. 1848–1912.

Black Oak Agricultural Society, St. John's, Berkeley [7v]. Meteorological journals and minutes (1842–62). 1842–1925.

Bluffton General Store [v]. Account book. 1852–57.

Bowen-Cook Papers [421]. Letters of Rev. Penuel Bowen, of Boston, Mass., who died on John's Island in 1788, his widow, his son (Rev. Nathaniel Bowen, who died in 1833), and his daughter (Mrs. John Cooke). 1772–1857.

Broughton Papers [49]. Letters and legal papers of Mulberry Plantation family. 1739–1854.

Brotherhood of St. Andrews, St. Philip's Chapter, Charleston [v]. Minute book. 1897–1902.

Campbell Papers [3v]. Accounts and letterbook of James B. Campbell family, political correspondence, and receipt book of Mary Bennett Campbell. 1833–88.

Carson, James P. [17]. Letters, clippings, photographs. 1858–92.

Charleston Alms House [36v]. Register (1841–56) and various records. 1801–1916.

Charleston Auditor's Office [11 boxes, 11v]. Various papers and documents re auditor's and treasurer's offices. 1854–1909.

Charleston Bible Society [box]. Records. 1863–1954.

Charleston Board of Commissioners for Streets and Lamps and for Opening and Widening Streets, Lanes and Alleys [2v]. Records. 1817–66.

Charleston Board of Fire Masters [16v]. Records. 1848–1914.

Charleston Board of School Commissioners [7v]. Includes minutes of previous body, Commission on Free Schools of St. Philip's and St. Michael's Parishes. 1812–1913.

Charleston City Directories [17v mfm]. Also printed copies for 1831, 1856, 1861, 1867–68, (1884+).

Charleston Civic Club [3 boxes, v]. Records. 1900–15.

Charleston Community Club [186]. Various papers of a club mainly for servicemen, 1917–19. 1917–35.

Charleston County Coroner's Office [8 feet]. Records. 1883–1948.

Charleston County Treasurer's Office [82v]. Records. 1880–1910.

Charleston Gas and Light Company [16]. Details re organization and operation. 1846–1943.

Charleston Light Dragoons [v]. Minutes. 1835–48.

Charleston Light Dragoons and Charleston Light Auxiliary [3v]. Records. 1875–1915.

Charleston Merchant's Daybook [v]. 1764–66.

Charleston Orphan House [18v]. Records. 1809–82.

Charleston Protestant Episcopal Female Domestic Missionary Society [2v]. Treasurer's books. 1857–63.

Charleston Survey Books [2v]. 1851.

Chesnut-Miller-Manning Papers [7 boxes]. Business and political data; chiefly papers of John Chesnut (1744–94), Stephen D. Miller (1820–38), and John Manning (1824–44). 1744–1900.

Cheves, Langdon [224 boxes, 31v]. Papers of three generations of Cheves family, also Middleton-Haskell family papers. Political, legal, genealogical, and military data with a large amount of family correspondence in the CW period. However main theme is land management through decades of war, depression, and change. 1777–1938.

Cheves-McCord-Miles Papers [69]. Personal letters of three generations of these families. 1825–71.

Coburn Family Papers [25]. Business papers of Peter K., Ann, and Simon Magood Coburn. 1834–94.

Coffin Point Plantation [3v]. Records giving details of management and data on navigation on St. Helena's Sound. 1800–21.

Cohen, Louis [24v]. Business records of Louis Cohen Drygoods Company. 1870–1905.

Commissioners of Forfeited Estates [v]. Records of sales held at Jacksonborough, Pocotaligo, and Georgetown. 1782–83.

Commissioners of Fortifications [v]. Journal. 1755–70.

Conner Papers [94 boxes, 87v]. Business and professional papers of three generations: William H., General James, and William H. Conner. 1843–1938.

Council of Safety [29]. Letters from various parishes and neighborhoods to the Council in Charleston. 1775. See *SCHM* (1900–2).

De Saussure, Henry Alexander [v]. Death records kept by him. See *SCHM* (1958). 1829–65.

De Saussure, Louis D. [20]. Letters and documents re De Saussure, concerned mainly with CW era. 1846–81.

DeSaussure, Wilmot G. [v]. Orderly book of Fourth Brigade, SC Militia. 1861–62.

Dirleton Plantation, Georgetown [v]. Accounts. 1859–66.

Dixon, John [31]. Letters and documents re proceedings by Federal government against this Bamberg postmaster. 1866–72.

Elliott, Captain Barnard [v]. Order book giving details of RW in Charleston area. 1775–78. See *City of Charleston Yearbook* (1889).

Enston Home [5v]. Records of Board of Commissioners. 1883–1946.

Fielden-Smyth Papers [193, 3v]. Letters and data re Colonel Henry Wemyss Fielden, Colonel John Johnson, Gerald Smythe, Mrs. Augustine T. Smythe, Mrs. Anton P. Wright, and David McCord Wright. 1851–1921.

First Regiment, SC [v]. Order book at Fort Moultrie and Charleston barracks, probably kept by Captain Roger Parker Saunders. 1777–78. Extracts in *SCHM* (1906–7).

Fourth Brigade, SC [v]. Orderly book, includes account of entertainment for Lafayette. 1822–28.

Ford-Ravenel Papers [5 boxes]. Chiefly papers of Dr. Edmund Ravenel, physician, scientist, and planter, as executor of Timothy Ford's estate. 1788–1866.

Ford, Timothy [v]. Diary telling of travels from New Jersey to SC. 1785–86. See *SCHM* (1912).

Gadsden, John [6 boxes]. Papers of the principal of Holy Communion Church Institute. 1852–90.

Gilman, Caroline Howard [109]. Family letters of SC author, especially during CW. Some have been published in *The Atlantic* (XXXVII) and excerpts may be found in Mary Scott Saint-Amand, *A Balcony in Charleston* (1941). 1810–80.

Good Hope Plantation, Orangeburg [v]. Records and business accounts. 1835–59.

Hasell, Dr. Andrew [v]. Georgetown account book. 1843–56.

Hasell-Flagg Papers [25v]. Georgetown plantation accounts: inventories, crop yields, wages, details of plantation management. 1828–1904.

Haskell, Sophia Lovell [v]. Teen-age girl's CW diary. 1862–66.

Heyward, Du Bose [20 boxes]. Chiefly material re his literary career, but some data on other members of family. 1880–1940.

Holmes, James Gadsden [65]. Various papers, mostly concerned with post-CW records of veterans. 1776–1903.

Hunt, Randall [v]. Journal describing travels from Charleston to Philadelphia. 1832.

Independent Congregational Church, Charleston [37v, 2 reels mfm]. Various records; many have been printed in *SCHM*. 1732–1912.

Izard, General George [v]. Autobiography. 1855.

Johnson, John (1829–1907) [9 inches]. Papers of a Charleston engineer, mainly CW letters. 1862–1906.

Laurens, Henry (1724–92) [670, 38v, 19 reels mfm]. Outstanding collection of papers of noted planter and diplomat; contains transactions with French ministers, Commissioners of Correspondence, journal of Council of Safety, and data on Indian affairs. Letters from Laurens (1747–87) and letters to Laurens (1777–84). 1747–96.

Laurens, John (1754–82) [85]. Aide-de-camp to Washington, minister to France. Correspondents include Washington, Franklin, Adams, and Hamilton. 1777–81.

Lee, Major Hutson [3 boxes]. Papers of Quartermaster, CSA. 1858–65.

Le Jau-Huger-Downes-Frost Families [v]. Various records. 1800–21.

Lords Commissioners for Trade and Plantations [64]. Various documents. 1719–42.

Louisville, Cincinnati & Charleston Railroad Company [v]. Report of president and directors. 1837.

McGrath, Andrew Gordon [3v]. Letterbooks, telegrams, orders, and messages of CW governor. 1864–65.

McMichael, P. A. [35, v]. Journal kept by Orangeburg native while fighting in Virginia; also letters to his wife. 1861–65.

Macbeth, Malcolm [50]. Berkeley County land papers and a few early 19th-cent. letters from Robert Macbeth of Union District to relatives in Scotland. 1699–1854.

Manigault Papers [442, 5v]. Collection covers four generations: Peter (1731–73), Gabriel (1758–1809), Charles (1795–1874), and Gabriel E. (1833–99). 1751–1873.

Maw, John F. [v]. Laboratory book re artillery, military stores, and military affairs. 1794.

Mazyck, Arthur [105]. Letters, various papers, notes on Carolina Rifle Club, and data on Charleston. 1840–83.

Middleton, Arthur (1742–83) [box]. Various papers and correspondence, mainly between Charleston and Philadelphia. 1775–82. See *SCHM* (1925–26).

Middleton Papers [26]. Primarily letters of Charles Cotesworth, Thomas, and Elizabeth Lucas Pinckney. 1745–1836.

Mulberry Plantation [4v]. Cooper River journals concerned with weather and crops; some notes on social life and public affairs. 1853–89.

New England Society [6v]. Papers of a society founded in Charleston in 1819 to perpetuate the New England heritage and aid needy New Englanders in the city. Contains biographical sketches of members. 1819–1933.

Palmetto Regiment [2v]. Roster and rolls, Mexican War. 1846.

Pinckney Family [2 feet]. Papers spanning five generations; early land grants, letters, receipts, diaries, plantation records. 1708–1878.

Pinckney, Mrs. Charles (Elizabeth Lucas) [17]. Various papers. 1775–82.

Pinckney-Huger Papers [25]. Letters of Charles Cotesworth Pinckney and Benjamin Huger. 1775–1863.

Pinckney, Thomas [7v]. Letterbooks of minister to England (1790–96) and personal letterbook (1813). 1790–1813.

Pineville Jockey Club [50]. Various papers. 1852–63.

Planter [v]. Steamer's journal and business records. 1861–63.

Poinsett-Campbell Papers [60]. Business and political papers, Joel R. Poinsett to James B. Campbell. 1833–47.

Poinsett, Joel R. (1779–1851) [25]. Documents re his career as Secretary of War, Congressman, and minister to Mexico. 1779–1851.

Police Association, St. John's and St. Stephen's and Pineville Association [4v]. Berkeley District records. 1823–40.

Poppenheim Letters [200]. CW correspondence of Christopher Pritchard and Mary Elinor (Bouknight) Poppenheim. 1860–65.

Porcher, Frederick Adolphus [v]. "History of the Santee Canal." 1875.

Porcher, John Stoney [38, 3v]. Papers re settlement of the estates of Francis Marion, Joseph Couturier, Theodore Gourdin, and Peter Gaillard. 1771–1883.

Protestant Episcopal Church, St. John's Berkeley [v mfm]. Records of vestry. 1725–1813.

Protestant Episcopal Church, St. John's, Berkeley [v mfm]. Vestry cash book; Bishop Howe's records of Cooper River planters. 1813–37.

Protestant Episcopal Church, St. Peter's, Charleston [v mfm]. Parish records. 1856–1912.

Protestant Episcopal Church, St. Philip's, Charleston [2 reels mfm]. Vestry minutes (1756–74) and records. 1713–1940.

Protestant Episcopal Church, St. Stephen's Chapel, Charleston [v mfm]. Parish records. 1754–1878.

Protestant Episcopal Church, Waccamaw, Georgetown [v mfm]. Parish register. 1819–1954.

Quakers [v mfm]. "A Book of Minutes Belonging to the Meeting of the People Called Quakers in Charleston, South Carolina." 1719–69.

Ravenel, Henry (1739–85) [2v]. Hanover daybook and ledgers. 1751–83.

Ravenel, Stephen (1770–1818) [v]. Travel journal (partial account) describing visit with President Thomas Jefferson in Washington and tour to Warrenton, N. C. 1803.

Read, Motte Alston [43 reels mfm]. Collection of genealogical data re primarily colonial families of the SC Low Country. Compiled c. 1920–40.

Richmond Plantation [v]. Cooper River overseer's daybook. 1859–60.

Rose Hill Plantation [3v]. Workbooks of Cumbahee River area. 1878.

Rutledge, Benjamin Huger [6 folders]. Deeds, wills, and letters of Pinckney-Rutledge families. 1689-1867.

S. S. McClellan [v]. Records of a US army transport. 1861–65.

St. David's Society [vr]. Minutes telling of efforts to establish St. David's Academy, Society Hill. 1777–1833.

St. John's Parish, Berkeley [3v]. Records of the commissioners of high roads. 1760–1853.

St. Thomas Hunting Club [v]. Minutes and rules of Cooper River Club, visitors listed. 1785–1801.

Sally, A. S., Jr. [box]. Memorabilia of Charleston social life, especially the St. Cecilia Society. 1898–1954.

Sanders-Broughton Papers [43, 5v]. Legal papers, inventories, letters of two prominent families. 1703–1836.

Saylor, David [v]. Receipt book of Charleston merchant. 1784–87.

Schirmer, Jacob Frederick (1803–80) [9v]. Journals of Charleston life, supplemented by his family after his death. Index on mfm. 1826–86.

Second and Third Regiments, SC Line [48]. Documents re supply and administration. 1779–84. Most items have been published in SCHM (1904–06).

Senf, Charles C. [v]. Report on Santee Canal. 1800. See SCHM (1927).

Seymour, R. W. [v]. Magistrate's docket book. 1829.

Simons, Alfred D. [v]. CW diary. 1864–65.

Smith, Lancelot [v mfm]. Strawberry Ferry ledger. 1777–79.

Smith, Oliver M. [v]. Attorney's docket book. 1834–39.

Smyth, John Adger [90]. Chiefly letters to his wife. 1861–64.

Smythe, Augustine T. [3 boxes]. Business and private correspondence, some CW letters. Includes data re politics and the settlement of the estate of Mrs. Louisa McCord, letters to Mrs. A. T. Smythe and to his sister, Miss Sara A. Smythe. 1853–1916.

Society for the Prevention of Cruelty to Animals, Charleston [v]. Minute book. 1880–1914.

Society for Relief of Orphans and Widows of Clergy of the Protestant Episcopal Church [5v]. Minutes and records. Some additional data (1762–1943) available on mfm. 1763–1891.

South Carolina, Army of [998]. Headquarters papers, letters, enlistments, reports. 1861–65.

South Carolina, Census Returns [7 reels mfm]. Selected schedules. 1800–50.

South Carolina, Entomological Society [10v]. Current records and minutes. 1951+.

South Carolina Gazette [v mfm]. Index. 1732–38.

South Carolina Jockey Club [v]. Receipt book. 1832–34.

Teague, B. T. [box]. Collection of miscellaneous documents, letters, and almanacs, some re Teague family and Aiken area. 1760–1894.

Trapier, Rev. Paul [v mfm]. Charleston autobiography. 1807–67.

Vanderhorst Family Papers [12 boxes]. Primarily letters from and to Mrs. Arnoldus Vanderhorst (Adele Allston), daughter of Robert F. W. Allston. 1736–1910.

Wagener, John H. A. [v]. "Memorandum & Notes on Artillery," manuscript written by Wagener in Virginia. 1861–63.

Wagner, Theodore D. [26]. Business letters of a Charleston firm, primarily concerned with SC cotton trade and CW blockade. 1853–63.

Washington Artillery [v]. Charleston orderbook. 1845–46.

Washington Papers [40, 2v]. Letters by William Washington and his family. 1841–77.

Webb, Daniel Cannon [6v]. Plantation journals re life in Charleston and management of lands east of the Ashley River. 1817–50.

Webber, Mabel L. [c. 700 folders]. Collection of SC genealogical material, primarily Low Country families.

Webster, Pelatiah [v]. Journal of voyage from Philadelphia to SC. 1765. See *Publications of the Southern History Association* (1898).

Weston Family Papers [216, v]. Georgetown District business papers, bills, and manuscript re Dr. Paul Weston and Francis Weston. 1786–1869.

White, John Blake [14v]. Includes sketchbook of a Benjamin West student, also manuscripts of several plays and lectures. 1800–48.

Willis, Major Edward [14, v]. Primarily CW letters and clippings. 1858–80.

Wragg Papers [8 boxes]. Business and land records, mostly re William Loughton Smith (1758–1812), and some personal letters. 1708–1848.

Yates Papers [198]. Family letters, mainly of Mrs. Elizabeth Ann (Saylor) Yates (Mrs. Joseph Yates). 1822–81.

South Carolina State Ports News—M 1946+

Official publication of the South Carolina State Ports Authority.

United States Corps of Engineers Library
  V 200   CP 15

This is a small reference collection that includes several hundred government pamphlets, numerous technical reports, and Corps of Engineers publications. It is primarily for the use of staff personnel.

United States Department of Commerce Field Services
  V 1,000   CP 75

Although not actually a library, this office has 80 file drawers of current material re Bureau of International Commerce, Bureau of the Census, Business & Defense Services Administration, and Office of Technical Services of the Department of Commerce. This is a working commercial library for those interested in foreign trade and has limited historical data on South Carolina census reports. This is also a sales office for US Government documents and publications and Patent Office materials.

CHERAW

Cheraw Chronicle—W 1946+

Matheson Memorial Library
  V 7,000   R 225   SC 150   CP 6

CHESTER

Chester County Free Public Library
  V 24,714   R 1,500   SC 900   CP 105   MFMR   CMPC

Collection includes 30 bound volumes of 19th-cent. newspapers. Among these are the *Charleston Southern Intelligencer* (1822–23), *Chester Reporter* 1876–1906, and *Chester Standard* 1854–57. The library also has the *Chester News* 1951+ and the *Chester Reporter* 1951+. A trunk in the library contains local genealogical data, church histories, and cemetery records. Of special interest are the sessional records of the Catholic Presbyterian Church (1840–59) and a two-volume genealogy of the McCalla Family.

Chester County Historical Society

Society has a small collection of books, documents, manuscripts, newspapers, maps, and magazines in Chester County Courthouse. Of special interest are Boyd's map of Chester District (1818), ledger of John F. McAfee's liquor business in Chester (1843–47), original roll of the Richburg "Catawba Guards" (1861), Minute Books of the Chester Building & Loan & Savings Institution (1889–95), eight maps of Chester (1917) giving complete data on the city, and several issues of *Soil of the South* (Columbus, Ga., 1853).

Chester News—W 1904+, [mfm] 1887–1909, 1915–39, 1963+
  Mann

Chester Reporter—W 1930+

CHESTERFIELD

Chesterfield Advertiser—W 1915+

Chesterfield Public Library
  V 2,000   R 100   SC 20   CP 5
Library has back files of the *Chesterfield Advertiser* 1957+.

CLEMSON

Agricultural Research—Q 1953+

Publication of the South Carolina Agricultural Experiment Station of Clemson University.

Agrarian—(semianually) 1942+

Published by School of Agriculture, Clemson University.

Bobbin and Beaker—Q 1942+

Published by School of Industrial Management and Textile Science, Clemson University.

Clemson Alumni News—M 1946+

Clemson Chronicle—Q 1960+
Publication of the Clemson Literary Society.

Clemson Extension Service Bulletin—(occasionally) 1891+

Clemson Messenger—W 1955+

Clemson University Library
   V 225,000   R 5,000   SC 8,000   CP 3,500   MCR   MFMR   PCE
   US GOVT DOC
Holdings include extensive periodical and serial collections, often
supplemented by microfilm files, the US Senate papers of James F.
Byrnes, rare book collection of B. A. Behrend [5,000v] (1900–40),
US government maps, numerous plantation accounts and records,
miscellaneous books from Benjamin R. Tillman's library [100v],
the Pendleton Farmers Society Library [100v], and materials re
area and University history. Among the newspaper files [mfm]
are: *Anderson Independent* 1956+, *[Charleston] News & Courier*
1949+, *[Columbia] State* 1960+, *Greenville News* 1947+, *New York
Times* 1930+, *Pendleton Messenger* (1807–43), and the *Wall Street
Journal* 1960+. In addition to items already cited, the library's
manuscript collection includes:

Beech Island Agricultural Society Papers [4vr]. Various records.
   1846–74.
Calhoun, John C. (1782–1850) [3,000]. Family papers, correspond-
   ence, and pamphlets. 1809–50.
Carrison, Henry George [44v]. Various papers. 1876–1933.
Clarke, Ephraim M. [3v]. Various papers. 1872–98.
Clemson, Thomas Green (1807–88) [1,000]. Personal correspond-
   ence and family papers. 1858–88.
Cralle, Richard K. (1800–64) [240]. Correspondence of journalist
   re Virginia and the South. c. 1830–60.
Greer [S. C.] Cottonseed Oil & Fertilizer Company [v]. Various
   records and papers. 1899–1902.
Lever, Asbury Francis [30 boxes]. Papers of member of US House
   of Representatives from SC. 1901–40.
Ravenel, Henry William (1814–87) [215]. Botanist's correspond-
   ence with numerous noted scientists. 1841–86.
Robson, J. N., & Son, Charleston [15v]. Account books of hay and
   grain merchants. 1866–1932.
State Agricultural Society of South Carolina [v]. Minutes. 1855–60.

State Alliance of South Carolina [2v]. Minutes. 1876–1909.
State Grange of South Carolina [v]. Minutes. 1873–1905.
Tillman, Benjamin Ryan (1847–1918) [85v, 215 boxes]. Papers of
    SC governor and senator. 1877–1919.

Locker Bulletin—M 1949+

Published by the South Carolina Frozen Food Association.

Saco-Lowell Research & Development Center Library
    V 250

Collection is comprised primarily of patents re the textile arts
and related patent reference materials. Various publications in this
field are received. Copies of some 250,000 US and British patents
re machines manufactured in Saco-Lowell shops are filed here.
British files date back to 1748, and US files to 1820. Copies of some
recent German patents are also maintained.

Slapstick—Q 1941+

Clemson University publication.

South Carolina Poultry Improvement Association, Yearbook—A
    1940+

Tiger—W (except summer) 1907+

Clemson University student newspaper.

CLINTON

Blue Stocking—W (except summer) 1925+

Presbyterian College student newspaper.

Clinton Chronicle—W [mfm] 1919+
    Mann   MFMR

Jacobs Brothers

This firm prints and distributes the following house organs and
fraternal publications and has files as indicated: *Along the Coast—*
W (in summer) 1958+, *Beta Club Journal—*M (publication of
National Beta Clubs) 1940+, *Chemstrand-Greenwood* (semi-

monthly house organ of Chemstrand plant) 1960+, *Clinton Cloth-maker*—M (publication of Clinton-Lydia Mills) 1951+, *Jack-sonette*—M (house organ of Jackson Mills) 1955+, *Joanna Way*—M (Joanna Mills publication) 1949–64, *Military Police Journal*—M (magazine of national organization) 1951+, *Quills*—M (house organ of Abney Mills) 1951+, *Texizer*—M (publication of Texize plant) 1961+.

Piedmont Churchman—M (except summer) 1924+

Published by the Committee on Christian Promotion, Episcopal Diocese of Upper South Carolina.

Presbyterian College and Community Library
   V 50,000   R 1,000   SC 1,000   CP 200   MCR   MFMR

Holdings include the William Plummer Jacobs Library of some 1,500 books and bound publications. This collection, housed separately, represents the private library of Jacobs (1848–1917), a prominent Presbyterian theologian. Other materials include the Jones Collection of Presbyterian Pamphlets [42v] (1830–60), Minutes of the Synod of South Carolina and the SC General Assembly (1845–1935), Journals of the Continental Congress 1776–89, and these newspaper files: *Atlanta Constitution* [mfm] (1868–76), *Blue Stocking* (Presbyterian College weekly) 1929+, [*Charleston*] *News & Courier* [mfm] (1873–89), *South Carolina Gazette* [mfm] 1732–82, and *Union Progress* 1900–18.

Presbyterian College Magazine—Q 1947+

South Carolina Trade & Industrial Education—Q 1951+

Thornwell Life—M 1933+

Published by the Thornwell Orphanage.

CLOVER

Clover Herald—W 1928+, [mfm] 1963+
   Mann   MFMR

Also has files of the *Palmetto Post* 1921.

York County Library
V 10,000   CP 15

COLUMBIA

Action Central—M 1964+

Publication of the Greater Columbia Chamber of Commerce; formerly titled *Columbia Chamber of Commerce in Action*, 1959–63.

Adult Education—M (except summer) 1951+

Publication of the Adult Education Association of the United States of America.

Allen University Library
   V 14,439   R 1,500   SC 50   CP 130   MCR   MFMR   PCE
Library is receiving the *New York Times* [mfm] 1963+.

Bell-Ringer—(6 times per year) 1954+

Publication of the South Carolina Mental Health Association.

Benedict College Library
   V 32,000   R 2,000   CP 400

Bobbin—M 1959+

National trade publication for the garment industry.

Business and Economic Review—M (except summer) 1954+

Report issued by the Bureau of Business and Economic Research, School of Business, University of South Carolina.

Camellia Journal—M 1945+

Camellian—Q 1950+

Cancer Wise—Q 1956+

Published by the South Carolina Cancer Society, which also distributes a monthly newsletter to various units throughout the state.

Carolina Cockpit—(issued 6 times per year) 1959+

Published by the NROTC, University of South Carolina.

Carolina Confidential—M 1957+

Gamecock Club magazine.

Carolina Highway—M 1946+

Published by the South Carolina State Highway Department.

Ce-Be-Cean 1932+

Student publication, Columbia Bible College.

Checklist of South Carolina State Publications—A 1950+

This guide to publications by departments, institutions, and agencies of the state of South Carolina is issued each year by the South Carolina Archives Department and the South Carolina State Library.

Columbia Bible College Library

  V 21,300 CP 360

This specialized library has substantial material on missions [24 file drawers] and an extensive supply of visual aids used in Bible teaching, Sunday School classes, and missionary work.

Columbia College Library

  V 34,000 R 1,600 SC 100 CP 261

Holdings include *Chemical Abstracts* 1962+, *Chemical Reviews* 1962+, *Psychological Abstracts* 1948+.

Columbia Hospital, Medical and Nursing Library

  V 3,000 CP 54

This library is operated by Columbia Hospital, Columbia Hospital School of Nursing, and the Columbia Medical Society of Richland County. Files are augmented by the photostatic loan service of the National Library of Medicine.

Columbia Museum of Art Library

  V 1,300 CP 15

This library, which is cataloged in the card files of the McKissick Library, U. S. C., also maintains a current file of auction catalogs, museum bulletins, and professional magazines.

Columbia Museum of Art News—M (September thru May) 1949+

Columbia Record—D [mfm] 1939+
  Micro Photo   MFMR

Comments—(issued eight times per year) 1959+
Published by the Christian Action Council.

Contracting in the Carolinas—M 1955+

Criterion—(issued five times per year) 1897+
Columbia College publication.

Crucible—(issued three times per year) 1960+
Published by students, University of South Carolina.

Education Report—Q 1957+
Published by the School of Education, University of South Carolina.

Epworth Record—M 1896+
Publication of the Epworth Children's Home.

Essays in Economics—(occasionally) 1955+
Published by the Bureau of Business and Economic Research, University of South Carolina.

Explicator—M 1940+
University of South Carolina publication.

Farm Credit Leader—Q 1961+
Published by the Farm Credit Banks of Columbia.

Gamecock—W (except summer) 1908+
University of South Carolina student newspaper.

Garden Club of South Carolina, Bulletin—(issued four times per year) 1936+

Garden Club of South Carolina, Yearbook—Q 1949+

Geologic Notes—Q 1946+

Published by the Division of Geology, South Carolina State Development Board.

Governmental Review—Q 1958+

Publication of the Bureau of Governmental Research and Service, University of South Carolina.

Horger Library, South Carolina State Hospital
  V 6,000   CP 73

Jaycees in Action—M 1937+

Official publication of the SC Junior Chamber of Commerce.

Key to Columbia—W 1950+

Magazine for tourists.

Library for Community Health Services, South Carolina State
  Hospital
  V 1,000   CP 30

Life Wires—M 1945+

Employee magazine of the South Carolina Electric and Gas Company; formerly titled *GET News.*

Lifelines—(issued six times per year) 1958+

Publication of the South Carolina Alcoholic Rehabilitation Board.

Lutheran Theological Southern Seminary Library
  V 30,000   R 5,000   CP 300   MCR   MFMR
Collection includes material on Lutherans, Baptists, and Methodists in the South, German Pietism during the 16th–18th centuries [1,000v], and the minutes of the SC (1804+) and other constituent Lutheran synods: North Carolina (1804+), Virginia (1829+), Tennessee (1820+), Georgia (1850+), Florida (1929+), and Southwest Virginia (1900+). (NOTE: The South Carolina Lutheran Synod Archives are located on Richland Street in Columbia.) Microfilm material includes 12 reels on early Baptists in

the South, the Annals of the Baptist State Convention of South Carolina (1821–1960), Minutes and Records of the First Baptist Church of Charleston (1806–75), the Minutes of the Annual Conference of the Methodist Church, South (1845–1941), and the *Corpus of American Lutheranism* [Units I–X]. This library is currently building up a Southern Lutheran History Collection. Part of this will be the personal library [150v] of Ernst L. Hazelius, president of the seminary 1839–1853.

Medical Professional Library, William S. Hall Psychiatric Institute
   V 1,895 CP 107 PCE
This small reference library, located at the SC State Hospital, specializes in neurology and psychiatry.

Merry Times—Q 1964+
House organ of Merry Brothers Brick and Tile Company, Augusta, Ga., published by the R. L. Bryan Company.

Motor Transportation Hi-Lights—M (1933–35) 1936+
Publication of the South Carolina Motor Transportation Association.

Names in South Carolina—(issued occasionally) 1954+
Publication of the Department of English, University of South Carolina.

New Horizons—(issued six times per year) 1959+
Published by the South Carolina Vocational Rehabilitation Department.

News for Public Libraries—M 1957+
Published by the South Carolina State Library Board; originally titled *News for Public Librarians.*

Palmetto Leaf—(twice a year) 1941+
Printed by the Southeastern Press for the South Carolina Dietetic Association. Originally a quarterly publication.

Palmetto Piper—M 1953+
Publication of the South Carolina Association of Plumbing, Heating, and Air Conditioning Contractors.

Palmetto Standard—Q 1949+

House organ of the Palmetto State Life Insurance Company.

Palmetto State Oil Marketers Association News—(issued six times per year) 1960+

Palmetto Times—W 1962+

Palmetto Variety—M 1952+

Publication of the South Carolina Mental Health Commission for State Park and Pineland divisions.

Public Welfare Statistics—M 1936+

Published by the South Carolina Department of Public Welfare.

Recorder—M 1936+

Publication of the Columbia Medical Society of Richland County.

Review of Architecture—Q 1957+

Published by Wing Publishers for the South Carolina Chapter of American Institute of Architects.

Richland County Public Library
    V 180,000   R 5,000   SC 800   CP 200   MFMR   MRP   PCE
Holdings include *War of the Rebellion,* 1,400 phonograph records with special listening facilities, extensive vertical file material, SC data, and these Columbia newspapers: *State* 1909+, [mfm] 1899+; *Record* [mfm] 1939+.

Richland Technical Education Center Library
    V 300   CP 50
Library is in process of development.

SCESC News—(issued bimonthly except summer) 1956+

Publication of the South Carolina Employment Security Commission.

South Carolina Academy of Science, Bulletin—A 1935+

South Carolina Department of Archives and History
V 6,000   CP 18   MFMR   MRP   PCE

The primary purpose of the Archives Department is the preservation and orderly arrangement of the public records of South Carolina as proprietary colony, royal province, and state. The department holds (1) either the originals or microfilm of all known records of South Carolina government up to 1785, the date which marks the formation of the counties and the start of their record-keeping; (2) the originals of all known records of state government to 1880 and many since that date; (3) microfilm of all surviving land and probate records and some court records of the counties to 1865 or later. Generally speaking, noncurrent government records should be sought at the Archives before applying to counties or individual state agencies.

The Archives has the original manuscript copies of all state constitutions (except that of 1895, which is still in effect and is kept in the office of the Secretary of State), engrossed laws of South Carolina (1691+), journals of various legislative bodies throughout the state's long history (1671+), and petitions, resolutions, and committee reports re the General Assembly (1788+) with a scattering of earlier papers. Notable are ten manuscript "Indian Books," 1710–18 and 1750–65 (publication in 3v nearly completed), reflecting South Carolina's long role as British imperial trader and diplomatist with the Southeastern Indians.

Executive documents are rather scanty, especially from the Revolutionary era through the CW. Significant exceptions are the letterbooks of Gov. John Drayton, 1800–2, 1808–10. Correspondence of the colonial governors with the home authorities can be found in "Records" in the British Public Record Office, published by the South Carolina Historical Society in the 1850's, and in more recently acquired microfilm of Colonial Office documents. Many of the executive papers of Reconstruction governors have survived; and several recent governors, notably Burnet R. Maybank and George Bell Timmerman, have transferred their records to the Archives.

Treasury records (1725+) consist of summary ledgers, journals, and infrequent cash books up to the Revolution; for the state period they are voluminous, of great variety, only roughly inventoried, and largely unexamined. Records of the Register of the Province (1671+) merge with the Records of the Register of Mesne Conveyances (1719+) in the Charleston County Courthouse, but are on microfilm in the Archives. Judicial records (1671+) grow out of the Journal of the Grand Council, the parent of all South Carolina courts: Common Pleas, Chancery, General Sessions, and Admiralty for the colonial period. The Auditor-General's office of the royal period left "Memorials" [14v] listing lands subject to quitrent, 1731–75. The Auditor-General of the early state period, a different officer with the same title, audited more than 9,000 RW claims, an invaluable collection of information for military service and the beginnings of state finance.

Most impressive of all the collections, however, are the records of the Secretary of the Province and the Secretary of State (1671+). Perhaps half of all the public records of South Carolina, both state and local documents, either have been made by these secretaries or stem from records which originated with them. They have been the great "recording officers" of South Carolina government.

The main trunk of Secretary's records consists of a series of volumes containing all sorts of documents. This series, officially called "Miscellaneous Records" after 1732, splits into a Charleston and a Columbia series during the period of dual state offices (1790–1862) and then continues as a single Columbia series in the Secretary of State's office to the present day. The Archives possesses 190v (1671–1903). A number of specialized series grow out of the "Miscellaneous Records." Among the earlier ones are "Wills" [16v], 1733–83; "Ship Registers" [2v], 1734–80; "Inventories" [20v], 1736–84; "Mortgages" [52v], 1736–1873; and "Marriage Settlements" [20v], 1785–1807. Later important offshoots include executive clemency records, corporation charters, eleemosynary charters, public officers bonds, and railroad record books.

The largest single group of documents inherited from the Secretary of State, however, are the land records of South Carolina. These consist of a Charleston and a Columbia series of recorded land grants [287v], actually growing out of the "Miscellaneous Records" as a specialized series in 1731, but recording grants made from 1674 to 1936. These are accompanied by 151 vols. of plats (systematically recorded from 1731 but containing surveys of earlier date) and by 196 boxes of unbound "duplicate plats" (for the most part surveys identical with those in the bound volumes but containing valuable endorsements).

Those wishing to consult the holdings of the Archives Department should note that the most recent records—approximately the last decade—are retained by various departments of state government. Also researchers should realize that only since 1960 has the Archives staff had adequate facilities in which to process the state's vast records. During South Carolina's long history many documents have been lost because of war, fire, and neglect, and others have become intermingled with those of a variety of departments. The staff is generally familiar with records up to 1860 and can usually provide a researcher with the information he desires, although only a few of the major record groups have been completely inventoried. The best known of these are legislative acts and journals, land records, RW audited accounts, and Confederate service records. It has been said that despite publication of more than one hundred books by the South Carolina State Historical Commission and the Archives Department, this body of material is "the largest single collection of unpublished official records" in the nation. For additional information the researcher should consult these publications:

List of Publications of the South Carolina Archives Department, February 1, 1957. 30 pp. Copies may be obtained from the Department.

Charles E. Lee, "South Carolina Archives," *University of South Carolina Governmental Review* (February 1964). A six-page analysis of the Archives by its director.

R. H. Woody, "The Public Records of South Carolina," *American Archivist* (October 1931).

South Carolina Historical Magazine (various issues). Beginning in January 1965, the Archives Department published the first of several brief reports on its activities and projects.

Copies of records of the British, Federal, and Confederate governments, although not strictly speaking part of the South Carolina Archives, have been acquired for the information they give concerning the history of the state and the development of its political institutions. And although nongovernmental papers are not actually a part of the Archives collection, its holdings do include some material of this kind. Among such papers are manuscripts used by Robert W. Gibbes when compiling his documentary history of the RW in South Carolina; a number of the maps, plats, and surveys made by Robert Mills and his associates for his famous *Atlas*; and a file of Manigault family papers (1783–1823).

The Archives maintains a small library of books, pamphlets, and periodicals chosen because they supplement or help one to understand the archival records that constitute the main holdings. The most important of these consist of guides and inventories of manuscript records re South Carolina in the National Archives and other depositories, the British Public Record Office's *Calendar of State Papers: Colonial* [43v], 1574–1737, *The Colonial Records of North Carolina* [14v], and *The Colonial Records of Georgia* [26v]. For other South Carolina materials and newspapers the researcher is referred to the nearby South Caroliniana Library.

Since 1906 this Department has published a variety of documents, records, and bibliographical studies and is currently publishing the papers of John C. Calhoun in cooperation with the University of South Carolina Press and the South Caroliniana Society. These published items (all on sale at the Achives) include:

Records of the British Public Record Office Relating to South Carolina (1663–1710) [5v]. There are 36 vols. in this series of transcripts, and the remaining 31 vols. are available on microfilm.
Selected Journals of the Council and Commons House of Assembly (1671–1765) [33v].
Records Relating to Indian Affairs (1710–54) [3v].
Warrants for Lands in South Carolina (1672–1711) [3v].
Miscellaneous Volumes [6v]. These relate to instructions from the Lords Proprietors (1685–1715), early records of the Secretary of the Province (1671–75), minutes of the Vestry of St. Helena's Parish (1726–1812), death notices in the *South Carolina Gazette* (1732–75), marriage notices in the *South Carolina & American General Gazette* (1766–81), and the *St. Augustine Expedition of 1740.*
Convention Journals [2v]. Records of the convention that ratified the US Constitution (1788) and the Constitutional Convention of South Carolina (1790). Journals of six other state-wide conventions (1832–95) were printed in conjunction with the proceedings at the time they were held.
Selected Journals of the General Assembly (1776–82) [4v].
Journals of the South Carolina Executive Councils of 1861 and 1862 [v]. This is the first volume of a new series: *State Records of South Carolina.*
Revolutionary War Records [20v]. These include audited claims against South Carolina and stub entries to indents issued in payment, journals of the commissioners of the Navy of South Carolina, the log of *H.M.S. Scorpion* (1775), Colonel William Hill's memoirs, documents re the RW in South Carolina, and an order book of the Third Regiment of South Carolina Line (1776–77).
Confederate War Records [5v].

Miscellaneous Records [2v]. Includes marriage notices from the *Charleston Courier* (1803–8) and selected letters of Robert Mills (1820–30).

These published materials also include a variety of bulletins, studies, bibliographies, reports, and circulars. Among the bulletins and studies are sixteen brief discussions of interesting aspects of South Carolina's past and a thorough study of banking in the state prior to 1860 by W. A. Clark [472 pp.]. These bibliographies include guides to the study of South Carolina history, an annual check-list of publications by the state government and its agencies (1950+), and a survey of published articles re South Carolina literature (1900–55).

Among materials available on microfilm are *Records of the British Public Record Office Relating to South Carolina* (1710–82) [6 reels with a general index], and *U. S. Census: Original Agriculture, Industry, Social Statistics, Mortality Schedules for South Carolina* (1850–80) [22 reels].

NOTE ON MICROFILM—The Archives Department has about 500 reels of microfilm in its collections. They are classified as follows:

1. Security films (negatives) of selected records in 9 of 46 county courthouses made for the counties by a commercial photographer and deposited in the Archives.
2. Positive copies of films of selected state and county records (20 of 46 counties) made by the Genealogical Society of Utah.
3. Positive copies of various records re South Carolina which are usually found in other depositories. These copies have been acquired by either gift or purchase.
4. Both negative and positive copies of records in the Archives Department made by the staff.

With the exception of negative files, these films are in constant use in the reading room and cannot be loaned to other Institutions. Lists of films are published periodically. The Archives Department is endeavoring to make available on 35 mm. positive film copies of records in its custody which have a high research value but are either too voluminous to be printed or will not be printed in the near future. Microfilm copies of some South Carolina records may be purchased from the Library of Congress. See *A Guide to the Microfilm Collection of Early State Records* (Washington, 1950) and *Supplement* (Washington, 1951). Microfilm available to researchers is listed below, with number of reels indicated in brackets.

Dates indicate the period in which most of the records fall. Special series falling outside the indicated main time period are mentioned in an underlying note. South Carolina county records consist primarily of deeds and estate papers (wills, inventories, and other probate records) up to 1865. Various court papers from some counties are also included.

South Carolina Institutions

1. Supreme Court of South Carolina [1]. Roster of Attorneys, 1809–1950.
2. Counties
   Abbeville [152]. 1782–1870. Includes records of the Commissioners of Location for Ninety-Six District south of Saluda.
   Anderson [440]. 1789–1880. Includes material on old Pendleton District, 1790–1828. There are also marriage records for Anderson County, 1911–56.
   Barnwell [99]. 1785–1865. Includes records of old Winton County, 1785–90. Also some Commissioners of Location records for old Orangeburg District. In addition: birth and death records, 1915–58; marriage records, 1911–59.
   Charleston [445]. 1671–1886. In addition: miscellaneous records vols. to 1954; dowers, 1796–1905; petitions for citizenship, 1796–1905; Confederate pension records, 1940–59; pension rolls, 1940–59.
   Chester [46]. 1785–1868.
   Darlington [87]. 1791–1895.
   Edgefield [178]. 1785–1888. In addition: coroner's records, 1891–1902; pension records, 1916–33.
   Fairfield [107]. 1785–1868.
   Greenville [59]. 1784–1880. Includes records of Commissioners of Location for Ninety-Six District north of Saluda, 1784–86.
   Horry [3]. 1803–84.
   Kershaw [10]. 1782–1868. Includes some wills from other counties of old Camden District, 1779–86.
   Lancaster [24]. 1787–1871.
   Laurens [23]. 1785–1867. In addition: marriage register, 1911–51.
   Lexington [22]. 1809–93. In addition: South Carolina state pension list by counties for year 1921.
   Marion [29]. 1800–88.
   Marlboro [28]. 1786–1881.
   Newberry [128]. 1785–1870. In addition: tax duplicates, 1940, 1945, 1948.
   Orangeburg [31]. 1865–1957. Record of earlier period consists of book of Commissioners Deeds (1824–35) re settlement of disputes over real property. Later period includes deeds,

wills, and plats. Also for early records see Barnwell, Edge-field, and Lexington Counties.
Pickens [65]. 1823–84. In addition: pensions of Confederate veterans and widows, 1922–56.
Richland [163]. 1787–1888.
Spartanburg [10]. 1816–64. In addition: pension applications of widows of veterans, 1923–35; pension applications of Confederate veterans, 1920–35.
Sumter [165]. 1784–1909.
Union [97]. 1785–1870. Includes a few court records of old Pinckney District.
Williamsburg [34]. 1806–79.
York [275]. 1785–1882.
3. Churches
   a. Records filmed at the Diocesan House Headquarters, Episcopal Diocese of South Carolina, Office of the Bishop, Charleston [6]. Organized in 1785.
   Miscellaneous Church Records, 1693–1905. Bishop's Register of various Churches, 1872–1912. Records from various Churches, 1786–1916. Register, Prince George Winyaw, 1813–1916. Vestry Book, St. Paul's, 1786–1864. Records of St. John's Parish, 1738–1874. Protestant Episcopal Church in South Carolina, State Convention Minute Book, 1804–20. Minutes of the Protestant Episcopal Society, 1810–62. Act of Incorporation, 1810 (with alterations, 1818). Protestant Episcopal Church in South Carolina, Journal of the Proceedings of the Annual Conventions, 1854–58, 1860, 1862–64, 1866–67.
   b. Protestant Episcopal Church records filmed in other parts of the state [12].
   Miscellaneous Church Records, 1715–1858. Register of the Church of the Redeemer, Orangeburg, also of the earliest Episcopal Church in Orangeburg and Amelia Township, 1739–1885. Records from St. Stephen's, St. John's, and St. Peter's Churches, 1754–1926; St. Stephen's and St. John's, Berkeley, 1754–1873; United Chapels of St. John and St. Stephens, 1828–90; St. Stephen's Chapel, Charleston, 1833–66; St. Stephen's Church, Charleston, 1866–80; St. Peter's Church, Charleston, 1892–1926. St. John's Parish, Berkeley, Vestry Minutes, 1731–1911 [3v], Register, 1872–1944, Vestry Cash Book, 1813–27, with various loose documents, (1807–31). Frederick Dalcho, *An Historical Account of the Protestant Episcopal Church in South Carolina . . .* (Charleston: E. Thayer, publisher, A. E. Miller, printer, 1820). Protestant Episcopal Society for the Advancement of Christianity in South Carolina: Cash Book, 1857–73; Episcopal Transactions, documents dated 1795–1871. St. John's, Colleton, Vestry Book, 1738–1874 [typescript]. Christ Church Parish, Vestry Minutes, 1708–59, 1797–1847; Register, 1700–84. Records

of St. Philip's Church, Charleston, 1713–1940. Records of the Chapel of the Holy Cross, Sullivan's Island, and of the Chapel of the Holy Cross at Moultrieville, 1891–1917. St. Helena's Parish, Beaufort, Register, 1725–1824.

c. From originals preserved in the Baptist Historical Collection, Furman University, Greenville [6].
Philadelphia Baptist Church, Pauline, Records, 1803–1957. Mountain Creek Baptist Church, Anderson County, Minute Book, 1798–1938. Secona Baptist Church, Greenville County, Minute Book, 1795–1938. Washington Baptist Church, Route 2, Pelzer, Minute Book, 1821–1911. Hopewell Baptist Church and Pacolet Baptist Churches, Greenville County, Notes and Correspondence of the Clerk of the Church, 1813–37. Minutes of Pacolet Baptist Church, 1787–1805, preceded by a sketch of Sandy River Baptist Church, of which Skull Shoals (Pacolet) was a branch.

d. Filmed at Darlington, 1963, by permission of the Pastor and Board of Deacons of the various churches [8].
Elim Baptist Church, Effingham, Minute Book, 1847–1927. Ebenezer Baptist Church, RFD, Florence, Minute Book, 1823–60. New Providence Baptist Church, RFD, Hartsville, Minute Book, 1808–1922. Mount Elon Baptist Church, Lydia, Minute Book, 1831–1943. Antioch Baptist Church, RFD, Society Hill, Minute Book, 1830–95. Lake Swamp Baptist Church, RFD, Timmonsville, Minute Book, 1834–55, 1868–1916. Sardis Baptist Church, RFD, Timmonsville, History of Sardis Baptist Church, 1840–1940 [typescript], Minute Book, 1863–73.

e. Filmed at Edgefield [5].
Bethany Baptist Church, Minute Book, 1810–1910, financial records, 1912–32, miscellaneous papers, 1890–1914. Edgefield Baptist Church, Minute Book, 1823–1920. Bethel Baptist Church, Minute Book, 1853–1908, list of pastors, 1909–35. Hortense Woodson and Church Historians, *History of Edgefield Baptist Association, 1807–1957* (Edgefield: The Edgefield Advertiser Press). Edgefield County Cemetery inscriptions, Mamie Norris Tillman and Hortense Woodson, compilers, *Inscriptions from Edgefield Village Baptist Cemetery Including Trinity Episcopal Church Section and Willowbrook Cemetery* (for Edgefield County Historical Society, 1958).

f. Filmed at Barnwell County Courthouse, Barnwell, [1]. Barnwell Baptist Church, records and minutes, 1803–1912.

g. Filmed at St. John's Lutheran Church, Charleston [1]. Record Book, (in German), 1765–87.

h. Filmed at South Carolina Archives Department, 1962 [1]. Stoney Creek Independent Presbyterian Church, Prince William's Parish, Records, 1722–1910.

4. South Carolina Historical Society: Henry Laurens Papers, 1748–81 [19].
5. Charleston Library Society: South Carolina Newspapers, 1732–82 [12]. *South Carolina Gazette,* 1732–75. *Gazette of the State of South Carolina,* 1777–80. *South Carolina Gazette and Country Journal,* 1765–68, 1773–75. *South Carolina and American General Gazette,* 1764–81. *Royal Gazette,* 1781–82. *Royal South Carolina Gazette,* 1780–82.
6. Kings Mountain National Park: Roster of Patriot Soldiers at the Battle of Kings Mountain, October 7, 1780 [1]. An unofficial "roster" assembled by Kings Mountain National Park. Filmed for the South Carolina Archives Department by W. L. McDowell, Jr., June 1964.

Other American Institutions

1. National Archives
   RG 53 Records of the Bureau of the Public Debt. Portions of the Register's Estimates and Statements, 1796–97 [1].
   United States District Court, Charleston Books, 1789–1861 [5]. Original court records deposited in the Federal Records Center, East Point, Georgia. Filmed for South Carolina Archives Department, April 1964.
   Records of the South Carolina Court of Admiralty (1716–95) [4].
   United States Census Records for South Carolina, 1800–80 [67].
   Records of the Commissioners of Claims (Southern Claims Commission) 1871–80 [2].
   Special Schedule of the 11th Census of the United States (1890) enumerating Union veterans and widows of Union veterans of the Civil War [1].
   Letters received by the Secretary of the Treasury from Collectors of Customs, 1833–69 [11].
   Correspondence of the Secretary of the Treasury with Collectors of Customs, 1789–1833 [1].
   Papers of the Continental Congress, 1774–89 [22]. Includes letters from Maj. Gen. Nathanael Greene, 1776–85.
   Consolidated index to compiled service records of Confederate soldiers [535].
   Compiled service records of Confederate soldiers who served in organizations raised directly by the Confederate government [1].
   Records relating to Confederate naval and marine personnel [7].
   Compiled service records of Confederate soldiers who served in organizations from the state of South Carolina [392].
   Index to RW pension applications and bounty land warrant files [15].
   Compiled service records of Confederate general and staff officers and nonregimental enlisted men [275].

Miscellaneous papers of the Continental Congress, 1774–89 [2]. Papers relating to specific states and deeds of cession of western lands with related documents (1779–1802). Credentials of the Delegates from each State to the Congress, 1774–89.

2. Library of Congress
   John Archdale Papers, 1690–1706 [1]. Manuscripts in the Library of Congress.
   Early State Records, 1671–1869 [39]. William S. Jenkins, compiler, and Lillian A. Hamrick, ed., *A Guide to the Microfilm Collection of Early State Records* (Library of Congress, 1950). South Carolina entries.

3. Harvard University
   Papers concerning the governorship of South Carolina, 1720–27 [1].
   Letters to, from, and concerning Francis Nicholson and the governorship after the revolution of 1719. Microfilm of private papers deposited in the Harvard University Library. Use only with permission of the Director of the South Carolina Archives.
   Report of the Surveyor General, 1770 [1].
   Manuscript of William Gerard DeBrahm, Surveyor for the Southern Department of North America, by commission of His Majesty George III, 26 June 1764.

4. New York Public Library
   Minutes of the Council of Safety, Feb. 28–March 26, 1776 [1]. Film made by the New York Public Library, 1960.

British Institutions

1. Public Record Office
   American Council of Learned Societies, British Manuscripts Project, 1663–1782 [87]. Includes all Carolina and South Carolina entries and one North Carolina entry.
   Shaftesbury Papers: Fundamental Constitutions for the Government of Carolina, 21 July 1669 [1].
   Papers re Carolina, Proprietary Period, 1663–1727 [2].
   War Office: Amherst Papers, 1756–1763 [2].
   Cornwallis Papers, 1779–82 [4].
   Papers of the Commanders-in-Chief at British Headquarters in America during the Revolution, 1775–83 [30]. Consists of documents transferred to Sir Guy Carleton by earlier commanders and those made during his command.

2. Bath, Library at Longleat: Coventry Papers, 1606–1705 [3]. Papers relating to Virginia, Barbados, and other colonies.

3. British Museum: Fundamental Constitutions of Carolina, March 1, 1669 [1]. Printed copy.

4. Christ Church Library, Oxford: Documents relating to South Carolina from Vol. 24 of the Wake Letters, 1716–25 [1].

5. Society for the Propagation of the Gospel in Foreign Parts, 1702–75 [7].
   Carolina Letters and Papers: A 1–17, 19-26 (1702–37); B 1, 4–5, 7, 9–16, 20 (1714–61); Fulham Manuscripts (South Carolina): Nos. 1, 7, 51–62, 67, 105, 115, 116, 125, 236, 245, 300 (1703–75); Lambeth Manuscripts: 1123 II No. 164, 1123 I No. 45; Photostats of the Society for the Propagation of the Gospel DeBray No. 334.

South Carolina Baptist Hospital Library
   V 1,600   CP 47
This library is primarily for the South Carolina Baptist Hospital School of Nursing, which is affiliated with Columbia College. Collection includes copies of articles published by hospital staff members.

South Carolina Business—M 1954+
Bulletin of the South Carolina State Chamber of Commerce.

South Carolina City—Q 1959+
Published by the Municipal Association of South Carolina.

South Carolina Civil Defense News Letter—M 1958+

South Carolina Clubwoman—M (except summer) 1955+
Published by the South Carolina Federation of Women's Clubs.

South Carolina Crop Reporting Service—M 1952+

South Carolina Dental Journal—M 1944+

South Carolina Education News—M 1918+
Publication of the South Carolina Education Association.

South Carolina Engineer—M 1937+
Published by the South Carolina Society of Engineers.

South Carolina Farmer—M 1944+
Published by the South Carolina Farm Bureau.

South Carolina Guidance News—Q 1950+

Published by the Office of Guidance Services, State Department of Education.

South Carolina High School Literary Yearbook—(24 issues per year) 1935+

Published by the School of General Studies, University of South Carolina.

South Carolina Historical Association, Proceedings—A 1931+

South Carolina Law Quarterly—Q 1948+

Published by the South Carolina Bar Association and the University of South Carolina Law School.

South Carolina Labor News—Q 1943+

South Carolina Magazine—M 1937+

At offices, 1106 Barnwell Street, editors also have copies of *Carolina Highways* 1945+, *Garden Club of South Carolina Magazine* 1955–63, *Review of Architecture* 1960+, *South Carolina Business and Professional Woman* 1945+, *South Carolina City* 1957+, *South Carolina Clubwoman* 1946+, *South Carolina Engineer* 1937+, and the *United Daughters of the Confederacy Magazine* 1946+.

South Carolina Magazine Corporation

This corporation prints, distributes, and retains limited files of these publications: *Carolina Highways*—M, *South Carolina City*—Q, and *South Carolina Magazine*—M (January issue of each year is a guide and directory to state and local governmental divisions).

South Carolina Market Bulletin—W 1934+

Published by the South Carolina State Department of Agriculture.

South Carolina Methodist Advocate—W 1837+

The *Advocate* office at 1420 Lady Street has microfilm files 1837–1900 and also copies of the *Wesleyan Journal* 1825–27. Essentially complete files of the *Advocate* can also be found at Wofford College and at Emory University.

South Carolina Nursing—Q 1948+

South Carolina Parent Teacher—(issued eight times per year) 1935+
Official publication of the South Carolina Congress of Parents and
Teachers.

South Carolina Pharmaceutical Association, Proceedings—A 1918+

South Carolina Reporter—W (when law cases are available)
The *Reporter*, published by R. L. Bryan, consists of advance sheets
of *South Carolina Reports* 1871+.

South Carolina Schools—(issued six times per year) 1949+
Official publication of the South Carolina Department of Education.

South Carolina State Development Board News—M 1959+

South Carolina State Library
V 275,000   CP 21   US GOVT   DOC
Located in the state capitol, this noncirculating legislative library
was established in 1814. It has a small but selective collection of
SC and CW data, up-to-date codes of all states, materials printed
by the state of South Carolina, selected Federal documents, and a
general reference section. This collection includes numerous clip-
pings, books, and papers of the late A. S. Salley. Of special interest
is his annotated set of the *South Carolina Historical and Genealogical
Magazine*. This library has files of the [*Columbia*] *State* 1891+,
[*Charleston*] *News & Courier* 1884+, *Yearbooks of the City of
Charleston* (1880–1951), and *Columbia City Directories* 1919+.

South Carolina State Library Board
V 65,000   R 3,537   SC 1,810   CP 278   MFMR   MRP   PCE
The South Carolina State Library Board coordinates and supplements the services of the public library system throughout the state.
Its collection of books and periodicals is available only through
interlibrary loan to the patrons of any public library. There is no
charge for such service, but the borrowing library is expected to
pay return postage and any insurance charges. The board also an-
swers reference questions, but this service does not extend to con-

test questions, genealogical research, medical or legal advice, or any type of information not normally given by public libraries. A file of material re history and development of various public libraries in SC is maintained at the board's headquarters. It includes numerous unpublished histories and sketches of various libraries. This material, which is indexed, does not circulate on loan but may be consulted by interested persons. The South Caroliniana Library and the State Library Board have developed a cooperative plan in genealogical research. A number of genealogical compendiums and reference works on family history have been purchased by the board and are available in the reading room of the South Caroliniana Library. The board also maintains a collection of books [c. 1,000] on art, art masterpieces, and architecture which is also available on interlibrary loan.

From time to time the board augments the holdings of various public libraries. See CAROLINA MATERIALS PROJECT (pp. 55–61). And the board also publishes guides to its own collection. *A Bibliography of Business, Technical, and Scientific Books Available on Interlibrary Loan from the South Carolina State Library Board* was compiled in 1964 by Charles H. Busha, reference consultant.

All of the board's periodical files are on microfilm and may be borrowed on interlibrary loan for two weeks. Photocopies of specific articles may also be obtained from the State Library Board. This collection, begun in 1958, includes 223 titles. The majority of those indexed in the *Readers' Guide to Periodical Literature* begin in 1952; those indexed in the *Applied Science and Technology Index,* in 1958. These magazines include: *Administrative Management* 1961+, *Advertising Age* 1958+, *Aircraft Engineering* 1958+, *Air Conditioning & Refrigeration* 1958+, *Air Conditioning, Heating & Ventilation* 1958+, *America* 1952+, *American Association of Petroleum Geologists Bulletin* 1958+, *American Business [Office Management]* 1958+, *American City* 1953+, *American Concrete Institute Journal* 1958+, *American Dyestuff Reporter* 1958+, *American Home* 1954+, *American Journal of Public Health* 1958+, *American Machinist* 1958+, *American Mercury* 1953+, *American Oil Chemists' Society Journal* 1958+, *American Scientist* 1958+, *American Society of Civil Engineers' Proceedings* 1958+, *American Water Works Association Journal* 1958+, *Americas* 1953+, *Antiques* 1953+, *Applied Hydraulics* 1958+, *Architectural Record* 1958+, *Archives of Environmental Health* 1960+, *Archives of Industrial Health* 1958–60,

The Atlantic 1953+, *Atomic Scientists' Bulletin* 1954+, *Audubon Magazine* 1953+, *Automation* 1958+, *Automobile Engineer* 1958+, *Automotive Industries* 1958+; *Bell Laboratories Record* 1958+, *Bell System Technical Journal* 1958+, *Best's Insurance News* 1958+, *Better Homes and Gardens* 1953+, *British Plastics* 1958, *Business Week* 1958+; *Catholic World* 1952+, *Changing Times* 1954+, *Chemical Engineering* 1958+, *Chemical Week* 1958+, *Civil Engineering* 1958+, *Coal Age* 1958+, *Combustion* 1958+, *Commentary* 1955+, *Commonweal* 1952+, *Compressed Air Magazine* 1958+, *Concrete* 1958+, *Consumer Reports* 1953+, *Consumers' Research Bulletin* 1953+, *Control Engineering* 1958+, *Coronet* 1954–61, *Current History* 1954+; *Design* 1953+, *Diesel Equipment Superintendent* 1958+, *Diesel Power* 1958–60, *Distribution Age* 1958+, *Dun's Review & Modern Industry* 1958+; *Economic Geology* 1958+, *Economist* 1958–59, *Electrical Communication* 1958+, *Electrical Construction & Maintenance* 1958+, *Electrical Engineering* 1958+, *Electrical Manufacturing* 1958–59, *Electrical World* 1958+, *Electro-Technology* 1960+, *Electronic Engineering* 1958, *Electronic Industries* 1958+, *Electronics* 1958+, *Electronics World* 1959+; *Factory Management & Maintenance* 1958+, *Fleet Owner* 1958+, *Flower Grower* 1954+, *Flying* 1953+, *Food Engineering* 1958+, *Food Technology* 1958+, *Foreign Affairs* 1952+, *Foreign Policy Bulletin* 1954+, *Foundry* 1958+, *Franklin Institute Journal* 1958+; *General Electric Review* 1958, *Geophysics* 1958+, *Graphic Arts Monthly* 1958+; *Harper's Magazine* 1953+, *Harvard Business Review* 1958+, *Heating, Piping & Air Conditioning* 1958+, *Holiday* 1953+, *Horn Book Magazine* 1954+, *House & Home* 1953+, *Hydraulics & Pneumatics* 1960+; *Illuminating Engineering* 1958+, *Industrial Arts & Vocational Education* 1953+, *Industrial & Labor Relations Review* 1958+, *Industrial Development & Manufacturers' Record* 1958+, *Industrial Finishing* 1958+, *Industrial Laboratories* 1958–59, *Industrial Marketing* 1958+, *Industrial Medicine & Surgery* 1958+, *Industrial Quality Control* 1958+, *Inland Printer* 1958+, *Institute of Petroleum Journal* 1958–59, *Instruments & Control Systems* 1958+, *Iron Age* 1958+, *International Conciliation* 1954+; *Journal of Accountancy* 1958+, *Journal of Applied Mechanics* 1958+, *Journal of Applied Physics* 1958+, *Journal of Geology* 1958+, *Journal of Marketing* 1958+, *Journal of Metals* 1958+, *Journal of Petroleum Technology* 1958+; *Ladies Home Journal* 1953+, *Life* 1958+; *McCall's Magazine* 1952+, *Machine Design* 1958+, *Maga-*

zine of Standards 1958+, *Management Review* 1958+, *Manufacturers' Record* 1958, *Material Handling Engineering* 1958+, *Mechanical Engineering* 1958+, *Metals Progress* 1958+, *Mining Engineering* 1958+, *Modern Packaging* 1958+, *Modern Plastics* 1958+, *Modern Textiles* 1958+, *Monthly Labor Review* 1953+, *Musical America* 1953+; *Nation* 1953+, *National Civic Review* 1959+, *National Municipal Review* 1958, *National Parent-Teacher* 1953+, *National Petroleum News* 1958+, *National Tax Journal* 1958+, *Nation's Business* 1954+, *Natural History* 1953+, *Nature Magazine* 1953+, *Negro History Bulletin* 1953+, *New Republic* 1953+, *Nucleonics* 1958+; *Office* 1958+, *Office Management* [*American Business*] 1960, *Oil & Gas Journal* 1958+, *Outdoor Life* 1954+; *Paper Trade Journal* 1958+, *Parent's Magazine* 1953+, *Personnel* 1958+, *Personnel & Guidance Journal* 1957+, *Personnel Journal* 1958+, *Petroleum Engineer* 1958–60, *Petroleum Management* 1961+, *Petroleum Refiner* 1958+, *Petroleum Week* 1958+, *Physics Today* 1958+, *Pit & Quarry* 1958+, *Plant Engineering* 1958+, *Plating* 1958+, *Plays* 1954+, *Poetry* 1957+, *Popular Mechanics* 1953+, *Popular Photography* 1953+, *Popular Science Monthly* 1953+, *Power* 1958+, *Power Engineering* 1958+, *Practical Home Economics* 1952+, *Printer's Ink* 1958+, *Product Engineering* 1958+, *Progressive Architecture* 1958+, *Public Management* 1958+, *Public Works* 1958+, *Publisher's Weekly* 1958+, *Pulp & Paper* 1958+; *Q. S. T.* 1958+; *R. C. A. Review* 1958+, *Radio-Electronics* 1958+, *Radio & Television News* 1953+, *Railway Age* 1958+, *Readers Digest* 1953+, *Recreation* 1953+, *Roads & Streets* 1958+, *Rock Products* 1958+, *Rotarian* 1953+, *Rubber Age* 1958+, *Rubber Chemistry & Technology* 1958+; *S.A.E. Journal* 1958+, *Safety Maintenance & Production* 1958+, *Sales Management* 1958+, *Saturday Evening Post* 1952+, *Saturday Review* 1953+, *School & Society* 1953+, *School Arts* 1952+, *School Life* 1953+, *Science Digest* 1953+, *Science News-Letter* 1954+, *Scientific American* 1953+, *Senior Scholastic* 1952+, *Sewage & Industrial Wastes* 1958–59, *Sky & Telescope* 1952+, *Society of Dyers & Colourists* 1958–59, *Society of Motion Picture & TV* 1958+, *Steel* 1958+, *Survey of Current Business* 1958+; *Taxes* 1958+, *Textile Industries* 1958+, *Textile Research Journal* 1958+, *Textile World* 1958+, *Theatre Arts* 1953+, *Time* 1958+, *Today's Health* 1953+, *Tool Engineer* 1958+; *United Nations Review* 1954+, *US Department of State Bulletin* 1955+, *US News & World Report* 1955+; *Vogue* 1952+; *Water & Sewage*

Works 1958+, *Water Pollution Control Federation Journal* 1960+, *Welding Engineer* 1958+, *Welding Journal* 1958+, *Wireless World* 1958–59, *Writer* 1953+; *Yachting* 1956+, *Yale Review* 1952+.

Carolina Materials Project

The books on this list were chosen by a panel of experts on South Carolina history as representing the essential books for the study of the State's history. The South Carolina State Library Board made available to one library in each congressional district any title on the list which the library did not own. Libraries receiving the grants have opened their South Carolina history collection to adult users in the congressional district. Most of the titles on the list are either out of print or available only in the rare book market. Those entries followed by an asterisk are available in Xerox editions from University Microfilms. The participating libraries are Colleton County Memorial Library, Aiken-Bamberg-Barnwell-Edgefield Regional Library, Greenwood City and County Public Library, Spartanburg Public Library, Chester County Free Library, Horry County Memorial Library, and Florence County Library.

Allen, Walter. *Governor Chamberlain's Administration in South Carolina; A Chapter of Reconstruction in the Southern States.* New York: Putnam, 1888.*

Andrews, Columbus. *Administrative County Government in South Carolina.* Chapel Hill: University of North Carolina Press, 1933.*

Bernheim, Gotthardt Dellmann. *History of the German Settlements and of the Lutheran Church in North and South Carolina.* Philadelphia: Lutheran Book Store, 1872.*

Boucher, Chauncey Samuel. *The Nullification Controversy in South Carolina.* Chicago: University of Chicago Press, 1916.*

Burton, E. Milby. *South Carolina Silversmiths, 1690–1860.* Charleston, S. C.: Charleston Museum, 1942.

Capers, Henry Dickson. *The Life and Times of C. G. Memminger.* Richmond: Everett Waddey, 1893.*

Carroll, Bartholomew Rivers, ed. *Historical Collections of South Carolina; embracing many rare and valuable pamphlets, and other documents, relating to the history of that state, from its first discovery to its independence in the year 1776.* New York: Harper, 1836. 2 vols.*

Chapman, John Abney. *History of Edgefield County from the Earliest Settlements to 1897.* Newberry, S. C.: E. H. Aull, 1897.*

Chreitzberg, Abel McKee. *Early Methodism in the Carolinas.* Nashville, Tenn.: Methodist Episcopal Church Publishing House, 1897.*

Coleman, James Karl. *State Administration in South Carolina.* New York: Columbia University Press, 1935.*

Crum, Mason. *Gullah: Negro Life in the Carolina Sea Islands.* Durham, N. C.: Duke University Press, 1940.*

Dalcho, Frederick. *An Historical Account of the Protestant Episcopal Church, in South Carolina, from the first settlement of the province, to the war of the revolution; with notices of the present state of the church in each parish and some account of the early civil history of Carolina . . . to which are added; the laws relating to religious worship; the journals and rules of the convention of South Carolina; the constitution and canons of the Protestant Episcopal Church, and the course of ecclesiastical studies; with an index and list of the subscribers.* Charleston, S. C.: S. Thayer, 1820.*

Doar, David. *Rice and Rice Planting in the South Carolina Low Country.* Charleston, S. C.: Charleston Museum, 1936.*

Draper, Lyman Copeland. *King's Mountain and Its Heroes: History of the Battle of King's Mountain, October 7th, 1780, and the Events Which Led to It.* Cincinnati, Ohio: P. G. Thomson, 1881.*

Drayton, John. *Memoirs of the American Revolution, from its commencement to the year 1776, inclusive; as relating to the state of South Carolina; and occasionally referring to the states of North Carolina and Georgia.* Charleston, S. C.: A. E. Miller, 1821. 2 vols.*

Drayton, John. *A View of South Carolina, as Respects Her Natural and Civil Concerns.* Charleston, S. C.: W. P. Young, 1802.*

Durham, Frank. *DuBose Heyward, the Man Who Wrote Porgy.* Columbia, S. C.: University of South Carolina Press, 1954*

Elliott, William. *Carolina Sports, by Land and Water; Including Incidents of Devilfishing, etc.* Charleston, S. C.: Burges & James, 1846.*

Elzas, Barnett Abraham. *The Jews of South Carolina.* Philadelphia: Lippincott, 1905.*

Fraser, Charles. *Reminiscences of Charleston, lately published in the Charleston Courier and now rev. and enl. by the author.* Charleston, S. C.: J. Russell, 1854.

Gallagher, Helen Mar (Pierce). *Robert Mills: Architect of the Washington Monument, 1781–1855.* New York: Columbia University Press, 1935.*

Garden, Alexander. *Anecdotes of the Revolutionary War in America, with sketches of character of persons the most distinguished in the southern states for civil and military services.* Charleston, S. C.: A. E. Miller, 1822.*

Garlington, J. C. *Men of the Time. Sketches of living notables; a biographical encyclopaedia of contemporaneous South Carolina leaders.* Spartanburg, S. C.: Garlington, 1902.*

Gibbes, Robert Wilson. *Documentary History of the American Revolution: consisting of letters and papers relating to the contest for liberty, chiefly in South Carolina. . . .* New York: Appleton, 1853–57. 3 vols.*

Great Britain. *Public Record Office. Records in the British Public record office relating to South Carolina, 1663–1710;* indexed by A. S. Salley. Printed for the Historical Commission of South Carolina by Foote & Davies Company of Atlanta. Ga., 1928–31; Columbia, S. C., Crowson-Stone Printing Company, 1946–47.

Green, Edwin Luther. *A History of Richland County.* Vol. 1, 1732–1805. Columbia, S. C.: R. L. Bryan, 1932.

Gregg, Alexander. *History of the Old Cheraws: containing an account of the aborigines of the Pedee, the first white settlements, their subsequent progress, civil changes, the struggle of the revolution, and growth of the country afterward, extending from about A. D. 1730 to 1810, with notices of families and sketches of individuals.* New York: Richardson, 1867.*

Gregorie, Anne King. *Thomas Sumter.* Columbia, S. C.: R. L. Bryan, 1931.

Hemphill, James Calvin. *Men of mark in South Carolina; ideals of American life: a collection of biographies of leading men of the state.* Washington: Men of Mark Publishing Co., 1907–9. 4 vols.*

Heyward, Duncan Clinch. *Seed from Madagascar.* Chapel Hill: University of North Carolina Press, 1937.*

Hirsch, Arthur Henry. *The Huguenots of Colonial South Carolina.* Durham, N. C.: Duke University Press, 1928.*

Houston, David Franklin. *A Critical Study of Nullification in South Carolina.* New York: Longmans, Green, 1896.*

Howe, George. *History of the Presbyterian Church in South Carolina.* Columbia, S. C.: Duffie & Chapman, 1870–83. 2 vols.*

Hughson, Shirley Carter. *The Carolina Pirates and Colonial Commerce, 1670–1740.* Baltimore: John Hopkins University Press, 1894.*

Hungerpiller, John C. *South Carolina literature, with biographical notes and critical comments, compiled, edited, and published by J. C. Hungerpiller.* Columbia, S. C.: R. L. Bryan, 1931.*

[Irving, John Beaufain]. *The South Carolina Jockey Club.* Charleston, S. C.: Russell & Jones, 1857.*

Jervey, Theodore Dehon. *Robert Y. Hayne and His Times.* New York: Macmillan, 1909.*

Johnson, Joseph. *Traditions and Reminiscenses Chiefly of the American Revolution in the South: including biographical sketches and anecdotes, few of which have been published, particularly of residents of the upper country.* Charleston, S. C.: Walker and James, 1851.*

Johnson, William. *Sketches of the Life and Correspondence of Nathanael Greene.* Charleston, S. C.: A. E. Miller, 1822. 2 vols.*

Johnston, Gideon. *Carolina Chronicle; the papers of Commissary Gideon Johnston, 1707–1716,* ed. with an introduction and notes by Frank J. Klingberg. Berkeley: Univ. of California Press, 1946.*

Jones, Frank Dudley, ed. *History of the Presbyterian Church in South Carolina since 1850.* Columbia: Synod of South Carolina and R. L. Bryan, 1926.

Kibler, Lillian Adele. *Benjamin F. Perry, South Carolina Unionist.* Durham, N. C.: Duke University Press, 1946.*

King, William L. *The Newspaper Press of Charleston, S. C.: a chronological and biographical history, embracing a period of one hundred and forty years.* Charleston, S. C.: Edward Perry, 1872.*

Kohn, August. *The Cotton Mills of South Carolina.* Columbia, S. C.: Department of Agriculture, Commerce, and Industries, 1907.*

Larsen, Christian L. *South Carolina's Natural Resources: a Study in Public Administration.* Columbia: University of South Carolina Press, 1947.*

Logan, John Henry. *A History of the Upper Country of South Carolina.* Repr. Spartanburg, S. C.: Reprint Co., 1960.

McCrady, Edward. *The History of South Carolina in the Revolution, 1775–1780.* New York: Macmillan, 1901.*

McCrady, Edward. *The History of South Carolina in the Revolution, 1780–1783.* New York: Macmillan, 1902.*

McCrady, Edward. *The History of South Carolina under the Proprietary Government, 1670–1719.* New York: Macmillan, 1897.*

McCrady, Edward. *The History of South Carolina under the Royal Government, 1719–1776.* New York: Macmillan, 1899.*

Malone, Dumas. *The Public Life of Thomas Cooper, 1783–1839.* Columbia: University of South Carolina Press, 1961.

Meriwether, Colyer. *History of Higher Education in South Carolina, with a Sketch of the Free School System.* Washington: Government Printing Office, 1889.*

Meriwether, Robert Lee. *The Expansion of South Carolina, 1729–1865.* Kingsport, Tenn.: Southern Publishers, 1940.

Mills, Robert. *Atlas of the State of South Carolina.* Facsimile edition with an introduction by Francis Marion Hutson. Columbia, S. C.: Bostick and Thornley, 1938.

Mills, Robert. *Statistics of South Carolina, Including a View of Its Natural, Civil, and Military History, General and Particular.* Charleston, S. C.: Hurlbut and Lloyd, 1826.*

Mitchell, Broadus. *William Gregg, Factory Master of the Old South.* Chapel Hill: University of North Carolina Press, 1928.*

Moultrie, William. *Memoirs of the American Revolution, so far as it related to the states of North and South Carolina and Georgia; compiled from the most authentic materials, the author's personal knowledge of the various events, and including an epistolatory correspondence on public affairs, with civil and military officers, of that period.* New York: Longworth, 1802. 2 vols.*

O'Connell, Jeremiah Joseph. *Catholicity in the Carolinas and Georgia; Leaves of Its History.* New York: D. & J. Sadler, [1879].*

O'Neall, John Belton. *The annals of Newberry, in two parts; part first by John Belton O'Neall . . . part second by John A. Chapman.* Newberry, S. C.: Aull & Houseal, 1892.*

O'Neall, John Belton. *Biographical Sketches of the Bench and Bar of South Carolina . . . to which is added . . . the rolls of attorneys* *admitted to practice*. Charleston, S. C.: S. G. Courtenay, 1859. 2 vols.*

Petigru, James Louis. *Life, Letters and Speeches of James Louis Petigru, the Union man of South Carolina . . . with an introduction by Gaillard Hunt*. Washington, D. C.: W. D. Lowdermilk, 1920.

Petty, Julian J. *The Growth and Distribution of Population in South Carolina*. Columbia, S. C.: prepared for State Planning Board, published by State Council for Defense, Industrial Development Committee, July 1943.*

Pringle, Mrs. Elizabeth Waties (Allston). *Chronicles of Chicora Wood*. New York: Scribner, 1922.

Ramsay, David. *The History of South Carolina, from its first settlement in 1670, to the year 1808 . . . by David Ramsay . . .* Charleston, S. C.: David Longworth for the author, 1809.

Ravenel, Harriott Horry Rutledge ("Mrs. St. Julien Ravenel"). *Eliza Pinckney*. New York: Scribner, 1896.*

Ravenel, Harriott Horry Rutledge ("Mrs. St. Julien Ravenel"). *Life and Times of William Lowndes of South Carolina, 1782–1822*. Boston, Mass.: Houghton, 1901.*

Rhea, Linda. *Hugh Swinton Legare, a Charleston Intellectual*. Chapel Hill: University of North Carolina Press, 1934.*

Richardson, James McDowell. *History of Greenville County, South Carolina, narrative and biographical*. Atlanta, Ga.: A. H. Cawston, 1930.*

Rivers, William James. *A Sketch of the History of South Carolina to the Close of the Proprietary Government by the Revolution of 1719*. Charleston, S. C.: McCarter, 1856.*

Robertson, Ben. *Red Hills and Cotton; an Upcountry Memory*. Columbia: University of South Carolina Press, 1960.

Salley, Alexander Samuel. *The History of Orangeburg County, South Carolina, from Its First Settlement to the Close of the Revolutionary War*. Orangeburg: R. L. Berry, Printer, 1898.*

Schaper, William August. *Sectionalism and Representation in South Carolina; a Sociological Study*. American Historical Association Report No. I (1900), pp. 237–463. Washington: Government Printing Office, 1901.*

Sellers, Leila. *Charleston Business on the Eve of the American Revolution*. Chapel Hill: University of North Carolina Press, 1934.*

Shipp, Albert Micajah. *History of Methodism in South Carolina*. Nashville, Ten.: Southern Methodist Publishing House, 1884.*

Simkins, Francis Butler. *Pitchfork Ben Tillman, South Carolinian*. Baton Rouge: Louisiana State University Press, 1944.

Simkins, Francis Butler. *South Carolina during Reconstruction*. Chapel Hill: University of North Carolina Press, 1932.*

Simkins, Francis Butler. *The Tillman Movement in South Carolina*. Durham, N. C.: Duke University Press, 1926.*

Simms, William Gilmore. *Letters*, ed. Mary C. Simms Oliphant, Alfred Taylor Odell, and T. C. Duncan Eaves; intro. by Donald

Davidson; biographical sketch by Alexander S. Salley. Columbia: University of South Carolina Press, 1952–56.
Singer, Charles Gregg. *South Carolina in the Confederation.* Philadelphia, 1941.*
Smith, Reed. *South Carolina Ballads, with a Study of the Tradition Ballad Today.* Cambridge, Mass.: Harvard University Press, 1928.*
Smith, William Roy. *South Carolina as a Royal Province, 1719–1776.* New York: Macmillan, 1903.*
South Carolina Dept. of Agriculture. *South Carolina. Resources and Population, Institutions and Industries.* Charleston, S. C.: Walker, Evans and Cogswell, 1833.*
South Carolina Historical Association. *Proceedings.* 1931+
South Carolina Historical Magazine. 1900+. Charleston, S. C.
South Carolina Historical Society. *Collections of the South Carolina Historical Society.* Charleston, 1857–97.*
South Carolina. Laws, Statutes, etc. *The Statutes at large of South Carolina (1682–1838).* Vols. I–V ed. Thomas Cooper; Vols. VI–X ed. David J. McCord. Columbia, S. C.: A. S. Johnston, 1838–41.*
South Carolina, University of. *South Carolina: Economic and Social Conditions in 1944.* Columbia: University of South Carolina Press, 1945.*
Stoney, Samuel Gaillard. *Plantations of the Carolina Low Country . . . edited by Albert Simons and Samuel Lapham, Jr. . . . with an introduction by John Mead Howells.* Charleston, S. C.: Carolina Art Association, 1938.
Taylor, Alrutheus A. *The Negro in South Carolina during Reconstruction.* Washington, D. C.: Association for Study of Negro Life and History, 1924.
Thomas, J. A. W. *A History of Marlboro County, with Traditions and Sketches of Numerous Families.* Atlanta, Ga.: Foote and Davies Co., 1897.*
Thomason, John Furman. *The Foundations of the Public Schools in South Carolina.* Columbia, S. C.: The State Co., 1925.
Townsend, Leah. *South Carolina Baptists, 1670–1805.* Florence, S. C.: Florence Printing Co., 1935.
Tuomey, Michael. *Report on the Geology of South Carolina.* Columbia, S. C.: A. S. Johnston for the State, 1848.*
Van Deusen, John George. *Economic Bases of Disunion in South Carolina.* New York: Columbia University Press, 1928.*
Vandiver, Mrs. Louise Ayer. *Traditions and History of Anderson County.* Atlanta, Ga.: Ruralist Press, 1928.*
Wallace, David Duncan. *The Life of Henry Laurens; with a Sketch of the Life of Lieutenant-Colonel John Laurens.* New York: Putnam, 1915.*
Wallace, David Duncan. *The South Carolina Constitution of 1895,* Bulletin of the University of South Carolina No. 197, February 15, 1927. Columbia, 1927.*

Wauchope, George Armstrong. *Literary South Carolina; a short account of the progress of literature and the principal writers and books from 1700 to 1923*, Bulletin of the University of South Carolina No. 133, Dec. 1, 1923. Columbia, 1923.*

Wauchope, George Armstrong, comp. *The Writers of South Carolina, with a Critical Introduction, Biographical Sketches, and Selections in Prose and Verse.* Columbia, S. C.: The State Co., 1910.*

Who's Who in South Carolina, a dictionary of contemporaries containing biographical notices of eminent men of South Carolina, ed. Geddings Harry Crawford. Columbia, S. C.: McCaw, 1921.*

Who's Who in South Carolina, a standard biographical reference book of South Carolina, 1934–35. Columbia, S. C.: Current Historical Association, 1935.*

Willis, Eola. *The Charleston Stage in the XVIII Century, with Social Settings of the Time.* Columbia, S. C.: The State Co., 1924.*

South Carolina Supreme Court Library

V 20,000   CP 20

This legal library is maintained in the state capitol for justices and judges of the state. It is open for public use, but materials cannot be loaned. Files include briefs and records of the South Carolina Supreme Court and a scrapbook of clippings re activities of the court.

South Carolina Wildlife—Q 1953+

Published by the South Carolina Wildlife Resources Department.

South Carolina Young Farmer and Future Farmer—Q 1950+

Publication of the South Carolina State Department of Agriculture.

Southeastern Press

This press prints, distributes, and retains limited files of these publications: *North Carolina Council of Women's Organizations*—A, *North Carolina Football Annual*—A, *Palmetto Leaf*—Q (publication of the Dietitic Association of South Carolina), *South Carolina Football Annual*—A. Also Southeastern Press has files of the *Jackson Journal*—W 1956–62, a civilian enterprise for military and civilian personnel at Fort Jackson.

Spotting the News—M 1935+

Published by the Southeastern Photoengravers Association.

Star Reporter—W 1963+

State—D [mfm] 1891+

Recordak and Micro Photo   MFMR

Sunday editions of this newspaper have contained from time to time (1949+) a separate feature section known as the *State Magazine.* Two indexes have been compiled and are available at many libraries. A subject index prepared by Susie Norwood McKeon, of Winthrop College, Rock Hill, covers the years 1949–53. An annual index prepared by Lila Grier, of Dreher High School, Columbia, covers the years 1949–56. Numerous libraries also have an early annual index to all issues of the *State* (1892–1912).

State Board of Health Monthly Newsletter—M 1948+

State Service Magazine—M 1950+

Publication of the South Carolina State Employees Association.

Student Nursing Education Library, South Carolina State Hospital

V 3,243   R 19   CP 23

Summary of Operations—M 1947+

Published by the South Carolina Employment Security Commission.

Trade Winds—(semiannually) 1948+

Publication of the South Carolina Area Trade School.

USC Perspective—Q 1960+

Issued ten times a year (1960–65), in June 1965 *USC Perspective* became a quarterly. Also at that time the *University of South Carolina Magazine* appeared. This publication and *USC Perspective* replace several previous University alumni magazines under a variety of titles (1920–59).

Unemployment Insurance Claims—W 1955+

South Carolina Employment Security Commission publication.

University of South Carolina, Law School Placement Bulletin—A
1958+

University of South Carolina Libraries
  V 566,516   R 15,000   CP 3,000   MCR   MFMR   MRP   PCE
  US GOVT DOC

This system includes six main divisions: McKissick, School of Education, School of General Studies, Law School, South Caroliniana, and Undergraduate. It serves all libraries at University extensions throughout the state. The general collection includes 15,816 reels of microfilm and 348,374 items of other micro materials. In addition to this entry for the entire library system and specifically re holdings at McKissick Library, this guide contains entries for each of the other major divisions and for the extension libraries.

McKissick Library

Currently establishing a rare book collection which is a heterogeneous assortment of titles (1800–60) from its shelves reflecting interests of scholars of those decades. See Elizabeth Doby English, *Special Collections in the McKissick Memorial Library, University of South Carolina* (Ann Arbor, 1952). This work describes some 700 titles printed prior to 1820, Confederate imprints, and limited editions. An interim supplement compiled by McCluer Sherrad (1961) is available at the library. Materials housed at McKissick Library include the following items:

MICROCARD SERIES—Chaucer [I, II], *Courier-Journal* [Louisville, Ky.] 1949–52, French Revolution Pamphlets, British Historical Manuscripts Commission Reports 1874+, Health and Physical Education, Kentucky Culture, Primary Records in Culture and Personality, 19th-cent. American Literature, 19th-cent. American Pamphlets, "Rolls Series" of Chronicles and Memorials of Great Britain and Ireland during the Middle Ages, and Debates of the US Congress 1824–37.

MISCELLANEOUS MICROFILM MATERIAL—Jeremiah Black Papers [Library of Congress, 36 reels] 1813–1904, Current Digest of the Soviet Press (1949–52), Despatches [sic] from US Ministers to Great Britain 1815–70, Diplomatic Instructions from the US Department of State to all Countries 1801–33, Diplomatic Instructions from the US Department of State to Great Britain 1829–40, 1863–71,

Diplomatic Instructions from the US Department of State to the Netherlands 1833–64, English Books 1475–1640 [941 reels], English Books 1640–1700 [117 reels], English Literary Periodicals, 17th to 19th centuries [662 reels], Facts on Film [40 reels], *Federal Register* 1936+, German Foreign Ministry Records 1914–18, German Foreign Office Records Received by the US Department of State 1919–33, International Military Tribunal for the Far East 1946–47 [12 reels], Abraham Lincoln Papers [Library of Congress, 97 reels] 1833–1916, Sears, Roebuck & Company Catalogs 1888+, Lyman Trumbull Papers [Library of Congress, 22 reels] 1855–94.

NEWSPAPERS ON MICROFILM—*China Weekly Review* 1917–51, *Christian Science Monitor* 1908–60, *Chung-Kuo Chi'ing Nien Pao* 1958–59, *Coming Nation* [Greensburg, Ind.] 1893–1901, *International Press Correspondent and World News* 1922–54, *Izvestia* 1958+, *Jen Min Jih Pao* 1954–62, *Kuang Ming Jih Pau* 1954–62, *Le Monde* 1952+, [London] *Times* 1785+, [London] *Times Literary Supplement* 1902+, *Manchester Guardian* 1821+, [New Orleans] *Morning Star and Catholic Messenger* 1868–79, *New York Herald* 1858–68, *New York Times* 1851+, *New York Tribune* 1857–68, *New York Weekly News* (1876), *Pravda* 1958+, [Richmond] *Enquirer* 1860–67, *Wall Street Journal* 1957+, [Washington] *National Intelligencer* (1840), *Virginia Gazette* 1736–80.

MICROPRINTS—American State Papers 1789–1838; British House of Commons: Sessional Papers 1731–1900, Journal 1547–1900; Early American Imprints 1639–1800; Russian Historical Sources [First Series, 1–19]; Three Centuries of English and American Plays; United Nations Documents and Officials Records 1946+; US Government: Non-Depository Publications 1953–61, Documents Serials Set 1–915, and Library of Congress Cyrillic Union Catalog.

School of Education Library
V 28,000   CP 156

School of General Studies Library

This library supplies films, filmstrips, recordings, books, plays, and related materials to high schools, teachers, students, clubs, and other interested groups. It also serves seven off-campus centers of the University throughout the state. See these annual bulletins: *Audio-Visual Aids Catalog, Package Library Service,* and *Play Library Service.*

Law School Library

V 54,357   CP 178

Collection includes proceedings and reports of the American Bar Association 1878+, selected court reports, and statutes of various states, New Zealand, Australia, Great Britain, and Canada.

South Caroliniana Library

This division of the University of South Carolina Library contains special materials in South Carolina history. Its collections include 1,270,000 manuscripts (1675+), approximately 45,000 books, pamphlets, and periodicals, and more than 4,500 reels of microfilm. The editorial offices for *The Papers of John C. Calhoun* are located in this building (some 40,000 photocopies of Calhoun documents collected by this agency will eventually become part of the library's manuscript holdings). The files of a substantial number of South Carolina newspapers, both original and microfilm copies, are found here (see pp. 138–45; national and international newspaper files are housed in McKissick Library), and the library has a complete file of all University of South Carolina theses and dissertations.

SPECIAL COLLECTIONS—Among these are 8,468 pictures indexed by person and place; a guide to portraits in public buildings and private homes throughout the state; a sheet music collection [10 boxes, c. 500 items] containing songs written about South Carolina or by South Carolinians (1800+); the A. S. Salley collection of the works of William Gilmore Simms [c. 400v]; and the Henry P. Kendall Collection of books, pamphlets, pictures, and maps of South Carolina and adjoining states (1580–1830). The Kendall maps are supplemented by the Library's own collection of 17th–20th-cent. maps. A file of 415 maps published by the Sanborn Map Company, 1884–1935, gives location and minute construction details of business establishments, churches, homes, schools, factories, hotels, and other insurable property in 88 cities and towns in SC.

MANUSCRIPTS—Filed and indexed by personal, corporate, or institutional names. Main entries in the manuscript catalog are also listed chronologically in a "Year File." The main catalog lists microfilmed materials and WPA transcripts of epitaphs and county records. There is also a subsidiary catalog of unprocessed materials, and entries drawn from this catalog in the following list may not be entirely accurate. Other inaccuracies and some duplication may have resulted in combining the main and subsidiary catalogs and in abbreviating the main catalog's fuller descriptions for this list. Future handling by the library staff of unprocessed material for permanent filing may result in changes in designation and description. Manuscripts listed here include all collections classified as one or more volumes [v] and those containing fifteen or more individual items. It is regrettable that thousands of choice items in smaller groups must be omitted. Thus an entry of [21] indicates twenty-one letters or papers; [21, v], twenty-one items and a single volume; [3v], three volumes. The letter "r" indicates that the item has been reproduced by some means other than microfilm (which is designated by mfm). Entries such as [125 mfm] or [3v mfm] show that the material is available only on microfilm; [125, also mfm] or [3v, also mfm] indicates both original and microfilm copies may be consulted. The dates of some individuals are cited in parentheses. Dates at the end of an entry indicate either the approximate years covered by the collection or, in some instances, the date of compilation or publication. Researchers should also consult the annual programs of the University South Caroliniana Society for detailed accounts of important manuscript acquisitions since 1951.

Abbeville Account Book [v]. Cokesbury, recipes and miscellaneous clippings. 1875.
Abbeville County [18vr]. WPA transcripts, Court of Equity and Judge of Probate records. 1772–1869.
Abbeville County [2vr, also mfm]. WPA transcripts of epitaphs: Episcopal Churchyard, Long Cane and Melrose Cemeteries.
Abbott, Martin L. [v mfm]. "Freedman's Bureau of S. C.," diss. Emory Univ., 1954.
Abney, Benjamin Lindsey [2v, 29 boxes]. Uncatalogued material. 1809–1910.
Adams Family [v mfm]. Genealogy, descendants of Joel and Grace Adams, Richland County. c. 1910.
Adams, James H. [vr]. Genealogy, "Adams Family of the Fork." 1905.
Addison, John [vr]. Edgefield County, family records. 1760–1900.
Addy, Lonnie B., Sr. [vr]. Lexington centennial. 1961.
Adger, James [vr]. Charleston letterbook, constitution of Charleston Independent Greens. 1809–19.
Adger-Smyth-Flinn [97]. Charleston, chiefly correspondence of Adger and Smyth families, especially John B. Adger (1810–99). 1830–94.

Agricultural and Mechanical Institute of Orangeburg [v]. Account book. 1878–79.
Aiken County [vr, also mfm]. WPA transcripts of epitaphs: Bethany Cemetery, Darien Baptist and First Baptist Churchyards, Glover Cemetery, Hammond Private Graveyard, Hardy's Baptist Church, Kimball Cemetery, Levels Baptist Churchyard, Methodist Cemetery [Montmorenci], Millbrook Baptist Church, Montmorenci Cemetery, North Augusta Cemetery, Old Langley Cemetery, St. John's Methodist, St. Thaddeus Episcopal Churchyard, Sweetwater Baptist Church, Turner-Hatcher, Wade, and Williams Families [private burying grounds].
Aiken Family [87, v]. Family letters, politics, CW, genealogy, diary of Mary Gale Aiken (1874–88), New Orleans, Winnsboro, and Mobile. 1832–97.
Aiken, Hugh K. [125]. Fairfield District, CW, business papers. 1833–64.
Aiken, W. E. [v]. SC College notes with list of Fairfield District physicians. 1845–52.
Aiton, Thomas [44]. Abbeville, Edgefield, CW. 1839, 1861–64.
Alder, Sikke [v]. Charleston Harbor pilot book. 1854–55.
Aldrich, James (1850–1901) [2v]. Clippings on Ellenton Riot. 1850–1910.
Aldrich, Robert (1844–1911) [v mfm]. Scrapbook of SC collegiate and political life. 1896–1910.
Allen, Orasmus D. [vr]. Barnwell letterbook. 1826–47.
Allendale County [2vr, also mfm]. WPA transcripts of epitaphs: Boyles Family Cemetery, Fairfax Cemetery, Family [sic] Burying Ground, Swallow Savannah Cemetery.
Allston-La Bruce Families [28]. Genealogy. 1680–1900.
Allston, Robert F. W. (1801–64) [14, 2v, 11vr]. Various papers re family, politics, education, plantation life. 1775–1895.
Alston Family [v]. Rose Hill Plantation recipe book. c. 1818.
American Association of University Women, SC Division [16v]. Records. 1924–63.
Ancrum, W. A. & Co., Camden [v]. Letterbook. 1878–80.
Anderson, Mrs. Charles G. [vr]. Selected epitaphs of Aiken, Calhoun, Lexington, Orangeburg, and Saluda Counties. 1953.
Anderson County [vr]. Historical sketches of Anderson College and Cokesbury Institute. 1911–25.
Anderson County [12vr]. WPA transcripts, various official court records. 1790–1935.
Anderson County [2vr, also mfm]. WPA transcripts of epitaphs: Baker's Creek Baptist Churchyard, Bennett Family Graveyard, Bethany Baptist Churchyard, Big Creek Cemetery, Boggs Burying Ground, Byrum Family Burying Ground, Cedar Grove Baptist Churchyard, Concord Baptist Cemetery, Concord Baptist Churchyard, Dorchester Baptist Churchyard, Eureka Baptist Churchyard, First Presbyterian Cemetery, Flat Rock Cemetery, Hopewell

Baptist Churchyard, Long Branch Cemetery, Midway Presbyterian Churchyard, Mt. Bethel Baptist Churchyard, Mt. Zion Presbyterian Churchyard, Neal's Creek Baptist Churchyard, Old Concord Presbyterian Churchyard, Old Hopewell Baptist Churchyard, Old Lewis Burying Ground, Pendleton Baptist Churchyard, Pendleton Methodist Churchyard, Presbyterian Church Cemetery, Rice Cemetery, St. Paul's Episcopal [Pendleton], Sandy Springs Methodist Church, Trinity Methodist Churchyard, Union Grove Methodist Churchyard, Watkins Family Burying Ground, Welcome Baptist Church Cemetery, Whitaker Smith Burying Ground, Whitefield Baptist Churchyard, Williamston Cemetery.

Anderson, Lily Strickland (1887–1958) [46]. Letters and articles re her career as a composer. 1937–47.

Anti-Saloon League, Camden [31]. Circulars and letters. 1919–20.

Arnett, G. Scott [19]. Walterboro business papers. 1897–1900.

Arnold, Annie S. [v]. Allendale, notes on Teachers' Institute at SC College. 1881–86.

Arthur, Benjamin F. (1826–70) [30]. Politics and CW. 1834–1942.

Arthur-Dogan Families [20]. Columbia and Union family letters. 1834, 1857–80.

Arthur Family [24]. Lexington County bills and receipts; Columbia Bridge Company accounts. 1810–63.

Ashmore, John D. (1819–71) [vr]. Sumter and Anderson County plantation journal. 1853–59.

Ashworth, Henry (1794–1880) [v]. Diary of an East Coast tour. 1857.

ARP Church, Hopewell, Chester County [5vr]. Records, some (1833–1910) available on microfilm. 1832–1939.

ARP Church, Union, Chester County [vr, also mfm]. Records. 1752–1939.

ARP Church, Thompson Street, Newberry [vr]. Records. 1854–81.

Association of SC Colleges [28, v]. Minutes and records. 1902–45.

Athenaeum Fire Insurance Company, Charleston [v]. Diagrams of various SC mills. 1855.

Atkinson, James [17, v]. Chester County bills and receipts. 1812–84.

Atlantic Coast Lumber Corporation, Georgetown [16,000]. Chiefly deeds in Berkeley, Florence, Georgetown, Marion, and Williamsburg Counties; also company records (1899–1942). 1716–1946.

Auld, Donald J. [26]. Family correspondence, Sumter and Manning area. 1867–1901.

Austin, E. [v]. Account book. 1857–63.

Babcock, Ferebe E. (b. 1897) [17]. Correspondence of Waverly Sanitarium Negro employees in World War II. 1941–44.

Babcock, Katherine Gion (1866–1943) [24, 2v]. Notes on hospital training in Boston (1888–90) and lectures at the SC State Hospital for the Insane. c. 1890.

Bachman, Mrs. W. K. [vr]. Letters, including account of the burning of Columbia. 1865.

Bacot, Ada [8, 7v]. CW diaries of life in Mars Bluff and service as a nurse in Charlottesville, Va. 1860–63. See *University South Caroliniana Society Program* (1965).

Bacot Family [78]. Family letters, Winnsboro and Charleston. 1854–1928.

Bailey, Thomas P. [20, 19v]. Medical account books of Georgetown; also, description of Leeds, England. 1853–95.

Baldwin, Thomas W. [v]. Notes on Baldwin family in SC in the 18th century. c. 1940.

Ball Family [v]. Birth-death register of Comingtree Plantation. 1849–96.

Ball Family [c. 1,000]. Various papers. Some of these are plantation records (1792–1890) available on microfilm. 1696–1864. See *SCHM* (1964) for an article by Richard Beale Davis re this collection.

Ball, Mrs. W. W. [3v]. Political clippings on Tillman campaigns. 1888–90.

Bank of Camden [v]. Account book. 1855–70.

Banks, Charles R. [v]. Genealogy of Banks, Long, Hauser, Early, Sanders, and Skinner families. 1943–44.

Banks, William [8v]. Scrapbooks. 1801–1917.

Bannon, John (1829–1913) [v]. Confederate priest, diary of activities in Mississippi. 1861–63.

Baptist Church, Allendale [v]. Records. 1868–1902.

Baptist Church, Antioch, Kershaw County [vr]. Marriage records. 1852–84.

Baptist Church, Barnwell, Barnwell County [vr, also mfm]. Records. 1803–1912.

Baptist Church, Barnwell Baptist Association [vr]. Records. 1867.

Baptist Church, Beaulah, Laurens County [vr]. Records. 1883–1904.

Baptist Church, Beech Branch, Hampton County [4v]. Records. Some of these are available on microfilm (1865–1918). 1814–1918.

Baptist Church, Bethabara, Laurens County [vr, also mfm]. Records. 1801–81.

Baptist Church, Bethel, Newberry County [vr, also mfm]. Records. 1841–1910.

Baptist Church, Bethesda, Kershaw County [v, also mfm]. Records. 1823–1905.

Baptist Church, Big Creek, Anderson County [vr, also mfm]. Records. 1801–1936.

Baptist Church, Black Creek, Beaufort County [vr, also mfm]. Records. 1828–1922.

Baptist Church, Bush River, Newberry County [v mfm]. Records. 1792–1923.

Baptist Church, Bushy Creek, Greenville County [vr, also mfm]. Records. 1794–1927.

Baptist Church, Camden [64]. Chiefly correspondence concerning centennial. 1907–33.

Baptist Church, Canaan, Orangeburg County [v, also mfm]. Records. 1823–1910.
Baptist Church, Cashaway, Craven County [vr, also mfm]. Records. 1756–78.
Baptist Church, Chestnut Ridge, Laurens County [2v, also mfm]. Records. 1816–1939.
Baptist Church, Christ, Horn's Creek [v mfm]. Records. 1824–54.
Baptist Church, Church of Christ, Abner Creek [vr, also mfm]. Records. 1834–70.
Baptist Church, Church of Christ, Mountain Creek [vr, also mfm]. Records. 1833–54.
Baptist Church, Church of Christ, Popular Springs [v]. Records. 1878–1911.
Baptist Church, Columbia [vr]. Sunday school records. 1876–78.
Baptist Church, Concord, Greenville County [vr]. Records. 1880–1903.
Baptist Church, Coosawatchie [v mfm]. Records. 1814–64.
Baptist Church, Ebenezer, Darlington County [2v, also mfm]. Records. 1823–1908.
Baptist Church, Elim, Effingham, Florence County [2v mfm]. Records. 1836–1927.
Baptist Church, Euhaw, Beaufort County [20, 2v]. Various papers and records. Some records (1831–75) have been microfilmed. 1831–1908.
Baptist Church, Fair Forest, Union County [vr, also mfm]. Records. 1820–99.
Baptist Church, First, Charleston [vr, also mfm]. Records. 1847–75.
Baptist Church, First, Columbia [vr, also mfm]. Records. 1809–40.
Baptist Church, Flint Hill, York County [3v, also mfm]. Records. 1792–1899.
Baptist Church, Great Saltketcher, Barnwell County [vr, also mfm]. Records. 1858–79.
Baptist Church, Gum Branch, Lower Fork of Lynches Creek, Chesterfield County [vr, also mfm]. 1796–1887.
Baptist Church, Hopewell, Chester County [vr]. Records. 1871–95.
Baptist Church, Horn's Creek, Edgefield County [v]. Records. 1824–59.
Baptist Church, Huntsville, Laurens County [v, also mfm]. Records. 1838–71.
Baptist Church, Kingstree, Williamsburg County [vr, also mfm]. Records. 1858–94.
Baptist Church, Little Pee Dee, Pauley's Creek, Horry County [vr]. Records. 1868–87.
Baptist Church, Mechanicsville, Darlington County [2v, also mfm]. Records. 1803–67.
Baptist Church, Milford, Greenville County [vr, also mfm]. Records. 1832–69.

Baptist Church, Mineral Springs, Marlboro County [vr]. Records. 1867–1905.
Baptist Church, Mount Aron, Allendale County [2vr, also mfm]. Records. 1839–1937.
Baptist Church, Mount Moriah, Camden [15]. Clippings, circulars and letters. 1922–34.
Baptist Church, Mount Pleasant, Laurens County [v]. Historical sketch. 1949.
Baptist Church, Mountain Creek, Spartanburg County [vr]. Records. 1833–54.
Baptist Church, Neal's Creek, Anderson County [vr, also mfm]. Records. 1832–1901.
Baptist Church, New Allendale, Allendale County [vr]. Records. 1882–1922.
Baptist Church, New Providence, Hartsville [vr, also mfm]. Records. 1808–1922.
Baptist Church, Old Mispah, Mars Bluff, Florence County [vr, also mfm]. Records. 1830–62.
Baptist Church, Padget's Creek, Union County [2vr, also mfm]. Records. 1784–1874.
Baptist Church, Perfect [vr, also mfm]. Records. 1859–1939.
Baptist Church, Pleasant Grove [v mfm]. Records. 1833–1955.
Baptist Church, Popular Springs, Union County [2v, also mfm]. Records. 1794–1937.
Baptist Church, Primitive, Beaver Dam, Kershaw County [v]. Records. 1844–82.
Baptist Church, Primitive, Crooked Run, Edgefield District [v]. Records. 1840–43.
Baptist Church, Prince William's, Hampton County [vr, also mfm]. Records. 1812–1937.
Baptist Church, Raburn Creek, Laurens County [vr, also mfm]. Records. 1828–1913.
Baptist Church, Salem, Marlboro County [3vr, also mfm]. Records. 1797–1930.
Baptist Church, Sandy Level, Fairfield County [vr, also mfm]. Records. 1817–1908.
Baptist Church, Sandy Run, Lexington District [vr]. Records. 1881–1909.
Baptist Church, Smyrna, Hampton County [vr]. Records. 1870–1927.
Baptist Church, Swift Creek, Kershaw County [v, also mfm]. Records. 1827–68.
Baptist Church, Thomas Memorial, Marlboro County [vr, also mfm]. Records. 1832–1924.
Baptist Church, Tyger River Association, Greenville County [vr]. Records. 1870.
Baptist Church, Union, Spartanburg County [vr, also mfm]. Records. 1804–43.

Baptist Church, Warrior's Creek, Laurens County [7v, vr]. Records, some (1843–96) are available on microfilm. 1843–1932.
Baptist Church, Welsh Neck, Society Hill [vr, also mfm]. Records. 1737–1952.
Barnwell County [20vr]. WPA transcripts, various court records. 1785–1936.
Barnwell County [vr, also mfm]. WPA transcripts of epitaphs: Baptist Churchyard [Barnwell], Baptist Churchyard [Blackville], Blackville Cemetery, Catholic Churchyard [Barnwell], Catholic and Methodist Churchyards [Blackville], Episcopal Churchyard [Barnwell], Friendship Churchyard [near Barnwell], Old Baptist Churchyard [Barnwell].
Barnwell, Edward H. (1832–1908) [48]. Material re Beaufort, Charleston, Pocataligo, and Kinston, N. C.; chiefly correspondence with his wife and details of his CW experiences. 1860–69.
Barnwell, Robert Woodward (1801–82) [42]. Reports and letters as a faculty member and president of SC College. 1835–79.
Barnwell, Robert Woodward (1831–63) [21]. Correspondence as SC College professor and superintendent of Confederate hospitals in Virginia. 1856–62.
Barton, Hettie C. [7vr]. Genealogical notes on Alverson/Anderson, Wheden/Whedon families. c. 1955.
Baruch, Bernard M. [15]. Clippings, letters, and addresses. 1926–58.
Baskin, William Peebles (b. 1904) [v mfm]. Bishopville scrapbook, activities as chairman of SC Democratic Party (1947–52); and [vr] transcript of testimony re rights of Negroes to enroll in SC Democratic Party (1948). 1947–52.
Bateman, J. M. [3v]. SC travel accounts. 1914–37.
Baxter, William and Fannie [33]. Newberry, business papers. 1835–88.
Bearden, Elizabeth, compiler [vr]. Contributors to the *Southern Review*. 1925.
Beaufort [v]. Photo album. 1890.
Beaufort College [v mfm]. Trustees minutes. 1795–1868.
Beaufort County [v]. Minutes and records of School District No. 1. 1925–30.
Beaufort County [4vr, also mfm]. WPA transcripts of epitaphs: First Tabernacle Baptist Churchyard, St. Peter's Catholic Churchyard, US National Cemetery, Jewish Cemetery, Old Sheldon, St. Peter's Church Graveyard, First Baptist Church Graveyard [Beaufort], Evergreen Cemetery [Beaufort], and one "unnamed" cemetery.
Beckett, R. C. (1845–1921) [v]. Beckett genealogy. 1958.
Bellinger, Edmund C. (1803–48) [v]. Estate records. 1848–64.
Belser, F. S. and L. H. [20]. Sumter and Charleston, business papers. 1848–69.
Berkeley County [2vr, also mfm]. WPA transcripts of epitaphs: Belle Isle Cemetery, Pooshee Plantation.
Bible Society of Charleston [v]. Treasurer's book. 1821–62.

Bicaise Company, The L. W., Charleston [3v]. Business records. 1892–1913.

Binda, Count Joseph Agememnon (1790–1864) [v]. Journal of husband of Fanny Sumter, daughter of Colonel Thomas Sumter, Jr., re London and Paris in 1824; also, entries re Miss Brownfield's Boarding and Day School, 1881–89. 1824–89. See *University South Caroliniana Society Program* (1965).

Black Creek Farmers' Club, Hartsville [v]. Records. 1860–73.

Black, J. H. [vr]. Scrapbook and notes. 1857–61.

Black, James M., Jr. [25r]. Humorous printed verse. 1944–48.

Black, John [357, 79v]. Mercantile accounts and records at Island Ford, Milton, Cedar Springs, and Wadsworthville School. 1790–1848.

Black, Joseph [58]. Manuscript and published poems. 1857–60.

Black Oak Agricultural Society, Berkeley County [vr]. Minutes. 1842, 1847–49.

Black Oak Calhoun Monument Association [v]. Records. 1853–72.

Blackville, Barnwell County [v]. Birth-death-marriage register. 1895–1919.

Blair, John [v]. Journal of voyage from Larne to Charleston. 1796.

Blake, Daniel [69]. Legal documents and letters, Beaufort and Charleston. 1795–1843.

Blake, Eugene Hood (b. 1886) [190]. Greenwood; newspaper articles and other materials re compulsory education, Thomas S. Lubbock, World War I, and various subjects of SC interest. 1914–60.

Blanding, A. Lucius [21, 2v]. Medical accounts and clippings; materials re Kentucky, Fountain Inn, and McFaddin family. 1889–1937.

Blanding, James Douglas (1821–1906) [40]. SC College in the 1840's, Reconstruction. 1834–1905.

Blanding, William (1773–1857) [128, 4v]. Diaries and correspondence re Massachusetts, Camden, Charleston, slavery, natural science, nullification, Indian mounds, and extensive East Coast travels. 1807–50.

Bleckley, S. [v]. Scrapbook. 1865.

Blease, Coleman Livingston (1868–1942) [19]. Newberry; chiefly clippings, leaflets, and handbills. 1914–61.

Blue Family [28, vr]. Family papers and genealogy. 1883–1945.

Boinest, Thaddeus S. [vr]. Diary as a farmer, official of Newberry College, and Lutheran minister. 1852–70.

Bolt, Margaret Eltinge [v]. Laurens County epitaphs. 1950.

Bomar, Edward Earle [v]. Diary re Legare Literary Society and education in Spartanburg County. 1875.

Bones Family [vr]. Genealogy. 1963.

Bonham, Milledge Luke (1815–90) [c. 4,000, vr]. Papers of CW governor, legal and business records of Edgefield District family, material re Mexican War and Reconstruction. Also data collected by grandson, Milledge Lipscomb Bonham, Jr., for unpublished biography of his grandfather. 1771–1940. See *University South Caroliniana Society Program* (1965).

Bonney, E. W. [24]. Camden, business papers. 1841–68.

Bost, Raymond Morris [vr]. "Religion and Medicine," paper read before SC Chapter, American Academy of General Practice. 1963.

Boyd, D. T. [vr]. Phosphate shipments from Beaufort. 1891–98.

Boyd, W. B. [v]. Accounts kept as Laurens County (?) doctor. 1858.

Bradley Family [1 box]. Chiefly Williamsburg land records. 1736–1808.

Bradley, Francis W. [14v]. Correspondence re SC dialects. 1949–53.

Branchville Vigilant Association [v]. Minutes and resolutions adopted as security against slaves. 1860–63.

Branson, Lanier [v]. Records of CW requisitions and post-CW law suits. 1865, 1872–73.

Bratton Family [186, 16v]. CW letters, correspondence, and business records of York County family; sketch of Brattonsville; data re Bratton, Lowry & Company and Bratton & Rainey; and DAR correspondence of Mrs. R. M. Bratton re Battle of King's Mountain and *USS South Carolina*. 1779, 1840–1953.

Breslauer-Lachicotte Company, Georgetown [10 boxes, 39v]. Records. 1864–1900.

Bresnihan, William F. [7 boxes]. Charleston business papers. 1887–1913.

Brice Family [v]. Winnsboro, genealogy. 1931.

Bristow, Louis Judson [410]. Columbia, Abbeville; papers re early years of Columbia Baptist Hospital. 1910–52.

Brookes, Iverson L. [280]. Business and personal papers re Edgefield, Charleston, Hamburg, Georgetown, Furman Institute, and his career as a Baptist minister. 1792–1872.

Brown Family [vr]. Genealogy, Spartanburg and Greenville Counties. 1963.

Brown, Joseph N. [895]. Various papers. 1857–1911.

Brown, Mary Davis (1822–1903) [7v]. York County, diary. 1854–59, 1867–1901.

Brown, William (d. 1757) [vr]. Genealogical notes on his descendants. 1945.

Broyles, Margaret Taliaferro [v]. Account book and journal of life in Tennessee. 1863–72.

Bruce, Jones, and Murchison Families [621, 4v]. Orangeburg, St. Matthews, Sumter; chiefly family letters on socioeconomic life. 1785–1956. See *University South Caroliniana Society Program* (1964).

Bruns, Henry M. [2v]. Scrapbooks of professor at College of Charleston. 1840–89.

Brunson, Joe E. (1847–1913) [13v]. Kingstree and Sumter letterbooks. 1882–1911.

Bryan, John (1753–1805) [v]. Genealogy. 1940.

B. T. and Company, Conway [v]. Account book with news clippings. 1860–87.

Bull, William A. (d. 1839) [153, v]. Life at Willington Academy and SC College, Seminole War, and plantation accounts. 1803–60.
Burney, William B. [49v]. Chemistry notebooks and textbooks. 1854–99.
Bullard and Burr, Camden [27]. Business papers. 1824–29.
Burts, Robert N. [v mfm]. "Public Career of Richard I. Manning" (diss. Vanderbilt Univ., 1957).
Bush, John [vr]. Barnwell District and Georgia, indentures and deeds. 1795–1867.
Butler, Andrew Pickens (1796–1857) [36]. Edgefield, various papers. 1847–55.
Butler Family [4v]. Family Bibles, genealogical records, and a scrapbook kept by Mrs. F. W. Pickens Butler and her daughter, Ellen I. Butler. Mrs. Butler's scrapbook (1861–1950) has been microfilmed. 1759–1953.
Butler, Francis Wilkinson Pickens (1858–1924) [176]. Letters to his wife, Lillian Jones Butler; papers re his medical practice. 1881–1938.
Butler, Lillian Jones (1870–1950) [vr]. Scrapbook re Pickens, Butler, Jones and allied families. 1821–1951.
Butler, Matthew Calbraith (1836–1909) [77]. Family letters, correspondence with John L. Manning, Stephen D. Lee, and Wade Hampton; US relations with Cuba. 1860–1926.
Butler (M. C.) & Youmans (Leroy) [8 boxes]. Edgefield attorneys' papers. 1850–1875.
Butler, Pierce (1744–1822) [25]. Papers re RW confiscated estates, slaves, Georgia Indians, and finances. 1775–1819.
Butler, Pierce Mason (1798–1847) [1,350]. Personal papers re his career as soldier (Seminole and Mexican Wars), banker, planter, Indian Agent, and governor of S. C. 1819–83. See *University South Caroliniana Society Program* (1957).
Byrnes, James Francis (b. 1879) [31, 5v]. Various papers re World War II, speeches at USC, and SC politics. 1935–62.
Caesar's Head Hotel [v]. Guest register. 1873–80.
Cain, J. C. [2v]. Geological notes and Somerset Plantation records. 1857–68.
Cain, Joseph P. [4v]. Records of Somerset Plantation. 1870–93.
Cain, William [184, 4v]. Pinopolis, plantation and household accounts. 1836–69.
Caldwell & Coleman, Columbia [4v]. Account books. 1844–62.
Caldwell, Howard Haine (1831–58) [17]. Notes on Caldwell as editor of the *Courant*. c. 1947.
Caldwell, James Fitz James (1837–1925) [v]. *History of a Brigade of South Carolinians . . . Gregg's . . . and McGowan's* with author's notes. 1866.
Caldwell, J. J. [v]. Columbia, business records. 1848–62.
Caldwell, P. C. [v]. Lexington County, business records. 1838–43.
Calhoun County [2vr, also mfm]. WPA transcripts of epitaphs: Cattle Creek Church, Cemetery [four miles southwest of Elloree],

David Wannamaker Cemetery, First Baptist Church Cemetery [St. Matthews], Heatly Cemetery, Keller Cemetery, Fort Motte Mizpah Baptist Church Cemetery, Old Cemetery [two miles east of Prospect Church], Old Cemetery [beside route 31], St. Matthews First Baptist Church Cemetery, St. Matthews Protestant Episcopal Church Cemetery, Tabernacle Cemetery, West Bethel Methodist Episcopal Church.

Calhoun, James Edward (1798–1889) [598]. Correspondence and papers re naval service, plantation affairs, gold mining, mills, railroad and land speculation, nullification, John C. Calhoun, and German colonization in SC. 1806–89.

Calhoun, John Caldwell (1782–1850) [30 boxes]. Uncatalogued letters consisting of correspondence of Calhoun and his immediate family. 1801–99.

Calhoun, John Caldwell (b. 1843) [431, 8v]. Anderson District land papers, CW reports, and military papers. 1786–1865.

Calhoun, Patrick (1821–58) [5, v]. Mexican War; account book of Quartermaster Department, Fort Lincoln, Texas. 1844–52.

Callcott, Wilfrid H. (b. 1895) [v]. Manuscript, biography of General Santa Anna with directions to the printer. 1936.

Cambridge Account Book [vr]. Mercantile records. 1835.

Camden Account Books [2v]. General merchandise accounts. 1828–55.

Camden Historical Society [v]. Records. 1904–16.

Camden Orphan Society [4v]. Records. 1786–1876.

Camden Riding and Driving Club [c. 40]. Records. 1923–28.

Camden Water, Light and Ice Company [v]. Stock certificates. 1901–2.

Campbell, James Butler (1808–33) [96]. Charleston legal and land papers, US District Tax Commission. 1826–1901.

Campbell, Simeon (d. 1912) [vr]. Diary, church records, and newspaper clippings. 1800–1912.

Canfield, Felicia [36]. Family letters re Charleston, Barnwell, Columbia, and Aiken. 1850–89.

Cannon, Aaron [2v]. Laurens County, diaries with mention of agricultural meetings and speech of Benjamin R. Tillman. 1886–87.

Cantey Family [320]. Business papers re plantations in Georgia and Alabama and construction of SC Railroad. 1771–1913.

Capers, Ellison (1837–1908) [70]. Chiefly correspondence with CW comrades re regimental history. 1862–1901.

Capers, William H. [42]. Legal papers of Sumter County sheriff. 1800–24, 1864.

Carlisle, James Henry (1825–1909) [2vr]. Published works with manuscript notes. 1842.

Carolina Biographical Association, Inc. [19]. Letters re *South Carolina and Her Builders.* 1928–29.

Carolina Military Institute [34r]. Printed matter re this Charlotte, N. C., school. 1873–1902.

Carrigan, Leach [2v]. Society Hill cotton buyer's records. 1836–38, 1849–63.
Carrigan, Samuel K. [2v]. Society Hill, daybook and salesbook. 1858–60.
Carrigan, William A. (1826–97) [476, 14v]. Society Hill business and plantation records. 1860–84.
Carroll, Charles R. [108]. Barnwell District, business and legal papers. 1857–88, 1926.
Carson, Caroline Petigru (1820–92) [16, 2v]. Original poems, clippings. 1852–87.
Carson, Martha Bray [v]. Epitaphs of area flooded by Santee-Cooper Project. 1942.
Carsten & Company, Charleston [v]. Receipt book. 1859–66.
Cash, Ellerbe Boggan Crawford (1823–88) [80, v]. Family, land, and business papers; correspondence re Cash-Shannon duel. 1805–1935.
Caston, W. Thurlow [v]. Scrapbook of his editorials in *Camden Journal.* 1849–50
Catesby, Mark (1682/3–1749) [28 mfm]. Charleston letters. 1722–25.
Cathcart, John H. [47, 12v]. Winnsboro and Columbia; business papers of Cathcart & Elliott, family correspondence, diaries, and school notes. 1858–95.
Catholic Church, Sisters of Our Lady of Mercy [vr]. "A Retrospect of the First Educational System in Sumter, South Carolina," St. Joseph's Academy. 1930.
Caughman-Hendrix Family [35]. Legal papers. 1803–1919.
Cayce Family [47]. Chiefly genealogical material. 1869–1956.
Certain, Mrs. Henry [v]. Scrapbook of poems. 1847–67.
Chafee & Company, Charleston [8,000, 27v]. Correspondence and accounts of this firm and its successor, Holmes & Company. c. 1880.
Chafee & O'Brien, Charleston [8v]. Business records. 1878–87.
Chafee, W. E. & Company, Charleston [v]. Ledger. 1887.
Chafee, William H. C. & Company, Charleston [3v]. Business records. 1887–89.
Chamberlain, Daniel Henry (1835–1907) [20]. Correspondence with Yates Snowden and John W. Alling with Snowden (1925) re Chamberlain's career in SC. 1877–1925.
Chamberlain, Valentine Burt [46 mfm]. Letters of a Connecticut CW prisoner in Columbia, S. C., jail. 1863–65.
Chandler, General S. B. [v]. Estate records. 1862–63.
Chandler, T. B. [v]. Personal account book. 1862–63.
Chapman, James K. [7v]. Pomaria, medical accounts and notes. 1868–88.
Chapman, William H. [77]. Chiefly notes on centennial celebration of the Palmetto Guards and their participation in CW. 1802–79.
Charles & Company, Darlington [70v]. Business records. 1839–1908.
Charles, A. L. [16]. Business papers. 1875–1909.

Libraries, Archives,

Charles Family [vr]. Thomas Charles genealogy. 1940.
Charleston [9v]. Register of Free Negroes. 1828–57.
Charleston [v]. Theatre programs. 1888–1905.
Charleston Account Book [v]. Cotton sales. 1849–52.
Charleston Bakery [v]. Order book. 1852–53.
Charleston County [160vr]. WPA transcripts, various court records
   including three volumes of US Admiralty Court journals (1787–
   1814). 1671–1935.
Charleston County [21vr, also mfm]. WPA transcripts of epitaphs:
   Bethany Cemetery, Bethel Methodist Episcopal Church [Charles-
   ton], "Stadium" Cemetery, Magnolia Cemetery, Old Circular
   Church Cemetery, French Huguenot Church Cemetery, Old
   First Baptist Church Cemetery, Presbyterian Churchyard [Edisto
   Island], Presbyterian Churchyard [James Island], St. Andrew's
   Episcopal Church Cemetery, St. Andrew's Lutheran Church Cem-
   etery, St. James Episcopal Church Cemetery [James Island],
   St. John's Episcopal Church Cemetery [Charleston], St. John's
   Lutheran Church Cemetery [Charleston], St. Lawrence Cemetery,
   German Artillery Memorial Association Cemetery, St. Mary's
   Church Cemetery, St. Patrick's Church Cemetery [Charleston],
   St. Paul's Episcopal Church Cemetery [Charleston], St. Peter's
   Episcopal Church Cemetery, St. Philip's Churchyard, St. Stephen's
   Chapel Cemetery, Scotch Presbyterian Church Cemetery, Second
   Presbyterian Church Cemetery, Styles Point Family Burying
   Ground [James Island], Trinity Episcopal Church Cemetery
   [Edisto Island], Trinity Methodist Church Cemetery [Charles-
   ton], Unitarian Church Cemetery [Charleston], Yeamen's Hall
   Cemetery [Goose Creek], German Cemetery.
Charleston Courier [67]. Price current sheets. 1836–39.
Charleston District [2v]. Commissioner of Locations records (1832–
   41) and miscellaneous legal records (1848–50). 1832–50.
Charleston Light Dragoons [3vr]. Records. 1835–59.
Charleston Navy Yard [19]. Chiefly papers re destroyer launchings.
   1932–47.
Charleston *News & Courier* [2v]. Clippings re material by and
   about Archibald Rutledge. 1921–22.
Charleston Scrapbook [v]. Newspaper clippings and notes. 1800–10.
Charleston Typographical Union [v]. Records. 1859–62.
Charleston, Ward No. 1 [v]. Account books and letters. 1807.
Cheraw Merchants Bank [4v]. Ledgers. 1849–63.
Cherry, Samuel S. [75]. Business papers. 1842–72.
Chesnut, James (1773–1866) [67]. Charleston, Camden, and Phila-
   delphia; chiefly household and plantation accounts. 1800–59. See
   also Williams-Chesnut-Manning Collection.
Chesnut, James (1815–85) [10, v]. Plantation papers, CW and post-
   CW accounts. 1832–85. See also Williams-Chesnut-Manning Col-
   lection.
Chester County [40 vr]. WPA transcripts of various court records.
   1768–1937.

Chester County Board of Commissioners [2v]. Minutes. 1850–72.

Chester, John and C. [v]. Sumterville daybook. 1830–32.

Chester Male Academy [19]. Miscellaneous records. 1853–72.

Cheves, Langdon (1776–1857) [25]. Correspondence as US Bank official and various personal papers. 1809–44.

Childs, Arney Robinson [c. 1,000]. Newspaper notes on sociopolitical life in SC. 1876–1912.

Childs Family [178, 3v]. Columbia genealogy and business papers of Lysander D. and William G. Childs. 1834–1912.

Childs, Frederick L. [44, vr]. CW correspondence and ordnance-artillery letterbook. 1857–65, 1901.

Chiles, John C. [vr]. Diary. 1860.

Chisolm Family [vr]. Genealogy. 1940.

Chisolm, Jean Flinn [122]. Clippings and letters. 1918–19.

Chisolm, William Garnett (1891–1955) [4v]. Manuscript notes for biography of Hugh Swinton Legare. 1913–52.

Christian Church, Browning, Brunson [vr]. Records. 1886–1927.

Christian Church, Enon, Hampton [vr]. Records. 1875–1911.

Ciples, Mrs. Sarah [19]. Camden, business and legal papers. 1847–67.

Clardy Family [116]. Laurens County, plantation and household records. 1833–88.

Clarendon County [2vr]. WPA transcripts, Judge of Probate records. 1871–96.

Clarendon County [9vr, also mfm]. WPA transcripts of epitaphs: Brown Family Cemetery, Butler Family Burying Ground, Calvary Baptist Churchyard, Conner Burial Ground, Elliott Family Cemetery, Evergreen Cemetery [Summerton], Home Branch Baptist Churchyard, Lawson Family Cemetery, Manning Cemetery, Paxville Cemetery, St. Paul's Cemetery, Ragin Family Cemetery, Summerton Baptist Cemetery, Ridgill Family Burying Ground, Tisdal Family Burying Ground, Trinity Methodist Churchyard.

Clark, Micajah Adolphus (1822–1905) [v]. Journal of travels from SC to Mississippi. 1857.

Clark, Washington Augustus (1842–1931) [277, 33v, 3vr]. CW material, plantation accounts, family documents, clippings, and speeches. 1767–1945.

Clayton, Narcissa [138]. Family letters. 1809–93.

Clayton, Robert Carter (1832–1911) [vr]. CW diary and notes. 1862–1949.

Clayton, W. F. [vr]. "Recital of our Services during the War for Southern Independence." c. 1870.

Clemson, Floride [vr, also mfm]. Diary. 1863–69.

Clemson, Thomas Green (1807–88) [vr]. Copies of letters in Clemson University collection. 1832–70.

Clifton Plantation [v]. Account book. 1878–80.

Clinkscales, Addison [2v]. Abbeville, account books. 1845–55.

Clinton, Henry [vr]. Copies of Charleston surrender papers in Clements Library. 1780.

Coates Family [vr]. Genealogy. c. 1957.
Cochran, Washington Smith (1803–62) [v]. Abbeville County, diary. 1860.
Coker Family [c. 170, c. 85v, 4 boxes]. Plantation and business records of a Society Hill-Hartsville family. 1831–1963. See also Lide-Coker Family.
Colclough, Alexander [v]. Clarendon County sheriff's receipt book. 1792–1820.
Colclough Family [vr]. Clarendon County, wills and receipt book. 1748–1820.
Colding, S. M. [v]. Letterbook of Savannah merchant re SC customers. 1867–80.
Coleman, John T. [437]. Chiefly family and business papers. 1833–90.
Colhoun, John Ewing (c. 1750–1802) [412]. Chiefly plantation and business papers and correspondence as US Senator. 1763–1822.
Colhoun, John Ewing (b. 1791) [43, vr]. Pendleton District and Charleston; commonplace book (1836–37), letters on plantation management. 1825–52.
Colhoun, William Ranson (1827–62) [v mfm]. Keowee Plantation account book. 1853–57.
College for Women, Columbia [22]. Chiefly programs. 1906–13.
Colleton County [2vr, also mfm]. WPA transcripts of epitaphs: Island Creek Cemetery.
Colleton County, Auditor [137 boxes]. Tax returns. 1868–1883.
Colleton County, Treasurer [c. 70v]. Tax receipts. 1868–1889.
Colleton County, Sheriff [57 boxes]. Records. 1807–1929.
Colleton Family [51]. Miscellaneous letters and papers re settlement of SC estate. 1684–1830.
Columbia Bank & Trust Company [v]. Business letters of J. C. Roath and others. 1871–72.
Columbia, Board of Water Commissioners [37, v]. Contracts, bills, and minutes. 1903–10.
Columbia Canal [55]. Land plats and legal papers. 1820–1901.
Columbia, Chamber of Commerce [38v, 9 boxes]. Scrapbooks (1920–55) and uncatalogued material. 1913–48.
Columbia City Council [971]. Records. 1908–13.
Columbia College [3v mfm]. Trustees minutes and student records. 1866–1921.
Columbia Comunity Chest [5v]. Chiefly scrapbooks. 1925–49.
Columbia & Eau Claire Electric Railway Company [v]. Directors' minutes. 1896–1901.
Columbia & Greenville Railroad [v]. Account book. 1850.
Columbia Ice House [v]. Ledger, daybook, and correspondence. 1866–74.
Columbia Medical Society [2 boxes, 24v]. Minutes and records. 1865–1942.
Columbia Medical Society, Women's Auxiliary [69]. Biographical data on deceased members. 1952–63.

Columbia Mills [vr]. Brief history. 1952.
Columbia Music Festival [v]. Miscellaneous programs. 1909–52.
Columbia Scrapbook [v]. Material re city life. 1911–13.
Columbia, Sesqui-Centennial Pageant and Christmas parades [47].
    Various papers. 1936–42.
Columbia Steamboat Company [v]. Minutes. 1856–59.
Columbia Theatre [34, v]. Programs. 1911–39.
Columbia Theological Seminary [3v]. Notebooks. 1872–83, 1927.
Columbia, Treasurer [v]. Register of bonds and scrip. 1881–92.
Commissioners of Free Schools [46]. Records. 1824–57.
Commissioners of Forfeited Estates [27r]. Lists for Ninety-Six and
    Camden Districts. 1783.
Confederate Scrapbook [v]. Newspaper clippings. 1889.
Confederate States Army, Engineers Department [72]. Miscellane-
    ous records of Charleston area. 1862–64.
Confederate States Army, Quartermasters Department [1,733].
    Chiefly letters and papers of Captain John Smythe Richardson,
    Assistant Quartermaster. 1864–65. See *University South Caro-
    liniana Society Program* (1962).
Confederate States Army, First Military District, SC [60 mfm].
    James Island papers. 1863.
Congregational Church, Circular Independent, Charleston [16v
    mfm]. Records. 1695–1935.
Connie Maxwell Orphanage, Greenwood [21]. Chiefly letters re
    contributors. 1902–28.
Connors, William John [3v mfm]. Clarendon and Lancaster Coun-
    ties, farm journals. 1821–43.
Conway, Bonds (1763–1843) [117]. Camden, chiefly papers re "free
    persons of color." 1800–1905.
Coogler, J. Gordon (1868–1901) [30r]. Editorials, poetry, and news
    articles by Coogler. 1894–1901.
Cook, Burrell Brown [v]. Genealogy. c. 1698–1774.
Cooper Limestone Institute, Gaffney [v]. Chiefly correspondence of
    R. O. Sams, joint principal. 1881–86.
Cooper, Thomas (1759–1839) [135, v]. Papers re career as pro-
    fessor and president of SC College. 1778–1951.
Copeland, D. Graham [vr, also mfm]. "Many Years After," genealo-
    gies of Bamberg and Orangeburg County families. 1940.
Cordes, John [vr]. Estate records. 1764–98.
Couper, William [vr]. Diary, chiefly re Fort Jackson in World War
    I. 1917–42.
Courtenay, William Ashmead (1831–1908) [731]. Chiefly re pub-
    lications by Courtenay, political events, and correspondence as
    mayor of Charleston for many years with such figures as Paul
    Hamilton Hayne, William Ellerbe Boggan Cash, Robert C. Win-
    throp, Hamilton Fish, and Oliver Wendell Holmes. Library has
    index of correspondents. 1872–93.
Covington, Frank Harlee [vr]. Cheraw, Charleston, North Carolina,
    and Alabama; family correspondence. 1837–1929.

Covington, Paul M. [3v]. Family correspondence, World War I. 1918–19.

Coward, Asbury [vr]. CW reminiscences. c. 1870.

Cox Family [2vr]. Family letters of Marlboro and Marion Districts, especially CW era. 1759–1884.

Coxe Family [973]. Uncatalogued material. 1787–1875.

Crafts, William (1787–1826) [vr]. Poems and biographical sketch. 1829.

Craig, S. J. [v]. Laurens County, daybook. 1877–80.

Crawford, John A. [70]. Columbia, legal papers. 1808–62.

Crews, T. B. [77]. Various papers. c. 1880–1911.

Crigler, Mrs. Henry Towles (Sara Gossett) [v]. "Education for Girls and Women in Upper South Carolina Prior to 1890 with Related Miscellanea." 1963.

Crolley, John A. (1847–1913) [23]. Marlboro and Darlington Counties, land and legal papers. 1872–1913.

Crosland, Edward (1850–85) [43]. Columbia, Bennettsville, and Lexington, Va.; chiefly letters as student at USC and Washington College. 1838–70.

Crosland Family [vr]. Bennettsville, catalogue of papers and biographical sketch of Dr. William Crosland. 1826–88.

Cross, Paul (d. 1784) [303, 4v]. Papers of a slave trader and tavern keeper. 1768–1803.

Crosswell, L. R. [v]. Oaks Plantation records. 1861–62.

Crow, Dorothy, compiler [v]. Notes on David and John Joachim Zubly, 1724–81.

Culbertson, Andrew [63]. Various papers. 1822–1930.

Culbertson, J. D. [22v]. Journals and daybooks. No date.

Cunningham, Anne Pamela [22]. Chiefly letters and clippings re preservation of Mount Vernon. 1857–74, 1935.

Cureton, Thomas Kirk, Jr. [vr]. "The Curetons of Lancaster County." 1949.

Curtis, Francis Orlando Seabrook (1844–1920) [vr]. Records of the Seabrook, Jenkins, and Grimball families. 1760–1900.

Daniel, J. W. [6 boxes]. Correspondence, clippings re his writings. c. 1920–35.

Daniel, James W. [v]. Notes on Southern Indians. 1934.

Daniel, William Lowndes [v]. Notes on SC College lectures by Maximilian La Borde. 1853.

DAR, USC Chapter [vr]. Records. 1957–61.

Dargan & Dargan, Darlington [v]. Law firm writ book. 1854–57.

Dargan, John J. [183]. Various Darlington area papers. 1885–1921.

Darlington Agricultural Society [2vr, also mfm]. Minutes. 1846–94.

Darlington County [33vr]. WPA transcripts of various county records. 1783–1893.

Darlington County [7vr, also mfm]. WPA transcripts of epitaphs: Antioch Baptist Cemetery [Hartsville], Bethel Methodist Church Cemetery, Bethlehem Methodist Cemetery [Hartsville], Centre Point Graveyard, Chapel Hill Baptist Cemetery, Damascus Graveyard, First Baptist Cemetery, First Baptist Church Cemetery [Hartsville], Grove Hill Cemetery, Jewish Cemetery, Kelleytown Baptist Church Cemetery, Magnolia Cemetery [Hartsville], Methodist Cemetery, Mount Elon Baptist Cemetery [Hartsville], New Providence Baptist Church Cemetery, Presbyterian Cemetery [two collections by same name], Swift Creek Baptist Cemetery [Hartsville], Wesley Chapel Methodist Cemetery [Lydia].

Darlington Riot [v]. Testimony at inquest. 1894.

Davidson, Chalmers Gaston (b. 1907) [26r]. Articles, autobiographical data, and reviews. 1937–52.

Davis, Edgar W. [1 box]. Davis genealogy. 1933–37.

Davis, Esther Serena Reynolds [vr]. "Memories of Mulberry." 1934.

Davis Family [76]. Chiefly clippings and legal notes re Clinton and Laurens area. 1847–83.

Davis, Harman (1740–1805) [vr]. Newberry County genealogy, some letters. 1860–88, 1937.

Davis, Henry C. [4 boxes]. Indexed catalogue to SC schools and teachers. No date.

Davis, Henry Campbell (1879–1951) [56, 18v]. Various papers including themes and SC College notes, information on Emma Willard School (1850–65), SC Female Collegiate Institute at Barhamville, and life in Charleston and Columbia. 1850–1950.

Davis, Henry Clarence (1857–1931) [4v]. Genealogy and military career. 1883–1928.

Davis, Herman [90]. Letters re Davis genealogy. 1933–37.

Davis, James M. [62]. Charleston, Columbia, Camden, and Wilmington, N. C.; business and legal papers 1866–77.

Davis, James W. [v]. Record of college expenses, probably at SC Medical College. 1857–58.

Davis, John Hainey (1795–1877) [v mfm]. Laurens doctor's records. 1827–43.

Davis, John M. [v]. Charleston receipt book. 1813–34.

Davis, Joseph Le Conte (1877–1912) [8, v]. Career as an electrical engineer. 1900–14.

Davis Military Academy [v]. Handbook. 1893–94.

Davis, Nora Marshall [vr]. Paper on "Fort Charlotte." 1943.

Davis, Richard [v]. Richland County daybook. 1845–47.

Davis, Robert Means (1849–1904) [1,811, 37v, 2 boxes], Diaries of Sally Le Conte (Mrs. Robert Means Davis), life in Columbia and California, SC College (1845–1900), scrapbooks, news articles, and speeches; also, post-Reconstruction politics in SC, Fairfield County, Mt. Zion Academy, SC Exposition, and SC Dispensary. 1845–1937.

Dawkins, Mary Poulton [v]. "Recollections of England." 1902.

Dawson, Francis Warrington (1840–89) [124]. Chiefly papers re operation of *News & Courier.* 1871–1914.

Dean, Edward F. [v]. Greenville diary with comments on the Mexican War. 1847.

Deas, Anne Simons [4v]. Life in Summerville area. 1893–1910.

Deas, Elias Horry [26]. Charleston, Comingtree Plantation, and Cordesville. 1845, 1865–67.

De Fontaine, Felix Gregory (1832–96) [v mfm]. Scrapbook and clippings of the "Personne" letters. 1861–64.

De La Vaux, Francis, Rev. [v]. Memorandum book re Beaufort and Flat Rock, N. C. 1818–47.

De Leon, Edwin (1829–91) [1,728, v mfm]. Diaries and writings concerning Confederate diplomacy; includes mfm copy of correspondence and clippings in the Library of Congress. 1820–1933.

De Leon, Thomas C. (1839–1914) [5 boxes, 8v]. CW letters, literary manuscripts, scrapbooks and plays. 1862–1943.

Delmar Ginning Company [v]. Account book. 1904–10.

Delmar Telephone Company, Leesville [v]. Account book. 1914–21.

Democratic Club, Charleston [v]. Minutes of Ward 4 club. 1868–79.

Democratic Club, Columbia [v]. Roll of Club #2, Ward 4. 1906.

Democratic Club, Greenville [v]. Membership roll. 1878.

Demosthenian Debating Society [v]. Minutes. 1842–43.

DeSaussure & Ford, Ninety-Six [v]. Law firm records. 1786–92.

DeSaussure, Daniel (1735–98) [20]. Charleston merchant's bonds. 1762–97.

DeSaussure Family [86]. Charleston and Camden business papers re John M. and Daniel L. DeSaussure and James M. Davis. 1825–79.

DeSaussure, Henry William (1763–1839) [23, v]. Information re Charleston, SC College, and John E. Calhoun's collegiate career. 1795–1834.

DeSaussure, John McPherson (1807–83) [2 boxes, 9v]. Kershaw County plantation accounts (1850–80) and business papers re Camden, Charleston, and Norden, Florida. 1833–80.

DeSaussure, William Ford (1792–1870) [30]. Chiefly letters of SC College trustee. 1825–68.

DeVeaux, Stephen G. [v]. Cooper River steamer account book. 1834–35.

Devereaux, V. M. [v]. Estate account book. 1879.

Dexter, Andrew Alfred [26, v]. Philadelphia, Montgomery, Charleston, and SC Railroad Company; business papers including saw mill account book. 1823–34.

Dibble, Samuel (1837–1913) [23]. Orangeburg, US Congressman. 1880–89.

Dillon County [5v, also mfm]. WPA transcripts of epitaphs: Bess Cemetery, Bethesda Methodist Church Cemetery [Latta], Buck Swamp [Bethea], Dothan Cemetery, Haillee Cemetery, Hays Burying Ground [Latta], Little Rock Cemetery, Magnolia Cemetery, Sweat Swamp Cemetery [Bethea], Union Cemetery [Bethea], William Rogers Cemetery.

Dillwyn, William [vr]. Charleston, travel diary. 1772–73.

Doar, James C. [98, 4v]. SC lectures, memoranda, and assorted papers. 1858–86.

Doar, Stephen Duvall (1805–72) [c. 400, 10v]. SC College lecture notes, Charleston legal and business papers. 1807–98.
Dogwood Garden Club, Columbia [6v]. Scrapbooks. 1935–47.
Dorchester County Papers [47 mfm]. St. George area items. 1836–1906.
Douglass, Garrie [51, v]. Newberry County notebook (1861), CW letters, and material re Columbia Female Seminary and Maybinton. 1861–90.
Dowdle Family [vr]. Genealogy, descendants of Robert and Mary Dowdle of Anderson County. 1945.
Downes, Elizabeth and Ann [v]. Georgetown account book. 1776–1819.
Dozier Family [v]. Genealogy. 1833–1936.
Drayton, John (1766–1822) [26, 4v]. Miscellaneous letters and notes. 1779–1943.
Drayton, William Henry (1732–90) [18]. Miscellaneous letters including some reproductions. 1785–1828.
Dreher, Godfrey (d. 1875) [v mfm]. Journal of sermons and ministerial activities in Lexington, Newberry, and Edgefield Counties. 1819–51.
DuBose & Laws, Charleston [v]. Daybook. 1819.
DuBose Family [v]. Descendants of "Issac DeBose who came from Dieppe, Normandy . . . to 1855 as far as known by Capt. John DuBose." 1873.
Duc, Henry A. [70, 9v]. Charleston business and legal papers. 1788–94.
Dudley, Paul H. [v]. Settlement of estate. 1832–34.
Duffie and Berry, Columbia [2v]. Drug store records. 1887–92.
Duffie, William Jefferson (1829–1901) [5v]. Columbia ledgers. 1870–1901.
Dugas-Kerblay Family [68]. Various papers in French re Paris and Edgefield County. 1754–1830.
Dugas, Lewis Frederick Edward [v]. Cotton merchant's letterbook with letters to Charleston, Augusta, and Apalachicola, Fla. 1845–47.
Dugas, Louis Alexander [v]. Doctor's prescription book. 1867–76.
Dukes, William Christopher (b. 1794) [6v mfm]. Charleston and Summerton; original poems, family papers, and CW. 1814–67.
Dulles Family [19r]. Genealogy of John Foster Dulles. 1749–1846.
Dulles, Joseph (c. 1754–1818) [v]. Journal of voyage from Charleston to England. 1808–10.
Dunbar, George Robinson [vr]. Barnwell County family Bible records. 1783–1928.
Dunlap, Cassen [v]. Lancaster District account book. 1811–12.
Dunlap, George [v]. Lancaster District, physician's account book. 1829–39.
Dunn, Sabritt Dotey (1862–1956) [75]. Winnsboro, SC College, and Mt. Zion Society. 1882–1950.
Dunovant, R. G. M. [16]. Chiefly CW letters. 1855–76.

Du Pont Family [vr]. Genealogy. c. 1940.
Durham, Francis Marion [4v, v mfm]. Copies of dissertation and published edition of *Du Bose Heyward: The Man Who Wrote Porgy;* manuscript of "Du Bose Heyward, Southerner and Artist" on mfm. 1954.
Durham, Samuel [v]. Spartanburg County household account book. 1835–40.
Eargle, S. O., & Company, Leesville [v]. Account book. 1904–9.
Earle, Bevins & Company [6vr]. Greenville District ledgers and accounts. 1834–39.
Earle, Ann (Mrs. John Baylis) [39]. Chiefly estate papers, Greenville. 1828–54.
Earle & Woodin [vr]. Account book. 1843–51.
Easterby, James Harold (1898–1960) [21v]. Notes on College of Charleston and *Three Wade Hamptons.* 1767–1935.
Easterling, Rebecca [91]. Orangeburg, Georgetown, Spartanburg, University of North Carolina, and CW. 1851–76.
Eaves, Nathaniel Ridley [232]. Chester, Mexican War, and CW. 1815–68.
Eckhard, Jacob [v mfm]. Portions of a choirmaster's book used at St. Michael's, Charleston. 1809–33.
Eclectic/Palmetto Club, Georgetown [v]. Minutes. 1883–89.
Edgefield Advertiser [34r]. Material re centennial issue. 1936.
Edgefield County [108vr]. WPA transcripts of various court records. 1785–1885, 1939–40.
Edgefield County [2vr, also mfm]. WPA transcripts of epitaphs: Baker Cemetery, Bethlehem Baptist Churchyard [now Asbury Methodist], Brick Church Cemetery, Catholic Cemetery, Ebenezer Cemetery, Harmony Cemetery, Hatcher Family Cemetery, Little River Baptist Cemetery, Mims-Tut Cemetery, Posey Cemetery, Willowbrook Cemetery.
Edgefield [v]. Tax Records. 1863.
Edie, John Rufus (d. 1888) [20]. Army life in Charleston. 1866–70.
Edings Family [vr]. Edisto Island genealogy. 1940.
Edings, William [23]. Charleston and Edisto Island bills and receipts. 1858–59.
Edisto Island Volunteers [vr]. Roster. 1776.
Edisto Social Club [v]. Minutes. 1893–99.
Edmunds, Gerald Palmer (1826–1930) [170, 1 box]. Clippings and manuscripts. c. 1900–10.
Edwards-Dawkins-Battise Families [c. 100]. Columbia and St. Matthews area; papers of a Negro family interested in school, church, and Masonic life. 1867–1938.
Edwards, Morgan (1722–95) [vr]. "Materials Towards a History of the Baptists in South Carolina." 1772.
Edwards, William Henry and Margaret McFadden [5v mfm]. Chester County scrapbooks, CW. 1856–1957.
Efird, Daniel (1824–91) [v mfm]. Journal of Lutheran activities in the Carolinas. 1849–59.

Elford, James M. (c. 1799–1840) [32]. Charleston and Boston, also material re *Marine Telegraph.* 1827–36.
Elliott Family [43]. Genealogy. 1898–1901.
Ellis Family [321]. Beaufort and Charleston papers. 1814–1939. See *University South Caroliniana Society Programs* (1960–62).
Elliott, William, Jr. (1872–1943) [c. 2,000]. Beaufort, Columbia, legal and political correspondence. 1898–1910.
Ellis, Richard A. [vr]. Barnwell County data; Chaplin and Sams genealogy. 1900.
Ellison, James [67]. Letters and miscellaneous papers. 1780–1914.
Elmore, Franklin Harper (1799–1850) [167]. Iron manufacturing in SC, military contracts, and family business matters. 1818–57.
Emanuel, Solomon [v]. Scrapbook of CW and Reconstruction; accounts of a Georgetown business firm. 1837–80.
English, Charles M. [76]. Charleston and Camden; chiefly business and legal papers of a Negro family; also, material re Jenkins Orphanage Institute and Republican party politics. 1898–1934.
English, Elizabeth Doby (b. 1887) [5vr, v mfm]. "Descendants of Joshua English, Irish Quaker" (also available on mfm); marriage-birth-death notices of the *Southern Chronicle* (1824), *Camden Chronicle* (1848–49), *Lancaster Ledger* (1853–54); and a Columbia College scrapbook (1909). 1824–1934.
English, Lucretia Price [v]. Negro autograph album, Scotia Seminary, Concord, N. C. 1883–84.
Enright, Rex (1901–60) [v]. Memorials. 1960.
Erlich Boot & Shoe Store, Columbia [v]. Account books. 1852–66.
Ervin Family [3vr]. Genealogy, descendants of Samuel James Ervin, Jr. 1941.
Ervin, John F. [v]. Mercantile accounts and Robert Ervin estate records. 1835–45.
Ervin, W. R. [154]. Chiefly accounts of an Allendale estate and student tuitions. 1840–85.
Ethredge, Mrs. Helen B. [v]. Saluda Garden Club Yearbook and various papers. 1944–52.
Eustis, Frederick A. [23]. Papers re Eustis plantation on Lady's Island. 1865–70.
Evans, David Reid (1769–1843) [15]. Fairfield congressman, War of 1812. 1795–1834.
Evans & Finley, Attorneys, Spartanburg [505]. Various papers. 1901–11.
Evans, John [v]. Journal of an Indian trader in the Carolinas. 1702–15.
Evans, John Gary (1863–1942) [c. 6,500]. Personal correspondence of Aiken politician, governor of SC (1894–97). 1882–1934.
Eveleigh, Thomas [2v]. Charleston and Philadelphia letterbooks. 1776–89.
Faber, John C. [2 boxes, 3v]. Chiefly letters from German correspondents, Isaac S. K. Bennett and family papers. 1814–1924.
Fairey, F. E. [v]. Branchville farm account book. 1876.

Fairey, F. W. (1823–95) [1,560, 14v]. Branchville, Charleston, and Orangeburg legal and business papers. 1828–91.

Fairfield Account Book [v]. Store records. 1791–93.

Fairfield County [57vr]. WPA transcripts of various court records. 1785–1899.

Fairfield County [7vr, also mfm]. WPA transcripts of epitaphs: Alston Family Cemetery, ARP Cemetery, Antioch Methodist Church Cemetery, Beaver Creek Baptist Church Cemetery, Bethel Church Cemetery [Old], Chappell Family Cemetery, Coleman Family Cemetery, Cook Family Cemetery, Cool Branch Methodist Church Cemetery, Episcopal Cemetery, Feaster Family Cemetery, Free Family Cemetery, Furman and Davis Family Cemetery, Horeb Presbyterian Church Cemetery [Old], Jeffares Family Cemetery, Lyles Family Cemetery [Old], Kirkland Family Cemetery, McMeekin Family Cemetery, Methodist Church Cemetery [Monticello], Methodist Cemetery, Pearson Family Cemetery, Presbyterian Cemetery, Shelton Family Cemetery, Shiloh Methodist Cemetery [Jenkinsville], Winnsboro Cemetery.

Fairfield District [v mfm]. Wills, 1787–1803.

Farmers' Alliance, Edgefield County [v]. Minutes. 1889–94.

Farmers' Club, Beech Island, Aiken County [2vr]. Records of ABC Farmers' Club. 1846–1934.

Farmers' Educational & Cooperative Union, Delmar [v]. Minutes. 1910–15.

Farmers' State Alliance [204, 4vr]. Minutes and records. 1888–1902.

Farr Family [23]. Various papers, chiefly CW era. 1837–88.

Feaster, T. D. [10v]. Fairfield daybooks and accounts, some genealogy. 1802–87.

Federal Court Building, Columbia [v]. Dedication and admission of SC lawyers to practice. 1936–38.

Fellowship Society, Charleston [17 reels mfm]. Records. 1762–1947.

Fennell, Samuel Franklin [v]. Walterboro deputy sheriff's records. 1920–33.

Ferguson & Miller, Columbia [260]. Blacksmith shop records. 1814–73.

Finigan, George W. [17]. Charleston receipts. 1855–95.

First Artillery Regiment, SC Militia [v]. Records. 1844–51.

Fishing Creek Canal [vr]. Toll records, Chester District. 1831–60.

Fitzsimons, Christopher [2v, also mfm]. Charleston letterbooks and business correspondence. 1799–1813.

Flinn, Andrew [v]. Records of Green River Plantation. 1840.

Flinn, J. W. [3v]. Scrapbooks of writings and recollections of Northern CW prisons. 1877–94

Florence County [10vr]. WPA transcripts of various court records. 1889–1939.

Florence Town Council [vr]. Minutes. 1874–79.

Ford Family [53]. Notes in almanacs kept by Jacob (?) Ford recording plantation and family records. 1809–43.

Fort Jackson [v]. Various papers. 1949.
Forum Club, Columbia [2 boxes, v]. Minutes and records. 1925–64.
Fox, John [458]. Lexington area papers, chiefly political. 1822–92.
Fox, John [3v]. Account books. 1858–74.
Francis, John [v]. Charleston receipt book. 1824–50.
Fraser, Alexander [v]. Charleston receipt book. 1761–62.
Fraser & Haynesworth, Sumter [2 boxes]. Law firm's papers and accounts. 1802–84.
Fraser & Trenholm Company [v]. Records. 1868.
Fraser, Thomas B. [2,479]. Sumter area papers. 1786–1902.
Fraser, Thomas B., Jr. [v]. Sumter letterbook. 1894–96.
Freeman, W. C. [v]. Columbia account book. 1860–66.
Freemasons, Columbia Commandry #2 [2v]. Records. 1902–18.
French Benevolent Society [1,420]. Various papers. 1816–93.
French Society, Charleston [70]. Business accounts. 1832–54.
Freneau, Peter [vr]. Copies of Charleston and Columbia materials in other archives. 1791–1805.
Freundschafts-Bund, Charleston [v]. Records. 1860–72.
Frierson, David E. (1818–96) [271, v, 48 mfm]. Presbyterian theological notes and sermons, some material on mfm. 1839–96.
Fripp Family [3v]. Beaufort records, diary of Alice Louise Fripp (1887–1903) and partial Ellis genealogy by Mrs. Nellie Hasell Fripp. 1887–1939.
Frost, J. D. [v]. Records of lumber cut for the Greenville & Columbia Railroad Company. 1850–53.
Fulmer-Clark Families [204]. Business papers and miscellaneous items. 1846–68.
Furman, Charles James McDonald (1863–1904) [424]. Life at SC College, Southern Indian archaeology, woman's suffrage, SC history, politics, and literature. 1877–1903.
Furman, Richard (1755–1825) [24, 39 mfm]. Various papers re Baptist education in SC. 1755–1825.
Gadsden, James (1788–1858) [53]. Material on SC railroads and Indian reservations. 1833–58.
Gaffney, Michael (d. 1854) [vr]. Journal with editorial comments. 1797–1854.
Gaillard, Samuel Porcher [7v]. Sumter plantation accounts; notes on Huguenot immigration. 1835–68.
Gaillard, Thomas [vr]. SC Huguenots and their descendants. 1848.
Gairdner, James & Edwin, & Company, Charleston [v]. Ledger. 1796–99.
Galphin, George [vr]. Notes on Fort Galphin and Silver Bluff. c. 1925.
Gandy, Darius [244]. Various papers. 1838–82.
Gardner, Elizabeth [v]. Autograph book, SC Female Collegiate Institute, Barhamville. 1851–53.
Garland, William H. [132]. Family letters re Charleston, Laurens, Sumter, and North Carolina. 1841–72.
Garlington, John [33]. Papers of Laurens clerk of courts. 1813–41.

Garnett, R. S. [37]. Military receipts and records, New York and
    California. 1854–56.
Gary, John Hillary (1840–63) [15]. SC College notes and family
    correspondence. 1859–63.
Gary, Martin Witherspoon (1831–81) [506]. Various uncatalogued
    papers. 1851–1927.
Gaston-Crawford Families [549, 2v]. Chiefly business and personal
    papers re Chester, college life in the Carolinas, and life in the
    Southeast. 1739, 1772–1933.
Gaston, John Thomas (1841–1911) [30]. Edgefield, CW, and Re-
    construction. 1849–1910. See *Confederate War Diary of John
    Thomas Gaston* (1960).
Gayer, John S. [61]. Financial papers. 1806–29.
Geddings, W. H. [v]. Clippings re Aiken as a health resort and
    some meteorological notes. 1880–94.
Gee, Wilson [31]. Correspondence re his master's thesis. No date.
Geiger, Edwin W. [212]. Berkeley, Orangeburg, and Lexington
    Counties; legal papers and inventories. 1741–1881.
Geiger, Lizzie K. [61]. Personal letters, Hampton campaign of 1876.
    1858–97.
Georgetown Board of Trade [30]. Various papers. 1900–15.
Georgetown Chamber of Commerce [v]. Data on area resources.
    1911–12.
Georgetown County [3vr]. WPA transcripts of various court records.
    1862–1912.
Georgetown County [3vr, also mfm]. WPA transcripts of epitaphs:
    Episcopal Cemetery, Hebrew Cemetery [Georgetown], Old Bap-
    tist Cemetery, Prince Frederick's Parish, Prince George's Winyaw.
Georgetown Merchant's Book [vr]. Ledger. 1819–27.
Georgetown Rifle Guards [v]. Records. 1874–80.
Georgetown Sunday School Association [1 box]. Records. 1897–99.
Georgia-Carolina Power Company [2v]. Operating agreements.
    1912.
German Friendly Society, Charleston [16vr]. Minutes. 1766–1858.
Gibbes Family [v]. Family Bible with records. 1835.
Gibbes, Lewis R. [vr]. Catalogue of phoenogamous plants in Co-
    lumbia area. 1835.
Gibbes, Robert Wilson (1809–66) [299, 3v]. Charleston and Co-
    lumbia business-legal papers, including "Autograph Book of the
    Revolution" containing 296 signatures and documents (1770–
    1836). 1803–66, 1931.
Gibbes, Wade Hampton (1836–1903) [99]. Columbia business
    papers, CW. 1862–1905.
Gibbes, William Hasell (1754–1834) [28]. Notes and legal papers,
    autobiography. 1755–1841.
Gibson, Thomas J. [4v]. Columbia account books. 1853–74.
Giessendanner Family [v, also vr]. Orangeburg church register of
    marriages, births, and deaths kept by John Ulrich and John
    Giessendanner. 1727–96.

Gilbert, Peter (1776–1812) [v]. *Buccolicks of Virgil* (1749) with notes on Gilbert and Petigru families. 1802–22.
Gilliland, W. H. [1,027, 4v]. Charleston pharmacist's records and papers. 1813–93.
Gillilands & Howell, Abbeville [v]. Various notes. 1844–46.
Gilman, Caroline Howard (1794–1888) [28]. Letters and poems. 1850–78.
Gilman, Samuel (1791–1858) [23]. Charleston sermon notes and comments on wife's [Caroline Howard Gilman] literary efforts. 1828–88, 1932–49.
Girardeau, John Lafayette (1825–98) [c. 200 mfm]. Charleston, poems and miscellaneous writings re ministerial career and work with Negro congregations. 1844–1936.
Girls of the Sixties [v]. Sketches and notes of CW era. 1864–1929.
Gist, Margaret Adams (1865–1949) [11, 13v]. Personal correspondence, SC history, minutes of York County Historical Society (1929-36), and data re York, Columbia, Charleston, and Gastonia, N. C. 1785–1943.
Gist, William Henry (1807–74) [26]. CW material. 1859–62.
Glass, P. B. [v]. *Southern Almanac* with notes. 1861.
Glenn, John A. [v]. Laurens daybook. 1849–77.
Glenn, Laurens [v]. SC College for Women memoir book. 1894.
Glover Family [c. 825]. Legal and business papers. 1732–1866.
Glover Family [6v]. Colleton County plantation records. 1824–65.
Glover-North Families [313]. Material re Columbia, Greenville, CW, Cedar Springs Institute, Charleston earthquake, Texas, Mexico, Central America, and the Mexican National Railway. 1836–1918.
Glover, Thomas Worth [78]. Orangeburg, chiefly SC House of Representatives papers and membership lists. 1692–1874.
Glymph, John [22]. Newberry District business accounts. 1838–60.
Godfrey, William R. [6v]. Cheraw business records and diary (1919). 1839–83, 1919.
Going Family [37]. Various papers re Union, Orangeburg, and Alabama. 1857–1958.
Golding, Carrie M. E. [2v]. Spartanburg Female College notes and scrapbooks. 1833, 1850–57.
Gonzales, Narcisco Gener (1858–1903) [72]. Personal papers including letters concerning political editorials and a scrapbook concerning his murder. 1895–1922.
Goodlet, R. P. & Sons, Greenville [4v]. Business records. 1844–65.
Goodwyn, A. R. [1 Box]. Various papers. 1836–1920.
Gordon Family [vr]. Genealogy. 1963.
Gordon, Joshua [v]. Witchcraft and disease remedies. 1784.
Goss, Frank [41]. Camden business papers. 1865–71.
Gott, Julia Sloan (b. 1841) [19]. Family letters and CW. 1794–1879.
Goulding Family [22r]. Genealogical records. No date.
Governor's Guards, Columbia [1 box, 11v]. Records and miscellaneous papers. 1850–99.
Graffenreid Family [v]. Genealogy. No date.

Graham, W. M. [v]. Deposit book. 1895–96.

Gramling, Michael [v]. Orangeburg plantation accounts. 1839–58.

Graniteville Manufacturing Company [27v]. Various records and accounts. 1824–1900.

Graves, John Temple [c. 315, 4v]. Family papers, correspondence as journalist and lecturer. 1840–1933.

Graydon, Ellis Garland [v]. SC College notes. 1867–72.

Grayson, William John (1788–1863) [3v]. CW diary, autobiography, and various notes. 1788–1863.

Great Southern Freight Line [v]. Charleston and New York. 1879.

Green, Edwin Luther (1870–1948) [106, 5v]. Notes re his writing career, especially material on George McDuffie. 1790–1934.

Green, Samuel [33]. New York and Columbia business papers. 1791–1813.

Green, Watson & Walsh, Sumter [v]. Cotton ledger. 1865–67.

Green, William (1713–78) [vr]. Black River and Bishopville family records. 1741–1955.

Greenville Chamber of Commerce [v]. Post-World War II plans. c. 1945.

Greenville County [46vr]. WPA transcripts of various court records. 1785–1894.

Greenville County [3vr, also mfm]. WPA transcripts of epitaphs: Springfield Cemetery, Christ Church Cemetery, Carter Family Burying Ground.

Greenville District [v]. Magistrate's records. 1848–52.

Greenville Ladies Association [3v]. Records. 1861–65.

Greenwood County [vr]. Historical sketch. 1939.

Greenwood County [vr, also mfm]. WPA transcripts of epitaphs: Rehoboth Church Cemetery.

Greenwood Mill Domestic Exhibition Society [2v]. Minutes. 1910–11.

Greer [vr]. Historical sketch of town. 1896.

Gregg, David (1783–1855) [11, v]. Pee Dee River navigation projects. 1826–66.

Gregg, J. Eli & Sons, Mars Bluff [37v]. Cotton accounts. 1842–1914.

Gregg, Maxcy (1814–62) [35, 2v]. Letters and papers re hunting, fishing, Mexican War, secession movement of the 1850's, and CW. 1835–62.

Gregg-Wallace Families [20]. Mars Bluff and Columbia business papers. 1860–1903.

Griffin, Harry [v]. Welsh Neck diary. c. 1800.

Griffin & Tullman Company [v]. Account book. 1850–53.

Griffin, William King & Company, Newberry [v]. Druggist's accounts. 1856–59.

Griggs, B. B. [24]. Columbia and Chattanooga, family letters. 1859–65.

Grimball, John (1748–1804) [24]. Charleston and Beaufort legal-business papers. 1756–1816.

Grimball, John Berkeley (1800–93) [86, v]. Family letters, CW, SC in the 1890's. 1816–95.
Grimball, Joseph [v]. Account book. 1777.
Grimké, Edward Montague (1832–95) [29]. Family letters, college life at The Citadel. 1850–68.
Grimké Family [28]. Background data. 1800–1920.
Grimké, St. Julien [2v]. Letterbooks. 1891–1908.
Guerin, Henry C. [102]. Charleston; chiefly correspondence as chief of CSA Subsistence Bureau in SC. 1843–1905.
Guignard Family [c. 3,000]. Personal papers, plantation and business records, 1795–1930. See Arney R. Childs, ed., *Planters and Business Men: The Guignard Family of Columbia*, (Columbia, 1957).
Hagood, J. E. [25]. Anderson and Greenville Counties, chiefly business and legal papers of Pickens County clerk of court. 1860–67.
Hagood, James [35]. Business papers, CW. 1857–72.
Hagood, James R. (1844–70) [vr]. Copy of CW memoirs. 1861–65.
Hallman, Elmer B. (b. 1865) [v mfm]. "Early Settlers of the Carolina Dutch Fork, 1744–60" (M.A. thesis, Wofford College, 1944).
Hamilton, James (1786–1857) [20]. Charleston merchant's papers with data on nullification. 1820–49.
Hamilton, Paul (1762–1816) [25, vr]. Various papers re Charleston and the War of 1812. 1802–12.
Hammett Family [53]. Charleston business papers. 1826–1904.
Hammett, William (d. 1803) [4, v]. Journal as Methodist minister. 1787–1803.
Hammond Collection [60, 170v, 36 boxes]. Personal papers, business and plantation records of James Henry, Marcus Claudius Marcellus (1814–76), Edward Spann (1834–1922), Harry, and James Henry (b. 1885) Hammond. 1795–1935.
Hammond & Lark, Hamburg [2v]. Account books. 1856–61.
Hampton, Wade I (1752–1835) [25]. Assorted personal papers. 1773–1834.
Hampton, Wade II (1791–1858) [22]. Legal and business papers. 1812–57.
Hampton, Wade III (1818–1902) [255]. Personal letters; CW, Reconstruction, and SC politics. 1843–1937.
Hanks, John [24]. Sumterville business records. 1826–37.
Hanks, L. B. [49]. Sumterville mercantile accounts. 1848–80.
Hare, Eargle & Company, Caughman [2,333, 12v]. Business ledgers and papers. 1880–1926.
Hare, J. W. [5v]. Account books. 1862–74.
Hare, William Henry (b. 1866) [88, 28v]. Edgefield and Lexington County legal papers, CW, personal papers as teacher, surveyor, news correspondent, telegraph operator, merchant, and mail carrier in Saluda and Lexington Counties; World War I letters and life in town of Delmar. 1871–1935.
Harllee, Louisa Jane (1838–1934) [v]. Recollections of SC Female Collegiate Institute, Barhamville. 1853–56.

Harris, T. A. [v]. Miscellaneous records of the Abbeville Methodist Church. 1854–89.

Harrison & Marshall, Greenville [v]. Scrapbook. 1869–71.

Hart, Oliver (1732–95) [252, 3vr]. Family letters, genealogy, and sermons. 1792–1831.

Hart, R. E. [v]. Furman University chemistry notes. 1895.

Hart, William Speight [vr]. CW letters. 1861–63.

Hartwell Project [v]. Plans for dam near Anderson. 1949.

Haskell, John C. [v]. Letters as attorney for Columbia & Greenville Railroad. 1883–87.

Hayne Family [vr]. Genealogy. c. 1940.

Hayne, Paul Hamilton (1830–86) [30]. SC literature, letters re William Gilmore Simms. 1860–88.

Hayne, Robert Young (1791–1839) [38]. Various personal papers. 1813–36.

Haynesworth, E. C. [v]. Records of Junction School, Sumter County, prepared by Hugh S. Thompson. 1880–81.

Haynesworth, Fraser & Cooper, Sumter [v]. Letterbook. 1870–71.

Haynesworth, W. F. B. [2,676]. Sumter and Cheraw personal papers. 1796–1880.

Hazard & Ayrault Company, Charleston [v]. Receipts. 1796–1805.

Hazard, Isaac Peace [34]. Charleston business letters. 1825–43.

Hebrew Orphan Society, Charleston [1 box, 3v]. Records. 1850–1938.

Hemphill, J. C. [31]. Charleston, Camden, and Washington, D. C.; correspondence re *Men of Our Time.* 1905–9.

Hemphill, James (b. 1813) [vr]. Genealogy and sketch of his life. c. 1880.

Hemphill, Robert W. [576, 5v mfm]. Political correspondence, speeches, scrapbooks. 1945–63.

Hennig, Helen Kohn [vr]. SC fine arts in 20th century. 1949.

Henry, Robert (1792–1856) [70]. Chiefly papers re life at SC College. 1823–55, 1948.

Henry, Samuel [vr]. Genealogy. 1945.

Herbert, R. Beverly (b. 1879) [vr]. Experiences with SC Department of Immigration. c. 1910.

Herd, E. Don, Jr. (b. 1932) [vr]. Typed copy of *Andrew Jackson, South Carolinian.* 1963.

Hesseltine & Chafee, Lancaster [v]. Receipt book. 1873–88.

Heyward, Charles (b. 1802) [v]. Slave accounts with emancipation records. 1858–65.

Heyward, Duncan Clinch (1864–1943) [938, 2v]. Myrtle Grove Plantation accounts and family papers. 1714–1917.

Heyward, Edward Barnwell [3v]. Plantation records. 1851–79.

Heyward, Thomas S. [15]. Genealogy. 1893–95.

Hibernian Society, Charleston [vr]. Minutes. 1827–47.

Higgins, Francis Bernard (1794–1863) [38]. Newberry District personal papers. 1773–1891.

Higginson, Thomas Wentworth (1823–1911) [v]. "The Baby of the Regiment," a short story. c. 1880.
Hill, J. Walter [21]. CW items. 1861–65.
Hill, Mrs. Susan B. [57, v]. Edgefield area genealogical notes. 1923–50.
Hines, Cornelia Ravenel [v mfm]. "Diary of James W. Moore." 1920–21.
Hodges Family [2v]. Walterboro genealogy. 1949.
Holland, Edwin C. [v]. Poems (1829). 1961.
Hollingsworth, John [32]. Business and plantation papers. 1816–71.
Holman, Olive Brownlee [vr]. Genealogical data on SC German-Swiss and Scotch-Irish. 1937.
Holmes, Edmund G. [83]. Charleston family and business papers. 1841–49, 1863.
Holmes, Eliza Ford Gibbes (1808–75) [52]. Charleston and Camden, family letters. 1859–1926.
Holmes, Emma E. [4vr]. Charleston journals. 1861–66.
Holmes, Henry M. [v]. Diary of CW surgeon. 1861–65.
Holmes, Reuben G. [151, v]. Beaufort, Massachusetts, and New Jersey business papers; Reconstruction data. 1851–79.
Holmes, W. E. [17v]. Charleston business accounts. 1883–1912.
Holst Family [41]. Papers re Chester and Copenhagen, Denmark. 1822–88.
Holt, William Joseph (1829–81) [110, 3v]. Papers re career as doctor, service in Crimea and CW; business papers of his father, Judge William White Holt. 1799–1908.
Honour, Theodore A. [180]. Charleston, CW material. 1859–65.
Hood, Ina R. [2v]. York County tavern accounts. 1839–56.
Hook, J. R. [v]. Columbia merchant's accounts. 1850.
Hooker, Edward (1785–1846) [2v]. Diary. 1805–8.
Hopewell Literary Association, Mars Bluff [v]. Records. 1881–83, 1903.
Hopkins Family [242r]. Business, personal and plantation papers, Richland District. 1763–1886.
Hopkins, James Ward (1832–64) [2v]. SC College, travels in North and Europe. 1848–67.
Hopkinson, James [402, 20v]. Charleston, Edisto Island, and France; family papers. 1847–1917.
Holbeck, John [v]. Charleston account book. 1865–69.
Horry County [20vr]. WPA transcripts of various court records. 1799–1907.
Horry County [6vr, also mfm]. WPA transcripts of epitaphs: Baker's Chapel Baptist Churchyard, Beaty's Burying Ground, Buck Graveyard of Hebron Church [Bucksville], First Baptist Church [Conway], Flemming's Field [Savannah Bluff], Green Sea Baptist Cemetery, Hebron Methodist Church Cemetery, Jack's Branch Graveyard, Kingston Presbyterian Church Cemetery [Conway], Lakeside Cemetery [Conway], Methodist Episcopal S o u t h Churchyard [Conway], Mincey Burying Ground, Old Camp Bury-

ing Ground, Pauley Swamp Baptist Cemetery, Pleasant View Baptist Cemetery, Kingston Presbyterian Churchyard [Conway], Singleton's Graveyard [Conway], Union Methodist Cemetery [Conway], Waccamaw Presbyterian Churchyard.

Horry, E. S. [v]. Georgetown County plantation accounts. 1866–69.

Horry Industrial School [73]. Minutes. 1919–28.

Horry, Paul T. [v]. Plantation account book. 1873–79.

Hort, Mary (b. 1796) [9v, 2v mfm]. Originals and copies of Sumter journals describing religious and social life; diary (1842–47) on mfm. 1830–71.

Hough & White, Society Hill [2v]. Daybooks. 1873–93.

Howe, William Bell White (1813–82) [v]. Theological lecture notes and poems. 1835–64.

Howland, Ward, [Spring] & Taft Company, Charleston [23]. Cotton correspondence. 1831–41.

Hoyt, James Allen (1877–1959) [c. 868, 22v, 12v mfm]. Chiefly correspondence of Hoyt and Arthur J. Morris of "Morris Plan" fame; some personal scrapbooks on mfm. 1865–1956.

Hucket, Héloise [v]. Drawing book of a French girl in Charleston. 1823.

Hucks Family [v]. Scrapbook. 1958–61.

Hudson, Edward [27]. Papers re damage and repair of British brig *Alexis*. 1823.

Hudson, Joshua Hilary (1832–1909) [6v]. Papers of a Bennettsville lawyer, Reconstruction. 1870–77.

Huey Family [v]. York District plantation, school, blacksmith, and medical accounts. 1857–76.

Huger, A. M. [v]. Letterbook of rice and cotton merchant. 1859–60.

Huger, Harriet H. [4v]. Journals, notebooks, scrapbooks. 1874–87.

Hughes, Frank Porcher [2v]. Notebook and *Index Rerum* with notes re College of Charleston. 1833–63.

Hughes, J. Gordon [c. 3,000]. Uncataloged. c. 1900–1940.

Humphries Family [vr]. Genealogy. 1965.

Hunicutt/Honeycutt Family [v]. Genealogy. c. 1960.

Hunt Family [25]. Greenville legal papers. 1784–1895.

Hunt, N. A. [54]. Charleston shoe company papers. 1867–86.

Hunt, Walter H. [19]. Various papers re SC College. 1900–5.

Hunter, Henry [19]. Settlement of Laurens District estate. 1806–27.

Huntersville Temperance Society, Laurens [v]. Records. 1842–46.

Hutchinson, John and Croswell, Sumterville [v]. Cash book. 1833–35.

Hutchinson, William [vr]. Darlington notebook. 1821–73.

Hutson, Charles Woodward (1840–1936) [62]. Letters from SC College to his family in Beaufort. 1856–60.

Hutson, F. M. [v]. "Plantation Negro of Today." 1943.

Hutton, Sybil V. Wilson [v mfm]. "Social Participation of Married Women in a South Carolina Mill Village." Master's thesis Univ. of Kentucky, 1948.

Hypatian Literary Society [v]. Secretary's book. 1956–58.
Independent Congregational [Circular] Church, Charleston [19vr]. Records. 1695–1935.
Industrial Home for Colored Children, Columbia [v]. Records. 1896–1907.
Industrial School for Boys, Florence [3v]. Records. 1947–50.
Industrial School for Girls, Columbia [3v]. Records. 1947–50.
Industrial School, John G. Richards, Columbia [4v]. Records. 1947–51.
Ingram & Webb, Charleston [v]. Receipts. 1859–73.
Irish Volunteer Company, Charleston [3v]. Records and minutes. 1798–1929.
Irvin, William (d. 1814) [50]. Camden and York legal papers. 1774–1828, 1897.
Izard Family [4 boxes]. Chiefly uncataloged papers of Ralph Izard (1742–1804), including photostatic and mfm copies of scrapbook (1897–1946) and letters (1778–80) in the E. C. Genet Collection, Library of Congress. 1765–1831.
Izard, Walter (b. 1828) [v]. SC College sketches. 1845.
James Island Agricultural Society [vr]. Minutes. 1872–1935.
Jameson, McElroy [366]. Various personal papers and family correspondence. 1847–1923.
Janney, Ellen C. [156, 75v]. Chiefly records of her Columbia school. 1856–1919.
Janney, James C. [186, 3v]. Records, personal letters, and accounts of Columbia hotel man and public hall owner. 1856–80.
Jefferies, Richard Manning (1889–1964) [14 boxes]. Papers as governor. 1942–43.
Jefferson Davis Memorial Association, Fort Mill [v]. Records. 1889–1906.
Jenkins, Charles S. [v]. Philadelphia, notes on walk commemorating SC signers of the Declaration of Independence. 1942.
Jenkins, John (1824–1905) [872]. Personal and business papers of Edisto Island planter family. 1775–1945. See *University South Caroliniana Society Program* (1955).
Jennings Family [v]. Bible records. 1814–57.
Jennings, Henry [3v]. Scrapbook, newspaper clippings re SC politics. 1888–92.
Jewish Synagogues [5vr]. SC records. 1750–1939.
Joanna Textile Mills [vr]. Special edition of *Clinton Chronicle*. 1947.
Johns Family [vr]. Genealogy. 1944.
Johnson, David (1782–1855) [61]. Chester, Columbia, Union; family letters. 1810–55, 1951–52.
Johnson, Ellen Cooper (b. 1844) [vr]. Memoirs of Horry and Conway Counties. 1962.
Johnson, William Bullein (1782–1862) [22, v]. Papers re Edgefield, Hamburg, and Baptist ministry. 1848–1922.
Johnson, William E. (1797–1871) [340]. Chiefly bills, receipts, and personal papers of president of Bank of Camden. 1837–71.

Johnson, William S. [v]. Mexican War journal. 1847–48.
Johnston, George Milligen [v]. *A Short Description of South Carolina* . . . (1763) with notes. 1770.
Johnston, Olin D. (1896–1965) [c. 400 boxes]. Uncatalogued papers of SC governor and US senator.
Johnston, William (1776–1840) [418, 4v]. Chiefly records and papers of rice plantation, Georgetown District. 1796–1958.
Johnstone Family [17]. Greenville and Flat Rock, N. C.; family correspondence. 1845–68.
Johnstone, Francis Withers [3vr]. Scrapbooks re agricultural experiments and CW. 1803–1940.
Johnstone, Isabel [2v]. Tombstone inscriptions and genealogical records. c. 1913.
Jones, Benjamin R. [v]. Medical account book. 1836–39.
Jones, Benson Miles (1843–76) [v]. Journal of trip from Charleston to Liverpool. 1860–62.
Jones, F. Dudley (b. 1874) [252, 1 box]. Clinton, botanical material, published articles, and notes. 1883–1946.
Jones, Iredell (1842–1914) [169, v]. Rock Hill, family letters, CW. 1797–1913.
Jones, James (1805–65) [v]. Letterbook of "Commissioner for Building the State House." 1855–61, 1892–1933.
Jones, Jane Bruce [20]. Charleston, Orangeburg, Columbia, family letters; Vesey Plot. 1784–1831.
Jones, Noah [v]. "Juvenile Composition . . . ." 1805–9.
Jones-Watts-Davis Families [611]. Business papers and family correspondence re Laurens District and Georgia. 1766–1915. See *University South Caroliniana Society Programs* (1963–64).
Jones, William [vr]. Arguments re seizure of American vessel *Molly* as a naval prize. 1795.
Joynes, Edward S. (1834–1917) [49]. Reports of his USC department and letters to Blondelle Malone. 1882–1917.
Kaigler, George [36]. Granby, Orangeburg, Sandy Run, and Georgia; chiefly business papers. 1796–1860.
Kaminer, Guilielma Melton [v]. "South Carolina Biography under Royal Government." 1926.
Keenan, Rowland A. [v]. Columbia daybook. 1873–75.
Keith, Alexander [v]. Georgetown commonplace book. 1730–40.
Keith, Elliott [v]. CW diary of Sullivan's Island and Virginia. 1862.
Keith, Frances G. Gibbes [Mrs. Oscar L.] (1880–1948) [c. 250]. Includes c. 27 vols. of her notes, poetry, sketches, and plays. 1898–1945.
Keith, Oscar L. [246]. Various papers. 1908–18.
Keith, Sylvanus [63]. Charleston business papers and school accounts. 1801–35.
Keitt, Ellison Summerfield (1831–1911) [57, v]. St. Matthews, business papers, letters, personal reminiscences; genealogy, and Ku Klux Klan. 1847–1900.
Keitt, Mrs. S. S. [50]. Personal letters. 1879–80.

Kellers, Edward Henry (1836–1906) [36, 2v]. Autographs, SC College notes, diary as CW surgeon. 1852–93.
Kelley Family [2v]. Kershaw estate inventory. 1862–84.
Kelley, Henrietta A. [v]. Charleston autograph book. 1859–65.
Kennedy, Robert McMillan, compiler [vr]. SC items in the *Gentleman's Magazine.* 1731–92.
Kerr, Elijah [v]. Chester account book. 1831–34, 1861–92.
Kerrison Family [75]. Charleston, Columbia, Spartanburg, CW. 1878–93. See *University South Caroliniana Program* (1963).
Kershaw Account Books [4v]. Camden and Hanging Rock taverns, general merchandise. 1816–68.
Kershaw County [32vr]. WPA transcripts of various court records. 1770–1877.
Kershaw County [vr, also mfm]. WPA transcripts of epitaphs: Ancrum Plot, Boykin Burying Ground, Chesnut Cemetery, Hammond Cemetery, Hanging Rock Church Cemetery, Kershaw Plot, Quaker Cemetery, Family Burying Ground [unidentified].
Kershaw County, Treasurer's Office [c. 5,000]. Miscellaneous records. 1926–46.
Kershaw, James [8v]. Camden diary with miscellaneous notes and observations. 1791–1825.
Kershaw, Joseph Brevard (1822–94) [147]. Chiefly CW papers, genealogy. 1766–1931.
Ketchin/Castchen, Thomas (1786–1855) [2v]. Sermons and biographical sketch. 1815, 1905.
Keyes, Julia L. [vr]. "Our Life in Brazil." 1867–70.
Kinard, James Efird [vr]. Sketch of Summer family and Pomaria plantation. 1942.
Kincaid-Anderson Families [2,575, 9v, v mfm]. Fairfield County papers, including scrapbook of Eugenia Anderson McMaster on mfm. 1767–1926. See *University South Caroliniana Society Program* (1959).
King, Isaac [v]. Bristol and London letters re Charleston. 1783–98.
King's Mountain Centennial Association [189]. Records and correspondence. 1880–1910.
King's Mountain Monument Association [v]. Minutes. 1909.
Kirkland, Thomas J. [4 boxes, v]. Miscellaneous Kershaw County papers; Clermont ledger (1776–90). 1756–1931.
Klein, J. J. [1,010, 2v]. Walterboro, Charleston, and Columbia business papers; Ku Klux Klan. 1843–84.
Klein, John M. [1 box, 40v]. Walterboro, mercantile and druggist account and letterbooks. 1851–1908.
Knight, Aaron (?) [vr]. Diary kept as Methodist minister, Chesterfield County. 1840–1921.
Knights of Honor, Edgefield Lodge [9 boxes]. Correspondence and records. 1873–1928.
Knights of Honor, Marlboro Lodge, Bennettsville [v]. Minutes. 1872–92.

Kohn, August (1868–1930) [2,630, 36v]. College notes, *News &
Courier* articles, family and business papers, information re Co-
lumbia, Ku Klux Klan, SC politics. 1882–1941.
Kohn, Theodore (1840–1902) [23v]. Orangeburg family and business papers. 1874–96.
Kosmos Club, Columbia [3 boxes, 6v]. Records and papers. 1905–
35.
La Borde, Maxmilian (1804–73) [62, v]. Thesis in Latin, SC Med-
ical College (1826), and papers re SC College. 1826–73.
Lacey, Robert Alexander (b. 1878) [vr]. "General Edward Lacey
and his Descendants." 1944.
Ladies Benevolent Society, Charleston [11vr]. Records. 1813–1935.
Laffitte, David Montague (1791–1869) [383, v, also v mfm]. Charles-
ton and Savannah receipts; Barnwell medical account book (1817–
37); original and mfm copies. 1817–60.
La Grove, Jacob and Peter [1 box]. Legal and business accounts.
1784–1870.
Lancaster County [12vr]. WPA transcripts of various court records.
1787–1869.
Lancaster County [3vr, also mfm]. WPA transcripts of epitaphs:
Old Presbyterian Cemetery, Cemetery near Hanging Rock, Con-
nors Family Burial Ground [Lancaster], West Side Cemetery
[Lancaster], Tirzah Cemetery.
Lander Club, Anderson [14]. Papers read at various meetings.
c. 1920.
Landrum, John Belton O'Neall [v]. Scrapbook. 1862–1910.
Larsen, George [25]. Records of CW commissary agent. 1863.
Laurens County [17vr]. WPA transcripts of various court records.
1766–1872.
Laurens County [vr, also mfm]. WPA transcripts of epitaphs:
Laurens Cemetery.
Laurens County Account Books [2v]. Mercantile records. 1839,
1849–50.
Laurens, Henry (1724–92) [29, 9v mfm]. Miscellaneous papers, in-
cluding RW material and Charleston letterbooks. 1762–92.
Law, Hugh Lide (1847–1918) [v]. USC lecture notes. 1866–67.
Law, Thomas Cassels (1811–88) [776, 3v, vr]. Darlington District
family correspondence and business papers; data re Thomas E.
Hart family. 1770–1899. See *University South Caroliniana Society
Programs* (1963–64).
Law, Thomas Cassels (1880–1962) [vr]. Hartsville diary. 1895–96.
Law, Thomas Hart (1838–1923) [vr]. Journal re Columbia Thelog-
ical Seminary and CW. 1860–65.
Lawton Family [c. 2,600, 7v]. Business and legal papers re Robert-
ville in Black Swamp, St. Peter's Parish, Beaufort District, and
Baptist records. Some material on mfm. 1733–1949. See *Uni-
versity South Caroliniana Programs* (1963–64).
Leaphart, John S. [334, 2v]. Columbia business records and family
papers. 1863–90.

Leaphart & Sloan, Columbia [v]. Grocers' account book. 1869–70.
Lebby, Robert (b. 1805) [3v]. Charleston scrapbooks. 1861–85.
Le Conte, Emma Florence (1848–1901) [2vr]. CW journal, Columbia genealogy. 1698–1865.
Le Conte Family [v mfm]. Genealogy. c. 1900.
Le Conte, John (1818–91) [28]. SC College reports. 1856–68, 1891.
Le Conte, Joseph (1823–1901) [78, 6v]. Genealogy, SC College, CW. 1847–1935.
Ledbetter Family [vr]. Genealogy of Ledbetter and Brazelton families. 1945.
Lee, Charles (1731–82) [v]. Letterbook. 1776.
Lee County [vr, also mfm]. WPA transcripts of epitaphs: Cyress Cemetery [Lynch's River].
Lee Family [18]. Columbia, Georgia, California, and Texas; personal letters. 1835–87.
Lee & Moise [61]. Legal papers. 1846–1905.
Lee, Robert Edward (1807–70) [16]. Chiefly CW items. 1845–66.
Legare Family [v mfm]. Genealogy. No date.
Legare, Hugh Swinton (1797–1843) [244, vr]. Various papers inluding memoir by Mary Legare Bullen. 1813–90.
Legare, J. B. [2v]. Charleston and Edisto Island account books. 1845–51, 1857.
Leland, Eliza Hibben and Eugenia Rebecca (Griffin) [v mfm]. Diaries. 1853, 1865–68.
Lemachs, Elizabeth A. [v]. Scrapbooks. 1853–1905.
Leroy & Wilson [v]. Store account book. 1861.
Lewis Family [197]. Horry County personal and business papers, material re SC colleges. 1743–1954.
Lewis, Mary L. [3v]. Columbia and Winthrop Training School notebooks. c. 1886.
Lexington Account Books [2v]. 1832–58.
Lexington County [53 mfm, 5v mfm]. Various papers on early history. 1955–63.
Lexington County, Sheriff's Office [vr]. Receipt book. 1806–17.
Lexington County, Superintendent of Education [c. 15,256]. Teachers' reports, pay certificates, and monthly records. 1869–1900.
Lexington County, Treasurer's Office [v]. Account book. 1871–81.
Lexington Dispatch-News [v]. Ledger and advertising accounts. 1917.
Lexington-Edgefield Telegraph Company [983, 2v]. Message reports and various records. 1892–1900.
Library Society, Georgetown [2vr]. Minutes. 1799–1814.
Lide-Coker Family [581]. Personal papers re Society Hill, Darlington, and Alabama. 1827–1914. See Fletcher M. Green, *The Lides Go South and West* (1952).
Lide, Robert Wilkins (1852–1940) [5v mfm]. Records kept as Baptist minister. 1875–1934.

Lieber, Francis (1800–72) [164, 3v]. Various personal papers re SC College and John C. Calhoun. 1808–79.

Lieber, Oscar Montgomery (1830–62) [22, 15v]. Notes used in writing *Mineralogical, Geological, and Agricultural Survey of South Carolina and Vocabulary of the Catawba Language;* also notes on trip to Labrador. 1850–62.

Lien Law [31]. Clippings and handbills. c. 1908.

"Light Wood Knot Herald & Daily Expositor" [v]. Facetious Columbia newspaper. 1837–38.

Lodebar, Marine School Ship [v]. Log book. 1861–62.

Loftis, Reuben [41 mfm]. CW material. 1862.

Longstreet, Augustus Baldwin (1790–1870) [25]. Columbia, various personal papers. 1793–1861.

Lott Family [51, 13v]. Family papers, including 20th-cent. diaries of Ella Lott Lamb. 1837–1938.

Louisville, Cincinnati & Charleston Railroad [v]. Engineering records. 1837–40.

Love, Walter T. [73r]. World War I pamphlets and brochures. 1917–19.

Love, William Dare [133, 4v]. Columbia and New York business receipts. 1855–1936.

Low, James P. [2v]. Letters of Blue Ridge Railroad Company engineer. 1870–75.

Lowder, John D. [16]. Business papers. 1881–1905.

Lowrance Company, Columbia [v]. Account book. 1893–1905.

Lowrance, J. Douglas [v]. Columbia scrapbook. 1887–93.

Lowrance, William Barr (b. 1841) [18]. Chiefly CW letters. 1859–78.

Lowry & Witherspoon, Yorkville [v]. Account book. 1889–98.

Lucas, A. H. [v]. Edgefield account book. 1868.

Lucas, John [36 mfm]. Charleston correspondence with British firms. 1840–43.

Lucas, M. D. [v]. Santee account book. 1880.

Lucas, Thomas Bennett [35, 5v]. Charleston and New York, chiefly legal papers. 1860–66.

Luck, George K. [17]. CW letters. 1862–65.

Lutheran Church, Bethlehem, Newberry County [vr, v mfm]. Records. 1816–1936.

Lutheran Church, Church of the Redeemer, Newberry [2vr, v mfm]. Minutes and historical sketch. 1854–99, 1953.

Lutheran Church, Conference [vr]. Minutes. 1939–40.

Lutheran Church, Epiphany, St. Matthews [v mfm]. Records. 1912–63.

Lutheran Church, German Protestant, Charleston [vr, also mfm]. Records. 1826–1937.

Lutheran Church, Grace, Prosperity, Newberry County [vr, also mfm]. Records. 1859–1936.

Lutheran Church, Incarnation, Columbia [c. 500 mfm]. Records. 1921–65.

Lutheran Church, New Central Conference of Evangelical Lutheran Synod, SC [vr]. Records. 1930–38.
Lutheran Church, St. Andrew's Evangelical, Columbia [2vr, v mfm]. Records. 1860–1938.
Lutheran Church, St. John's Evangelical, Charleston [26vr, 5v mfm]. Records. 1778–1937.
Lutheran Church, St. Luke's, Stoney Battery, Newberry District [vr, also mfm]. Records. 1932–57.
Lutheran Church, St. Mark's, Ft. Motte [v mfm]. Records. 1895–1924.
Lutheran Church, St. Matthew's, Orangeburg [v, v mfm]. Records. 1767–1897.
Lutheran Church, St. Philip's, Newberry County [vr]. Records. 1881–1923.
Lutheran Church, Zion, Lexington County [2v mfm]. Records. 1861–1929.
Lyles, W. H., Jr. [v]. Diary kept at Janney School, Columbia. 1901.
McAfee, John T. [c. 111]. Papers of a Chester businessman. 1830–79.
McAliley, Mary [49]. Chiefly Columbia school letters. 1848–1901.
McBee, William Pinckney [105]. Family correspondence, SC railroads, politics. 1819–1937.
McBryde, John McLaren (1841–1923) [12v]. Chiefly business papers of USC president. 1883–1945.
McBryde, Sarah C. [2v]. McBryde and Livingston genealogy, Fairfield County epitaphs. 1948–50.
McCants, James B. (1814–80) [118]. Winnsboro, Columbia, and Charleston legal papers. 1844–80.
McCay, Charles F. [32]. SC College data. 1856–69.
McClain, John [v]. "South Carolina Grain Production." 1840–80.
McClintock, Euphemia (1870–1953) [18]. Papers re her career as educator. 1922–60.
McConnel & Kennedy, Manchester, England [684 mfm]. Business papers re rice and cotton; letters to Charleston, Savannah, and New Orleans. 1819–26.
McCord Family [vr]. Letters and clippings re David J., David R., Louisa S., and Langdon Cheves McCord. 1845–99.
McCrady Family [203, 6 v, also mfm]. Charleston, Columbia Chester, and Manchester letters; chiefly correspondence of Edward McCrady, Sr., and his wife, Louisa Rebecca Lane McCrady, and son, Edward, Jr. 1821–1907. See *University South Caroliniana Society Program* (1961).
McCreery, W. W. [v]. Pocotaligo Confederate letterbook. 1862.
McCreight, James and Robert J., Winnsboro [v]. Account book. 1827–45.
McCrorey, J. L. [vr]. Maryland CW diary. 1864.
McCullough, E. H. [31, v]. Chiefly papers re railroad service, commonplace book. 1876–1920.
McCullough, John DeWitt (1822–1902) [v]. Records kept as Episcopal minister. 1848–65.

McCullough, Rosanna [v]. Arithmetic and poetry book. 1825–32.

McDavid Family [vr]. Genealogy. c. 1962.

McDowell, Davison (1784–1842) [59, v]. Ireland and Georgetown, SC politics, War of 1812. 1767–1836.

McDowell, Sue [v]. Camden CW journal. 1861.

McDuffie, George (1790–1851) [55, 48r, vr]. Various papers re Columbia, Cherry Hill, Washington, D. C., and tariff debates. 1822–1948.

McGaw Family [29]. Sumterville, Orangeburg, and Richmond, Va., including CW letters. 1859–67.

McGowan, Samuel (1819–97) [20]. Chiefly political correspondence. 1857–60.

McGowan, Samuel (1870–1934) [76, vr]. Strother genealogy, memoranda as chief of SC State Highway Department, especially "billboard controversy." 1920–37.

McGraw, Marshal [105]. Chiefly correspondence from out-of-state relatives, CW and Reconstruction. 1842–1905.

McIlhenny, Ada A. (1836–74) [140]. Chiefly business letters re Charleston, New York, Paris. 1841–64.

McIntosh, Edward [v]. SC College notes. 1857–58.

McIntosh, James H. (b. 1866) [577, 8v]. Chiefly addresses and correspondence as president of the SC Medical Association and the Tri-State Medical Association. 1840–1938.

McIver, Robert Boyd (b. 1892) [vr]. Reprint of article with biographical data. 1952.

McIver, Sarah Witherspoon Ervin [vr]. Darlington social diary. 1854–89.

McJunkin, Joseph (1755–1846) [vr]. RW memoir. No date.

McKay, Robert [v]. "South Carolina Redeemed," Reconstruction material, and clippings. 1865–87.

McKee, John [vr]. Letters as Indian agent in Alabama. 1793–1843.

McKensie, Richard Daniel [15]. Charleston and New York papers re his estate. 1859.

McKie, Thomas Jefferson (1828–98) [69, 8v]. Edgefield medical data and CW material; diaries, postal and farm accounts. 1824–1903.

McKissick, A. Foster [2v]. SC College notes. 1888–89.

McKissick, James Rion (1884–1944) [2 boxes]. Various papers of USC president. 1800–1944.

McLaurin, D. B. and J. J. Chandler, Sumter [40]. Various papers. 1846–54.

McLaurin, John Lowndes (1860–1934) [3v]. Scrapbooks of US senator. 1914–27.

McLean, John Knox (b. 1835) [137]. Chiefly letters of CW surgeon. 1820–67.

McLees, John (1812–82) [435, v]. Letters and papers of a Presbyterian minister, student diary at Columbia Theological Seminary, and data re work among Negroes of Greenwood and Pickens Counties. 1838–1918.

McLendon, Baxter F. [45]. Newspaper clippings of sermons and an endorsement of Coleman L. Blease for governor (1922). 1922–25.

McLendon Family [vr]. Genealogy. 1787–81.

McLeod, Thomas G. [148]. Sumter business papers. 1803–79.

McMahan, John Joseph (1865–1936) [41v]. Columbia and Fairfield County; SC educator and political reformer. 1847–1934.

McMaster, Fitz Hugh (1867–1952) [2vr]. Various papers including "USC Class of 1885." 1940–64.

McMaster, Fitz William (1826–99) [1,705, 20v, 2vr]. Chiefly Columbia business and legal papers, CW, Republican post-Reconstruction politics. 1753–1929.

McMaster, Helen Graham [2v]. Columbia scrapbooks of poems, CW. 1864–1924.

McMaster, John (1787–1864) [30, 2v]. Winnsboro business papers. 1814–78.

McMaster, Richard Nott [vr]. CW letters. 1861–65.

McMillan, Lewis Kennedy [vr]. Orangeburg, clippings and notes on "Inside Germany." 1949.

McPheeters, William M. (b. 1854) [2v]. Various papers including notes kept at Columbia Theological Seminary. 1876–1911.

Macfarlan, Allan (1820—69) [145]. Chiefly Cheraw and Charleston business papers, CW. 1818–69.

Macfie, James [v]. Columbia account book. 1836–37.

Mackay Family [82]. Material re nullification and CW; family correspondence from Pocotaligo, Charleston, McPhersonville, and Orangeburg. 1822–1926.

Madden, Mabra [728]. Various personal papers and plantation accounts. 1774–1879.

Magnolia Cemetery, Charleston [2v]. Burial records. No date.

Magrath, Andrew Gordon (1813–93) [137]. CW, correspondence with Confederate leaders. 1861–79.

Magrath, Selina E. Bollin [v]. "Burning of the Ursiline Convent . . . 17 February, 1865." 1929, 1933.

Magrath, William Joy (1817–1902) [10, 23v]. Charleston, papers as president of South Carolina Railroad. 1861–94.

Maham, Hezekiah [vr]. Appraisals of Berkeley County estates. 1767–90.

Mahlstedt, Louis D. [19, v]. Monthly reports and accounts of Charleston County liquor dispenser. 1896–1900.

Mairs, Jane B. [vr]. Laurens County genealogy. 1874–89.

Malone, Blondelle Octavia Edwards (1877–1951) [3,340]. Correspondence and various personal papers. 1800–1956. See Louise Jones Du Bose, *Enigma; the Career of Blondelle Malone in Art and Society* (1963).

Malone, Peter Jehu (1844–73) [262, 2vr]. Papers re Woodlands, works of William Gilmore Simms, and poetry. 1823–1930.

Manigault, Charles Izard (1795–1874) [v, 3vr]. Reminiscences, family accounts, and catalog of personal library. 1776–1872.

Libraries, Archives,

Manigault, Gabriel Edward (1833–99) [vr]. Charleston reminiscences and travel accounts. 1836–99.
Manigault Family [937]. Charleston papers. 1750–1884.
Manigault, Louis (1828–99) [3vr]. Charleston genealogy and travel accounts. 1850–99.
Manning, Brown [22]. Manchester and Camden financial papers. 1873–76.
Manning, John Laurence (1816–89) [42, vr]. Various papers including CW items and biographical sketch. 1834–1962. See also Williams-Chesnut-Manning collection.
Manning, Richard Irvine (1859–1931) [c. 17,000, 20v]. Plantation, business records and correspondence. 1897–1931.
Manning-Richardson-Cantey Families [vr]. Genealogy. 1700–1925.
Manning Times [vr]. Centennial edition, Manning and Clarendon Counties. 1955.
Manning, Wyndham M. [c. 16,000, 57v]. Business accounts, clippings, SC political life (1934–42). 1920–42.
Marion County [8vr]. WPA transcripts of various court records. 1796–1888.
Marion County [2vr, also mfm]. WPA transcripts of epitaphs: Centenary Methodist Churchyard, Davis Family Cemetery [Britton's Neck], First Methodist Church [Marion], Giles Family Cemetery, Goldbold-Haselden-Ellerbee Cemetery, Legette Family Cemetery [China Grove Plantation], Munnerlyn Graveyard, Rosehill Cemetery [Marion], Tabernacle Churchyard, Miscellaneous Epitaphs.
Marion, Francis (1732–95) [24]. Chiefly RW papers. 1761–1858.
Marion, Gabriel [v]. Incomplete manuscript and notes. 1774–78.
Marlboro County [vr]. Various records. 1787–1853.
Marlboro County [20vr]. WPA transcripts of various court records. 1785–1882.
Marlboro County [7vr, also mfm]. WPA transcripts of epitaphs: Adams Cemetery, Beauty Spot Cemetery, Beaverdam Cemetery, Bennett Graveyard, Bethel Churchyard, Breeden Graveyard, David Graveyard, Drake Graveyard, Easterby Cemetery, Easterling Graveyard, Fletcher's Cemetery, Fletcher Graveyard, Hamer Burial Ground, Hebron Cemetery, Hodges Cemetery, Holy Road Cemetery, Lester Cemetery, Liles Graveyard, Manship Graveyard, Moore Cemetery, Mossy Bay Cemetery, Munford Cemetery, Murchison Cemetery, Old Welsh Neck Cemetery, Parker's Cemetery, Parnassus Cemetery, Robertson and Ellerbee Cemetery, Rogers Cemetery, Salem Cemetery, Saw Mill Churchyard, Smyrna Cemetery, Spears and Edens Graveyard, Tatum Cemetery, Webster Cemetery.
Marple, Alfred (b. 1830) [vr]. Union officer's diary and letters; Beaufort, Folly and Morris Islands, and Hilton Head. 1863–64.
Marshall, Adam [v]. Greenville receipt book. 1799–1809.
Marshall, J. Foster [v]. CW data. 1862.

Martin, C. J. [v]. "History and Development of Negro Education in South Carolina." 1949.

Martin, James L. [v]. Journal. 1866–68.

Martin, William (b. 1807) [3v]. Diary and reminiscences of a Columbia Methodist minister. 1807–88.

Martin, Mrs. William (b. 1807) [2v]. Columbia scrapbook and autobiography. 1860–80.

Martin, William Dickerson (1789–1833) [v]. Journal of trip from Edgefield to Litchfield, Conn. 1809.

Martindale, C. O., Jr. [v]. USC thesis: "Psychology, Its Scope and Value." 1893.

Masons, Carolina Chapter, Charleston [v]. Ledger. 1867–72.

Masons, Pomaria Lodge No. 151 [v]. Records. 1869–71.

Masons, Solomon's Lodge No. 1, Charleston [4v]. Minutes and ledger. 1841–90.

Mathews, John Raven (1788–1867) [43]. Charleston business papers. 1802–51.

Mathis, Samuel [v]. Camden plantation journal and RW. 1781.

Maverick-Van Wyck Families [202, 3v]. Ninety-Six and Alabama, some genealogy. 1772–1889. See *University South Caroliniana Society Program* (1954).

Maxcy, Johnathan (1768–1820) [32]. Columbia and SC College. 1812–1943.

Mazyck Family [209, v, vr]. Charleston business papers and Bible records, chiefly papers of Henry Broughton Mazyck (d. 1835). 1748–1889.

Meachum, Joshua [v]. Plantation management book. 1820–28.

Meachum, J. M. [v]. Receipt book. 1888.

Meachum, Miriam D. [v mfm]. Catholic University thesis: "A Checklist of South Carolina Imprints, 1811–18." 1962.

Means-English-Doby Families [345, 4vr]. Material re CW, Fairfield and Richland Counties. 1828–1950. See *University South Caroliniana Society Program* (1963).

Means, Mary Hart (1835–1916) [2 boxes, 3v]. Family papers representing the Coalter, Davis, Bates, Means and Poelnitz connections, Fairfield District. 1837–1906.

Meares, Richard A. (1858–1946) [795, vr]. Chiefly concerned with Rural Electrification Administration. 1858–1946.

Medical Officers, Confederate Army and Navy, Association of [vr]. Records and biographies. 1874–75.

Medical Society of SC [14 mfm, 3v mfm, 7vr]. Various papers, minutes, and records. 1780–1924.

Meighen, J. [116]. Bills and receipts. 1834–80.

Melton, Samuel W. (1830–99) [181]. Material re Columbia, Charleston, and various points in Virginia and North Carolina during CW. 1860–78.

Memminger, Christopher Gustavus (1803–88) [16]. Various personal papers. 1830–80.

Merchants Steamboat Company, Cheraw [3v]. Account books. 1836–53.

Meriwether, Colyer (d. 1920) [c. 143, 3v]. Scrapbooks and papers re proposed biography of Thomas Cooper; material on life in Washington, Japan, and Philippines; Grange and other farm movements. 1835–1920.

Meriwether-McKie-Griffin Families [vr]. Genealogy. 1963.

Meriwether, Margaret Babcock [v]. Data re South Caroliniana Library collection. 1941–43.

Meriwether, R. E. [v]. Receipt book. 1883.

Meriwether, Robert Lee (1865–90) [v]. Farm account book. 1885–1900.

Meriwether, Zachary [v]. Account book. 1816–17.

Methodist Church: see entries under three headings in the South Caroliniana Library files: Methodist Church, Methodist Episcopal Church, and Methodist Church, South.

Methodist Church, Bennettsville [v mfm]. Records. 1846–1925.

Methodist Church, Black River and Kingstree Circuits [vr, also mfm]. Records. 1857–69.

Methodist Church, Bramlettes, Laurens County [3v]. Records. 1842–78.

Methodist Church, Camden [6vr, 3v mfm]. Minutes. 1818–1907.

Methodist Church, Camden Station [3vr]. Records. 1828–94.

Methodist Church, Central, Newberry [vr]. Records. 1868–1901.

Methodist Church, Cypress, Darlington [4v mfm]. Sunday School records. 1853–99.

Methodist Church, Darlington [v mfm]. Records. 1841–67.

Methodist Church, Darlington Circuit, Florence County [2v]. Minutes. 1831–78.

Methodist Church, Duncan Memorial, Georgetown [vr]. Marriage-baptism records. 1811–46.

Methodist Church, Lynchburg [v, also v mfm]. Records. 1855–1938.

Methodist Church, Lynch's Creek Circuit, Darlington County [v, v mfm]. Records. 1787–1897.

Methodist Church, Mars Bluff [v]. Records of Missionary Society. 1890–1915.

Methodist Church, Newberry [3vr, v mfm]. Records. 1820–83.

Methodist Church [South], Newberry County [vr, v mfm]. Records (1823–70) and church register (1873–86). 1823–86.

Methodist Church, New Hope, Chester County [vr, v mfm]. Records. 1832–1931.

Methodist Church, Parnassus, Marlboro County [vr]. Records. 1883–1915.

Methodist Church, Sandy River, Fairfield County [vr, also mfm]. Records. 1810–74.

Methodist Church, South Cypress, Charleston County [v]. Records. 1844–88.

Methodist Church [South], Saint Paul's [v]. Records. 1891–1914.

Methodist Church, Swallow Savannah [2vr, also mfm]. Records. 1856–89.
Methodist Church, Tabernacle [vr, also mfm]. Records. 1861–88.
Methodist Church, Trinity, Charleston [3v, v mfm]. Assorted records. 1792–1888.
Methodist Church, Waccamaw Circuit, Horry County [vr, also mfm]. Records. 1836–55.
Methodist Church, Washington Street, Columbia [23, v, also v mfm]. Various records, biographical sketches, pictures. 1831–86, 1923–39.
Methodist Church, Upper SC Conference [16v]. Minutes. 1917–40.
Middleton Family [811, v]. Charleston, Columbia, New York, and Bristol, R. I.; family letters. 1789, 1817–1921.
Miller, Archibald Edward (b. 1785) [vr]. Data on *Miller's Almanacs*, Charleston. 1785–1878.
Miller, John Blount (1782–1851) [4v]. Sumter scrapbooks and legal data. 1796–1857.
Milligan, James [v]. Charleston bills for lodgings. 1785–86.
Mills, Robert (1781–1855) [30, v]. Various papers re SC architect and atlas compiler. 1827–1963.
Minshall, Rachel Hemphill [vr]. Abbeville County historical sketches. 1923.
Miot, C. H. [v]. Account book. 1848–74.
Mitchell, Samuel Chiles (1864–1948) [117v]. Papers of USC president, including those of Andrew Charles Moore, acting president. 1908–13.
Moncrieffe, James [v]. Charleston letterbook of a British soldier. 1780–82.
Montgomery, John Henry (1833–1902) [v mfm]. Letterbook of cotton mill executive. 1899–1901.
Montgomery, Mabel [572]. World War II letters of Marion County servicemen to editor of the *Marion Mail*. 1943–45.
Moody Family [14v]. Sumter business records, some CW material. 1817–80.
Moore, Arthur C. [22, v]. Columbia and New Orleans daybooks and accounts, some CW data. 1837–74.
Moore, Charles Andrew (1866–1928) [72, 9v]. Notes on biology, botany, and zoology; material re USC, Columbia, and SC Agricultural Experimental Station. 1890–1921.
Moore Family [49 mfm]. Spartanburg family letters and genealogy. 1774–1882.
Moore Family [166]. Various papers. 1804–1931.
Moore, James Washington (1837–1912) [15v]. CW, Reconstruction, Darlington Riot. 1861–1912.
Moore, Mrs. J. A. [v]. Columbia business accounts, CW diary. 1848–63.
Moore, John A. [v]. Columbia business ledger. 1859–60.
Moore, John A. [v]. Farm accounts. 1866.
Moore, John Burchell [v]. University of Virginia law notes. 1850.

Moore & Lacoste, Cheraw [18]. Georgetown and Charleston business correspondence. 1825–26.
Moore, Mary [21]. Charleston bills and accounts. 1816–22.
Moore, Richard [2v]. Ledgers and notes. 1792–1833.
Moore, Stephen (1734–99) [50]. Various RW papers. 1763–97.
Moore, Mrs. W. Bedford and Mrs. Wyatt A. Taylor [v]. Genealogy of Calhoun, Vince, Finley, Hext-Dunbar, Bellinger-Bull-Duncan, Jones, and Caldwell families; compiled for DAR. 1950.
Moragne, Mary Elizabeth (1816–1903) [28, v, vr]. Incomplete Abbeville journal and letters. 1836–42. Edited by Delle Mullen Craven as *The Neglected Thread* . . . (1951).
Morgan, James Morris (1845–1928) [67]. Various papers re Washington, Panama, Texas, and Egypt. 1769–1927.
Morris, John B. [vr]. Documents re *South Carolinians Speak: A Moderate Approach to Race Relations.* 1957–58.
Morris, Thomas [116]. Charleston and Philadelphia business letters. 1783–96.
Morrow, James [355]. Business papers and material re Davidson College, Charleston, CW, Perry's expedition to Japan, and Philadelphia. 1838–1938.
Morse, Agur T. [v]. Sumterville tannery daybook. 1829–30.
Morse, Josiah (1879–1946) [40, v]. Letters and material re USC Psychology Department and race relations in the South. 1903–52.
Moses, F. J. [v]. Reference book of Euphennian Society debates, Charleston. 1821.
Moses, Franklin Israel (compiler) (d. 1877) [v]. Index to SC Assembly acts. No. date.
Motte Family [122]. Charleston business papers. 1791–1892.
Mouchet Family [vr]. Genealogy. 1958.
Moultrie, Alexander [v]. Commonplace book. 1750.
Moultrie Family [vr]. Genealogy. 1714–1927.
Moultrie, William (1730–1805) [721, 44 mfm]. Various business and family papers re Charleston and Summerville. 1747–1940.
Moultrieville, Sullivan's Island [3v]. City Treasurer's account book (1870–79) and poll book (1878–82). 1870–82.
Mounsey, Thomas [70]. Chiefly legal documents. 1822–29.
Mount Hope School, Ridgeway [2v]. Records. 1878–92.
Mount Tabor High School [v, vr]. Newberry County, minutes. 1885–91.
Mount Zion Society, Winnsboro [5vr]. Minutes. 1783–1933.
Muckenfuss Family [72, v]. Legal papers. 1797–1880.
Muckenfuss, H. and B., Charleston [7v]. Business accounts. 1838–52.
Muckenfuss, H. W. [3v]. Charleston business records. 1824–37.
Muckenfuss, H. W. & J. H. Steinmeyer, Charleston [v]. Business records. 1838–39.
Muckenfuss, Henry [2v]. Charleston business records. 1810–23.
Muckenfuss, W. M. [3v]. Charleston business records. 1891–1901.
Muller Diary [v]. In German. c. 1848.

Muller, Gerhard (1815–91) [82]. Family, business and political letters and papers, Lexington District. 1832–73.
Munnerlyn, Mrs. Henry J., compiler [vr]. Marlboro County marriage licenses. 1788–1826.
Munnerlyn, Mrs. Henry J., compiler [2vr]. Marlboro County genealogical data. 1951.
Murray and McIntosh, Camden [v]. Inventory book. 1835.
Murrell, William [4v]. Old Camden District and Claremont County mercantile records. 1784–1812.
Napier, Rapilyea, Bennett & Company, Columbia [v]. Law ledger. 1823–25.
Napier, Thomas (c. 1777–1860) [263, 5v]. Charleston, New York, rice milling, and slavery. 1803–60, 1947.
Nash, Reuben [vr]. Officers and men in War of 1812. 1814.
National Conference of Social Work [vr]. SC area report. 1947.
National Resources Planning Board [v]. Committee on Conservation of Cultural Resources. 1941–42.
Neely, William W. [vr]. "Ecological Changes in South Carolina Farmlands of Benefit to Wildlife." 1940.
Nesbitt Family [c. 200]. Genealogical records. 1940–61.
Nesbitt, Robert [v]. Medical account book. 1796–1804.
Netherlands Fire Insurance Company [v]. Policy register containing roll of Company G, 20th Regiment, SC Volunteers, CSA. 1885–1908.
Nettles, Joseph Edward [v]. SC College geology notes. 1859.
New Century Club, Columbia [v]. Yearbooks. 1901–5.
Newberry Account Book, Glymphville [v]. General store accounts. 1857–59.
Newberry County [41vr]. WPA transcripts of various court records. 1776–1887.
Newberry County [vr, also mfm]. WPA transcripts of epitaphs: Asford Cemetery [Strother's Bridge], Baxter Cemetery [Newberry], Boland Burying Ground, Nance Graveyard [near Cannonsville], Newberry Village Graveyard, Reagin and Kinard Cemetery, Rosemont Graveyard, King's Creek Presbyterian Church Cemetery, St. Paul's Lutheran Church Cemetery.
News & Courier, Charleston [3v]. Business records and prices current sheets. 1877–90.
Nickles, Mary [v]. Readings in SC history for high schools. 1939.
Nixon, William [v]. Camden receipt book. 1810–32.
Noble Family [149, v]. Various papers. 1751–1879, 1920–22.
Noisette Family [76]. Charleston legal papers and land transfers. 1841–73, 1937–39.
Nott, Henry Junius (1797–1837) [24]. SC College reports and plans for South Pacific exploration. 1830–37, 1951.
Obear Family [3,319]. Various papers re Winnsboro, England, and Australia. 1834–1941. See *University South Caroliniana Program* (1964).

111

Libraries, Archives,

Ogilby, William [v]. British consul's reports on Charleston economic life. 1833.
Ogilvie, John W. [1 box, 5v]. Allendale and Barnwell medical account books and notes, family letters. 1845–85.
Oliphant, William [143]. Various papers. 1809–32.
Oliver, E. R. (b. 1883) [v]. Address of Southern Railway vice-president to Columbia Rotary Club. 1945.
Olney, Richard [v mfm]. Copies of correspondence (in Library of Congress) with Latin American ministers. 1880–90.
O'Neil, Bernard [v]. Charleston account book. 1874–76.
O'Neil, John [50]. Material re Lynchburg, *Alabama* claims, and Reconstruction; some foreign correspondence. 1867–95, 1903.
Orangeburg Collegiate Institute [vr]. History and records of school and alumni. 1895–1963.
Orangeburg Conscription Rolls [v]. Data on registrants. 1864.
Orangeburg County [2vr]. WPA transcripts of various court records. 1824–37.
Orangeburg County Jail [75]. Copies of records. 1867–68.
Orangeburg Jewish Community [vr]. Newspaper clippings; also, material re Kohn family, Camden, Aiken, and Greenville. 1927.
Orphan Aid Society, Charleston [19]. Various papers. 1909–27.
Orr, James L. (1822–73) [18]. Various papers. 1850–68.
Osmut, John [v]. CW diary. 1863.
Ostendorff, J. M. [v]. Charleston receipt book. 1841–71.
Oswald Family [v]. Beaufort accounts. 1808–46.
Oswald-Sams Families [25]. Genealogy. 1784–1851.
Overman, Flora Keith [v]. Keith genealogy. 1929–30.
Owens, L. G. [30]. Various papers. 1898–1908.
Owens, Loulie Latimer [vr]. SC Baptist historical pageants. 1938, 1945, 1947.
Owings, Osmond Young [60]. Columbia, water power development on the Saluda River. 1921–31.
Pack, Joseph (d. 1862) and Andrew [45]. Material on CW and SC Institution for the Blind. 1859–72.
Padgett, Lucas C. [v]. Walterboro business accounts. 1913–33.
Paine and Lucas [16]. Business papers. 1850–54.
Palmer, Benjamin Morgan (1818–1902) [v]. Notes on lectures in Columbia. 1850–52.
Palmer Family [1,501, 4v, 6vr]. Berkeley County plantation accounts and records; Pineville Academy. 1720–1938.
Palmer, Hattie Amelia [v]. Columbia poetry collection. 1849–50.
Palmer, Joseph [vr]. Wood Pond and Springfield plantation accounts, Pineville. 1810–94.
Palmetto Steam Fire Engine Company, Columbia [v]. Minute book and miscellaneous papers. 1895–1914.
Palmetto Weekly Press Association [vr]. Records. 1939–42.
Pardue, Joseph S. (1833–54) [19]. Writings of Chester County native at Davidson College. 1851–53.
Parent-Teacher Association, John's Island [vr]. Minutes. 1924–31.

Parker Family [26]. Charleston, also some foreign letters. 1820–84.
Parker, Francis S. [3v]. Plantation records. 1846–65.
Parker, Henry Middleton (d. 1926) [66]. Biographical data and letters re missionary life in Liberia. 1859–1943.
Parker, John R. [9vr]. Account book and diaries. 1859–1911.
Parker, Niles G. [294]. Records of SC treasurer. 1868–69.
Parnassaus Temperance Society [v]. Proceedings. 1840–43.
Patrons of Husbandry, Goshen Hill [41]. Minutes. 1873–74.
Patrons of Husbandry, State Grange [2v]. Minutes. 1873–1905.
Patrons of Husbandry, Tom's Creek, Lexington County [65]. Records. 1870–77.
Patterson, Giles J. (1827–91) [vr]. SC College journal. 1846–47.
Patterson, Joel [v]. Toll accounts, Seneca (?) River. 1856–65.
Peacock Papers [222]. Material re Shaller and Sosnowski families, Timrod, and SC College. No dates.
Pearson, William Franklin [vr]. Abbeville District marriage register. 1861–93.
Pegues, Rebecca Ann Evans [v mfm]. Chesterfield County diary. 1837–84.
Pelot, Francis [vr]. Genealogy. 1734–1848.
Pelzer Manufacturing Company [7v]. Records and accounts. 1896–1924.
Pemberton, James [v mfm]. Diary of trip to SC (original in Library of Congress). 1745.
Pendleton County [10vr]. WPA transcripts of various court records. 1790–1816.
Pendleton Farmers' Society, Anderson County [vr]. 1824–1930.
Pendleton Female Academy, Anderson County [196vr]. Accounts and business papers. 1827–1904.
Pendleton Social Library Society, Anderson County [vr]. Records. 1828–34.
Pendleton Sunday School Society, Anderson County [v]. Minutes. 1819–38.
Penman, J. and E., & Company, Charleston [v]. Merchants' daybook. 1794.
Penn, Annie and Georgia [2v]. Albums. 1846–59.
Perry, Benjamin Franklin (1805–86) [101, v, v mfm]. Various papers and documents. 1760–1886, 1910. See *University South Carolinana Society Program* (1963).
Peterkin, Julia (1880–1961) [49, vr]. Various papers re literary career; University of Georgia thesis by Marilyn Price Maddox on Miss Peterkin and her work (1956). 1929–61.
Petigru, James Louis (1789–1863) [43, vr]. Charleston and SC politics. 1834–1902.
Phi Beta Kappa, USC [v]. Addresses by J. Heyward Gibbes. 1936, 1947.
Phillips, John [v]. Sumter District blacksmith's accounts. 1860–62.
Pickens, Andrew (1739–1817) [18, v]. Various papers. 1781–1809.

Pickens, Andrew, Jr. (1779–1838) [15, v]. Various papers. 1779–
1826.
Pickens County [6vr]. WPA transcripts of various court records.
1828–85.
Pickens County [vr, also mfm]. WPA transcripts of epitaphs: Bethel
Presbyterian Cemetery, Choenee Baptist Cemetery [Tomassee],
Day Burying Ground, Mountain Grove Southern Baptist Church-
yard, Nicholson Family Graveyard, Old Stone Churchyard,
Oolenoy Churchyard, Pickens Mill Cemetery, Presbyterian
Churchyard, Secona Southern Baptist Churchyard, Sunrise Cem-
etery.
Pickens Family [3 vr, v mfm]. Genealogical data. 1781–1960.
Pickens, Francis Wilkerson (1805–69) [70, 5v, vr, v mfm]. Various
business papers, letters, and speeches; CW and plantation ac-
counts; data on Russia and US Congress. 1830–70.
Pinckney, Caroline [v]. "Extract Book." 1852–63.
Pinckney, Charles (1699–1758) [46]. Charleston receipts and legal
papers. 1735–52.
Pinckney, Charles (1757–1824) [28]. Various papers re Charleston
and Spain. 1779–1822.
Pinckney, Charles Cotesworth (1746–1825) [69]. Various papers re
Charleston, Philadelphia, and France. 1779–1829.
Pinckney, Charles Cotesworth, Jr. (1839–1909) [93, 6v]. Papers re
Charleston, Columbia, Prussia, phosphates, secession, and CW.
1860–1922.
Pinckney Family [v]. Charleston and Columbia accounts. 1872–84.
Pinckney, Harriott (1776–1866) [26]. Chiefly plantation correspond-
ence. 1854–61.
Pinckney, James S. [108, v]. Various papers. 1850–1904.
Pinckney, Lawrence M. [8v]. WPA publications re SC. 1935–40.
Pinckney, Thomas (1750–1828) [42, vr]. Various papers re Charles-
ton, Europe, and RW; some plantation accounts. 1780–1835.
Plantation Journal, Barnwell District [v]. Brief, but thorough ac-
count. 1838–44.
Poinsett, Joel Roberts (1779–1851) [40]. Political campaign of 1824,
Mexico, Washington, and Charleston. 1804–50.
Pope & Haskell [v]. Record book of Greenville & Columbia railroad
cases. c. 1883.
Porcher-Ford Families [401, 6vr]. Genealogy, business accounts, and
family correspondence re Charleston, Aiken, Atlanta, and Abbeville District. 1797–1925.
Porcher, Francis Peyre (1825–95) [21, 2v]. Charleston, medicine,
and botany. 1850–1935.
Porcher, Frederick Adolphus (1809–88) [62]. Charleston, Greenville, CW; family correspondence. 1862–1922.
Porcher, John Palmer [154]. St. John's, Berkeley, and Charleston;
business papers. 1831–72.

Porcher, Octavius Theodore [2 boxes, 2v]. Family letters and papers, journal and lecture notes as Willington teacher; Pineville and Pinopolis. 1850–73.

Porcher, Octavius Theodore (1865–1940) [37v]. Greenwood, Bennettsville, Sewanee, Willington, and Pendleton; diaries, original poetry, personal accounts. 1885–1940.

Porcher, Philip [vr]. Rice and indigo accounts re St. Stephen's Parish, Cedar Springs, and Charleston. 1770–1800.

Porcher, Philip E. [v]. Genealogy and inventory of John Cordes' estate. 1764–99, 1850.

Porcher, Samuel De Bose [105, 4v]. Abbeville, Willington, Charleston, and Porter Academy; family papers. 1845–95.

Porcher, Thomas Davis [2v]. Farm records and material re Porter Academy. 1885–88.

Porcher, Benjamin Faneuil (1808–68) [v]. Scrapbook re his writings in Charleston newspapers. 1849–50.

Posey Family [v]. Genealogy. 1948.

Pou and Senn, Columbia [1 box]. Business papers. 1840–99.

Pourtales, Marie Boozer, Countess de (c. 1850–1908) [14]. Various papers. 1878–1955.

Pratt, Elizabeth [v]. School letters from Salem, N. C., to her family in Union. 1834–35.

Presbyterian Church [2vr]. Miscellaneous records. c. 1935.

Presbyterian Church, Aimwell, Ridgeway [vr]. Recollections of work of church women. c. 1915.

Presbyterian Church, Aveleigh, Newberry District [vr, also mfm]. Records. 1835–53.

Presbyterian Church, Bennettsville [vr, v mfm]. Records. 1855–98.

Presbyterian Church, Bethel, Williamsburg District [vr, also mfm]. minutes. 1811–28.

Presbyterian Church, Bethesda, Camden [vr, v mfm]. Records. 1806–1937.

Presbyterian Church, Bethesda, York County [v]. History. 1769–1885.

Presbyterian Church, Cannon Creek, Newberry County [vr]. Records. 1875–95.

Presbyterian Church, Darlington [vr, also mfm]. Records. 1827–53.

Presbyterian Church, Fairview, Greenville [vr, also v mfm]. Centenial. 1768–1886.

Presbyterian Church, First, Columbia [743, 42v, 3v mfm]. Various records and papers. 1827–1952.

Presbyterian Church, First, Greer [vr]. Minutes. 1924–39.

Presbyterian Church, Fishing Creek, Chester County [2vr, v mfm]. Records and minutes. 1799–1937.

Presbyterian Church, Georgetown [vr]. Records. 1897–1926.

Presbyterian Church, Greer [vr]. Records of Ladies Aid Society. 1901–24.

Presbyterian Church, James Island [vr, also mfm]. Records. 1833–45.

Presbyterian Church, John's and Wadamalaw Islands [vr, also v mfm]. Records. 1856–1911.

Presbyterian Church, Kingston, Horry County [2vr]. Minutes. 1903–36.

Presbyterian Church, Marlboro County [v mfm]. Records. 1833–1924.

Presbyterian Church, Mount Tabor, Greer [3vr, v mfm]. Records. 1841–1912.

Presbyterian Church, Ninety-Six [vr, also v mfm]. Records. 1860–1936.

Presbyterian Church, Old Buffalo [vr, also v mfm]. Records. 1833–1924.

Presbyterian Church, Pleasant Grove, Chester County [2vr, v mfm]. Records. 1847–1929.

Presbyterian Church, Salem, Black River [3vr, also mfm]. Records. 1759–1860.

Presbyterian Church, Second, Charleston [9vr, also mfm]. Records. 1809–1908.

Presbyterian Church, Smyrna, Blenheim, Marlboro County [vr]. Records. 1833–1924.

Presbyterian Church, Stoney Creek, Independent, Prince William Parish [v mfm]. 1722–1910.

Presbyterian Church, Union [vr]. Records. 1864–1938.

Presbyterian Church, Williamsburg, Kingstree [2vr, also mfm]. Records. 1834–1931.

Presbyterian High School [2v]. Catalogues. 1894–96.

Press & Standard, Walterboro [v]. Daybook. 1929–32.

Preston, William Campbell (1794–1860) [190, 2v, 3 reels mfm]. Autobiography edited and published as *Reminiscences of William C. Preston* (1933); various personal papers re Columbia and Washington; mfm copies of material in South Caroliniana Library and Huntington Library. 1817–1935.

Preston, Mrs. William C. (d. 1847) [vr]. Poetry album and diary. 1829–1909.

Price, Richard L. [49]. Camden, chiefly receipts as treasurer of Negro Masonic order. 1895–1910.

Prince, George Edward (1855–1923) [v mfm]. Scrapbook. 1923.

Pringle, James R. & Son, Charleston [13, 2v]. Receipts, cotton and grain reports to E. B. Cantey of Camden. 1857–74.

Pritchard, S. C. [vr]. "SC's Militant Agrarian" (M.A. thesis, Longwood College, 1965). Biography of David Wyatt Aiken (1828–1887).

Protestant Episcopal Church [3vr]. Miscellaneous information and history. c. 1935.

Protestant Episcopal Church [c. 40]. Notes on SC bishops. 1957–61.

Protestant Episcopal Church, All Saints, Waccamaw [vr, also v mfm]. Records. 1819–1954.

Protestant Episcopal Church, Allendale [vr]. Records. 1874–1900.

Protestant Episcopal Church, Charleston County [v mfm]. Records. 1754–90.
Protestant Episcopal Church, Christ Church, Charleston [vr, also mfm]. Records. 1694–1936.
Protestant Episcopal Church, Christ Church Society, Florence County [vr]. Records. 1907–8.
Protestant Episcopal Church, Church of the Atonement, Blacksburg [vr]. Material re reconstruction plans. 1958.
Protestant Episcopal Church, Church of the Holy Apostles, Barnwell [v mfm]. Records. 1848–1957.
Protestant Episcopal Church, Church of the Holy Comforter, Sumter [vr]. Newspaper articles concerning the church. 1934–35.
Protestant Episcopal Church, Church of the Redeemer, Orangeburg [vr, also mfm]. Records. 1739–1885.
Protestant Episcopal Church, Edmundburg Chapel, Charleston [v, also mfm]. Records. 1854–56.
Protestant Episcopal Church, Grace, Camden [vr]. Records. 1830–1938.
Protestant Episcopal Church, Holy Cross, Stateburg [3vr, also v mfm]. Records. 1770–1936.
Protestant Episcopal Church, North Santee [v]. Minutes and records. 1853–62.
Protestant Episcopal Church, Prince Frederick's, Plantersville, Georgetown County [vr]. Records. 1846–1935.
Protestant Episcopal Church, Prince Frederick's, Winyah, Charleston County [vr, also mfm]. Records, including Black River. 1729–63.
Protestant Episcopal Church, Prince George's, Winyah, Georgetown County [vr, also mfm]. Records. 1813–1916.
Protestant Episcopal Church, St. Bartholomew's Parish, Colleton County [vr, also mfm]. Records. 1840–54.
Protestant Episcopal Church, St. David's Parish, Cheraw [2vr, also mfm]. Records. 1768–1832.
Protestant Episcopal Church, St. James' Parish, Santee [vr, also mfm]. Records. 1806–86.
Protestant Episcopal Church, St. John's, John's Island [vr]. Records. 1874–1917.
Protestant Episcopal Church, St. John's Parish, Berkeley County [2vr, 3 reels mfm]. Records. 1753–1853.
Protestant Episcopal Church, St. John's Parish, Colleton County [vr, also mfm]. Records. 1738–1874.
Protestant Episcopal Church, St. Luke's Parish, Charleston [2vr]. Records. 1866–1905.
Protestant Episcopal Church, St. Luke's, Newberry [vr, also mfm]. Records. 1846–1923.
Protestant Episcopal Church, St. Luke's, Clarendon [vr, also mfm]. Records. 1840–1936.
Protestant Episcopal Church, St. Matthew's Parish, Calhoun County [vr, also mfm]. Records. 1767–1838.

117

Protestant Episcopal Church, St. Michael's, Charleston [4vr, 2v mfm]. Records. 1759–1930.
Protestant Episcopal Church, St. Paul's, Charleston [v, also mfm]. Records and church history. 1810–79.
Protestant Episcopal Church, St. Peter's [2vr]. Church books. 1874–1930.
Protestant Episcopal Church, St. Philip's, Charleston [18, 9vr, 2 reels mfm]. Church books and assorted papers. 1732–1910.
Protestant Episcopal Church, St. Philip's, Bradford Springs, Charleston County [vr]. Church book. 1846–55.
Protestant Episcopal Church, St. Stephen's, Craven County [vr, also mfm]. Records. 1754–1885.
Protestant Episcopal Church, St. Stephen's and St. John's, Charleston [10vr, 2v mfm]. Records. 1754–1935.
Protestant Episcopal Church, St. Thomas and St. Dennis, Berkeley County [vr, also mfm]. 1693–1794.
Protestant Episcopal Church, Trinity, Columbia [2v mfm]. Records. 1860–1925.
Protestant Episcopal Church, Wambaw Church, St. James, Santee [2vr]. Church books. 1887–1935.
Pugh, Evan (1729–1802) [7vr]. Diary and journals of Baptist minister with material re Cheraw, Chesterfield, Darlington, Charleston, and Georgetown. 1762–1841.
Quill Club, Columbia [4v]. Records. 1922–30.
Quinn, Frederick J. E. [v]. York County arithmetic book with practice pages. 1827.
R & D Railroad Company [v]. Letterbook of company's SC attorney. 1888–89.
Rainey, Samuel L. [v]. York County blacksmith's account book. 1829–31.
Ramsay, David (1749–1815) [15]. Various papers of SC historian. 1782–1815.
Rast Family [72]. Various papers re Texas and Charleston, chiefly CW letters. 1854–94.
Ratchford, Joseph [v]. Chester blacksmith's accounts. 1825–33.
Ravenel, Daniel James (1788–1814) [v]. Charleston legal receipts, plantation data, and various papers. 1788–1868.
Ravenel, Henry W. (1814–87) [98, 13v]. Pooshee, Hampton Hill, Columbia, Aiken, and New York; journals and letters. 1844–87.
Ravenel, John (1793–1862) [57]. Charleston, Morristown, N. J., and nullification controversy; various papers. 1815–61, 1915.
Raymond, Henry Hunter (1822–76) [42]. Family letters concerning life in Charleston and New York. 1822–76.
Read Family [309]. Charleston, Newport, and New York; family correspondence. 1724–1843.
Reardon, G. W. [v]. Account book of Sumter postmaster. c. 1890.
Reconstruction Scrapbook [v]. Indexed SC newspaper clippings. 1865–77.

Reeder, Thomas and William [70]. CW letters to Charleston, Virginia, and data re blockade running. 1861–65.

Reeves, Mrs. Edward Le Roy [vr]. Clippings of SC political life, including data on Cash-Shannon duel. 1876–80.

Reid, John Sharp [v]. Genealogy; Reids of Chesterfield County and Anson County, N. C. 1951.

Reid, William Moultrie (1798–1884) [2,024]. Charleston, Sumter, Columbia, SC preparatory schools and colleges, Presbyterian Church, and CW. 1800–1916.

Renwick, William W. [2,159]. Family papers, Union, Newberry and Laurens Districts. 1791–1886.

Revill, Janie [vr]. SC Byrd/Bird/Burd genealogy (1716–1852). c. 1940.

Reynolds, Dr. Samuel M. [v]. Marion District medical accounts. 1853–59.

Rhett Family [v]. Genealogy. c. 1914.

Rhett, Robert Barnwell (1800–76) [65, v mfm]. Family correspondence re CW and copy of University of Florida dissertation on Rhett (1954). 1832–89, 1954.

Rhodes, Nathaniel [v]. "Observations on General Doctrine of Fevers." 1800.

Rice, B. H. & Company, Columbia [v]. Journal. 1870.

Rice, W. D. [13, v]. SC Baptist accounts of Bible distribution during CW. 1861–64.

Richardson Family [2vr]. Epitaphs of Sumter and Clarendon Counties. 1927, 1936.

Richardson, James S. G. [v]. Notes on law cases. c. 1845.

Richardson, John Smythe (1828–94) [574, 7v]. Sumter District, Washington, CW; family papers. 1809–90. See *University South Caroliniana Society Program* (1962).

Richardson, Richard [32]. Prince Frederick's Parish land papers. 1735–1806, 1880.

Richardson, Thomas E. [44 boxes, 65v]. Miscellaneous papers re law, Sumter Manufacturing Company, and CW. 1701–1929.

Richardson, William G. (1773–1849) [3v]. Sumter ledgers, legal and family papers. 1800–48.

Richardson, William H. B. [90]. Various papers re Charleston and Columbia. 1826–63.

Richland County [v]. Magistrate's Court records. 1847–50.

Richland County [24]. Plats surveyed by M. L. Braswell. 1875–1905.

Richland County [3vr]. WPA transcripts of various court records. 1787–1885.

Richland County [10vr, also mfm]. WPA transcripts of epitaphs: Crescent Hill Baptist Cemetery, Ebenezer Lutheran Cemetery, Elmwood Cemetery, First Baptist Churchyard, First Presbyterian Churchyard, St. Peter's Catholic Cemetery, St. Peter's Churchyard, Taylor Cemetery, Trinity Episcopal Churchyard, Washington Street Methodist Churchyard.

Richland County Memorial Association [v]. Treasurer's records. 1886–94.

Richland County Women's Auxiliary, South Carolina Medical Association [v mfm]. Biographies of Columbia doctors. c. 1950–65.

Richland Democratic Club [v]. Minutes. 1876–80.

Richland Rifle Club, Columbia [2v]. Records. 1874.

Rion, James Henry (1828–86) [3v]. SC College pamphlets. 1846–78.

Rivers-Bultman Outfitting Company, Sumter [v]. Bank records. 1913–15.

Rivers, William James (1822–1909) [c. 265, 5v]. Charleston, Columbia, Chestertown, Md., SC College, and SC history. 1841–1909.

Roach, Mary [17]. Barnwell and Charleston family letters and bonds. 1868–86.

Robert, Henry Martyn (1837–1923) [33]. Various papers and clippings. No date.

Robertson and Clayton Families [1 box]. Various papers. 1851–1918.

Robertville, Beaufort District [vr]. Notes on history of Black Swamp region. c. 1950.

Robinson, John Andrew [301, v]. CW, Reconstruction, Due West Grange, Abbeville Medical Society, and Jefferson Medical College; family papers. 1858–76.

Robson, J. W. & Son [544, v]. Business papers and records. 1854–1936.

Rogers, John [v]. Union District plantation records. 1821–39.

Routh, S. S. [v]. Branchville receipt book. 1837–39.

Royal Society of Arts, London [264 mfm]. Papers re America, especially SC. 1755–1840.

Russell, R. E. [24]. Bills and receipts. 1845–57.

Rutherford Family [vr]. Genealogy. 1959.

Rutledge, Edward (1749–1800) [51]. Charleston, Columbia, Savannah, and Nathanael Greene's estate. 1774–1808.

Rutledge Family [84]. Charleston, Orangeburg, Richmond, Va., nullification, and CW; family papers. 1796–1862.

Rutledge, John (1739–1800) [30]. Georgetown, Columbia, Charleston, and RW. 1776–93.

St. David's Academy, Society Hill [vr]. Records. 1822–24.

St. Paul's Parish, Stono [v]. Minutes of the Board of Road Commissioners. 1783–1839.

Salley, Alexander Samuel, Jr. (1871–1961) [c. 20,000]. Chiefly correspondence as secretary of the SC Historical Society and secretary and state historian of the SC Historical Commission. 1885–1961.

Sams Family [c. 130, 35v]. Genealogical notes and papers re Beaufort, Columbia, Barnwell, Allendale, Gaffney, Edgefield, and Reconstruction. 1700–1934.

Sams, Stanhope [2v]. Newspaper clippings. 1931–33.

Sanders, Louis [v]. Sandersville sales account book. 1872–74.

Sanders, Thomas W. [v]. Stateburg daybook. 1838.
Sanders, William [36]. Camden business papers. 1849–74.
Sanders, William (d. 1875) [35]. Sumter area accounts. 1828–78.
Sargent, Samuel S. [v]. Turner family of Kentucky. 1946.
Sartor, D. R. [vr]. Medical lecture notes and plantation data. 1841–42.
Sartor, Samuel S. (b. 1843) [vr]. CW reminiscences. 1928.
Sass, George Herbert (1845–1908) [59]. Data re life in the South and his literary efforts. 1859–1907, 1933.
Saunders Family [vr]. Saunders/Sanders genealogical and legal notes, Charleston. 1939.
Savage, Joe [2v]. Account book and daybook. 1897–1902.
Sawyer, Frederick Adolphus (b. 1822) [25]. Routine letters, biographical sketch, and material re Washington, Columbia, and Charleston. 1848, 1868–73.
Saye Family [31]. Material re agricultural life, religion, Union, Chester, Tennessee, and Georgia. 1835–46.
Scarborough, William Harrison (1812–71) [2vr]. Diary of Italian tour and daily business accounts. 1857–70.
Schirmer Brothers, Charleston [12v]. Accounts and journals. 1855–1929.
Schulz, John [3v]. Daybook and cotton records. 1811–24.
Schweizerische Landesbibliothek [15vr, also mfm]. Documents re Swiss emigration to SC. 1711–54.
Seabrook Family [3 boxes]. Papers re Charleston, Cokesbury, and Pendleton; chiefly CW letters from various army camps. 1838–1914.
Seabrook, Isaac DuBose [v]. "Race Relations in South Carolina." 1895.
Seabrook, William [v]. Freight account book. 1857.
Seaver, J. Montgomery [v]. Keith family genealogy. 1930.
Seibels, Edwin Grenville (1866–1954) [vr]. Paper re trip to Russia in 1911. 1933.
Seibels Family [253, 3v]. Chiefly correspondence of John Temple Seibels (d. 1853) with his family and friends in Columbia, Greenville, Spartanburg, Charleston, and Orangeburg. 1780–1945.
Seventh South Carolina Battalion, Company A [vr]. CW roll prepared by B. S. Lucas. 1861–65.
Shaffer, Edward Terry Hendri (b. 1880) [4v mfm]. Material re CW and Walterboro area. c. 1935.
Shand, Louly (1870–1961) [2v]. Columbia scrapbooks. 1874–1950.
Shand, Mary Wright (1876–1953) [v]. Columbia scrapbook. 1894–1902.
Shanklin Papers [200]. Chiefly letters of J. S. Shanklin re Beaufort County Training School; various school records. 1899–1957.
Shannon, William McWillie (1822–80) [v]. Guardian records. 1840–62.
Sharpe, E. and Company [2v]. SC railroad books. 1860–64.
Shaw, A. E. [2v]. Doctor's accounts. 1844–46, 1870.

Shaw, John M. [21r]. Camden receipts. 1828–82.

Sheppard Brothers (J. C. and Orlando), Edgefield [183 boxes]. Business papers. 1875–1935.

Sheppard Family [22]. Charleston and CW. 1860–78, 1922.

Sheppard, J. C. and Orlando [16 boxes]. Business, legal, political, and family papers, Edgefield. 1850–1935.

Sherfessee, Louis (1842–1904) [13 mfm]. CW material. 1894–1924.

Sigourney Society, Female High School, Limestone Springs [vr]. Records. 1848–52.

Simms, William Gilmore (1806–70) [c. 1,000]. Correspondence and various papers re literary career. 1830–1963.

Simons Family [61, vr]. Charleston, Columbia, Stateburg, and New York; correspondence of James Simons's descendants. 1798–1874.

Simons, Katherine Drayton Mayrant (b. 1892) [3v]. Scrapbooks on three of her novels. 1948–50.

Simons, Mrs. H. H. [v]. Account of the burning of Columbia. 1865.

Simons, James [1 box]. Papers of Charleston lawyer. 1819–90.

Simons, Jane Kealhofer (Mrs. Arthur St. Julian) [v]. Columbia Art Association programs, Hampton-Preston Home clippings. 1940–44.

Simons, Keating (1753–1834) [32]. Charleston papers re his estate. 1758–1855.

Simons-Lucas Families [vr]. Genealogy, descendants of Benjamin Simons of Charleston. 1770–1902.

Simons, Thomas Young (1828–78) [17, v]. Papers re Charleston, Caesar's Head, and fire insurance. 1853–76.

Simonton, Charles Henry (1829–1904) [v]. Clippings re his judicial decisions. 1887–93.

Simonton Family [v, 2vr]. Genealogy, scrapbook, clippings. 1860–73.

Simpson Family [2v mfm]. Genealogy. No date.

Simpson, J. Wistar [v]. Catalogue of Euphradian Society, SC College, with personal notes. 1842.

Simpson, John (d. 1808) [37]. Chester and Camden; bills, receipts, various papers. 1774–94.

Simpson, John W. [v]. Blacksmith and mill work accounts. 1844–51.

Simpson, William Dunlap (1823–90) [3,147]. Laurens and Columbia; legal and family papers, some CW material. 1816–94.

Sims, James Marion (1813–83) [23]. Various papers. 1828–1947.

Singletary, Robert L. [17]. Mars Bluff and SC railroads. 1873–75.

Singleton-Deveaux Families [137]. Various papers. Library has calendar. 1784–1931.

Singleton Family [19]. Sumter District letters re business, horse racing, slaves, and land; several items from European correspondents including Angelica Van Buren and Mary Singleton McDuffie. 1812–56.

Singleton, Matthew (1730–87) [19]. RW papers, Sumter District. 1778–79.

Singleton, Richard (1776–1852) [37]. Columbia, New York, Liverpool, University of Virginia; various family matters. 1821–52, 1931.

Sixth Regiment, South Carolina Volunteer Cavalry [v]. Order book of Company F. 1863–64.
Sloan, Benjamin [23]. Letters re retirement as USC president. 1908.
Smith, Annie Brunson [v]. Charleston diary and scrapbook. 1874–95.
Smith, Daniel H. [20]. Charleston and Kingstree business papers. 1848–69.
Smith, E. P. [c. 1,800]. Spartanburg District, papers of postmaster at Smith's Store. 1807–1907.
Smith, Elihu P. [27]. South Carolina Manufacturing Company receipts. 1834–48.
Smith, Family [57, v, 6vr]. Various papers and notes from which *Mason Smith Family Letters, 1860–68* was published. c. 1860–68.
Smith, Lafayette [v]. Sumter County store account. 1892–1915.
Smith, Lancelot [v mfm]. Strawberry Ferry ledger. 1777–79.
Smith, Mendel Lafayette (1870–1934) [108 boxes, 2v]. Columbia legal accounts and diary (1911), various papers re Kershaw County, USC, University of Virginia, World War I, sports, fraternal and religious organizations, addresses and legal-political correspondence. 1888–1934.
Smith, M. W. [v]. Account book. 1878–1908.
Smith, Norman Murray (b. 1883) [17]. Various documents. 1900–52.
Smith, Samuel Porcher (1841–1915) [vr]. Genealogy. 1915.
Smith-Screven Families [v]. Genealogy. c. 1961.
Smith, W. H. [v]. CW experiences. 1862–63.
Smith, William Loughton (1758–1812) [vr, 78 mfm]. Copies of correspondence, some as European diplomat. 1792–1802.
Smyth-Flinn Families [2 boxes]. Various papers. 1838–95.
Smyth, Thomas [v]. Manual for Second Presbyterian Church, Charleston, with notes. 1838.
Smythe, Augustine Thomas (1842–1914) [3vr]. Charleston correspondence, CW reminiscences. 1860–1914.
Smythe, Louisa McCord (1845–1928) [vr]. Recollections of Pendleton, Columbia, Charleston, Fort Motte, SC College, and Reconstruction. c. 1928.
Smythe, Thomas (1808–73) [vr]. Reminiscences of interview with P. T. Beauregard. No date.
Snowden and Salley, Charleston [3v]. Book store records. 1902.
Snowden, Mary Amarinthia (1819–98) [631, v]. Chiefly re her Confederate activities, Charleston and Columbia. 1846–1958.
Snowden, Yates (1858–1933) [c. 46 boxes]. Various papers, scrapbooks, and correspondence. Library has index. 1904–32.
Social Survey Club, Columbia [3v]. Minutes, programs and papers. 1919–41.
Society Hill Pomological Club [vr]. Records. 1868–72.
Society for Orphan and Destitute Children, Columbia [2v]. Records. 1839–1937.
Solomon, Kate Cecile [2v]. Miscellaneous scrapbooks. 1863–66.

Sondley, D. R. [v]. Abbeville letterbook, chiefly letters to Charleston cotton merchant. 1870–72.

Sons of the American Revolution, Mississippi Society of [vr]. Directory. 1909–49.

Sons of Confederate Veterans, Camp Henry Buist, Charleston [v]. Members' records. c. 1900.

Sons of Temperance, Bennettsville [vr]. Records. 1866–81.

Sons of Temperance, Marion [v]. Records. 1849–54.

Sosnowski-Shaller Families [3 boxes, 6v]. Genealogy, letters, clippings. 1828–1932.

South Carolina Academies and Private Schools [13]. Various papers. 1855–1941.

South Carolina Agricultural Society, Charleston County [3v]. Records. 1825–1935.

South Carolina Association of Women Deans and Counselors [1 box]. Records. 1931–62.

South Carolina Bookplates [3v]. Collection. 1744–1940.

South Carolina College Cadets [17]. Various papers, including some CW data. No date.

South Carolina College Conference [v]. Reports. 1945.

South Carolina Conscript Department, Columbia [v]. Headquarters order book. 1863–65.

South Carolina Convention [v]. Minutes. 1862–63.

South Carolina Council of Social Studies [314]. Records. 1948–58.

South Carolina County and District Boundaries [v]. Laws relative to. 1785–1902.

South Carolina Department of Education [v]. Report of R. L. Bryan Company, managers of Central Textbook Depository. 1911–17.

South Carolina Entomological Society [v]. Minutes. 1962–63.

South Carolina Experiment Station [v]. Records. 1888–90.

South Carolina Federation of Business and Professional Woman's Clubs [54v]. Records. 1925–62.

South Carolina Federation of Temple Sisterhoods [9v]. Various papers and records. 1931–54.

South Carolina Federation of Women's Club [2v]. Historical essays. 1929–33.

South Carolina Female Collegiate Institute, Barhamville and Columbia [111]. Chiefly student letters to families and friends. 1828–1929.

South Carolina [25, v]. Ship's log and data re ship's bell. 1781–82, 1945.

South Carolina General Assembly [74]. Various papers. 1802–91.

South Carolina Governor's Office [2v]. Statutes re county appointments. 1926–39.

South Carolina High School Newspapers [v]. Collection. 1936–39.

South Carolina Historical Association [114]. Various papers. 1948–51.

South Carolina Historical Commission [vr]. Marker inscriptions. 1937–42.

South Carolina Hospital Bureau, Charlottesville and Richmond, Va. [3v]. Records. 1861–62.

South Carolina Industrial School for Boys, Florence [v]. Records. 1950–51.

South Carolina Industrial School for White Girls, Columbia [v]. Records. 1950–51.

South Carolina Inter-Collegiate Oratorial Association [52]. Various papers. 1937–39.

South Carolina Interstate and West Indian Exposition [2v]. Records of Georgetown Commissioners. 1901–2.

South Carolina League of Women Voters [29, v, 2 boxes]. Records. 1913–30.

South Carolina Militia, Fort Marion [21 mfm]. Reports and records. 1814–15.

South Carolina Militia, Fourth Brigade [240]. Charleston records. 1734–1879.

South Carolina Militia, Second Regiment [113, v, also mfm]. Paymaster and other War of 1812 records. 1814–15.

South Carolina Militia, Thirteenth Regiment [55]. Colleton District papers. 1830–37.

South Carolina Monuments and Markers [v]. Compilation. 1955–62.

South Carolina Penitentiary [c. 34,000]. Records and various papers. 1867–1921.

South Carolina Penitentiary [58 boxes, c. 93v]. Records. 1867–98.

South Carolina Revolutionary War Pensioners [4vr]. Summary of National Archives records. 1947–56.

South Carolina Revolutionary War Records [1 reel mfm]. Selected materials from the Draper Collection. 1777–81.

South Carolina Rural Electrification Association [v]. Reports of A. R. Wellwood and others. 1933.

South Carolina Society, Charleston [3v]. Minutes. 1865–88.

South Carolina State Agricultural Society, Columbia [vr]. Records. 1855–60.

South Carolina State Agricultural & Mechanical College, Orangeburg [5v]. Annual reports. 1948–51.

South Carolina State Alliance [v]. "Rejection" book. 1890.

South Carolina State Board of Health [v]. Directory of SC camps. 1949.

South Carolina State Council for Defense [11v]. Civilian defense papers. 1940–44.

South Carolina State Dispensary [25]. Various papers. 1889–1937.

South Carolina State Dispensary, Kershaw County [3v]. Records. 1904.

South Carolina State Government [7vr]. Report by Griffenhagan & Associates. 1920.

South Carolina State Highway Department [89]. Papers re Rural Electrification program. 1933–36, 1958.
South Carolina State Hospital [v mfm]. Scrapbook. 1957.
South Carolina State Planning Board [13v]. Industrial and economic survey of these counties: Beaufort, Chester, Darlington, Greenville, Greenwood, Horry, Lexington, Marlboro, Newberry, Oconee, Richland, Spartanburg, and York. 1943.
South Carolina State and Provincial Currency and Scrip [172]. Various issues. 1723–1886.
South Carolina Tax Returns [c. 120v]. c. 1865–80.
South Carolina Treasury Department [v]. Accounts. 1802.
South Carolina Volunteers, Eighth Regiment [v]. Accounts. 1861, 1873–74.
South Carolina Volunteers, Fifteenth Regiment [v]. Record book. 1860–65.
South Carolina Volunteers, First Artillery, Company E [v]. Records. 1862.
South Carolina Volunteers, Fourteenth Regiment, Company D [vr]. Records. 1861–65.
South Carolina Volunteers, Fourth Regiment [v]. Records. 1861–62.
South Carolina Volunteers, Holcombe's Legion, Company C [vr]. Records. 1861–65.
South Carolina Volunteers, Orr's Regiment [v mfm]. Records. 1861–86.
South Carolina Volunteers, Palmetto Regiment [v]. Accounts. 1846–48.
South Carolina Volunteers, Second Regiment Artillery, Company E [2v]. Records. 1862–64.
South Carolina Volunteers, Third Regiment, Rebel Troop [v]. Order book. 1862–64.
Spain (A. C.) and Richardson (J. S. G.), Attorneys, Sumter [5 boxes]. Business and legal papers. 1803–1912.
Sparkman, W. E. (d. 1946) [vr]. Georgetown plantation accounts. 1844–88.
Spartanburg Account Book [v]. Anonymous. 1816.
Spartanburg Account Book [v mfm]. Copy of original in Alabama Archives. 1837–38.
Spartanburg County [vr]. Description of Glenn Springs. 1847.
Spartanburg County [51vr]. WPA transcripts of various court records. 1785–1887.
Spartanburg County [2vr, also mfm]. WPA transcripts of epitaphs: Oakwood Cemetery, Magnolia Cemetery [Spartanburg].
Spencer, Elisha S. [9v]. Lynchburg and Willow Grove daybooks. 1850–55.
Spigener, J. Sims [v]. Gadsden farm record. 1905.
Spratt Family [2vr]. York County history and genealogy. 1875, 1908.

Spratt, Thomas D. [vr]. "Recollections of the Spratt Family." 1730–1875.

Stafford, Benjamin Spicer (1853–1943) [1 reel mfm]. Memoirs re Robertville, Missouri, Texas, Arkansas, and Oklahoma. c. 1931.

Stapleton, John [113]. St. Helena Island plantations, Bull family. 1790–1839.

Stateburg Literary and Musical Society [v]. Historical sketch. 1885–1949.

Steamer *Anson* [vr]. Record of Darlington County shipments. 1840–42.

Steinmeyer, John Henry [vr]. CW diary re Marion Rifles, Charleston, and Tennessee. 1860–65.

Stevens, Edward L. [13, v]. Notes on Potter's Raid by a US Army officer. 1865.

Stevens, Neil T. [v]. Notes on Henry W. Ravenel. 1920–26.

Stewart, Charles (d. 1818) [26]. Various papers by his heirs. 1832–1946.

Stewart, Clark B. (d. 1885) [12vr]. Various papers re Laurens, Columbia, CW, Presbyterian ministry. 1836–85.

Stoeber, Edward M. (b. 1838) [37]. Material re Negro troops in CW and Sea Islands during Reconstruction. 1864–69.

Stokes, William (b. 1833) [498, v]. Various papers, chiefly letters (1855–68). 1792–1885.

Stoll Family [vr]. Charleston genealogy. 1931.

Stout, John (1842–94) [490]. Family correspondence and letters from leaders in Southern Baptist Convention. 1861–1912.

Stratton, John Paul (1857–1936) [8 boxes, 2v]. Scrapbooks, clippings on agriculture, history, and biography. 1886–1913.

Strawberry Agricultural Society, Strawberry, St. John's, Berkeley [31 mfm]. Records. 1847–59.

Stroman, Jacob [22]. Various papers re Columbia area and CW. 1842–64.

Stubbs, Thomas M. [vr]. Early Sumter newspapers and their editors. 1947.

Stuckey, A. B. [v]. Sumter legal letterbook. 1898–1906.

Summer, Henry [v]. Diary of trip from Newberry to St. Augustine. 1837.

Sumter County [50vr]. WPA transcripts of various court records. 1774–1876.

Sumter County [8vr, also mfm]. WPA transcripts of epitaphs: Andrews Chapel Methodist Churchyard, Bethel Baptist Churchyard, Bethel Cemetery, Bradford Springs Cemetery, Fulton Cemetery, Hodge Burial Ground, Jewish Cemetery, Providence Baptist Churchyard, Reynolds Burying Ground, St. Lawrence Catholic Church Cemetery, St. Mark's Episcopal Church Cemetery, Skinner Cemetery, Sumter Cemetery, Weeks Cemetery.

Sumter County, Appeals to South Carolina Supreme Court [2v]. 1871–74.

Sumter County, Auditor's Book [v]. c. 1880.

Libraries, Archives,

Sumter County, Commissioner of [2v]. Letterbooks. 1879–81, 1892.
Sumter County, Pension Board [v]. Minutes. 1901.
Sumter District, Court of General Sessions [2v]. Records. 1827–57.
Sumter Manufacturing Company [v]. Information re stock. 1895.
Sumter Music House [4v]. Ledgers. 1891–1911.
Sumter Post Office [v]. Accounts. 1890–94.
Sumter Riflemen [v]. Minutes. 1849–58.
Sumter Telephone Company [2v]. Accounts. 1901–2.
Sumter, Thomas (1734–1832) [78, vr]. Various business and personal papers. 1764–1853, 1931, 1951.
Sumter, Mrs. Thomas, Jr. (Natalie DeLage) [2 boxes]. Diary and letters, chiefly in French. 1793–1842.
Sumterville Library Society [2v]. Records. 1809–10, 1845.
Surles, Flora B. [2vr]. Report of records copied by WPA for USC Library. 1935–38.
Swaffield, W. C. [2,685, 33v]. Columbia insurance agency records. 1869–1911.
Swearingen, John Eldred (1875–1957) [1,709, v mfm]. Various papers re Edgefield and Columbia. 1772–1963. See *University South Caroliniana Society Program* (1961).
Talbert, John F. (d. 1898) [8, 6v]. Edgefield and CW. 1838–98.
Taylor, Alexander Ross (1812–88) [v]. Columbia scrapbook, RW and Taylor family. 1877.
Taylor Family [61]. Notes on Colonel Thomas Taylor (b. 1826), genealogy, and recipes. 1825–1906.
Taylor, James [vr]. Land papers. 1795–1805.
Taylor, John (1842–1912) [79, v]. CW papers; Columbia, Johnson's Island, and Granby plantation. 1863–79.
Taylor, Sally Elmore (b. 1829) [vr]. Memoirs. 1909–10.
Taylor, Wyatt A. [v]. Council-manager government in Columbia. 1951.
Templeton, William A. (1836–1903) [25, v]. Various papers re York, Sullivan's Island, Arkansas, Texas, and CW. 1847–80.
Templeton, William Cater [3v]. Mercantile records, Tylersville, Laurens County. 1872–1916.
Thacher, Davis [v]. Account of trip from Massachusetts to Charleston. 1816–18.
Thee, J. Herman (1893–1949) [vr]. Suggestions for permanent registration in SC. c. 1949.
Third Regiment, South Carolina State Troops, War of 1812 [vr]. Roll book. 1812.
Thomas, A. S. [13v]. Furniture company records. 1893–1906.
Thomas, Charles E. [v]. Journal of transcontinental trip by General Wade Hampton and party, clippings and accounts. 1893.
Thomas Family [1,462, 45v]. Early 18th century letters of Samuel Thomas reporting to England on work for the Society for Propagation of the Gospel in Foreign Parts; diaries, account books, records of plantation life in Fairfield District, CW, sermons and family correspondence re Greenville, Edisto Island, St. John's,

Berkeley, and Ridgeway. Letters re CW, travel in both Europe and US, St. Mary's, Winthrop and Converse Colleges, and politics. 1702–1955. See *University South Caroliniana Society Program* (1956, 1965).

Thomas, John Alexander William (1822–96) [v]. *History of Marlboro County*, with notes. 1897.

Thomas, John Peyre (1796–1859) [v mfm]. Diary. 1827–56.

Thomas P. Salmond [70]. Records of Charleston to Florida steamer. 1837–45.

Thomas, Robert Gibbes [4v]. Original and typed copy of "William Moultrie, Arms and the Man. . . ." 1932.

Thomas, Stephen [vr]. Family records. 1736–1915.

Thompson, Hugh Smith (1836–1904) [1 box, vr]. Various papers re Columbia, Greenville, SC education, politics, and personal affairs. 1856–1923, 1937.

Thompson, O. G. [2v]. Laurens ledgers. 1833–37.

Thompson, Waddy (1798–1868) [26]. Augusta, Mexican War, Tennessee, Alabama, plantation and political life. 1817–48.

Thomson Family [2vr]. Chiefly data on William Thomson and the Battle of Fort Moultrie. 1807–1909.

Thomson, Marian [vr]. Genealogy, Midway plantation. c. 1900.

Thornwell, James Henley (1812–62) [572, 8v]. Various papers re work as SC College president, editor, and Presbyterian minister. 1828–81, 1904. See *University South Caroliniana Society Program* (1960, 1964).

Thurmond, James Strom (b. 1902) [c. 250, 163 boxes]. Uncatalogued material; chiefly correspondence, speeches, clippings and other data re term as governor and presidential campaign of 1948. 1947–62.

Tidwell, John Pressley [v]. Notebook. 1807.

Tilghman, Bell Woods [c. 200]. Notes re U. S. Grant's attitude towards the South during Reconstruction. No date.

Tillman, Benjamin Ryan (1847–1918) [3vr]. Biographical sketch and clippings. 1865–1940.

Timmerman, George Bell (b. 1912) [vr]. Various addresses. 1955–56.

Timrod, Henry (1828–67) [90, v mfm]. Charleston, Bluffton, and his literary career. 1851–1937.

Tindal, J. W. [25]. CW letters. 1864.

Tindal, John [87]. Sumter business papers. 1828–64.

Tomb, James H. [vr]. CW memoirs, Charleston, submarines. 1861–64.

Tompkins Family [vr]. Genealogy. c. 1940.

Toombs, Robert [vr]. CW letterbook. 1861.

Town Theatre, Columbia [4v]. Records, scrapbooks, and programs. 1917–54.

Townes Family [520, 6vr]. Abbeville, Greenville, Pendleton, and Columbia; various papers and family correspondence. 1829–54.

Townsend Family [vr]. Charleston, extracts of genealogical records. 1922.

Townshend, D. H. [v]. Notebook on Joseph Le Conte's lectures. 1860.

Trenholm Family [67]. Charleston, genealogy of Trenholm and Mc-Beth families. 1829–1916.

Trenholm, George Alfred (1806–76) [77, vr]. CW, Richmond, Va., Columbia, and Lee's retreat. 1864–1923.

Trescott, William Henry [11 boxes, v]. Various papers. 1761–1937.

Trezevant, Daniel Heyward (1796–1873) [3vr]. Accounts of Columbia estates, CW. 1796–1873.

Trezevant Family [36]. Columbia and Charleston, legal and business papers. 1831–88.

Trezevant, James Davis [4v]. Orangeburg plantation accounts, Hampton campaign (1876). 1845–78.

Troy, James F. [c. 35, 9v]. Scrapbooks and various accounts. 1839–1900.

Trumble, James [2v]. Receipts and cotton records. 1854, 1881–85.

Tucker, Cornelia Dabney [v mfm]. Charleston scrapbook, Republican Party politics, crusade for secret ballot, and teaching of government in SC schools. 1928–62.

Tucker, Starling [vr]. Officers and men under his command. 1811.

Turner Family [v]. Bible records. 1815–1958.

Turquand-McCord Families [vr]. Genealogy. 1583–1829.

Twiss, Thomas S. (b. 1804) [67]. SC College data. 1835–46.

Union Bible Society, Beaufort [23]. Records. 1853–62.

Union Bible Society, Richland and Fairfield Counties [v]. Minutes. 1871–1934.

Union Bible Society, Union County [v]. List of members. 1857.

Union County [46vr]. WPA transcripts of various court records. 1777–1939.

Union County [vr, also mfm]. WPA transcripts of epitaphs: Episcopal Cemetery, Forest Lawn Cemetery, Grace Methodist Cemetery, Presbyterian Cemetery, Rosemont Cemetery [Union], Garner Cemetery, Gallman Cemetery, Foster Methodist Chapel [near Kelton], Mt. Joy Baptist Church Cemetery, Rehoboth Baptist Church Cemetery, Sardis Methodist Church Cemetery, Gillas Baptist Church Cemetery, Mt. Tabor Presbyterian Church Cemetery, Site of Pinckneyville Courthouse, Wesley Chapel Cemetery, Phillipi Baptist Church Cemetery, Boganville Methodist Church Cemetery, Putnam Baptist Church Cemetery, Upper Fairforest Cemetery [also called "Duck Pond"], City Cemetery, Hawkins Cemetery, New Hope Methodist Church Cemetery, Fairforest Presbyterian Church Cemetery, Padgett Corner Baptist Church Cemetery, Enoree Church Cemetery, West Springs Baptist Church Cemetery.

United Confederate Veterans, Darlington [v]. Ladies book. 1922.

United Confederate Veterans [v]. Minutes of fortieth reunion. 1931.

United Confederate Veterans [v]. Military service records of Camp Hampton, Richland County. 1861–65.

United Confederate Veterans [v]. Records of Abner Perrin Camp, Edgefield. 1893–99.

United Confederate Veterans [v]. SC Division, Charleston; records. 1895–1902.

United Confederate Veterans [2v]. Survivors' Association, minutes and records. 1887–1923.

United Daughters of the Confederacy, Marion [2v]. Records. 1896–1919.

United Daughters of the Confederacy, Secessionville Chapter, James Island [3v]. Records. 1906–27.

United Sons of Confederate Veterans [3v]. Greenville and Columbia records. 1896–97.

United States Army, Department of the South [206]. Miscellaneous records re Beaufort, Folly Island, and Hilton Head. 1862–65.

United States Army, First Brigade, First Division [v]. Virginia and Folly Island order book. 1862–63.

United States Army, Quartermaster's Department [v]. Summary of persons employed at Hilton Head. 1862.

United States Atomic Energy Commission, Savannah River [vr]. Record of relocation of graves in area. 1964.

United States Daughters of 1812, South Carolina Society, Andrew Jackson Chapter [4vr]. Lineage records. 1812–15.

United States Interior Department [vr]. Appraisal of Clark Hill Reservoir. 1948.

United States Navy [v mfm]. South Caroliniana Library letters selected for RW Naval Papers Collection. 1957.

United States Pensioners [v]. Receipts of pensions paid at Charleston. 1824–28.

United States Post Office, Columbia [25]. Various papers concerning operations. 1865–85.

United States Treasury, War Finance Committee [8v]. SC loan drives. 1944.

University of South Carolina [3,166, 53v, 2vr, 7 boxes]. Various papers and documents, chiefly papers of the Dean of the University and the Dean of Women (1932–44). 1804–1960.

University of South Carolina, Alpha Delta Pi Sorority [v]. Scrapbook. 1927–34.

University of South Carolina, Alumni [7vr]. Records collected by Professor Charles Moore for his *Roll of South Carolina College Students*. 1905.

University of South Carolina, Alumni Association [5v]. Records. 1887–91, 1920–54.

University of South Carolina, Bain Humanities Society [53]. Records. 1941–53.

University of South Carolina, Barefoot Day [198r]. Investigation of disturbances. 1938.

University of South Carolina, Blue Key Fraternity [v]. Minutes. 1927–44.
University of South Carolina, Citations of Honorary Degrees [16]. 1957–60.
University of South Carolina, Civic Club [v]. Constitution and minutes. 1911–16.
University of South Carolina, Clariosophic Society [129v]. Records. 1806–1959.
University of South Carolina, Deans of Faculty and of Women [c. 100]. Various papers. 1934–45.
University of South Carolina, Euphradian Society [67v]. Various records and debates. 1806–1960.
University of South Carolina, Examinations [v]. Various copies. 1855–77.
University of South Carolina, Executive Committee [v]. Minutes. 1846–67.
University of South Carolina, Experimental Station [v]. Library holdings. c. 1890.
University of South Carolina, Extension Division [vr]. Radio series, "Know South Carolina." 1939–40.
University of South Carolina, Faculty [22v]. Minutes and records. 1805–1904.
University of South Carolina, _Garnet and Black_ [v]. Correspondence. 1933–34.
University of South Carolina, Graduate History Club [6v]. Records. 1930–55, 1957–63.
University of South Carolina, History Department [848]. Various papers. 1923–51.
University of South Carolina, Honor Council [v]. Register and pledge. 1938–40.
University of South Carolina, Hypatian Literary Society [3v]. Records. 1917–58.
University of South Carolina, Irving Cricket Club [v]. Constitution and scrapbook. 1860–67.
University of South Carolina, Library [85v]. Various papers and Records. 1800–1946.
University of South Carolina, News Service [4v mfm]. Scrapbooks. 1947–63.
University of South Carolina, Phi Beta Kappa [29]. Records. 1936–43.
University of South Carolina, Polumethian Club [v]. Roll book. 1935–36.
University of South Carolina, President's Advisory Committee [125]. Chiefly correspondence with faculty. 1936–40.
University of South Carolina, Register of Students [23v]. 1805–1956.
University of South Carolina, Registrar [vr]. Record of enrollment. 1833–52.

University of South Carolina, Roosevelt-Garner Club [v]. Roll book. 1932.
University of South Carolina, Schedule Committee [75]. Interdepartmental correspondence. 1925–42.
University of South Carolina, School of Education [vr]. Report of study on 12-year school program. 1944.
University of South Carolina, Shakespeare Pageants [29]. Various papers. 1916.
University of South Carolina, South Caroliniana Library [12, 50v]. Various papers and records. 1936–63.
University of South Carolina, Steward's Hall [16v]. Records. 1883–1903.
University of South Carolina, Treasurer's Records [148v]. Various papers and accounts. 1835–1903.
University of South Carolina, Trustees [14v mfm]. Minutes. 1801–1925.
University of South Carolina, Wardlaw Club [v]. Constitution and minutes. 1928–38.
University of South Carolina, YMCA [v, vr]. Correspondence and and annual report (1941–42). 1941–56.
University South Caroliniana Society [127, 1 box]. Charter and various papers. 1927–61.
Van Buren, Angelica Singleton (1816–77) [2v]. European journals. 1854–55.
Van Wyck Family [vr]. Genealogy. c. 1890.
Vance, Allan [16]. Business papers and correspondence re Spring Grove, Laurens, Charleston, and Washington College, Va. 1841–60.
Vanderford, Alonzo Adams (d. 1864) [118, v]. Cheraw and Chesterfield, chiefly family letters and CW correspondence. 1853–76.
Vedder, Charles S. [18v]. Charleston sermons, scrapbook, accounts, and diary. 1848–1912.
Venable, Charles Scott (1827–1900) [v]. Diary and memorandum book re CW and SC College. 1858–62.
Verner, James Spencer (1817–1933) [1 box]. Various papers. 1884–1933.
Verner, John, Jr. [v]. Records of Pendleton District magistrate. 1798–1827.
Verner, Samuel Phillips [3 boxes]. Various papers re African expeditions and writings. 1890–1906.
Vernon, Ida [v]. Mineral notes taken at Laurensville Female College. 1863.
Verstille, Tristram [67]. Robertville, Savannah, and New York; business and family correspondence. Library has calendar. 1811–60.
Vigilant Fire Engine Company, Charleston [v]. Records. 1855–61.
WIS Radio Station, Columbia [vr]. "Palmetto Landmarks" programs. 1947–49.
W———, M. W. [6v]. Charleston sermons. 1849–57.

Waccamaw Mercantile Company [3v]. Letterbooks. c. 1902.
Wade, E. W. [v]. Lumber account book. 1860–65.
Wade, John Rives [v]. Greek textbook with notes, USC. 1885.
Waites, Thomas [v]. Georgetown legal notes. 1784–88.
Waites, Thomas [45]. Business receipts. c. 1810.
Walker, George Edward (1826–63) [c. 200 mfm]. Chiefly architectural data re Columbia and Charleston. 1843–1910.
Walker, William Alexander (1819–82) [v]. Chester legal accounts. 1858–79.
Waller, Creswell A. C. [74]. Abbeville, Virginia, CW, and Reconstruction; various family papers. 1822–1918.
Ward, James A. [v]. Philadelphia notebook of medical lectures. 1807.
Wardlaw, George [v]. Translation of "Cicero's Oration for Marcellus." 1927.
Wardlaw, Patterson (1858–1948) [4 boxes, 7v]. Addresses, notes on Greek lectures, University of Virginia. 1881.
Wardlaw, Robert Henry (b. 1807) [vr, v mfm]. Recollection of Abbeville and Long Cane Presbyterian Church (1885–86) and mfm copy of family records. 1847–1915.
Waring, Joseph Ioor (b. 1897) [v mfm]. "History of South Carolina Medicine." 1963.
Waring, Joseph Ioor [v]. Account book and plantation records. 1852–65.
Waring, Thomas S. [60]. CW, John's Island, Richmond, Va., New York, and emigration to South America. 1849–94.
Washington Artillery [2v]. Charleston records. 1862.
Washington Light Artillery [26vr]. Charleston records. 1807–1936.
Washington National Monument Association [v]. Contributions from SC Third Congressional District. 1850.
Waterman, Thomas T. [v]. Survey of proposed Santee-Pinopolis reservoir area. 1939.
Watts, J. L. [16, 2v]. Miscellaneous accounts. c. 1861.
Watts, Beaufort Taylor [283]. SC and national politics, Colombia, and Russia. 1822–79.
Wauchope, George A. (1862–1943) [111]. Lecture notes, student reports, and clippings. 1904–40.
Waverly Supply Company, Waverly Mills [v]. Letterbook. 1903–4.
Wayside Hospital, Charleston [v]. Order and letterbook. 1862–63.
Wayside Hospital, Columbia [v]. Daybook. 1862–65.
Weatherly, T. J. [v]. Doctor's CW diary (Virginia). 1864–65.
Weathers, John T. [v]. Transcribed grammar. 1821.
Webb, Robert D. [v]. Chemistry notes, University of Virginia. 1847–50.
Wednesday Club, Laurens [v]. Yearbook. 1942–43.
Wednesday Club, Sumter [v]. Minutes. 1886–88.
Wells, James L. (d. 1881). CW diary of Northern prison life. 1861–65.
Westwood Plantation [vr]. Overseer's accounts. 1822–1917.

Whaley, E. C. [v]. Miscellaneous clippings. 1850.
Whaley, E. Mikell [109, 3v]. Edisto Island land accounts and legal papers. 1763–1887.
Whaling, Thornton (1858–1938) [v]. Miscellaneous records of a Lexington, Va., minister. 1902–25.
Whetstone Family [2 boxes]. Lexington and Orangeburg Districts, chiefly correspondence of Nathan C. and William C. Whetstone as students at Cokesbury School and medical school, as teacher and doctor. 1843–84.
Whitaker Family [38, v]. Family and business papers. 1819–87.
White, A. B. [v]. SC College lecture notes. 1857.
White Family [v]. Lexington County German Bible with birth-death records. 1826–34.
White & Haynesworth [vr]. Memorandum book. 1864.
White, Joseph [vr]. Fort Mill genealogy. c. 1951.
White, Mrs. Mary Virginia Saunders [vr]. Biographical sketch of General Richard Heron Anderson (1821–79). 1942.
White Mercantile Company, Abbeville [c. 260v]. Business accounts. 1865–1911.
White, William Cozby [19, 6v]. Chiefly Citadel material, including diary of his first college year. 1898–1902.
Whitman, H. A. [v]. Scrapbook re removal of Dr. W. J. Alexander from SC College faculty because of Unitarianism. 1891.
Whitner, William Church (1864–1940) [v mfm]. Clippings re development of hydroelectric power in SC. 1897–1940.
Wideman-Brown Families [126, 2v]. Abbeville, Anderson, McCormick, Williamson, Anderson College, and Washington, D. C.; letters and clippings. 1830–1954.
Wiggs Family [vr]. Genealogy. 1700–1900.
Wiggs, W. Hutson [v]. SC College lecture notes. 1854–55.
Wightman, William May (1808–82) [50]. Chiefly correspondence as Methodist minister. 1830–97.
Wildman, Zalmon (1775–1835) [68]. Charleston hat business, life in SC. 1812–20.
Wilkes, Samuel Morrison (d. 1861) [79]. Anderson, Columbia, and Charleston, W. Va.; chiefly letters to wife as SC legislator and CW soldier. 1851–64, 1921, 1963.
Wilkinson Family [340, 3v]. Various papers. 1831–1926.
Williams, Alfred Brockenbrough (1856–1930) [v]. Scrapbook, including articles on the Hampton campaign (1876). 1926.
Williams, Belle (1872–1952) [70]. Chiefly genealogical notes. 1809–1945.
Williams-Chesnut-Manning Collection [c. 2,850]. Various papers. 1682–1929. See *University South Caroliniana Society Program* (1962) for partial description.
Williams & Cohen [v]. Account book of fines. 1857–65.
Williams, David Rogerson (1776–1830) [36, v]. Charleston, Columbia, Society Hill, Rocky River Springs, state and national politics. 1808–35. See also Williams-Chesnut-Manning Collection.

Williams, William G. [v]. Letterbook of engineer for Louisville, Cincinnati, & Charleston Railroad. 1837.

Williamsburg County [19vr]. WPA transcripts of various court records. 1814–1937.

Williamsburg County [4vr, also mfm]. WPA transcripts of epitaphs: Baptist Black Mingo Churchyard, Baptist Cemetery, Baptist Churchyard, Bethany Baptist Churchyard, Bethesda Methodist Churchyard, Black Mingo Presbyterian Cemetery, Britton's Burying Ground, New Market Cemetery, Popular Hill Freewill Baptist Cemetery, Richburg Burying Ground, Sutton Methodist Churchyard, Union Presbyterian Churchyard, Williamsburg Cemetery [Kingstree], Witherspoon Burying Ground, Cedar Lane Cemetery, Frierson Burying Ground, Grenoch Cemetery, Indiantown Cemetery, McDonald Burying Ground, McLary Burying Ground, Midway Presbyterian Churchyard, Mt. Hope Cemetery [Greeleyville], Mt. Vernon Methodist Cemetery.

Williamson, Andrew (d. 1786) [26]. Camden, Monck's Corner, Augusta, and RW campaigns. 1778–79.

Williamson, Thomas [40]. Chiefly poems and clippings. c. 1940–60.

Willington Temperance Society [vr]. Constitution and bylaws. c. 1839.

Willis, Edward [v]. Data on Charleston phosphate industry. 1843–77.

Willson, John O. [3v]. Charleston plantation journals. 1845–61.

Willson, John Owen (1845–1923) [30]. Various personal papers including Methodist license to preach. 1873–1950.

Wilson, Furman Edwards [v mfm]. Records kept as doctor. 1885–87.

Wilson, Hugh [v]. Scrapbook and incomplete memoir, Abbeville. 1860–1908.

Wilson, John A. [v]. SC College scrapbook. 1858–81.

Wilson & Lee, Darlington [v]. Store account. 1856.

Wilson, Leroy [v]. Store account. 1861.

Wilson, Robert [vr]. Biographical sketch of J. L. E. W. Shecut (1770–1836). c. 1900.

Wilson, W. E. [vr]. CW diary re North Carolina and Virginia. 1862.

Wilson, William L. [vr]. Darlington business ledger. 1856.

Wilson, Woodrow (1856–1924) [15]. Chiefly letters re celebration of Wilson's birthday. 1924–30.

Wingard, James Samuel [v]. Memorandum book and notes. 1834.

Wingard, Simon P. (1829–1909) [c. 1,000, 7v]. Various papers. 1806–1945.

Wingfield Drug Store [255, 8v]. Columbia accounts. 1919–41.

Winn, Richard (1750–1818) [2v mfm]. Papers re Yazoo lands from Draper Collection and RW notes from Georgia records, Library of Congress. 1780–90.

Winthrop College [v]. Scrapbook. 1917–33.

Winyah Fire Engine Company, Georgetown [v]. Minutes. 1854–61.

Winyah Library Society, Georgetown [v]. Minutes. 1799–1814.

Witherspoon, B. J. [v]. *Fancy Tactics* (1814) with notes. 1856.
Witherspoon Family [2 boxes]. Chiefly family letters, legal and business papers and correspondence of Robert Witherspoon as State Treasurer, Congressman and member of SC Legislature. 1777–1909.
Witherspoon, J. H. [2v]. Lancaster account books. 1834–55.
Wofford College [4v]. Daybooks and ledgers. 1840–70.
Wofford, Dr. F. E. [4v]. Account books. 1832–66.
Woman's Christian Temperance Union of South Carolina [16, vr]. Correspondence re 28th annual convention and history of organization. 1880–1939.
Woman's World Fair Club of South Carolina [v]. Records. 1892–93.
Woodburn Farm, Pendleton [vr]. Records. 1853.
Woodman of the World, Charleston [1,372]. Various records. 1895–1909.
Woodrow, James (1828–1907) [c. 100, 25v, 3vr]. Papers re Columbia, Charleston, Macon, Ga., and *Southern Presbyterian Review* account books. 1848–97.
Woodruff, Caldwell [vr]. "Life of James Simons . . . and his son, Charles Dewar Simons, first chemistry professor, University of South Carolina." 1942.
Woodson, Agatha A. [2v]. Notes on Joseph Abney, Mexican War clippings. 1848.
Woodward Family [31]. Fairfield District land papers and letters. 1770–1856.
Woodward, William [v]. Records of Philadelphia book dealer and publisher with data on SC customers. 1801–2.
Wooton, J. A. [v]. Charleston account book. 1830–41.
Works Progress Administration, Writers Project [c. 5,000]. Various papers. c. 1935.
Wright, Minnie Lee [v]. Columbia, collection of personal essays. 1877.
Wrightman-Stoll-Dibble Families [4vr]. Charleston genealogy. c. 1928.
Wylie & Agurs, Chester [4v]. Ledgers. 1876–1904.
Yeadon, Richard (1802–70) [14, v]. Scrapbook, clippings of editorials, letters. 1857–70.
Yeargin, Mary [c. 140]. Letters and papers. 1890–94.
York County [22vr]. WPA transcripts of various court records. 1770–1891.
York County [2vr, also mfm]. WPA transcripts of epitaphs: Rose Hill Cemetery, Adah Church Cemetery, Old Unity Church Cemetery.
Youmans, Leroy F. [v]. Political scrapbook. 1876–86.
Young American Fire Company, Columbia [v]. Records. 1875–76.
Young Family [94]. Camden, Philadelphia, France, Florida, and CW; various papers. 1809–92.
Young, Henry Clinton [16]. Various papers, Laurens. 1836–68.

Young Ladies Hospital Association, Columbia [v]. Records. 1861–96.
Young Mens Christian Association, Columbia [21]. Various papers. 1910–25.
Young, Pauline [vr]. Abbeville; Norris family genealogy. 1948.
Young, Thomas John (1803–52) [v]. Diary of assistant rector, St. Michael's Episcopal Church. 1850.

SOUTH CAROLINA NEWSPAPERS—There are extensive files of both original and microfilm copies of newspapers published in the state. Newspapers are listed here in alphabetical and geographical order with those which incorporate the place of publication in the title appearing first. Dates within parentheses indicate incomplete files for years cited. If dates appear without parentheses, the file is essentially complete. A plus sign [+] shows that the Library continues to receive that newspaper. Microfilm copies may be borrowed through interlibrary loan. If the number of reels of microfilm is not specified, the collection consists of one full reel or less; if there are more than one reel, the total number is indicated.

Abbeville Medium (1878–1915), [mfm] (1878–1909).
Abbeville Messenger (1886–87), [mfm] (1886–87).
Abbeville Press & Banner (1873–1924), [mfm] (1873–1924).
Abbeville Scimitar (1914–17).
Abbeville Press & Banner & Abbeville Medium (1927–48), [mfm] (1927–28).
Aiken Journal (1874).
Aiken Recorder (1882–1907), [2 mfm] (1882–1907).
Aiken Standard & Review (1935–50) 1951+.
Aiken Standard & South Carolina Gazette (1915–35), [7 mfm] (1915–35).
Aiken Tribune (1873–74), [mfm] 1875.
Aiken: *Courier-Journal* (1875–78), [mfm] (1877–78); *Journal & Review* (1880–1935), [17 mfm] (1885–1935).
Allendale County Citizen (1930–38), [mfm] (1930–38).
Anderson Daily Intelligencer 1914–16, [5 mfm] 1914–16.
Anderson Daily Mail (1900–45) 1949+, [46 mfm] 1945–49.
Anderson Daily Tribune (1920–24).
Anderson Gazette [mfm] 1843–48.
Anderson Independent [& Tribune] (1924–43), [185+ mfm] 1924, 1944+.
Anderson Intelligencer (1860–1915), [12 mfm] (1860–1915).
Anderson Journal (1882–89).
Anderson: *Blease's Weekly* (1925–26); *Highland Sentinel* [mfm] 1840–43; *People's Advocate* (1892–1915), [5 mfm] (1892–1915); *South Carolina Baptist* [mfm] (1866–68).
Andrews News (1918–21), [2 mfm] (1918–21).

Bamberg County Times (1902, 1930–38), [mfm] (1930–38).
Bamberg Herald (1891–1955), [mfm] (1891–1932).
[*Barnwell*] *People* (1877–1913), [2 mfm] (1877–1913).
Barnwell People-Sentinel (1930–41), [mfm] (1930–41).
Barnwell Sentinel (1861–1914), [mfm] (1861–1914).
Batesburg Advocate (1901–11), [2 mfm] (1901–11).
Batesburg Herald & Leesville News-Advocate (1914–17), [2 mfm] (1914–17).
Batesburg: *Enterprise* (1910–12), [mfm] (1910–12); *People's Advocate* [mfm] (1895); *Summerland Headlight* (1924–25), [mfm] (1924–25); *This Way* (1894–95), [mfm] (1894–95); *Twin City News* 1925–35, [mfm] (1925).
Beaufort County News [mfm] (1939).
Beaufort Gazette (1914–51) 1952+.
Beaufort Tribune & Port Royal Commercial [mfm] 1877.
Belton News (1941–42), [mfm] (1941–42).
Bennettsville Banner (1891–94).
Bennettsville: *Marlboro Democrat* (1885–1911), [3 mfm] (1885–1911); *Marlboro Herald-Advocate* 1951+; *Pee Dee Advocate* (1895–1951), [11 mfm] (1895–1939); *Pee Dee Daily* (1913–14), [2 mfm] (1913–14).
Bethune Observer (1914–23).
Bishopville Leader & Vindicator [*Lee County Vindicator*] (1903–22), [mfm] (1903–22).
Bishopville: *Lee County Messenger* (1924–35) 1936+, [3 mfm] (1930–39).
Branchville Journal (1909–11), [mfm] (1909–11).
Camden & Lancaster Beacon (1831–32).
Camden Chronicle (1913–43), [18 mfm] (1891–1950).
Camden Commercial Courier (1837–38).
Camden Confederate (1861–65).
Camden Daily Journal (1864).
Camden Gazette [*& Mercantile Advertiser*] (1816–22).
Camden Journal (1850–91).
Camden Journal [*& Southern Whig*] 1826–37.
Camden News (1909–12).
Camden: *Kershaw Gazette* (1873–87); *People* (1905–9); *South Carolina Temperance Advocate* (1853–54); *Southern Chronicle* [*Camden Gazette . . . Aegis . . . Literary & Political Register*] (1822–25); *Wateree Messenger* (1888–1934).
Chapin: *Carolina News* (1897–1903), [mfm] (1897–1903).
Charleston American (1917–23).
Charleston County Record (1931–32).
Charleston [*Daily*] *Courier* (1803–73); [97 mfm] 1803–73; also has triweekly edition (1832–70).
Charleston Daily News (1865–73).
Charleston Dispatch (1886–88).
Charleston Evening News (1847–61), [mfm] (1849).
Charleston Evening Post [378+ mfm] 1894+.

139

Charleston Evening Post & Commercial & Political Gazette 1815–16.
Charleston Gazette [mfm] 1778–80.
Charleston Gazette & Mercantile Advertiser (1814).
Charleston Journal of Commerce (1876–78).
Charleston Mercury [triweekly] (1857–68), [daily] (1880–84).
Charleston Mercury [& *Morning Advertiser*] (1823–68), [45 mfm]
 1822–59.
Charleston Observer (1832–45).
Charleston Weekly Standard (1855–58).
Charleston: *Biblical Recorder & Southern Watchman* [mfm] 1838–
 40; *Brigadier* (1954–61); *Bull Dog* (1932–47); *Carolina Gazette*
 (1799–1836); *Carolina Weekly Messenger* (1807–9); *City Gazette*
 [& *Commercial Advertiser* . . . *Daily Advertiser*] (1795–1826),
 [29 mfm] (1787–1832); *Columbian Herald* (title varies) [mfm]
 (1793–96); *Common Sense* (1909, 1914–15); *Daily Republican*
 (1869–71); *Gazette of the State of South Carolina* [mfm] 1777–80;
 Investigator (1812–13), [mfm] 1812–13; *News & Courier* [459+
 mfm] 1873+; *Royal Gazette* [2 mfm] 1781–82; *Royal South Carolina Gazette* [mfm] 1780–82; *South Carolina & American General
 Gazette* [3 mfm] 1764–81; *South Carolina Gazette* (1735–36),
 [7 mfm] 1732–75; *South Carolina Gazette & Country Journal*
 [3 mfm] 1765–75; *South Carolina State Gazette & Timothy's
 [and Mason's] Daily Advertiser* [4 mfm] (1794–1802); *Southern
 Baptist* [6 mfm] 1847–60; *Southern Baptist & General Intelligencer*
 [mfm] 1835–36; *Southern [Evangelical] Intelligencer* [mfm]
 1822–23; *Southern Patriot* [& *Commercial Advertiser*] (1814–48),
 [20 mfm] (1815–44); *Southern Presbyterian* (1852–57); *Southern
 Watchman & General Intelligencer* [mfm] (1837–38); *State
 Gazette of South Carolina* (1785–93), [3 mfm] 1789–93; *State
 Rights & Free Trade Evening Post* [3 mfm] 1831–33; *Strength
 of the People* [mfm] (1809–10); *Times* (1804–16), [mfm] 1803;
 United States Catholic Miscellany [14 mfm] 1822–61; *Weekly
 News* [& *Courier*] (1877–1910); *Wesleyan Journal* (1825–27);
 World [& *Sunday Budget*] (1888–91), [5 mfm] 1889–91.
Cheraw Chronicle (1932–41).
Cheraw Gazette (1835–36).
Cheraw Intelligencer & Southern Register (1823–24).
Cheraw: *Farmer's Gazette* [& *Cheraw Advertiser*] (1839–45).
Chester Bulletin [*State Bulletin*] (1880–92), [11+ mfm] (1880–91),
 1915–39, 1963+.
Chester News (1922–50) 1951+, [2 mfm] (1922–32).
Chester Reporter (1870–1935), [2 mfm] (1870–1935).
Chester Standard [*Palmetto Standard*] (1851–68), [2 mfm] (1851–
 64).
Chester: *Lantern* (1897–1913), [4 mfm] (1898–1913); *Semi-Weekly
 News* (1914–15).
Chesterfield Advertiser (1904–44), [mfm] (1904–34).
Clemson: *Tiger* (1937–61).
Clinton Chronicle (1929–32), [23+ mfm] 1919+.

Clinton Enterprise (1887–88), [mfm] (1887–88).
Clinton: *Blue Stocking* [mfm] (1928, 1935); *Sentinel* (1936–37), [mfm] (1936–37); *Southern Presbyterian* (1893–1902), [mfm] (1895–97, 1902).
Clover Herald [1+ mfm] 1963+.
Columbia Banner (1853–63).
Columbia [Daily] Record (1885–1924), [167+ mfm] (1898–1932) 1939+.
Columbia Daily Register 1875–98, [13 mfm] 1875–87.
Columbia Daily Union (1871–74).
Columbia [Free Press &] Hive [mfm] (1831–32).
Columbia Hi-Life (1926–44).
Columbia Journal (1893–94).
Columbia Telescope [& South Carolina State Journal . . . Southern Political & Literary Register] (1815–39).
Columbia: *Carolina Free Press* (1923–40); *Carolina Motor News* (1931–33); *Christian Neighbor* (1868–1900); *Confederate Baptist* (1862–64), [mfm] (1862–65); *Cotton Plant* [also published in Greenville and Orangeburg] (1893–95); *Courant* (1859); *Daily Carolina Times* (1855–58); *Daily Index [Court Bulletin]* (1915); *Daily Phoenix* (1865–77); *Daily Southern Guardian* (1858–70); *Daily Telegraph* (1847–51); *Evening News* (1895–96); *[Evening] Palmetto Yeoman* (1881–85); *Examiner* (1855–56); *Gamecock* 1908+; *Palmetto Leader* (1926–44); *Palmetto Progress* (1939–41); *Palmetto-State Banner* (1847–52); *Palmetto Times* (1962–64); *Reporter* (1910–12); *South Carolina Gazette* 1925–30; *South Carolina Republican* (1869–70); *South Carolina State Gazette & Columbian Advertiser* (1801–28); *South Carolina Teacher* 1939–42; *South Carolina Temperance Advocate [& Register of Agricultural & General Literature]* (1840–51); *South Carolinian* (1838–73); *Southern Christian Advocate* [also published in Charleston, Augusta, and Macon, Ga.] 1837–71, 1878–1947, [15 mfm] 1837–1900; *Southern Christian Herald* (1834–36); *Southern Chronicle* (1840–47); *Southern Indicator* (1913–24); *Southern Presbyterian* (1862–93); *Southern Times [& State Gazette . . . & South Carolina Gazette]* (1830–38); *State* [419+ mfm] 1891+; *Trade Review* 1919–20; *Tri-Weekly Carolina Times* (1855–58); *Tri-Weekly Phoenix* (1866–75); *Tri-Weekly [South] Carolinian* (1849–65); *Tri-Weekly Southern Guardian* (1858–64); *University Weekly News* (1915–26); *Way of Faith* (1894–96); *Weekly Gleaner* (1868–71).
Conway: *Field* (1913–32) 1954+, [mfm] (1924–28); *Horry Herald* (1916–35), [21 mfm] 1887–1954; *Horry News* [mfm] (1871–77); *Telephone* [mfm] (1879–80).
Darlington Flag (1851–52), [mfm] (1851–52).
Darlington News [3 mfm] (1878–95).
Darlington Press [& New Era] [mfm] (1905–7).
Darlington: *New Era* [mfm] (1865); *News & Press* (1911–52) 1953+, [9 mfm] 1911–39.

Dillon Herald (1904–36) 1937+, [11 mfm] (1904–39).
Due West Telescope (1856–63), [mfm] (1856–63).
Due West: *Associate Reformed Presbyterian* (1876–77, 1889); *Erskine Mirror* (1934–39), [mfm] (1934–39).
Easley Messenger (1885–87).
Easley Progress (1912–44).
Edgefield Advertiser (1837–1911) 1912+, [11 mfm] (1836–1902).
Edgefield Chronicle (1881–1925), [2 mfm] 1881–92.
Edgefield: *Carolinian* (1829–31); *Palmetto White Ribbon* (1907–40).
Fairfax Enterprise (1898–1905).
Florence Daily Times (1894–1924), [3 mfm] (1894–1923).
Florence Messenger [mfm] 1893–95.
Florence Morning News [Review] (1923), [138+ mfm] 1924+.
Florence Times [2 mfm] (1894–95).
Florence: *Centenary* [mfm] (1890–92); *Times-Messenger* [2 mfm] (1896–99).
Fort Mill Times (1914–35).
Gaffney Ledger (1896–1937); [16+ mfm] 1954+.
Gaffney: *Cherokee Times* (1923–29).
Georgetown Advocate (1902–3).
Georgetown American [mfm] (1839–41).
Georgetown Daily Item (1907–12).
Georgetown Enquirer (1880–82), [2 mfm] 1880–89.
Georgetown Gazette (title varies) [mfm] (1798–1816).
Georgetown Herald (1918).
Georgetown Semi-Weekly Times [mfm] 1895–96.
Georgetown Times (1880–1948) 1949+.
Georgetown Times-Index (1920–21).
Georgetown Union [mfm] 1837–39.
Georgetown: *Coastal Chronicle* (1922–27); *Pee Dee Times* [mfm] 1854–58; *Progressive Democrat* (1914–15); *Sunday Outlook* (1901–7); *Winyah Observer* [2 mfm] (1841–52); *Winyaw Intelligencer* [mfm] (1817–35).
Greenville [County] Observer 1930–36.
Greenville Enterprise [& Mountaineer] 1866–89, 1892, [mfm] (1817–80).
Greenville Mountaineer (1834–67), [4 mfm] 1829–50.
Greenville News (1874–1934), [182+ mfm] 1942+.
Greenville Piedmont (1912–40), [193+ mfm] 1941+.
Greenville Republican [mfm] 1826–28.
Greenville Weekly News (1878–88).
Greenville: *Baptist Courier* (1882–97); *Cotton Plant* [also published in Columbia and Orangeburg] (1887–1902); *Hornet* (1929–42); *Patriot & Mountaineer* 1856–61; *Southern Enterprise* (1861–69), [mfm] (1871–80); *Southern Patriot* [mfm] 1851–53.
Greenwood [Daily] Journal (1912–19), [9 mfm] (1895–1917).
Greenwood Index [13 mfm] (1897–1918).
Greenwood Index-Journal [140+ mfm] 1919+.

Greenwood: *Dixie Schools* (1900).
Greer Citizen (1922–32).
Greer Tribune (1929–33).
Hampton County Guardian (1882–1949).
Hartsville Messenger (1911–52).
Hartsville: *Periscope* (1935–43).
Hemingway Journal (1940).
Honea Path Plaindealer (1886–87).
Johnston Herald (1932–39).
Johnston News (1903–5).
Johnston: [*Edgefield*] *Weekly Monitor* (1881–1903).
Kershaw Era (1903–35).
Kingstree: *County Record* (1909–35) 1937+.
Lake City News (1917–54).
Lake City: *Times-Herald* (1950–60) 1961+.
Lancaster Ledger (1853–85).
Lancaster News (1912–59).
Lancaster Review (1882–1905).
Laurens Advertiser (1885–1935).
Laurens [*-ville*] *Herald* (1848–1932).
Laurens: *Tiger Life* (1938–39).
Leesville News (1906–11).
Leesville Sun (1905–6).
Leesville Twin-County News [*Batesburg-Leesville News*] 1913–23.
Leesville: *News-Advocate* (1911–13).
Lexington Dispatch (1873–1905).
Lexington Dispatch-News (1917–44) 1962+.
Lexington News (1915–17).
Lexington: *Cotton News* (1922–23); *South Carolina Temperance Standard* (1854–55).
McColl Dispatch (1924–25).
McColl: *Marlboro Times* (1909–10).
McCormick Messenger (1904–49).
Manning Times 1885–91, 1894+.
Manning: *Clarendon Banner* (1860–65); *Clarendon Enterprise* 1882–87.
Marion Star (1878–1937).
Moncks Corner: *Berkeley Democrat* (1928–49).
Mullins Enterprise (1914–49).
Myrtle Beach News (1936–41).
Newberry Herald 1865–84.
Newberry Herald & News (1884–1935).
Newberry Observer (1886–1940).
Newberry: *Conservatist* (1858–61); *Evening Telegram* (1904); *Indian* (1934–40); *Lutheran Visitor* (1887–99); [*Rising*] *Sun* (1858–65).
Orangeburg Democrat (1879–81), [mfm] (1881).
Orangeburg Evening News 1904–11 (1912).
Orangeburg News (1867–75).

Orangeburg News [& *Times*] (1875–81).
Orangeburg Times (1872–75).
Orangeburg Times & Democrat (1881–1911), [114+ mfm] (1881–1937) 1938+.
Orangeburg: *Carolina Times* (1866–67); *Collegian* (1933, 1955–61); *Edisto Clarion* (1878); *Enterprise* [& *Alliance Monitor*] (1890–94); *Free Citizen* (1875–76); *Southron* (1856–60); *Taxpayer* (1877–78); *Weekly Dispatch* (1894–95).
Pageland Journal (1923–35).
Pendleton Messenger [*Miller's Weekly Messenger*] (1818–23) 1826–51, [5 mfm] (1807–43).
Pickens Sentinel (1876–1935) 1936+.
Pickens: *Keowee Courier* (1854–68); *People's Journal* (1894–1903); *Sentinel Journal* (1903–11).
Port Royal Standard & Commercial (1875–76).
Port Royal: *New South* (1862–64); *Palmetto Post* (1882–95).
Pottersville: *Edgefield Hive* 1830.
Ridgeland: *Jasper County Record* (1928–44).
Ridgeway: *Fairfield News* (1914).
Rock Hill Evening Herald [149+ mfm] 1912+.
Rock Hill Herald [13 mfm] 1880–1911.
Rock Hill Journal [mfm] 1901–4.
Rock Hill Record [31 mfm] 1904–30.
Rock Hill: *Johnsonian* (1924–56).
St. George: *Dorchester County Record* (1927–34); *Dorchester Eagle* (1911–32); *Dorchester Eagle-Record* (1932–42).
St. Matthews: *Calhoun Advance* (1906–19, 1928); *Calhoun Times* (1922–30) 1931–45; *Cotton News* (1923–26).
Saluda Advocate (1896–1900).
Saluda Sentinel (1895–1903).
Saluda Standard (1902) 1903–35.
Spartanburg [*Daily*] *Herald* (1875–1943), [128+ mfm] 1905–8, 1950+.
Spartanburg Express (1857–66), [mfm] 1857.
Spartanburg Journal [& *Carolina Spartan*] (1906–49), [75+ mfm] 1902–9, 1950+.
Spartanburg: *Carolina Spartan* (1856–1904), [15 mfm] (1849–93); *Old Gold & Black* (1929–42); *Parley-Voo* (1924–35); *Scribbler* (1935–44); *Sun & Carolina Citizen* (1924–25).
Summerville Scene (1950–52) 1953+.
Summit: *Our News Letter* 1894–1906.
Sumter Advance (1882–93).
Sumter Banner (1846–55).
Sumter Daily Item (1894–1940) 1941–59, [9+ mfm] 1960+.
Sumter District Reporter (1885–86).
Sumter Herald (1892–1944), [20 mfm] 1896–1949.
Sumter High News (1937–44).
Sumter News 1866–73.
Sumter Watchman [*Black River Watchman*] (1855–81).

Sumter: *Evening News* (1904–5); *Freeman* (1892–1904); *Semi-Weekly Watchman* (1863); *Southern Whig* (1832–33); *Temperance Worker* (1883–87); *Tri-Weekly Watchman* (1860–62); *True Southron* 1873–81; *Watchman & Southron* 1881–1918.
Una: *News Review* (1936+).
Union Daily Progress (1925).
Union Progress (1900–25).
Union Times 1875–1950; [11 mfm] 1936–42.
[*Weekly*] *Union Times* (1875–1917).
Walhalla: *Keowee Courier* (1868–1933) 1934+.
Walterboro: *Press & Standard* (1901–35) 1936+; [32+ mfm] (1891–1905) 1906+.
Ware Shoals Life (1926–34).
Westminster: *Tugaloo Tribune* (1913–52).
Winnsboro: *Fairfield Herald* (1849–76); *News & Herald* (1876–1933) 1934+; *Fairfield Register* (1856–61); *Tri-Weekly News* (1865–72).
Yemassee: *Hampton County Democrat* (1938–40).
York Enterprise (1888–89).
York: *Encyclopedia* (1825–26), [mfm] (1825–26); *Pioneer* [*& Yorkville Advertiser*] *Advertiser . . . & Commercial Register* (1823–26), [mfm] (1823–24); *Yorkville Compiler* (1840–41), [mfm] 1840–41; *Yorkville Enquirer* (1855–1942), [3+ mfm] 1925–28, 1963+; *Yorkville Miscellany* 1851–54, [mfm] 1851–54.

Undergraduate Library
V 35,000   R 1,800   CP 50

This is a library for browsing and study. No periodical files are retained.

Veteran's Administration Hospital Library
V 10,000   CP 170

Collection includes a general library and a medical section. In the latter there are some 3,000 books and a twenty-year file of professional journals. Currently 130 medical journals are received. Library has direct telephone connections with all VA hospital libraries in the nation. Also, back files of pertinent published material can be obtained through Medical Library Association Exchange.

Wing Publications

This company prints, distributes, and retains limited files of the following publications:

Carolina Sportsman—Q

Hose and Nozzle—(issued six times per year by the Firemen's Association of North Carolina)
North Carolina Gardener—(issued five times per year by the Garden Clubs of North Carolina)
Review of Architecture—Q
Southern Gardens—Q
South Carolina Business and Professional Woman—(issued three times per year)
South Carolina Clubwoman—M (except summer)
South Carolina Engineer—(semiannually)
South Carolina Law—(issued six times per year by the Law Enforcement Officers' Association)
South Carolina Nursing—Q
State Service—Q
Tarheel Woman—M (publication of the Business and Professional Women of North Carolina)

CONWAY

Conway Field—W 1952+

Horry County Memorial Library

V 49,074   R 5,270   SC 1,635   CP 156   MFMR   PCE   CMPC

Newspaper files include:

Conway Field 1949+
Horry County News 1949–52
Horry County News and Loris Sentinel 1952–54
Horry Herald 1949+, also [mfm] 1892–1954
Horry News [mfm] 1874–77
Loris Sentinel 1955+
Myrtle Beach News (1949–61)
Myrtle Beach Daily News (1955–56)
Myrtle Beach Sun 1952–61
Myrtle Beach Sun-News 1961+

MANUSCRIPTS—Among the library's holdings are fourteen Norton composition books (1935–50), microfilm copies of two Norton histories of Horry County (1926, 1935), James A. Norton's field notebook of World War I battlefield diseases and injuries and his pocket account book (c. 1904), general store ledger of G. R. Congdon (1856–58), unidentified physician's ledger (1856–70), Conway Methodist Church Sunday School Records (1888–89) and Conference Minutes (1888–98), Register [3v] of Conway Station Methodist Episcopal Church South (1871–1907), and Quarterly Conference

Records [4v] of Conwayboro Change, Marion District (1836–55, 1879–81, 1888–91, 1904–7).

Horry Herald—W 1935+

University of South Carolina, Coastal Center Library
   V 2,500   R 300   SC 50   CP 50

DARLINGTON

Darlington County Circulating Library
   V 28,550   R 153

Darlington County Courthouse, Judge's Chambers Library
   V 10,000

Darlington County Historical Society

A vault in the Darlington Public Library contains a small collection of books, papers, and random newspapers re local history. Among these items are the Minutes of the Darlington Guards (1882), copies of Evan Pugh's diary (1762–67) and William Hutchinson's journal (1819–72), and Woods Dargan's *Chronicle* to area servicemen (1942–43).

Darlington News & Press—W 1928+

Also prints *Lake City News* and *Lake City Times-Herald,* but retains no files of these publications.

Darlington Public Library
   V 23,656   R 1,350   SC 668   CP 64
Collection includes minutes of several local clubs and these newspaper files:

[Columbia] *State* 1925–30
Darlington News & Press 1914+
Darlington News 1878–88
Darlington Flag 1856–57

Also, this library has an assortment of state and national newspapers containing material re the "Darlington Riot" of 1894.

147

DENMARK

Edisto News—W 1959+

Printed by *Barnwell People-Sentinel.*

Voorhees Junior College Library
    V 10,639   R 500   SC 25   CP 106
Clipping file includes data on juvenile delinquency, Negro life and history, and other subjects of special interest. Library has special religious collection (Episcopal Church) and several letters from Clinton B. Voorhees (the founder) to Booker T. Washington concerning plans to establish the college.

DILLON

Dillon Herald—W 1904+

DONALDS

Abbeville County Library
    V 13,950   R 26   SC 30

DUE WEST

Associate Reformed Presbyterian—W (1884–1922) 1923+

Erskine Bulletin—Q 1955+

Erskine College Library
    V 33,000   R 1,000   SC 500   CP 200   MFMR
In addition to various college and ARP publications, this library has files of the *Abbeville Press and Banner* 1846+, minutes of the ARP Synod 1812+, selected English and music recordings, farm diaries of John Pratt (1913–53), data re Due West Female College and Bryson College (at Fayetteville, Tenn.), and files of the *Due West Weekly* (1949–56).

Erskine Mirror—(semimonthly except summer) 1927+

Erskine College publication.

Erskine Theological Seminary Library

V 14,000   R 1,400   CP 100

Files contain the Glasgow Collection (c. 400v) on the history of the church of Scotland. This library separated from the Erskine College Library in 1958 and is currently replenishing its periodical files and general holdings.

DUNCAN

Cyrovac Division Library, W. R. Grace & Company

V 1,000   R 500   CP 100   MFMR

Collection includes a mechanized information retrieval system covering internal reports of W. R. Grace & Company and periodical references to plastic film technology for food packaging (5,000 documents), *Thomas' Register* complete with *Thomas' Micro-Catalogs*, and an extensive file of pertinent commercial catalogs.

EASLEY

Easley Progress—W (1902–34) 1934+

Pickens County Library

V 24,000   R 500   SC 100   CP 51

Collection includes data on the early history of Easley and a special file of gardening material (c. 200 titles).

EDGEFIELD

Edgefield Advertiser—W 1937+

Oakley Park

Home of General Martin Witherspoon Gary (1831–81), this UDC "Red Shirt Shrine" contains memorabilia, materials re SC history, some 200 CW letters, and about 200 books.

FLORENCE

Florence County Historical Society

A small collection [500 items] of photographs, scrapbooks, early maps, and town records (1874–1900) is housed in the Florence Museum of Art.

Florence-Darlington Area Technical Education Center Library
Library in process of development.

Florence Morning News—D [mfm] 1924+
Micro Photo   MFMR

Florence Public Library
V 30,367   R 1,244   SC 1,235   CP 127   PCE   CMPC
Collection includes an extensive vertical file on state and local history,
some 40 vols. of printed travel accounts (1800–50), and files of
these newspapers: *Darlington News* (1886–95), [*Florence*] *Centenary* (1891–92), *Florence Evening Star* (1939–41), *Florence Morning News* [*Review*] 1925+, [*Florence*] *Times-Messenger* (1896–97),
Florence Weekly (1957–58), *New York Illustrated News* (1853),
South Carolina Gazette & General Advertiser (1784).

Journal of the South Carolina Medical Association—M 1904+
Business offices are in Florence, editorial offices at 82 Rutledge
Street, Charleston.

University of South Carolina at Florence Library
V 2,000   R 300   SC 100   CP 50

FORT MILL

Fort Mill Public Library
V 2,395   CP 3

Fort Mill Times—W (1910–43) 1943+

FORT JACKSON

Fort Jackson Leader—(biweekly) 1962+

Post Hospital Medical Library
V 2,200   CP 100
Collection includes some 1,300 books and a substantial number of
bound medical journals 1950+. Library cooperates with VA hospital
library nearby.

Post Library System
V 70,000   R 3,000   CP 176

This post system consists of the main library and three branches, with special emphasis on military science, current affairs, history, and books and periodicals in foreign languages. The collection includes some material re history of Fort Jackson (1917+).

FOUNTAIN INN

Fountain Inn Tribune—W 1928+

FROGMORE

Laura M. Towne Library
V 5,382   R 86   SC 31   CP 6

Cooperates with the Regional Library for the Blind, Raleigh, North Carolina.

GAFFNEY

Cherokee County Public Library
V 52,017   R 3,500   SC 1,000   CP 50   MFMR

Collection includes 145 vols. of the DAR lineage books (1897–1921) and the June Carr collection of photographs re Gaffney (1906–20).

Gaffney Ledger—W 1894+, [mfm] 1954+
Mann

Grit and Steel—M 1898+

Gamecock publication of the De Camp Publishing Company.

Limestone College Library
V 28,000   R 1,700   CP 190

GEORGETOWN

Georgetown County Memorial Library
V 27,000   R 3,000   SC 500   CP 40

Holdings include the *Georgetown Times* [*Index*] 1920+ and the Oswald scrapbook on SC churches. Also housed in the library

151

building is the Winyah Indigo Society Collection, an outstanding file of newspapers, magazines, and documents re local history. This society was chartered at the Court of St. James in 1753; and although considerable material was lost during the 1860's, some 18th- and early 19th-cent. items remain. The total collection includes some 1,500 books, about 100 vols. of bound newspapers, several rare atlases, *War of the Rebellion,* and the register of visitors to the Georgetown booth at the Charleston Exposition (1901–2). Among the newspapers are the following files:

Albion [New York City] 1828–41
Andrews [S. C.] *News* 1918–21
Carolina Field [Georgetown] 1905
[*Charleston*] *Tri-Weekly Courier* 1861–62
Coastal Chronicle [Andrews, S. C.] 1922–24
Freeman's Journal, or the North-American Intelligencer [Philadelphia] 1787–88
Gazetter & New Daily Advertiser [London] 1768
Georgetown [S. C.] *American* 1840
Georgetown [S. C.] *Daily Item* 1907–12
Georgetown [S. C.] *Enquirer* 1880–90
Georgetown [S. C.] *Gazette* 1801
Georgetown [S. C.] *Progressive Democrat* 1913–16
Georgetown [S. C.] *Union* 1837–39
Georgetown [S. C.] *Times* 1895–1923
New York Journal & Patriotic Register 1791–94, 1796–97
New York Journal & Weekly Register 1789–92
Pee Dee Times [Georgetown, S. C.] 1853–58
Pennsylvania Gazette [Philadelphia] 1787
Sunday Outlook [Georgetown, S. C.] 1901–11
U. S. Telegraph [Washington, D. C.] 1830–31
Winyah Intelligencer [Georgetown, S. C.] 1819
Winyah Observer [Georgetown, S. C.] 1841–53

Georgetown Times—W 1954+

Southern Naval & Maritime Museum

A collection of records, artifacts, and historical documents re South Atlantic marine life is being developed.

GRANITEVILLE

Graniteville Bulletin—M 1942+

Employee publication of the Graniteville Company.

GREAT FALLS

Great Falls Reporter—W 1957+

GREENVILLE

American Textile Reporter—W

Published in Boston. This local office keeps back files for only two years.

Baptist Courier—W (1912–19) 1920+

Furman University Library has both original and microfilm files 1869+.

Bob Jones University Library

V 100,000 R 8,000 CP 500 MCR MFMR PCE

Collection includes substantial material in art (especially Renaissance), religious life (nondenominational), and American and English history and literature. The library has the *New York Times* [mfm] 1944+.

Bulletin of the Greenville County Medical Society—M 1936+

Carolina Christian—M 1959+

Published by the Church of Christ; formerly the *Carolina Messenger of Truth*.

Carolina Economist—M 1964+

Leaflet distributed by the South Carolina National Bank.

Commentator—(issued semimonthly) 1938+

House organ of Union Bleachery of Cone Mills. Began publication as a weekly.

Fellowship News—1934+

Published by Bob Jones University.

Furman Echo—(issued three times per year) 1951+

Furman University literary publication.

Furman University Library

V 115,000   R 3,000   SC 2,000   CP 580   MCR   MFMR   MRP
PCE   US GOVT DOC

Holdings include the South Carolina Baptist Historical Society Collection [900v]; files of the *Greenville Civil & Commercial Journal* (1921–26), *Hartford* [Conn.] *Courant* 1855, and *New York Mirror* 1829–42; and these mfm materials: diaries and daybooks of Isaac Backus (1724–1806), originals owned by the Andover-Newton Historical Society; Draper Manuscripts [11 reels] re the Southeast, including papers of Thomas Sumter; papers of James Dawkins (1785–1843), a Wilkinsville (S. C.) cotton planter; family papers and correspondence of Basil Manly (1825–92), president of the Southern Baptist Theological Seminary, and his brother, Reverend Charles Manly (1837–1924); records of the British Public Record Office re SC 1663–1782, with general index to transcripts in SC Archives; records of the annual sessions of the Southern Baptist Convention 1845–74, with an index to proceedings 1845–1953; minutes of the State Convention of the Baptist Denomination in SC 1821+; and annual reports of the state conventions of the SC Baptist Woman's Missionary Union 1882—1954. The library has mfm copies of the minutes and records of numerous SC Baptist associations. Few of these are complete; many of them are taken from originals in the collections of the SC Baptist Historical Society. Among them are: Abbeville, Aiken, Antioch, Barnwell, Barnwell and Bamberg, Beaverdam, Berea, Bethel, Black River, Broad River, Carolina, Charleston, Chester, Chesterfield, Colleton, Columbia, Dorchester, Edgefield, Edisto, Enoree, Fairfield, Florence, Fork, Fork Shoal, Greenville, Kershaw, Lake Swamp, Laurens, Lexington, Marion, Moriah, North Enoree River, North Greenville, North Spartanburg, Orangeburg, Pickens, Pee Dee, Piedmont, Reedy River, Ridge, Rocky River, Saluda, Salem, Santee Sauldam, Savannah River, Screven, Southeast, Spartan, Spartanburg, Twelve Mile, Tumbling Shoals, Tyger River, Union Waccamaw, Welsh Neck, and York. There are also records on mfm of some 35 specific churches. Most of this data is 19th-cent. material from the Piedmont. The following newspapers are on mfm:

Baptist Courier 1869+
Edgefield Advertiser 1836–1902
Greenville Enterprise (1871–80)
Greenville News 1942+
Greenville Piedmont 1941+

[*Greenville*] *Piedmont & Mountaineer* 1829–50
Greenville Republican 1826–28
Latter Day Luminary (Baptist) 1818–26
New York Times 1954+
Pendleton Messenger (1807–43)
Religious Herald 1828–97
Southern Intelligencer 1819–26
Southern Baptist 1846–60, 1866–68
Southern Patriot 1732–82
Southern Watchman & General Intelligencer 1835–38
The library also has *Debates of the US Congress* [mc] 1824–37.

Furman University Magazine—Q 1951+

Furman University Studies—(semiannually) 1919+

Published by Furman University as part of its quarterly series, the *Furman University Bulletin.*

Greenville County Courthouse, Law Court Library
V 7,000

Greenville County Library
V 175,516   R 5,000   SC 2,000   CP 200   MFMR   MRP PCE
Holdings include *War of the Rebellion,* an extensive clipping-pamphlet file on state and local history, scattered files of several local 19th-cent. newspapers: *Daily News, Enterprise,* and *Mountaineer,* files of the *Greenville Civil and Commercial Journal* 1922–26, *Greenville News* 1944+, and *Greenville Piedmont* 1944+. There are special collections in these fields: art [200v], business-technical [200v], genealogy [200v], and textiles [600v]. Reference resources include *Applied Science and Technology* 1958+, *Business Periodicals Index* 1960+, *Essay and General Literature Index* 1900+, *Library of Congress Catalog,* and the *National Union Catalog.*

Greenville General Hospital, Medical Library
V 3,500   R 700   CP 130   MFMR
This collection, sponsored by the Greenville County Medical Society and Greenville General Hospital, includes over 500 taped lectures re pediatrics, obstetrics, surgery, anesthesiology, and hospital management. Also back files of pertinent magazines can be obtained through the Medical Library Association Exchange.

Greenville General Hospital, School of Nursing Library
V 2,100   CP 126

Greenville News—D (1881–1900) 1900+, [mfm] 1938+
Micro Photo   MFMR
Has mfm copies of numerous newspapers published in Greenville, 1826–53. Mann Film Laboratories is currently filming random back copies of the *News.*

Greenville Observer—W (1951–52) 1963+

Greenville Piedmont—D 1926+, [mfm] 1936+
Micro Photo   MFMR
Mann Film Laboratories is currently filming random back copies of the *Piedmont.*

Greenville Technical Education Center Library
V 250
Library currently is in process of development.

Hornet—W (except summer) 1916+
Furman University publication.

Liberty Legion—(issued semimonthly) 1948+
House organ of the Liberty Life Insurance Company. A small newspaper for the home office of the company is also published.

Printopics—M 1930+
Published by Provence-Jarrard Company and circulated free to customers and prospects.

Textile World—M 1945+
A McGraw-Hill publication which also maintains editorial offices in New York City.

Voice of the Alumni News—(eight times per year) 1942+
Publication of Bob Jones University.

GREENWOOD

Chemstrand Plant Library
V 500   CP 53

Collection emphasizes textiles, chemistry, mathematics, and statistics.

Connie Maxwell—Q 1909+
Publication of the Connie Maxwell Children's Home.

Greenwood City and County Public Library
V 47,042   R 3,200   SC 500   CP 96   MFMR   PCE   CMPC

Holdings include a collection on SC history and genealogy deposited by the Star Fort DAR Chapter, a file of material on local history compiled by the Greenwood County Historical Society, and copies of the *Greenwood Index-Journal* 1933–42, [mfm] 1941+. Eventually the *Index-Journal* plans to give the library filmed copies of files of both the *Index* and the *Journal* dating from the 1890's.

Greenwood Index-Journal—D [mfm] 1895+
Micro Photo   MFMR

Lander College Library
V 32,000   R 3,000   SC 1,000   CP 350   MFMR   PCE

Holdings include 350 phonograph records, *Greenwood Index-Journal* [mfm] 1961+, *Biological Abstracts* 1960+, and a special collection provided by the Federated Garden Clubs of Greenwood. The official state library of the DAR—a file of books, microfilms, and genealogical data—is on deposit here.

News for South Carolina Local Historical Societies—Q 1964+
Published by the Confederation of South Carolina Local Historical Societies.

Park's Floral Magazine—M 1901+
Printed in Greenwood; editorial offices are at Libonia, Franklin County, Pennsylvania.

Self Memorial Hospital Library
V 800   CP 28

Collection includes 400 vols. of bound medical journals.

GREER

Greer Citizen—W (1918–42) 1942+

HAMPTON

Hampton County Guardian—W 1912+
Printed by Weeklies Publisher, Inc., Allendale. Files are located in Judge of Probate's vault, Hampton County Courthouse.

HARTSVILLE

Coker College Library
V 37,055   R 1,539   SC 1,000   CP 196   MFMR
In addition to materials re the Coker family, Coker College, and its predecessor [Welsh Neck Baptist High School], this library has some manuscripts of Elizabeth Boatwright Coker, several personal recollections of CW, *War of the Rebellion, Arents Tobacco Collection,* daybooks of a Society Hill firm [S. H. Pressley 1845–53 and Pressley & Griffin 1856–66], and these newspaper files: *Hartsville Messenger* 1942+, *New York Times* [mfm] 1963+, and the *New York Weekly Tribune* 1861–63. Files also include *Biological Abstracts* 1963+.

Hartsville Messenger—W (1893–1921) 1921+

Hartsville Memorial Library
V 18,000   R 450   SC 300   CP 45
Collection contains some general data on local history and the *Hartsville Messenger* 1938+.

Periscope—M (except summer) 1922+
Coker College publication.

Sonoco News—M 1942+
Published for employees of Sonoco Products of Hartsville.

HONEA PATH

Honea Path Chronicle—W 1945+

INMAN

Inman Times—W (1921–27) 1956+

JOHNSTON

Ridge Citizen—W 1947+

Has files of the *Newberry Herald & News* 1896–1925.

KERSHAW

Kershaw Memorial Library
  V 8,846   CP 7

Library has a small collection of reference and SC material and maintains current files of the *Kershaw News Era*.

Kershaw News Era—W 1946+

KINGSTREE

County Record—W 1890+

Kingstree Carnegie Library
  V 10,662   R 250   SC 250   CP 13

Collection includes *War of the Rebellion* and the *County Record* 1942+.

LAKE CITY

Lake City News—W

Because of limited space, retains back copies for only about two years. Printed by *Darlington News & Press*.

Lake City Public Library
  V 3,000   R 160   SC 60   CP 30

Collection includes some file material on local history.

Lake City Times-Herald—W

Because of limited space, retains back copies for only about two years. Printed by *Darlington News & Press*.

LANCASTER

Carolina Museum

This is a general museum emphasizing local history and the CW. Of special interest are CW letters of Congressman Samuel Dibble and the Minutes of the Lancasterville Presbyterian Church, 1835–99.

Lancaster County Historical Society

This collection includes extensive data on the Lancaster Center of the University of South Carolina, a file of some 300 items re the SC Up Country, and local genealogical data.

Lancaster County Historical Commission

Courthouse museum has retired county records, genealogical data, and materials re area history.

Lancaster News—W 1920+

Also has files of *Chester Reporter* 1920+ and *Springs Bulletin* (Springs Cotton Mills) 1947+.

Springs Bulletin—(published every other week) 1943+

Publication of Springs Cotton Mills.

Lancaster County Library
 V 30,660 R 1,126 SC 584 CP 34

Collection includes a DAR cabinet with some 500 vols., pamphlets, scrapbooks on local history, and files of the *Lancaster Ledger* (1852–60) and *Lancaster News* 1936+.

University of South Carolina, Lancaster Center Library
 V 6,000 R 500 SC 200 CP 50 MFMR

Collection includes the private library of former Congressman J. P. Richards. The library is retaining all copies of current periodicals received 1959+. It also has files of the *Wall Street Journal* 1961+ and *National Observer* 1961+.

LANDRUM

Landrum Leader—W (1955–57) 1958+

LANGLEY

United Merchants & Manufacturers Research Center Library
V 100   CP 50
This facility was established in 1962. Plans are underway to expand the library with increased holdings in chemistry, textiles, and related subjects.

LATTA

Dillon County Library
V 60,111   R 250   SC 175   CP 35
Holdings include local genealogical data, 20 WPA scrapbooks on area history, and these newspaper files: [*Marion*] *Crescent* (1866–70), *Dillon Herald* 1935+, and *Latta Observer* (1952–57) 1962+. These manuscripts are on file: C. B. Allen, "History of Latta Schools" (1958); John B. Eleazer, "Latta Library: Its Relation to Education in Dillon County" (1941); Mrs. L. T. McCollum, "Deaths & Marriages from the *Marion Star*, 1852–69" and "Some Cemetery Inscriptions of Marion & Dillon Counties" [2v] (1956–57); John L. McLucas, "My Trip to Russia" (1959); and Malcolm McNair, "Letters from Europe" (1939).

Latta Observer—W (1938–60) 1960+

LAURENS

Laurens Advertiser—W (1880–89) 1890+

Laurens County Library
V 37,615   R 1,500   SC 500   CP 25
Holdings include a DAR library [100v], a special SC deposit, and a substantial pamphlet collection re local history.

LEXINGTON

Lexington Dispatch-News—W (1894–1933) 1934+

LIBERTY

Liberty Monitor—W 1959+

LORIS

Loris Sentinel—W 1952+

McCOLL

McColl Messenger—W

Keeps no back files.

McCORMICK

McCormick County Library
  V 2,507

McCormick Messenger—W (1904–53) 1954+

MANNING

Manning Library
  V 4,000   R 50   SC 125
Manning Times—W (1892–1938) 1939+

MARION

Marion County Library
  V 8,437   R 50

Marion County Memorial Hospital Library
A small medical library is in the process of development.

Marion Public Library
  V 17,000   R 500   SC 150   CP 66
Collection includes back files of the *Marion Star* (1852–1930) 1931+
and the [Columbia] *State* 1962+, cemetery records of Marion and
Dillon Counties [2v], local genealogical material, a UDC cabinet
of the discontinued "Blue Savannah" chapter, and some 150 books
on SC life from the libraries of Judge C. A. Woods and A. M. Stack-
house. The library also has these scrapbooks on area history: Owls'
Book Club (1910–50), American Legion Auxiliary 1919+, and the
records of civic improvement during the "Finer Carolinas" contests.

Marion Star—W (1913–44) 1945+

MONCKS CORNER

Berkeley County Library
  V 15,000   R 830   SC 525   CP 28

Berkeley Democrat—W 1935+

MULLINS

Mullins Enterprise—W 1953+

Mullins Public Library
  V 6,000   R 400   SC 200   CP 40
Collections include *War of the Rebellion,* UDC and DAR scrapbooks re local history, and files of the *Mullins Enterprise* 1948+.

MYRTLE BEACH

Chapin Memorial Library
  V 12,507   R 325   SC 230   CP 53
Collection includes scrapbooks on local history 1954+.

Guide Magazine Group—W (March thru September) 1956+
Resort publication for tourists.

Myrtle Beach Air Force Base Library
  V 13,000   R 250   SC 50   CP 175

Myrtle Beach Sun-News—W 1952+

NEWBERRY

Indian—W (except summer) 1929+
Newberry College newspaper.

Newberry College Library
  V 41,000   R 3,000   CP 374   MCR   MFMR
Holdings include material on area and college history, CW data, archives of the Florida Lutheran Synod, the Dr. T. H. Dreher

Collection [1,000v], an Anglo-Saxon Collection [50v], letters re Newberry Mills, Lutheran Theological Seminary records, and materials re the Classical and Theological Seminary of Lexington. There are also files of the *Stylus* (Newberry College) 1900–30; *Evangelical Lutheran Intelligencer* (Frederick, Md.) 1826–29; and the *New York Times* 1954+. Reference files contain *Biological Abstracts* 1962+ and *Sociological Abstracts* 1963+.

Newberry Observer—W 1882+

Newberry-Saluda Regional Library
   V 30,677   R 500   SC 150   CP 27   MFMR
Collection includes some records, genealogical data, and area history files sponsored by local clubs and organizations.

Newberry Sun—W 1936+

South Carolina Lutheran—M 1919+

South Carolina Musician—Q 1946+
Printed by the *Newberry Sun* for the South Carolina Music Educators' Association.

Studies in Short Fiction—Q 1963+
Publication of Newberry College.

NICHOLS
Nichols Public Library
   V 5,070   R 112

NORTH AUGUSTA
North Augusta Star—W 1954+

NORTH CHARLESTON
Berkeley-Charleston-Dorchester Technical Education Center
   Library
Library is in process of development.

Charleston Air Force Base Library
V 20,000 CP 105

Charleston Naval Base Library
V 7,218 CP 60

North Charleston Banner—W 1960+

West Virginia Pulp & Paper Company, Information Services Center
V 4,500 CP 150 MFMR PCE
This is West Virginia Pulp & Paper's depository for reports, books, magazines, patents, and translations. It serves as a technical information center for all company divisions. Some 50,000 company reports are microfilmed and indexed. Files contain:

Analytical Abstracts 1954–60
Applied Science & Technology Index 1958+
British Plastics Federation Abstracts 1963+
Business Periodicals Index 1958+
Ceramic Abstracts 1954–56
Chemische Berichte 1961+
Das Papier (1949–53) 1955+
Holzforschung 1948+
Industrial Arts Index (1945–58)
Norsk Skogindustri 1947+
Packaging Abstracts 1946+
Paperi Ja Puu 1946+
Printing Abstracts 1946+
Svensk Pappers-tidning 1945+
Wochenblatt für Papierfabrikation 1947+

ORANGEBURG

Claflin College Library
V 21,000 R 1,000 SC 500 CP 352 MFMR
This library cooperates closely with the South Carolina State College Library nearby. It has special holdings re Negro life and history and these newspaper files: *New York Times* [mfm] 1962+ and [Columbia] *State* [mfm] 1962+. Its collections also contain *Chemical Abstracts* 1960+.

Collegian—(issued eight times per year) 1920+
South Carolina State College publication.

Orangeburg County Free Library
V 27,132   R 2,162   SC 1,188   CP 36
Holdings contain *War of the Rebellion* and 25 manuscripts re local history and regional genealogy.

Orangeburg County Historical Society
Collection is currently divided between County Treasurer's office, Southern National Bank vault, and the Old Dixie Club Library building; however plans are underway to erect a society building complete with fireproof vault. When completed, all materials will be deposited there. Materials include numerous maps and pictures re the Orangeburg area, some 250 books, Minutes of the Road Commissioners of Orangeburg Parish (1824–68), records of early 19th-cent. equity cases for Orangeburg District, and some papers and documents of A. S. Salley. D. Marchant Culler, a member of the Society, is currently working on a history of Orangeburg District to 1870 supplementing Salley's published works.

Orangeburg Regional Hospital, Medical Library
V 1,500   CP 25

Orangeburg Times & Democrat—D [mfm] 1878+
Micro Photo   MFMR

South Carolina State College Library
V 66,416   R 10,000   SC 200   CP 50   MCR   MFMR   PCE   US GOVT DOC
Collection includes the personal library [100v] and some papers of Thomas E. Miller, first president (1896–1911), some 1,200 vols. on Negro life and history, a vertical file of material on college activities, an extensive mfm file of periodicals, and these newspapers on mfm: *New York Times* 1939+ and *Orangeburg Times & Democrat* 1953+.

South Carolina State College, Law School Library
V 21,000   CP 50

Southern Methodist Junior College Library
V 5,100   R 1,000   CP 180
Collections include files of these newspapers 1961+: *State, News & Courier, Orangeburg Times & Democrat,* and the *Spartanburg Herald.*

PAGELAND

Pageland Journal—W 1911+

South Carolina Farmer—M 1945+

PARRIS ISLAND

United States Marine Corps Recruit Depot Library
  V 18,000   R 500   SC 100   CP 85
Collection includes special material re Marine Corps history and files of these publications: *Boot* (depot weekly) 1952+, *Leatherneck* 1951+, and *Marine Corps Gazette* 1946+.

PENDLETON

Tri-County Technical Education Center Library
  V 300
Library is in process of development.

PICKENS

Pickens County Historical Society

A small collection of relics, curios, and a few documents is housed in the local courthouse. Among these items are several letters written by General Andrew Pickens.

Pickens Sentinel—W 1930+

PIEDMONT

Saluda Valley Record—W 1962+

RIDGELAND

Jasper County News—W 1957+

ROCK HILL

Anthology—A 1964+
Student literary publication, Winthrop College.

Carolina Camellia Bulletin—(issued three times per year) 1959+

Carolina Camellias—(issued three times per year) 1949+

Publication of the Camellia Society of North and South Carolina, Georgia, and Virginia.

Celanese Fibers Company Library
   V 1,200   CP 25

This specialized collection contains these periodicals:

Analyst 1960+
Analytical Abstracts 1954+
Analytical Chemistry 1947+
Analytical Chimica Acta 1947+
Chemical Abstracts 1945+
Industrial & Engineering Chemistry 1946+

This company maintains a larger research center and library in nearby Charlotte, N. C. [V 3,300   CP 145   MFMR   MRP   PCE]. Its periodical files include:

American Chemical Society Journal 1924+
Chemical Abstracts 1935+
Industrial & Engineering Chemistry 1941+
Journal of the Society of Dyers & Colourists (1940–44) 1946+
Journal of the Textile Institute 1946+
Textile Organon 1933+

Clinton Junior College Library
   V 7,000   R 600   CP 25

Friendship Junior College Library
   V 12,000   R 200   CP 65

Files include some material on history of the College. Library is receiving and retaining (1961+) these newspapers: *Afro-American* [Baltimore], *Charlotte Observer, New York Times,* and the *Pittsburgh Courier.*

Johnsonian—W (except summer) 1923+

Winthrop College publication.

Rock Hill Evening Herald—D [mfm] 1880+
   Micro Photo MFMR

Also has these local newspapers on mfm:

Catawba Index (1897)
Rock Hill Evening Journal 1901–4
Rock Hill Record 1904–30
Rock Hill Weekly Sun (1897)
Yorkville Enquirer 1925–28

Rock Hill Public Library

   V 47,963   R 4,879   SC 2,186   CP 143   MFMR   PCE

This library has an outstanding collection of materials re Catawba Indians consisting of manuscripts, chronological and subject bibliographies, mfm material, newspaper clippings, maps, and correspondence. The collection is cited in the bibliography of W. C. Sturtevant, ethnologist of the Smithsonian Institution. The library also has a DAR cabinet and an extensive indexed clipping file on state and local history (c. 15,000 items). The following newspaper files are on mfm:

Catawba Index (1897)
Pinckney Whig (1833)
Rock Hill Evening Herald 1880–1914, 1955+
Rock Hill Journal 1901–4
Rock Hill Record 1904–10 (1915–23)
Yorkville Enquirer (1855–99) 1925–28
Yorkville Pioneer 1823–24

Winthrop Alumnae Magazine—Q 1962+

Winthrop College publication.

Winthrop College Library

   V 190,000   R 5,000   SC 2,500   CP 900   MCR   MFMR   PCE
   US GOVT DOC

Holdings include data on the history of the college and papers of David B. Johnson (1856–1928), founder of the institution and its first president 1886–1928; Draper Manuscripts [135 reels mfm]; selected 19th-cent. SC census schedules 1850–80 [22 reels mfm]; Records of the British Public Record Office re SC 1710–82 (indexed) [6 reels mfm]; Facts on Film 1954+ [68+ reels mfm]; documentary of John F. Kennedy's assassination [11 reels mfm]; and the files of these newspapers:

Charleston Courier [mfm] 1803–73
[Charleston] *News & Courier* [mfm] 1873–99, 1941+
Charleston Gazette [mfm] 1778–80
Gazette of the State of South Carolina [mfm] 1777–80

[London] *Times Education Supplement* [mfm] 1956+
[London] *Times Literary Supplement* 1958+
New York Times 1934, 1936–52, [mfm] 1952+
Orangeburg Times & Democrat 1948–55, [mfm] 1956+
Rock Hill Evening Herald 1946–55, [mfm] 1952+
Royal Gazette of the State of South Carolina [mfm] 1777–80
Royal South Carolina Gazette [mfm] 1780–82
South Carolina and American General Gazette [mfm] 1764–81
South Carolina Gazette [mfm] 1732–75
South Carolina Gazette and Country Journal [mfm] 1765–75
Wall Street Journal [mfm] 1965+
Yorkville Enquirer [mfm] 1858–67

York County Technical Education Center Library

Library is in process of development.

ST. GEORGE

Dorchester County Library

V 15,000   R 311   SC 250   CP 5

Dorchester Eagle-Record—W (1928–34) 1934+

Also has files of the *Summerville Journal* (1924–25)

ST. MATTHEWS

Calhoun County Historical Commission
MFMR

Extensive material on local history is housed in the Calhoun County Library. This collection includes cemetery records, family Bible records, some SC material, miscellaneous 19th-cent. newspapers, and genealogical data compiled by Mrs. F. C. Cain and continued by Mrs. Herbert Ulmer. Microfilm material includes the 1850 Census of Orangeburg District, records of the Clerk of Courts and Judge of Probate of Calhoun County 1908+, and sermons of Rev. Paul Turquand, first priest of St. Matthews Parish (1766–86). Files also contain back issues of the *Calhoun Times* 1938+. Among the manuscripts are:

Baker Family Records and Deeds [100]. 1730–1850.
Hamden Hall Plantation Manuscripts [70]. Records of the Thomson-Heatly families. 1730–1860.

Houser, David (1798–1876) [1,000]. Letters, account books, and family papers of the last senator from St. Matthews Parish. 1800–90.

Keitt, Lawrence M. (1824–64) [250]. Manuscripts, clippings, relics re the career of this fire-eating Congressman and CW leader. 1840–65.

Calhoun County Public Library
V 23,527   R 389   SC 566   CP 31

Calhoun Times—W 1920+

SALUDA

County Sentinel—W 1954

Also prints the *Saluda Standard,* but retains no files.

Saluda Standard—W

Retains random back files.

SENECA

Journal & Tribune—W (1905–48) 1949+

SOCIETY HILL

Society Hill Library
V 3,000

Collection includes some 1,500 vols. purchased in 1822 by the Society Hill Library Society. These are mainly encyclopedias and 18th-cent. works on travel and biography. There are also random files of early 19th-cent. periodicals.

SPARTANBURG

Beaumonte—M 1942+

House organ of Beaumont Mills.

Concept—Q 1893+

Converse College literary publication.

171

Conversationalist—(semimonthly except summer) 1924+
Converse College publication.

Converse College Library
   V 68,000   R 4,000   CP 200   MCR   MFMR
Holdings include some 7,000 musical scores, the Louise Haskell
Daly Collection of poetry and art books [200v], the A. B. Taylor
Collection of Prize Books awarded to scholars at British schools
[1,250v], files of the *Manchester Guardian Weekly* 1947+, a reprint
of the *American Weekly Mercury* 1719–23, and mfm files of the
Carolina Spartan 1849–93 and the *Charleston* [*Daily*] *Courier*
1852–73.

Deering Milliken Research Corporation Library
   V 3,000   CP 175   MFMR   PCE
The technical-reference holdings of this library include the complete catalog and shelf list [21v] of the resources of the Institute
of Textile Technology, Charlottesville, Va. This library is a member
of the Atlanta-Athens Catalog and has access to the holdings of
other members. Although materials do not circulate, the library
is open to the public.

Guide & Textile Tribune—W 1948+

Old Gold and Black—W (except summer) 1915+
Wofford College publication.

South Carolina County Information Digest and Directory—A 1960+
Published by the South Carolina Association of County Roads.

South Carolina Librarian—M 1954+

Spartan Shield—M 1945+
House organ of Spartan Mills.

Spartan Weekly—W 1965+

Spartanburg County Library

V 110,334   R 2,000   SC 1,500   CP 140   MFMR   MRP   PCE
CMPC

Collection includes a few local manuscripts, DAR lineage books, and a SC room which has *War of the Rebellion*, numerous church histories, and other local data. The library maintains back files of these newspapers: *Carolina Spartan* (1849–76), [Columbia] *State* 1960+, *Spartanburg Herald* (1900–29) 1930+, and *Spartanburg Journal* (1915–21) 1960+.

Spartanburg County Historical Association Museum

Collection contains numerous artifacts and a few documents re local history.

Spartanburg County Technical Education Center Library

V 500   CP 30

Library is in process of development.

Spartanburg General Hospital, Medical Library

V 423   CP 82   PCE

Library has some 425 tapes of medical lectures [Audio-Visual]. Also back files of pertinent magazines can be obtained through Medical Library Association Exchange.

Spartanburg General Hospital, School of Nursing Library

V 1,400   CP 30

Spartanburg Herald—D (1905–10) 1911+, [mfm] 1950+

Micro Photo   MFMR

Spartanburg Journal—D (1912) 1913+, [mfm] 1950+

Micro Photo   MFMR

Spartanburg Junior College Library

V 10,992   R 625   CP 78

Startex Prints—M 1945+

House organ of Spartan Mills.

WSPA News—M 1956+

Published by Station WSPA.

Wofford College Library

V 75,000   R 3,000   CP 400   MCR   MFMR   MRP   PCE

Holdings include material on college history; private library of Dr. James H. Carlisle (third president), 1875–1902; and these mfm files:

Carolina Spartan (1837–93)
Charleston Courier 1803–73
Charleston Gazette 1778–80
Charleston Mercury (1860–65)
[Charleston] *News & Courier* 1873–96
Daily Advocate [Methodist Episcopal Church, South] (1882–1956)
Daily National Intelligencer (1859)
Edgefield Advertiser 1836–1901
Gazette of the State of South Carolina 1777–80
Greenville Enterprise [& *Mountaineer*] 1871–80
Greenville Republican & Mountaineer 1826–50
New York Times 1851+
Records of the Charleston Board of Police 1780–82
[Richmond, Va.] *Enquirer* (1859)
Royal [*South Carolina*] *Gazette* 1781–82
South Carolina & American General Gazette 1764–81
South Carolina Census Records (1800–60)
South Carolina Gazette 1732–75
South Carolina Gazette & Country Journal 1765–75
Southern Patriot [Greenville] 1851–53
Spartanburg Express (1857)
Spartanburg Herald 1950+
Spartanburg Journal 1950+

Reference files contain *Biological Abstracts* 1949+. This library houses the collection of the Historical Society of the South Carolina Conference of the Methodist Church. These materials include minutes, books, church records, letters, receipts, church ledgers, and manuscripts 1795+.

STATE PARK

Palmetto State Hospital Library

V 5,000   CP 10

Socasan Piper—M 1926+

Publication of patients at South Carolina Sanitorium.

South Carolina Sanitorium Library
  V 9,000   CP 53

SUMMERVILLE

Summerville Scene—W 1946+

Timrod Library
  V 18,000   R 6,000   SC 300   CP 6

SUMTER

Carnegie Public Library
  V 50,526   R 700   SC 150   CP 57
Although this library has no special collections, it has unusual holdings in mental health, abnormal psychology, philosophy, painting, and fine arts.

Clemson University at Sumter Library
  V 1,000   R 50   CP 115   MFMR
A new library which opened in 1966.

Morris College Library
  V 8,000   R 500   CP 85
Collection includes some 200 vols. on Negro life and *Chemical Abstracts* 1954+.

Shaw Air Force Base Library
  V 22,000   R 200   CP 287
This library has extensive collections in aerial photography, aircraft maintenance, air force history (especially World War II and the Korean war), and materials re escape, survival, and evasion of the enemy.

Sumter Area Technical Education Center Library
  V 300
Library is in process of development.

Sumter Item—D 1922+, [mfm] 1960+
  Micro Photo   MFMR

Tuomey Hospital, School of Nursing Library
V 938   CP 11
The files of this reference library include *Nursing Outlook* 1956–62.

TIGERVILLE

North Greenville Junior College Library
V 13,000   R 1,000   CP 140
Collection includes some 700 vols. from the private library of William Arthur Sheppard, SC author.

TIMMONSVILLE

Timmonsville Weekly—W 1964+

UNA

Una News Review—W 1929+

UNION

Carnegie Free Library
V 8,410   R 123   CP 53
Library has records of Union County wills (1777–1848), *New York Times* 1960+, and considerable uncatalogued material belonging to the local historical society.

Union County Free Library
V 9,878   CP 8

Union County Historical Society
Some collected materials re local history can be found in the Clerk of Court's office.

Union Daily Times—D (1850–1935) 1936+

Union Regional Campus (USC) Library
V 2,700   R 550   SC 93   CP 49

WALHALLA

Keowee Courier—(1849–99) 1900+

Oconee County Library
V 40,000   R 400   SC 490   CP 30   PCE
Library currently receives eight local, state, and national newspapers, and back files are maintained from six months to one year.

WALTERBORO

Colleton County Memorial Library
V 23,000   R 1,134   SC 400   CP 44   MFMR   CMPC
Collection includes 5,400 vols. of the Walterboro Library Society (founded in 1820) which merged with the county system in 1955. Among these books are some 18th- and 19th-cent. imprints, records of the Court of Sessions held at Jacksonborough (1816–22), and random volumes of *Littell's, Edinburgh Review,* and other 19th-cent. periodicals. The library also has the [Walterboro] *Press & Standard* [mfm] 1873+.

Press & Standard—W (1895–1904) 1905+, [mfm] 1905+
    Mann   MFMR

WARE SHOALS

Community Foundation Library
V 13,863   R 310   SC 20   CP 25
This Library, owned by the Riegel Textile Corporation, is operated for the benefit of employees and the general public. It cooperates with the Greenwood County Library and the South Carolina State Library Board. Back files of most periodicals are maintained for six years.

Ware Shoals Life—W (1946–47) 1947+

WEST COLUMBIA

West Columbia-Cayce Journal—W 1956+

WESTMINSTER

Westminster News—W 1952+

WHITMIRE

Whitmire News—W 1957+

WILLIAMSTON

Williamston Journal—W 1955+

WILLISTON

Williston Way—W 1961+

Printed by the *Barnwell People-Sentinel.*

WINNSBORO

Fairfield County Courthouse, Law Library
V 240

Fairfield County Library
V 21,249   R 265   SC 55   CP 25

Collection includes material re local history, a DAR file, and copies of the Winnsboro *News & Herald* 1943–49.

News & Herald—W (1920–42) 1943+

US Rubber Company, Textile Division Development Center Library
V 1,200   CP 25

A reference library of materials in fields of chemistry, textiles, dyeing, mechanical engineering, water pollution, statistics, and industrial management. Library also has considerable information from fiber manufacturers. Holdings include the *Index of Patents* [annual] 1946+, *Journal of the Society of Dyers & Colourists* 1956+, and the *American Dyestuff Reporter* 1943+.

WOODRUFF

Woodruff News—W 1950+

YEMASSEE

Hampton County Democrat—W 1963+

YORK

Reminder—M (except summer) 1951+
Published by the Episcopal Church Home for Children.

South Carolina Turkey News—Q 1953+
Published by the South Carolina Turkey Federation.

Yorkville Enquirer—W 1928+, [mfm] 1963+
Mann

York Township Free Library
V 4,166   SC 100   CP 10

OUT-OF-STATE PUBLICATIONS RE SOUTH CAROLINA

ASHEVILLE, N. C.

Climatological Data—M 1897+
Material re SC published by the US Department of Commerce.

ATLANTA, GA.

South Carolina Farm and Ranch—M 1964+

CHARLOTTE, N. C.

Pica—M 1961+
Published by the Printing Industry of the Carolinas.

Semaphore—M 1946+
Publication of Piedmont & Northern Railway.

Southern Hospitals—M 1934+

Southern Textile News—W 1944+

EPES, ALA.

South Carolina Genealogical Register—Q 1963+

RALEIGH, N. C.

Carolina Cooperator—M 1921+

Formerly the *Carolina Cotton Grower*. Contains news of rural life in North and South Carolina.

SALISBURY, N. C.

Carolina Kiwanian—M 1921+

Kiwanis magazine for North and South Carolina.

PART TWO

Periodical Files Begun prior to 1941

SYMBOLS AND ABBREVIATIONS
USED IN PART TWO

( )	Incomplete file for the years indicated.
+	Publications currently being received.
[mfm]	Microfilm copies
[mc]	Microcard copies
Sc	South Carolina State Library, Columbia
ScA	South Carolina Archives Department, Columbia
ScABBE	Aiken-Bamberg-Barnwell-Edgefield Regional Library, Aiken [main office]
ScAHJ	Allendale-Hampton-Jasper Regional Library, Allendale [main office]
ScAikSr	Technical Information Service Library, Savannah River Laboratory, Aiken
ScBatL	Lexington County Circulating Library, Batesburg
ScBenM	Marlboro County Public Library, Bennettsville
ScC	Charleston Library Society, Charleston
ScCamDu	May Plant Technical Library [Du Pont], Camden
ScCC	College of Charleston, Charleston
ScCCit	The Citadel, Charleston
ScCDhs	Dalcho Historical Society, Charleston
ScCenW	Central Wesleyan Junior College, Central
ScChar	Charleston County Library, Charleston
ScChes	Chester County Free Library, Chester
ScCHis	South Carolina Historical Society, Charleston
ScCHu	Huguenot Society of South Carolina, Charleston
ScCleSl	Saco-Lowell Research and Development Center, Clemson

183

ScCleU	Clemson University, Clemson
ScClP	Presbyterian College, Clinton
ScCM	South Carolina Medical College, Charleston
ScCMus	Charleston Museum, Charleston
ScCoAl	Allen University, Columbia
ScCoBe	Benedict College, Columbia
ScCoBi	Columbia Bible College, Columbia
ScCoCo	Columbia College, Columbia
ScCoHo	Medical-Nursing Library, Columbia Hospital, Columbia
ScConH	Horry County Memorial Library, Conway
ScCoR	Richland County Public Library, Columbia
ScCoSn	Student Nursing Education Library, South Carolina State Hospital, Columbia
ScCoT	Lutheran Theological Southern Seminary, Columbia
ScCoWsh	Medical Professional Library, William S. Hall Psychiatric Institute, Columbia
ScCSf	St. Francis Xavier Hospital School of Nursing, Charleston
ScDarl	Darlington Public Library, Darlington
ScDenV	Voorhees Junior College, Denmark
ScDuCy	Cyrovac Division, W. R. Grace & Company, Duncan
ScDwErs	Erskine College, Due West
ScDwErs-T	Erskine Theological Seminary, Due West
ScFlor	Florence Public Library, Florence
ScGaLi	Limestone College, Gaffney
ScGBj	Bob Jones University, Greenville
ScGeor	Georgetown County Memorial Library, Georgetown
ScGF	Furman University, Greenville
ScGGh	Greenville General Hospital, Greenville
ScGGh-N	School of Nursing, Greenville General Hospital, Greenville

184

ScGrev	Greenville County Library, Greenville
ScGrew	Greenwood City-County Library, Greenwood
ScGwLa	Lander College, Greenwood
ScHart	Hartsville Township Memorial Library, Hartsville
ScHCok	Coker College, Hartsville
ScKing	Kingstree Carnegie Library, Kingstree
ScLaD	Dillon County Library, Latta
ScLanc	Lancaster County Library, Lancaster
ScLaur	Laurens County Library, Laurens
ScMar	Marion Public Library, Marion
ScMoB	Berkeley County Library, Moncks Corner
ScMyB	Chapin Memorial Library, Myrtle Beach
ScNcWv	West Virginia Pulp and Paper Company, North Charleston
ScNewb	Newberry College, Newberry
ScOran	Orangeburg County Free Library, Orangeburg
ScOrCl	Claflin College, Orangeburg
ScOrRh	Robert Lide Medical Library, Orangeburg Regional Hospital, Orangeburg
ScOrSc	South Carolina State College, Orangeburg
ScRhCel	Celanese Fibers Company, Rock Hill
ScRhP	Rock Hill Public Library, Rock Hill
ScRhW	Winthrop College, Rock Hill
Sc-SC	South Carolina Supreme Court Library, Columbia
ScSoH	Society Hill Library, Society Hill
ScSpar	Spartanburg Public Library, Spartanburg
ScSpC	Converse College, Spartanburg
ScSpDm	Deering-Milliken Research Corporation, Spartanburg
ScSpGh-N	School of Nursing, Spartanburg General Hospital, Spartanburg
ScSpJr	Spartanburg Junior College, Spartanburg

ScSpW	Wofford College, Spartanburg
ScStM	Calhoun County Public Library, St. Matthews
ScStpSan	South Carolina Sanitorium, State Park
ScSum	Carnegie Free Library, Sumter
ScSumM	Morris College, Sumter
ScSumT	Toumey Hospital, Sumter
ScTiNg	North Greenville Junior College, Tigerville
ScU	University of South Carolina, Columbia
ScU-Lanc	Lancaster Center, University of South Carolina, Lancaster
ScWaC	Colleton County Memorial Library, Walterboro
ScWinF	Fairfield County Library, Winnsboro
ScWinR	Textile Division Development Center, U. S. Rubber Company, Winnsboro
ScWs	Community Free Library, Ware Shoals
ScYork	York Township Library, York

SAMPLE ENTRIES

Ayshire Digest. ScCleU 1940+

[This indicates that the Clemson University Library has a complete file of this publication beginning in 1940 and continuing to the present.]

Canadian Historical Review. ScGF (1923–32); ScU 1920+

[The Furman University Library has an incomplete file of this Review from 1923 to 1932; the University of South Carolina Library has a complete file beginning in 1920 and continuing to the present.]

Ladies Port Folio. ScU [mfm] (1820)

[The University of South Carolina Library has an incomplete file of this publication for the year 1820 on microfilm.]

Ladies Repository. ScHCok (1852–70); ScU 1841, also [mfm] 1841–50

[Coker College Library has an incomplete file from 1852 to 1870; the University of South Carolina has a complete file for the year 1841 and also has microfilm files dating from 1841 to 1850.]

Botanical Abstracts. ScCleU 1875+, some files on mc; ScU 1918–26

[Clemson University Library has these Abstracts from 1875 to the present and is currently receiving them, but some files are on microcard; the University of South Carolina Library has a file from 1918 to 1926.]

ALPHABETIC LIST OF PERIODICAL TITLES

A

Abbeville Medical Society Proceedings. ScCM 1880

Abolition Intelligencer and Missionary Magazine. ScU [mfm] 1822–23

Abolitionist, or Record of the New England Anti-Slavery Society. ScU [mfm] 1833

Abstracts of Bacteriology [Biological Abstracts]. ScCM 1917–25; ScCleU 1922–25

Academician. ScU [mfm] 1818–20

Académie de Littérature et Beaux-Arts, Mémoires. ScC 1798–1803

Académie des Sciences, Mémoires des Sciences Mathématiques et Physiques. ScC 1798–1801

Académie des Sciences, Morales et Politiques, Mémoires. ScC 1798–1803

Académie des Sciences, Paris, Comptes-Rendus Hebdomadaires des Séances. ScCleU 1835+; ScCM 1836–1933 (1938–44) 1947+; ScGF [mc] 1835–80; ScU 1835–80 (1884) 1900–47 (1949) 1951+

Académie des Sciences, Paris, Mémoires. ScU (1813–62)

Académie Royale des Inscriptions et Belles Lettres, Histoire et Mémoires. ScC 1729–93

Academy. ScSpW (1896–97)

Academy of Natural Sciences of Philadelphia, Journal. ScC (1817–99); ScU 1817–42, 1847–1918

Academy of Natural Sciences of Philadelphia, Monographs. ScU 1935+

Academy of Natural Sciences of Philadelphia, Proceedings. ScCleU 1841+; ScU 1841–1913

Academy of Political Science, Proceedings. ScCC 1941–52; ScCCit (1930+); ScCleU 1922+; ScGF 1922+; ScRhW 1932+; ScSpW 1917–19, 1937+; ScU 1917–36.

Accent. ScU 1940–59

Accountants Digest. ScU 1935+

Accounting Review. ScU 1926+

189

Acoustical Society of America, Journal. ScCCit (1936+); ScCleU 1929+; ScU 1929+

Acta Arithmetica. ScU 1936–39

Acta Biologica Belgica. ScCM 1941–43

Acta Chirurgica Scandinavica. ScCM (1919–52) 1953+

Acta Dermato-Venereologica. ScCM 1937–39

Acta Mathematica. ScU 1882+

Acta Medica Scandinavica. ScCM (1921–37) 1938+

Acta Ophthalmologica. ScCM (1925+)

Acta Paediatrica. ScCM (1930–50) 1951+

Acta Pathologica et Microbiologica Scandinavica. ScCM (1924–52) 1953+, also *Supplements*

Acta Physiologica Scandinavica. ScCM 1940+, also *Supplements*

Acta Psychiatrica et Neurologica Scandinavica. ScCM (1927–54) 1955+

Acta Radiologica. ScCM (1921–39) 1940+

Acta Unio Internationalis contra Cancrum. ScCM (1937) 1952+

Addisonia. ScCleU 1916+

Adult Education Bulletin. ScRhW 1940–50

Advanced Management. ScCleU 1939+

Adventurer. ScC 1792

Adviser. ScU (1809–14), also [mfm] 1809–15

Advisory Leaflet [London]. ScCleU (1926+)

Advocate of Peace and the Christian Patriot. ScU [mfm] 1828–29

Advocate of Peace and Universal Brotherhood. ScU [mfm] 1837–50

Advocate of Science. ScU [mfm] 1833–34

Advocate of Science and Annals of Natural History. ScU [mfm] 1834–35

Aero Digest. ScGrev (1939–44); ScU 1932–56

Aeronaut. ScU [mfm] 1816–22

Aesculapian. ScCM 1908–10

Aesculapian Register. ScU [mfm] (1824)

African Intelligencer. ScU [mfm] (1820)

African Repository. ScU [mfm] 1825–50

African Repository and Colonial Journal. ScU [mfm] (1825)

Agrarian. ScCleU 1938–58, 1960+

Agricultural Education. ScCleU (1929+)

Agricultural Education Bulletin of Clemson College. ScCleU 1925–39

Agricultural Engineering. ScCleU 1920+

Agricultural Gazette of New South Wales. ScCleU 1913+
Agricultural History. ScCleU 1927+; ScSpC 1939–51; ScU 1927+
Agricultural Journal of India. ScCleU (1907–30)
Agricultural Journal of the Union of South Africa. ScCleU 1912–14
Agricultural Leaders Digest. ScCleU 1935–63
Agricultural Museum. ScU [mfm] 1810–12
Agricultural News Letter. ScCleU 1936+; ScU 1936–48
Agriculture Journal of the British Ministry of Agriculture. ScCleU 1939+
Ainsworth's Magazine. ScU [mfm] 1842–54
Air Facts. ScCC 1940–47
Akademie der Wissenschaften, Munich, Mathematisch-Naturwissenschaftliche Abteilung, Abhandlungen. ScU 1929+
Akademie der Wissenschaften, Munich, Mathematisch-Naturwissenschaftliche Abteilung, Sitzungsberichte. ScU 1871+
Akademiia Nauk S.S.S.R., Leningrad, Commentarii Academiae Scientiarum Imperialis Petrolpolitanae. ScU 1726–34
Akademiia Nauk S.S.S.R., Leningrad, Comptes Rendus (Doklady) International Edition, New Series. ScU 1933+
Akademiia Nauk S.S.S.R., Leningrad, Matematicheskii Institut Imeni V. A. Steklova, Trudy. ScU 1932+
Alabama Academy of Sciences, Journal. ScU 1924+
Alabama Geological Survey Bulletin. ScCleU 1886+
Alabama Geological Survey, Monographs. ScCleU (1883–1928)
Alabama Medical Association, Journal. ScCM (1931) 1933+
Albany Law Journal. ScU 1870–81
Albany Medical Annals. ScCM (1906–37)
Albion; or British, Colonial, and Foreign Weekly Gazette. ScU [mfm] 1822–25
All-Pets Magazine. ScU (1934–35)
Allis Chalmers Electrical Review. ScU 1936+
Almoner, a Periodical Religious Publication. ScU [mfm] (1815)
Amaranth, or Masonic Garland. ScU [mfm] 1828–29
Amerasia. ScCleU 1937–47; ScU 1937–47
America [Asociacion de Escritores y Artistas Americanos]. ScU (1939–45)
American Academy of Arts and Sciences, Memoirs. ScCleU 1908–31; ScU (1780–1815), also [mfm] 1780–1850
American Academy of Medicine, Bulletin. ScCM (1910–14)

American Academy of Ophthalmology and Oto-Laryngology, Transactions. ScCM 1906+; ScGGh (1911–31) 1944+

American Academy of Political and Social Science, Annals. ScCCit (1908+); ScCleU 1890+; ScGBj 1938+; ScGF 1908+; ScGrev 1919+; ScHCok (1931–39) 1940+; ScNewb 1911+; ScOrSc 1939+; ScRhW 1892+; ScSpC (1929–31) 1946+; ScSpW 1905+; ScU 1890+

American Agriculturalist. ScCleU (1841–1906) 1952+; ScU [mfm] 1842–50

American Almanac and Repository of Useful Knowledge. ScU 1830–54

American Annals of Education. ScU [mfm] 1826–39

American Annual Register. ScU 1825–32

American Anthropological Association, Memoirs. ScU (1912) 1937+

American Anthropologist. ScCMus 1900–34; ScU 1899+

American Antiquarian Society, Proceedings. ScCHis 1900+; ScU 1887+

American Antiquity. ScSpW 1935–47; ScU 1935+

American Apollo. ScU [mfm] 1792–94

American Architect [Architectural Record]. ScA 1931+; ScC 1933–38; ScCleU 1907, 1921–25, 1929–37; ScU 1928–38

American Archivist. ScA 1938+; ScCC 1938–51; ScCleU 1938+

American Art Annual. ScCleU (1898–1948)

American Artisan. ScU (1920–53)

American Artist. ScHCok 1940+; ScU 1940+

American Association for the Advancement of Science, Proceedings. ScC (1850–99); ScCleU 1848–1948; ScCM (1884–1934); ScCMus (1850–1925); ScU 1848–73, 1887–1915 (1921+)

American Association of Collegiate Registrars, Bulletin and Journal [College and University]. ScCleU 1930+; ScU 1930+

American Association of Colleges of Pharmacy, Proceedings. ScCM 1925–35; ScU 1900–35

American Association of Genito–Urinary Surgeons, Transactions. ScCM (1907–35) 1962+

American Association of Medical Milk Commissioners, Proceedings. ScCleU 1917–30

American Association of Museums, Museum News. ScCMus 1924+, library also has *Museum Work* 1918–26

American Association of Obstetricians and Gynecologists, Transactions. ScCM (1902–27) 1931+

American Association of Petroleum Geologists, Bulletin. ScSpW 1923+; ScU 1917+

American Association of Psychiatric Social Workers Newsletter [Journal of Psychiatric Social Work]. ScU 1940–55

American Association of School Administrators, Official Report. ScCleU (1904–32) 1935+; ScU (1874+)

American Association of School Administrators, Yearbook. ScCleU 1925–60; ScU 1923–60

American Association of State Highway Officials, Standard Specifications for Highway Materials. ScU (1935–47)

American Association of Teachers Colleges, Yearbook. ScU 1925–31

American Association of Textile Chemists and Colorists, Yearbook. ScCleU 1925–46

American Association of University Professors, Bulletin. ScCCit 1941+; ScCleU 1915+; ScGF 1919+; ScRhW 1931+; ScU 1915+

American Association of University Women, Journal. ScCleU 1930+; ScGF 1928+; ScHCok 1929+; ScRhW 1925+; ScSpC (1928–57); ScU 1923+

American Athenaeum, a Repository of Belles Lettres, Science, and the Arts. ScU [mfm] 1825–26

American Aviation [Airlift]. ScCleU 1940+

American Bankers' Association of New York, Proceedings. ScU (1907–13)

American Baptist Messenger and Missionary Intelligencer. ScU 1817–18, also [mfm] 1817–25

American Bar Association, Journal. ScU 1915+

American Bee Journal. ScCleU 1915, 1917+

American Berkshire Association, Record. ScCleU 1915–19

American Biology Teacher. ScChar (1930–50)

American Breeders Magazine. ScU 1910–13

American Builder. ScGrev 1938+

American Butter [Dairy] Review. ScCleU 1940+

American Cattle Producer. ScCleU 1939+

American Ceramic Society, Bulletin. ScCleU 1922+, library also has *Journal* and *Abstracts* 1918+ and *Transactions* 1899–1917

American Chemical Journal. ScCleU 1879+; ScU 1879–1913

American Chemical Society, Journal. ScCamDu 1919+; ScCC (1941–44) 1945+; ScCCit 1879+; ScCleU 1879+; ScClP 1916+; ScCM (1879–1903) 1906+; ScGaLi 1929+; ScGF 1879+; ScOrSc 1900+; ScRhCel 1928+; ScRhW 1919+; ScSpC 1926+; ScSpDm 1910+; ScSpW 1891–1903, 1911–21, 1926+; ScU 1879+

American Chemical Society, Proceedings. ScU (1876–78) 1879+
American Child. ScU 1919–22, 1927+
American Childhood. ScRhW 1926–58
American Cinematographer. ScCCit 1940–57
American City. ScChar 1932+; ScCCit 1927–38, 1955+; ScGrev (1919+); ScRhW 1929+; ScU 1912+
American Civil Liberties Union, Report. ScU (1940+)
American Climatological Association, Proceedings. ScCM (1897–1948) 1957+
American Collector. ScCMus 1939–45
American College of Dentists, Journal. ScCM 1934–52, 1955
American College of Surgeons, Bulletin. ScCM 1918+
American Concrete Institute Proceedings [Journal]. ScU (1930–33) 1937+
American Conference of Pharmaceutical Faculties, Proceedings. ScCM (1903–23)
American Cookery. ScRhW 1932–47
American Cooperation. ScCleU 1926+
American Cotton Grower. ScCleU (1935–40)
American Council of Learned Societies Devoted to Humanistic Studies, Bulletin. ScU (1920+)
American Country Life Association, Proceedings. ScCleU 1919+; ScU (1919–46)
American [Creamery and] Produce Review. ScCleU 1927+
American Critic and General Review. ScU [mfm] (1820)
American Cultivator. ScU [mfm] 1839–50
American Dental Association, Journal. ScCM (1917–18) 1921+
American Dietetic Association, Journal. ScCM (1931–51) 1953+; ScRhW (1932+)
American Druggist. ScCM 1927+; ScU 1925–26, 1928+
American Eagle Magazine. ScU [mfm] (1847)
American Eclectic. ScGF 1842; ScSpW 1841–42; ScU [mfm] 1841–42
American Economic Association, Publications. ScU 1886–1904
American Economic Review. ScCCit 1937–41, 1960+; ScCleU 1911+; ScClP 1937–41, 1960+; ScCoBe 1924+; ScGF 1915, 1920+; ScNewb 1940+; ScRhW 1911+; ScSpC 1937–61; ScSpW 1911+; ScU 1911+
American Education Association, Quarterly Journal. ScU [mfm] 1843–46

American Educational Digest. ScRhW 1923–28

American Egg and Poultry Review [Poultry Meat]. ScCleU 1940+

American Electric Railway Association, Proceedings. ScCleU 1926–31

American Electrician Journal [Electrical World]. ScCleU 1897–1904; ScU 1896–98

American Electrochemical Society, Transactions. ScCleU 1902–32; ScU 1902–30

American Entomological Society, Memoirs. ScCleU 1916+

American Entomological Society, Transactions. ScCMus 1867–1905; ScCleU 1872+

American Engineer and Railroad Journal. ScCleU 1893–1902

American Ethnological Society, Monographs. ScU (1940+)

American Expositor. ScU [mfm] (1950)

American Farm Equipment. ScCleU (1924) 1925–32

American Farmer. ScC (1819–27); ScCCit (1872–73); ScCMus 1821–22; ScU (1819–32) 1856–58, also [mfm] 1819–25

American Farmers Magazine. ScU [mfm] 1848–59

American Farming. ScCleU 1919–23

American Federationist. ScRhW 1941+; ScU 1934+

American Fern Journal. ScU 1911+

American Fertilizer [Farm Chemicals]. ScCleU (1894+); ScU 1923+

American Fisheries Society, Transactions. ScCleU (1909+)

American Florist Journal. ScCleU (1912–16)

American Folklore Society, Memoirs of American Folklore. ScU (1910+)

American Forestry. ScCleU (1901–23)

American Forests [Forest Life, Forestry and Irrigation]. ScCC (1938–49); ScCleU (1904–9) 1924+; ScCMus (1900–26); ScRhW 1941–61

American Fruit Grower. ScCleU 1922+

American Genetic Association, Annual Report [Journal of Heredity]. ScCleU 1903–8; ScU 1905–12

American Geographic Society, Bulletin. ScCMus 1876–1908

American Geographical Society of New York, Bulletin. ScU 1859–1915, library also has *Special Publications* 1915+

American Geologist. ScU 1888–1905

American Geophysical Union, Transactions. ScCleU 1920+; ScU 1929+

American German Review. ScU 1934+

American Gleaner and Virginia Magazine. ScU [mfm] (1807)

American Guernsey Cattle Club, Herd Register. ScCleU 1896–1905

American Gynecological and Obstetrical Journal. ScCM 1891–1901

American Gynecological Journal. ScCM 1892–93

American Gynecological Society, Transactions. ScCM (1876–1939); ScU (1880) 1887–1922

American Heart Journal. ScCleU 1938+; ScCM 1925+; ScGGh 1936+

American Hereford Journal. ScCleU (1928+)

American Historical Review. ScA 1931+; ScC 1895+; ScCC 1909+; ScCCit 1898+; ScCHis 1902–59; ScCleU 1895+; ScClP 1928+; ScCoCo 1936+; ScDwErs 1905+; ScGaLi (1904–6) 1940+; ScGBj 1938+; ScGF 1895+; ScHCok (1929–31) 1932+; ScNewb 1940+; ScOrSc 1910+; ScRhW 1895+; ScSpC 1906+; ScSpW1900+; ScU 1895+

American Home. ScCleU 1928+; ScCoCo 1937+; ScGBj (1935–43) 1944+; ScGrev 1928+; ScGrew 1934–41; ScLaD 1930+; ScNewb 1940+; ScOran 1938–59; ScRhP 1934+; ScRhW 1928+

American Hospital Association, Bulletin. ScCM 1928–35

American Illustrated Method Magazine. ScSpW 1900–2

American Institute of Chemical Engineers, Transactions [Chemical Engineering Progress]. ScCleU 1920+; ScNcWv 1917–46; ScU 1908+

American Institute of the City of New York, Annual Report. ScU 1865–71

American Institute of the City of New York, Transactions. ScCleU (1844–71)

American Institute of Electrical Engineers, Proceedings [Electrical Engineering]. ScU 1905–30

American Institute of Electrical Engineers, Transactions. ScCleU 1893+; ScU 1885+

American Institute of Electrical Engineers, Yearbook. ScCleU 1920–28

American Institute of Mining, Metallurgical and Petroleum Engineers, Transactions. ScCCit (1899–1933) 1934+; ScCleU (1876+); ScU (1871+)

American Interplanetary Society Bulletin [AIAA Journal]. ScCleU 1930–32; ScU 1930–32

American Irish Historical Society, Journal. ScU (1912–15) 1919–32

American Jersey Cattle Club. ScCleU 1897–1915

Amercian Jewish Committee, Annual Report. ScU (1936+)

American Jewish History Society Publications. ScCHis (1897–1947) 1948+

American Journal. ScU (1828)

American Journal of Anatomy. ScCM 1901+

American Journal of Archaeology. ScCMus (1920–43); ScRhW 1931+; ScSpC 1941–61; ScSpW 1940+; ScU 1897+

American Journal of Botany. ScCC 1938–50; ScCleU 1914+; ScCM 1928–29; ScCMus 1914–31; ScGF 1928+; ScHCok 1927+; ScOrSc 1914+; ScU 1914+

American Journal of Cancer. ScCM 1930–40; ScGGh (1933–38)

American Journal of Clinical Pathology. ScCleU 1936+; ScCM 1931+; ScGGh 1938+

American Journal of Digestive Diseases [and Nutrition]. ScCM 1934+; ScGGh 1935+

American Journal of Diseases of Children. ScCM 1911+; ScCoHo (1930+); ScGGh (1911–14) 1924+

American Journal of Economics and Sociology. ScCleU 1941+; ScSpW 1941+; ScU 1941–56, 1963+

American Journal of Education. ScC 1826–28, 1855–56; ScU [mfm] 1855–82

American Journal of Homoeopathia. ScU [mfm] (1835)

American Journal of Homoeopathy. ScU [mfm] 1838–39, 1846–54

American Journal of Hygiene. ScCM 1921+; ScU (1921–44) 1946+

American Journal of Insanity. ScCM 1844–93, 1915; ScU 1844–94

American Journal of International Law. ScCCit 1937+; ScU 1907+

American Journal of Mathematics. ScU 1899–1910, 1917+

American Journal of Medical Sciences. ScCM 1828+; ScGGh (1906) 1911+; ScU [mfm] 1827–50

American Journal of Mental Deficiency. ScU 1941+

American Journal of Nursing. ScCM 1918+; ScCoHo 1916+; ScCoSn (1925+); ScCSf 1933+; ScGGh–N 1900+; ScSpGh 1925+; ScSumT 1936+; ScU 1900+

American Journal of Obstetrics [and Gynecology]. ScCM 1868+; ScCoHo 1930+; ScGGh 1932+

American Journal of Ophthalmology. ScCM (1886–1916) 1917+; ScCoHo 1931–32

American Journal of Orthopsychiatry. ScCM (1930–45) 1946+; ScU 1932–33, 1937+

American Journal of Orthodontics and Oral Surgery. ScCM (1932–58) 1959+

American Journal of Pathology. ScCM 1925+; ScGGh 1938+

American Journal of Pharmaceutical Education. ScCM 1937+; ScU 1937+

American Journal of Pharmacy. ScCM (1830–1906) 1907+; ScU 1928+, also [mfm] (1825–27) 1829–52

American Journal of Philology. ScSpC 1884, 1909–12; ScSpW 1885–1902; ScU 1880+

American Journal of Physical Anthropology. ScCM 1918–40, 1959+

American Journal of Physics. ScCC 1940–51; ScCCit 1940+; ScCleU 1940+; ScOrSc 1940+; ScU 1940+

American Journal of Physiology. ScCleU 1926+, some files on mc; ScCM 1898+; ScOrSc 1938+; ScU (1901–4) 1939+

American Journal of Psychiatry. ScCM 1934+; ScCoWsh 1921+; ScU 1929+

American Journal of Psychoanalysis. ScU 1941+

American Journal of Psychology. ScCCit 1935+; ScGBj 1938–57; ScGF 1887+; ScRhW 1920+; ScSpC 1927+; ScU 1887+

American Journal of Public Health. ScCleU 1918+; ScCM 1912+; ScCoHo (1931–48); ScHCok 1923–36; ScOrSc 1931+; ScRhW 1930+; ScU (1911–27) 1928+

American Journal of Public Hygiene. ScCM (1908–10)

American Journal of Religious Psychology and Education. ScU 1904–11

American Journal of Roentgenology, Radium Therapy and Nuclear Medicine. ScCM (1913–14) 1915+; ScCoHo 1930+; ScGGh (1931–38) 1939+

American Journal of Science. ScC (1819–30) 1840–59; ScCC 1939–57; ScOrSc 1940+; ScU 1818+

American Journal of Semitic Language and Literature. ScCoT [mfm] 1884–91

American Journal of Sociology. ScCC (1932–40) 1941+; ScCCit 1939+; ScCleU (1895–1916) 1917+; ScCoBe 1910+; ScCoCo (1921–40) 1941+; ScDwErs 1939+; ScGF 1923+; ScGrev 1919–32; ScHCok 1940+; ScOrCl (1927–60); ScOrSc 1901–5, 1925+; ScRhW 1918+; ScSpC (1929–47) 1948+; ScSpW 1925+; ScU 1895+

American Journal of Surgery. ScCM (1905–25) 1926+; ScGGh 1927+; ScOrRh 1937+

American Journal of Syphilis. ScCM 1917–54; ScCoHo 1930–32

American Journal of Tropical Medicine [and Hygiene]. ScCleU (1921–37) 1938+; ScCM 1921–51; ScCoHo 1931–32

American Journal of Veterinary Research. ScCleU 1940+

American Judicature Society Journal. ScU 1928+

American Jurist and Law Magazine. ScU 1843–46

American Labor Legislation Review. ScU 1911–42

American Laborer. ScU [mfm] (1842–43)

American Ladies Magazine. ScU [mfm] 1828–36

American Laryngological, Rhinological and Otological Society, Transactions. ScCM (1904+)

American Law Journal. ScU [mfm] 1808–17

American Law Review [United States Law Review]. ScU (1885–1929)

American Law School Review. ScU (1902–47)

American Legion Magazine. ScU [monthly] (1927+), [weekly] (1923–26)

American Library Association, Bulletin. ScCC 1936+; ScChar 1933+; ScCCit 1936+; ScCleU 1926+; ScCoAl 1931+; ScCoCo (1937–52) 1953+; ScGF 1907+; ScNewb 1935+; ScRhW 1926+; ScU 1907+

American Library Association, Proceedings. ScU (1899+)

American Literary Magazine. ScU 1847–49

American Literature. ScCCit 1929+; ScCleU 1929+; ScCoBe 1930+; ScCoCo (1929–39) 1939+; ScDwErs 1929+; ScGF 1929+; ScHCok 1941+; ScNewb 1939+; ScRhW 1929+; ScSpC 1929+; ScSpW 1929+; ScU 1929+; ScU-Lanc 1929+

American Lutheran Survey. ScCoT 1914–29

American Machinist. ScCleU (1902–47) 1948+; ScU 1931+

American Magazine. ScCleU (1908–56); ScClP (1908–54); ScFlor 1926–29; ScGBj 1932–56; ScGF 1906–8, 1910–14; ScGrev 1919–56; ScHCok 1905–14; ScLaD 1931–56; ScRhP 1933, 1936; ScRhW 1919–56; ScU 1905–56

American Magazine [Albany, N. Y.]. ScU [mfm] 1815–16, 1841–42

American Magazine [Boston]. ScU [mfm] 1743–46

American Magazine [Brooklyn]. ScU 1887–88

American Magazine [New York]. ScU [mfm] 1787–88

American Magazine [Philadelphia]. ScU [mfm] (1751) 1757–58, 1769

American Magazine of Art [Magazine of Art]. ScC 1931–36; ScChar 1933–36; ScCleU 1931–36; ScCMus (1910–36); ScGrev 1934–36; ScRhW 1929–36; ScU 1916–36
American Magazine of Wonders. ScU [mfm] 1809
American Masonic Register. ScU [mfm] 1820–23
American Mathematical Monthly. ScC 1938+; ScCCit (1923) 1926+; ScCleU 1894; ScHCok (1922–45) 1958+; ScRhW 1939+; ScSpC 1936+; ScSpW 1941+; ScU (1894–1901) 1914+
American Mathematical Society, Bulletin. ScCCit 1926+; ScSpW 1929+; ScRhW 1924–27, 1944+; ScU 1894+
American Mathematical Society, Transactions. ScU 1900+, also *Translations* 1929+
American Mechanics Magazine. ScU [mfm] (1825–26)
American Medical and Philosophical Register. ScU [mfm] 1810–14
American Medical Association, Bulletin. ScCM (1907–23) 1924–36
American Medical Association, Journal. ScCCit 1938+; ScCleU 1926+; ScCM 1883+; ScCoHo 1930+; ScCoWsh 1921+; ScGGh (1910–24) 1925+; ScOrRh 1940+; ScU 1928+
American Medical Association, Transactions. ScCM (1848–82)
American Medical Association, Transactions: Diseases of Children. ScCM (1906–32)
American Medical Association, Transactions: Genito-Urinary Diseases. ScCM 1912–18
American Medical Association, Transactions: Laryngology, Otology and Rhinology. ScCM 1908–18, 1920–34
American Medical Association, Transactions: Ophthalmology. ScCM (1907–38)
American Medical Association, Transactions: Surgery. ScCM (1907–24)
American Medical Association, Transactions: Urology. ScCM 1921–31
American Medical Intelligencer. ScCM (1838–40); ScU [mfm] 1837–42
American Medical Recorder. ScU [mfm] 1818–29
American Medical Review. ScU [mfm] 1824–26
American Medicine. ScCM (1901–36)
American Mercury. ScChar 1933+; ScCleU 1924+; ScCoR 1926+; ScGBj 1938+; ScGrev 1924+; ScHCok 1935+; ScNewb 1938+; ScOrCl 1937+; ScOrSc 1925–49, 1955–59; ScRhW 1924+; ScSpW 1924–33, 1952+; ScU 1924+

American Metropolitan Magazine. ScU [mfm] (1849)
American Microscopical Society, Transactions. ScCleU (1895) 1915+
American Midland Naturalist. ScCleU 1909+; ScCMus 1909–48;
ScU 1909–50, 1953+
American Military History Foundation Journal. ScCCit 1937–40
American Military Institute. ScCCit 1937–40
American Milk [Dairy] Review. ScCleU 1940+
American Mineralogical Journal. ScU (1810–11), also [mfm] 1810–
14
American Mineralogist. ScCleU 1918+, some files on mc; ScU
1916+
American Monitor, or the Republican Magazine. ScU [mfm] (1785)
American Monthly Magazine [D.A.R.]. ScCleU 1908–13
American Monthly Magazine [New York]. ScGF (1829–38); ScU
[mfm] 1833–38
American Monthly Magazine [Philadelphia]. ScU [mfm] (1824)
American Monthly Magazine and Critical Review. ScU [mfm]
1817–19
American Monthly Review. ScGF 1832–33
American Monthly Review, or Literary Journal. ScU [mfm] (1795)
American Monthly Review of Reviews. ScCCit 1914–17; ScCleU
(1897–1907)
American Moral and Sentimental Magazine. ScU [mfm] 1797–98
American Museum, or Universal Magazine. ScC (1787–98); ScCM
(1788); ScGF 1787–92; ScU (1787–91), also [mfm] 1787–92
American Museum Novitates. ScCleU 1921+
American Museum of Literature and Arts. ScU [mfm] 1838–39
American Museum of Natural History, Bulletin. ScCleU (1897–
1924) 1925+; ScCMus (1881–1942)
American Museum of Natural History, Journal. ScCMus 1900+;
ScU 1914+
American Musical Magazine. ScU [mfm] 1786–87, 1800–1
American Naturalist. ScC 1905–11; ScCleU 1867+; ScCMus 1867–
1910; ScU 1868+
American Neurological Association, Transactions. ScCM (1919–24)
1926–50, 1954+
American Nut Journal. ScCleU (1916–31)
American Ophthalmological Society, Transactions. ScCM (1888–
1905)
American Organist. ScCoCo (1937+)

American Oriental Society, Journal. ScGBj 1934–55; ScU (1851–1909) 1911+

American Oxonian. ScU 1914+

American Peat Society, Journal. ScCleU 1908–22

American Pediatric Society, Transactions. ScCM (1891–1938)

American Peoples Journal of Science, Literature, and Art. ScU [mfm] (1850)

American Petroleum Institute [Petroleum Facts and Figures]. ScU 1929+

American Pharmaceutical Association, Journal. ScCM 1940+; ScU 1912+

American Pharmaceutical Association, Journal [Scientific Edition]. ScCM 1912+

American Pharmaceutical Association, Proceedings. ScCM 1851–1911; ScU 1857–1911

American Pharmaceutical Association, Yearbook. ScCM 1912–34

American Philological Association, Transactions and Proceedings. ScU (1873–91) 1896–1945

American Philosophical Association, Proceedings and Addresses. ScU 1926+

American Philosophical Society, Memoirs. ScU 1935+

American Philosophical Society, Proceedings. ScCHis 1900+; ScCleU 1876+; ScCMus 1854–99; ScU (1843+)

American Philosophical Society, Transactions. ScC 1789–1809, 1818–53; ScCleU 1892+; ScU (1818+)

American Philosophical Society, Yearbook. ScCleU 1941+

American Photography. ScCC 1941–50; ScCCit 1938–49; ScChar 1933–35; ScCoR 1936–51; ScGrev 1936–53; ScRhW 1940–53

American Physical Education Review. ScU 1896–1929

American Physical Society, Bulletin. ScU 1925+

American Physics Teacher [American Journal of Physics]. ScCC 1938–39; ScCCit 1933–39; ScCleU 1933–39; ScOrSc 1933–39; ScU 1933–39

American Physiological Society, Proceedings. ScCM (1934–41)

American Pioneer. ScU [mfm] 1842–43

American Planning and Civic Annual. ScU (1931) 1934–57

American Poet. ScRhW 1941–43

American Poetry. ScSpC 1929–32

American Political Science Review. ScCCit 1931+; ScCleU (1912–16) 1917+; ScGF 1916–17, 1920+; ScU 1906+

American Potato Journal. ScCleU 1923+
American Poultry Advocate. ScCleU 1924–26
American Prison Association, Proceedings. ScU (1910–23)
American Proctologic Society, Transactions. ScCM (1909–55); ScU 1926–28
American Produce Review. ScCleU 1938+, split into several sections in 1939, library has to date
American Professional Pharmacist. ScCM (1936) 1937+; ScU 1938+
American Psychoanalytic Association, Bulletin. ScCM 1937–40
American Psychological Journal. ScCM 1870–72
American Quarterly Observer. ScU [mfm] 1833–34
American Quarterly of Roentgenology. ScCM (1906–13)
American Quarterly Register. ScU [mfm] 1827–43
American Quarterly Review. ScC (1827–37); ScGF (1827–33); ScU (1827–37), also [mfm] 1827–37
American Railway Association, Signal Section Proceedings. ScCleU 1922–28
American Railway Engineering Association, Proceedings. ScCleU 1924–28; ScU (1912–42)
American Register. ScC 1807–9; ScGF 1807–10; ScU 1806–10, also [mfm] 1806–10, 1817
American Remembrancer. ScU (1795)
American Repertory of Arts, Sciences and Manufactures. ScU [mfm] 1840–42
American Review. ScCCit 1933–36; ScChar 1933–37; ScCleU 1933–37; ScGF 1933–37; ScGrev 1933–37; ScGrew 1933–35; ScSpC 1933–37; ScU 1933–37
American Review and Literary Journal. ScC 1801–2; ScGF 1801–2; ScU [mfm] 1801–2
American Review of History and Politics. ScC 1811–12; ScGF 1811–12; ScU (1811), also [mfm] 1811–12
American Review of Reviews. ScCleU 1908–28; ScCoCo 1907–24; ScFlor 1926–29; ScHCok 1899–1937
American Review of Tuberculosis. ScCM (1917) 1918–59; ScStpSan 1924+
American Review on the Soviet Union. ScU (1939–47)
American Rose Society, Annual. ScCleU 1917+
American Scandinavian Review. ScSpC 1940–51; ScU 1913+

American Scholar. ScCCit 1939+; ScCleU 1932+; ScClP (1932–55); ScDwErs 1932+; ScGF 1932+; ScHCok 1939+; ScOrCl 1932+; ScRhW 1932+; ScSpC 1932+ ScSpW 1932+; ScU 1932+

American School and University. ScU (1930–49) 1951+

American School and University, Yearbook. ScCleU 1938–59

American School Board Journal. ScCleU (1924–29) 1930+; ScGF (1919+); ScRhW 1941+; ScU 1917+

American Scientist [Sigma Xi Quarterly]. ScU 1931+

American Society for Agricultural Engineers, Transactions. ScCleU (1910–25) 1927–31

American Society for Control of Cancer, Bulletin. ScCM 1931–43

American Society for Horticultural Science, Proceedings. ScCleU 1903+

American Society for Metals, Transactions. ScCleU 1934–44, 1961+; ScU 1921+

American Society for Promoting the Civilization and General Improvement of Indian Tribes. ScU [mfm] (1824)

American Society for Testing and Materials, Bulletin. ScCleU 1927+; ScU 1931+

American Society for Testing and Materials, Index. ScCleU 1928+

American Society for Testing and Materials, Proceedings. ScCCit 1908–30; ScCleU 1904, 1906+; ScNcWv 1938+; ScU 1915+

American Society for Testing and Materials, Standards. ScCCit (1910–46); ScCleU 1910+; ScU (1926–35)

American Society for Testing and Materials, Yearbook. ScCleU 1910+

American Society of Agronomy, Proceedings and Journal [Agronomy Journal]. ScCleU 1907+

American Society of Animal Production, Proceedings [Journal of Animal Science]. ScCleU 1917+

American Society of Biological Chemists, Proceedings. ScCM (1910–41)

American Society of Church History, Papers. ScCoT [mfm] 1888–96

American Society of Civil Engineers, Proceedings. ScCleU 1892+; ScU (1925–27) 1929+. NOTE: *Proceedings* split into several sections in 1949; both libraries have to date.

American Society of Civil Engineers, Transactions. ScCCit 1879+; ScCleU (1878–96) 1897+; ScU (1892–97) 1900+

American Society of Civil Engineers, Yearbook. ScCleU 1913–32
American Society of Heating, Ventilating [and Air Conditioning]
Engineers, Transactions. ScCleU 1895+; ScU 1933+
American Society of International Law, Proceedings. ScU 1907+
American Society of Legion of Honor Magazine. ScU 1939+
American Society of Mechanical Engineers, Oil and Gas Division,
Proceedings. ScCleU 1934–48
American Society of Mechanical Engineers, Transactions. ScCCit
(1905–26); ScCleU 1880+; ScU 1882+. NOTE: *Transactions* split
into several parts in 1959; ScCleU and ScU have to date.
American Society of Municipal Engineers, Proceedings. ScU (1908–
30)
American Society of Newspaper Editors, Proceedings. ScU (1923+)
American Sociological Review. ScCleU 1936+; ScGaLi 1941+;
ScGF 1936+; ScOrSc 1939+; ScRhW 1936+; ScU 1936+
American Sociological Society, Publications. ScU (1906–27)
American Soil Survey Association, Report. ScCleU 1921+
American Speech. ScCleU (1926–40) 1941+; ScGBj (1939–46)
1947+; ScRhW 1925+; ScSpC 1940+; ScU 1925+
American Statistical Association, Journal. ScCleU 1898+; ScRhW
1940; ScU 1888+
American Surgical Association, Transactions. ScCM (1881–1940)
1947+
American Teacher. ScU (1927+)
American Turf Register and Sporting Magazine. ScU [mfm] 1829–
44
American Universal Magazine. ScU [mfm] 1797–98
American Veterinary Medical Association, Journal. ScCleU (1915–
19) 1920+
American Veterinary Review. ScCleU (1897–1915)
American Waterworks Association, Journal. ScCleU (1921–37)
1938+; ScU (1934) 1939+
American Waterworks Association, Proceedings. ScCleU (1926–60)
1961+; ScCM 1908–13
American Whig Review. ScGF 1845–52; ScU [mfm] 1845–52
American Wildlife [North American Wildlife and Natural Resources
Conference, Transactions]. ScCleU 1939+
American Wool and Cotton [Textile] Reporter. ScCleU (1909–46)
1947+

Anais Paulistas de Medicina e Cirurgia [São Paulo]. ScCM (1934–46) 1947+

Analectic Magazine. ScC (1813–20); ScCM (1815); ScGF (1814–18); ScU 1813–18, also [mfm] 1813–20

Analyist, or Mathematical Museum. ScU [mfm] (1808–14)

Analyst. ScCleU 1876+

Analytical Chemistry. ScCC 1929–59; ScCleU 1929+; ScGF 1929+; ScSpC 1929–50

Analytical Review. ScC 1791–92; ScU [mfm] 1788–98

Anatomical Record. ScCleU 1916+; ScCM 1906+; ScU (1906–37) 1950+

Anatomische Gesellschaft [Jena Verhandlungen]. ScU 1888–1920 (1925–26) 1928+

Anatomischer Anzieger. ScCM (1887+); ScU 1886–1932

Anderson County [S. C.] Hospital, Bulletin. ScCM 1939–41

Andover Review. ScU 1884–93

Anesthesia Abstracts. ScCM (1937–56)

Anesthesia and Analgesia. ScCM (1922–25) 1926+

Anesthesiology. ScCM 1940+

Anglia, Zeitschrift für Englische Philologie. ScU 1877–1951, 1956+, library also has *Beiblatt* 1890–1944 and *Supplementheft* 1894–1909

Anglo-American Magazine. ScGF (1853); ScU [mfm] 1843–47

Anglo-Saxon [Newberry College]. ScU (1926–32)

Anglo-Saxon Review. ScC 1899–1901

Animal Breeding Abstracts. ScCleU (1935–43) 1944+

Annalen der Physik. ScCleU 1940–43, 1947+, some files on mc; ScU 1799–1824, 1869+

Annalen der Physik, Ergänzungsbände. ScU 1848–78

Annalen der Physik und Chemie, Beiblätter [Annalen der Physik, Beiblätter]. ScU 1877–1919

Annales Bryologici, Yearbook [Annales Cryptogamici et Phytopathologici]. ScCleU 1928–39

Annales de Chimie. ScCleU 1914+

Annales de Dermatologie et de Syphilographie. ScCM (1930–46)

Annales d'Endocrinologie. ScCM (1939–46)

Annales de Géographie. ScU (1916–42)

Annales de l'Institut Pasteur. ScCM 1898–1906 (1911–50) 1951+

Annales de Medicine [Paris]. ScCM (1920–38)

Annales des Sciences Naturelles. ScCMus 1827–28

Annales Mycologici [Sydowia]. ScCleU [mc] 1903+
Annales Philosophiques, Politiques et Littéraires [Philadelphia].
ScU [mfm] (1807)
Annalists. ScU 1916–40
Annals of Agriculture and Other Useful Arts. ScC 1784–1806
Annals of Anatomy and Surgery. ScCM 1881–83
Annals of Applied Biology. ScCleU 1914+
Annals of Applied Botany. ScCleU (1914–27) 1928+
Annals of Botany. ScCleU 1888–1907, 1909+
Annals of Clinical Medicine. ScCM 1922–27
Annals of Collective Economy. ScCleU 1925–40
Annals of Dentistry. ScCM (1935–53)
Annals of Electricity, Magnetism and Chemistry. ScU 1836–43
Annals of Internal Medicine. ScCM 1927+; ScCoHo (1935+); Sc-
GGh 1933+
Annals of Mathematical Statistics. ScCleU 1930+; ScU 1930+
Annals of Mathematics. ScU 1884+
Annals of Mathematics Studies. ScU (1940+)
Annals of Medical History. ScCM 1917–42
Annals of Medical Practice. ScCM 1887–88
Annals of Nature [Lexington, Ky.]. ScU [mfm] (1820)
Annals of New York Academy of Sciences. ScCM (1933+)
Annals of Ophthalmology. ScCM (1892–1917)
Annals of Otology, Rhinology and Laryngology. ScCM 1897–1907
(1908) 1909+; ScCoHo 1930+
Annals of Philosophy. ScU 1813–16
Annals of Picket-Thomson Research Laboratory. ScCM 1926–31
Annals of Roentgenology. ScCM (1922+)
Annals of Surgery. ScCM 1885+; ScCoHo 1930+; ScGGh (1919–
36) 1937+
Annals of Tropical Medicine and Parasitology. ScCleU 1930+;
ScCM 1919+
Année Philologique. ScSpC 1924–59
Année Sociologique. ScU 1896–1912
Annuaire des Ventes du Livres. ScU 1918–31
Annuaire de Documentation Coloniale Comparée. ScU 1927–35
Annuaire International de Legislation Agricole. ScCleU 1911–25
Annual Law Register of the United States. ScU [mfm] 1821–22
Annual of Scientific Discovery. ScU 1850–54
Annual of the Universal Medical Sciences. ScU 1888–93

Annual Record of Science and Industry. ScCM 1874–75
Annual Register. ScC 1758–88 (1790–1816) 1818–59; ScCleU 1760–88; ScCM (1760–75) 1776–78; ScGeor 1760–1802; ScSpW 1758–1811; ScU 1758+
Annual Review. ScC 1802–3
Annual Review of Biochemistry. ScCleU 1932+; ScCM 1932+; ScU 1932+
Annual Review of Physiology. ScCM 1939+; ScU 1939+
Annual Trade Review [Charleston]. ScCMus 1885–90
Anthologia Hibernica. ScU 1793–94
Antiquarisk Tidsskrift. ScCHu (1905–24)
Antioch Review. ScCleU 1941+; ScU 1941+
Antiquity. ScCleU 1935+
Antiques. ScChar 1932+; ScCMus 1922+; ScMar (1929–39); ScRhP 1941+; ScSpar 1940+; ScU 1922–30, 1952+
Anti-Saloon League of America, Proceedings. ScU (1913–30)
Anti-Saloon League of America, Yearbook. ScU (1909–31)
Anti-Slavery Examiner. ScU [mfm] 1836–45
Anti-Slavery Record. ScU [mfm] 1835–37
Anti-Slavery Reporter. ScU [mfm] (1833)
Antivenin Institute of America, Bulletin. ScCM 1927–32
Apollian. ScCM (1837–42)
Apollo. ScCleU 1931–48
Apothecary. ScU 1938+
Appletons' Journal. ScCleU 1869–75; ScFlor (1867–71); ScRhW (1869–72); ScSpW 1870–72; ScU (1874–75)
Appletons' Mechanics Magazine and Engineers' Journal. ScU 1851–53
Applied Anthropology [Human Organization]. ScCleU 1941+
Applied Chemistry Reports. ScNcWv 1938–45
Aquariana. ScU (1932–33)
Aquarium. ScU 1912–14 (1932+)
Aquarium Journal. ScU (1933–35) 1938–55
Aquarium News. ScU 1934–37
Aquatic Life. ScU 1915–42, 1951+
Arbeitsphysiologie. ScCM (1931–54)
Archaeologica. ScU 1770–1800
Architect. ScCleU 1923–30
Architectural Concrete. ScU (1935–47)

Architectural Forum. ScCleU 1917–64; ScOrSc 1939, 1941–49, 1959–64; ScU 1929–31, 1935–59

Architectural Record. ScC (1907–37) 1938+; ScChar 1934+; ScCCit (1913–50); ScCleU 1891+; ScGrev 1930+; ScU 1891+

Architectural Review. ScCleU 1926–32, 1952+

Architecture. ScCleU 1923–36

Archiv der Pharmazie und Berichte der Deutschen Pharmazeutischen Gesellschaft. ScCM (1926–51) 1952+

Archiv für Anatomie, Physiologie und Wissenschaftliche Medicin. ScCM (1938)

Archiv für Anatomie und Physiologie. ScCM (1902)

Archiv für die Gesamte Physiologie. ScCM (1929–43)

Archiv für Elektrotechnik. ScCleU 1913–31

Archiv für Kinderheilkunde. ScCM (1931–32)

Archiv für Klinische Chirurgie. ScCM (1880–1940)

Archiv für Kreislaufforschung. ScCM (1937)

Archiv für Laryngologie und Rhinologie. ScCM (1893–1915)

Archiv für Naturgeschichte. ScU 1835–56

Archiv für Psychiatrie und Nervenkrankheiten. ScCM (1932)

Archiv für Reformationsgeschichte. ScU 1903–48, 1962+

Archiv für Verdauungs-Krankheiten [Gastroenterologia]. ScCM (1895–1909)

Archives d'Anatomie Microscopique et Morphologie Experimentale. ScCM (1936–50)

Archives d'Historie Doctrinale et Littéraire du Moyen Âge. ScU 1931–36, 1940+

Archives des Maladies du Cœur, des Vaisseaux et du Sang. ScCM (1938+)

Archives Internationales de Pharmacodynamie et de Therapie. ScCM 1938+

Archives Internationales de Physiologie. ScCM (1925–43)

Archives of Dermatology and Syphilology. ScCM 1920+; ScCoHo (1932+); ScGGh 1926+

Archives of Disease in Children. ScCM 1926+

Archives of General Psychiatry. ScGGh (1937+)

Archives of Internal Medicine. ScCM 1903+; ScCoHo 1930+; ScGGh (1911–44) 1945+

Archives of Maryland. ScU 1883+

Archives of Medical Hydrology. ScCM 1925–39

Archives of Medicine. ScCM 1879–81

Archives of Neurology and Psychiatry. ScCM 1919–59; ScCoHo 1930+

Archives of Ophthalmology. ScCM (1869–1919) 1920+; ScCoHo 1934–54

Archives of Otolaryngology. ScCM 1925+; ScCoHo (1934+); ScGGh 1934+

Archives of Otology. ScCM (1882–1903)

Archives of Pathology. ScCM 1926+

Archives of Pediatrics. ScCM (1889–97) 1898–1962; ScCoHo 1931+; ScGGh (1911–53)

Archives of Physical Therapy. ScCM 1920–44

Archives of Surgery. ScCM 1920+; SoCoHo (1930+); ScGGh (1921–47) 1948+

Archives of Useful Knowledge. ScU [mfm] 1810–13

Arcturus. ScGF 1841

Arena. ScU 1889–1909

Argosy. ScRhW 1866–67

Aristidean. ScU [mfm] (1845)

Aristotelian Society for the Systematic Study of Philosophy, Proceedings. ScU 1918+

Arkansas Academy of Science, Proceedings. ScU 1941+

Arkansas Medical Society, Journal. ScCM (1906+)

Arminian Magazine. ScSpW 1789; ScU [mfm] 1789–90

Army and Navy Chronicle. ScU [mfm] 1835–42

Army and Navy Chronicle and Scientific Repository. ScU [mfm] 1843–44

Army Medical Bulletin. ScCM (1925–32)

Arnoldia. ScCleU 1941+

Ars Medici. ScCM (1922–39)

Art Amateur. ScU 1880–85

Art and Archaeology. ScC 1914–33; ScCCit (1925–29); ScCMus 1922–31; ScHCok 1930–32; ScRhW 1914–34; ScU 1914–34

Art and Progress. ScU 1911–16

Art Bulletin. ScCC (1924–40) 1941–50; ScGBj 1941+; ScU (1919–48)

Art Digest [Arts Magazine]. ScCleU 1940+; ScCMus 1926–38; ScHCok 1927–52; ScSpC 1936–53; ScU 1926+

Art Journal. ScC (1851–83); ScCleU (1847–80); ScClP (1876–81); ScU (1875–83)

Art News. ScCC 1939–51; ScU 1938+

Art Work of Charleston. ScCC 1893

Arthur's Magazine. ScU [mfm] 1844–46

Artist, a Monthly Lady's Book. ScU [mfm] 1842–43

Arts and Decoration. ScCleU (1918–42); ScCoR (1919–39); ScRhW 1919–42; ScU 1914–15, 1922–41

Asia. ScCCit 1925–46; ScChar (1927–29) 1940–46; ScClP (1939–46); ScCoR 1935–46; ScGF 1923–32; ScGrev 1920–46; ScRhW 1922–46; ScSpC 1939–46; ScSpW 1935–45; ScU 1917–46

Asiatic Annual Register. ScC 1799–1802

Asiatic Society of Bengal [Calcutta], Asiatic Researches. ScU 1799–1839

Asiatic Society of Japan, Transactions. ScU (1893–1921)

Associate Reformed Presbyterian. ScDwErs 1911+; ScU (1882–1950)

Associate Reformed Presbyterian Journal of Missions. ScU (1915–49)

Association for Promoting the Discovery of the Interior Parts of Africa, Proceedings. ScC (1788)

Association for Research in Nervous and Mental Diseases, Proceedings. ScCM 1941+

Association for the Study of Negro Life and History, Annual Report. ScU (1924–38)

Association of American Colleges, Bulletin [Liberal Education]. ScCCit 1931+; ScCleU 1928+; ScGF 1925+; ScOrSc 1939+; ScRhW 1916+; ScSpC 1928+; ScSpW 1927+; ScU 1918+

Association of American Geographers, Annals. ScU 1911+

Association of American Medical Colleges, Bulletin. ScCM 1926–28

Association of American Medical Colleges, Journal. ScCM 1929–50

Association of American Physicians, Transactions. ScC (1886–1947); ScCM 1886+

Association of American Universities, Proceedings. ScU 1900–32, 1943+

Association of Colleges and Preparatory Schools of the Southern States, Proceedings. ScCC (1898–99); ScCleU (1899–1910)

Association of Colleges and Secondary Schools of the Southern States, Proceedings. ScCleU 1910–32

Association of Engineering Societies, Journal. ScCleU 1884–1915

Association of Land Grant Colleges and Universities, Proceedings [American Association of . . .]. ScCleU 1910+

Association of Official Agricultural Chemists, Journal. ScCleU 1915+; ScCM 1930–44; ScOrSc 1940–45, 1950+; ScU (1915–49) 1953+

Association of Official Seed Analysts of North America, Proceedings. ScCleU 1919+

Association of Southern Agricultural Workers, Proceedings. ScCleU (1902–11) 1927+

Astronautics [Jet Propulsion]. ScCleU 1932–44; ScU 1932–44

Astronomical Journal. ScU (1849–1916) 1920+

Astronomical Society of the Pacific, Leaflet. ScCleU 1925+

Astrophysical Journal. ScCleU 1895–99, 1955+

Athenaeum [New Haven]. ScU [mfm] (1814)

Athenaeum, a Journal of Literature, Science, the Fine Arts, Music and the Drama. ScC 1901–19; ScU 1909–17

Athenaeum, or Spirit of the English Magazines. ScC (1817–22); ScU [mfm] 1817–25

Athenian Magazine. ScU [mfm] 1691–97

Athenian News or Dunton's Oracle. ScU [mfm] (1710)

Athenian Oracle. ScU [mfm] 1703–10

Athletic Journal. ScCleU (1929–61) 1962+; ScNewb 1939+; ScU (1928–29) 1931+

Atkinsons Casket. ScU (1832–33)

Atlantic Magazine. ScU 1824–25

Atlantic, The. ScC 1857+; ScCC 1920+; ScCenW (1920+); ScCCit (1900–34) 1935+; ScChar (1858–1930) 1931+; ScChes 1940+; ScCleU 1857+; ScClP 1913+; ScCoBe 1857+; ScCoCo (1900–20) 1921+; ScCoR 1913+; ScDarl 1911+; ScDwErs 1925+; ScFlor 1926–29; ScGaLi 1904+; ScGBj 1857–76, 1934+; ScGF 1857+; ScGrev 1917+; ScGrew 1922+; ScGwLa 1936+; ScHCok 1900+; ScLaD 1940+; ScNewb 1875+; ScOrSc 1933+; ScRhP 1920–22, 1924+; ScRhW 1857+; ScSpar 1930+; ScSpC 1857+; ScSpW 1857+; ScSum 1935+; ScTiNg (1925+); ScU 1857+

Atlantic Souvenir. ScU 1828

Audubon Field Notes. ScSpC 1941+

Audubon Magazine. ScCleU 1941+; ScRhW 1941+; ScU 1941+

Augustana Quarterly. ScCoT 1922+, some files on mfm

Auk. ScCleU 1887+; ScCMus 1884+; ScU (1907–57)

Australia, Historical Records. ScU (1914+)

Australian and New Zealand Journal of Surgery. ScCM (1939+)

Australian Journal of Experimental Biology and Medical Science.
   ScCM (1928–46) 1947+
Australian Law Journal. ScU 1928+
Australian Museum, Records of the. ScCMus (1929+)
Australian Veterinary Journal. ScCleU 1941+
Automobile Trade Journal. ScCleU (1927–35)
Automotive Industries. ScCleU 1930+
Aviation [Aviation Week, Aviation Week and Space Technology].
   ScCCit 1939–46, 1959+; ScCleU (1923–47) 1948+; ScU 1916+
Ayer Clinical Laboratory of Pennsylvania Hospital, Bulletin. ScCM
   (1903–10) 1924+
Ayrshire Digest. ScCleU 1940+

B

Bacteriological Reviews. ScCleU 1937+; ScCM 1937+
Baking Technology. ScCleU 1925–26
Balance and State Journal [Albany]. ScU [mfm] 1802–11
Balance Sheet. ScRhW 1939+
Baltimore Bulletin of Education. ScNewb 1941+; ScU 1924+
Baltimore Literary and Religious Magazine. ScU [mfm] 1835–41
Baltimore Literary Monument. ScU [mfm] 1838–39
Baltimore Medical and Philosophical Lyceum. ScU [mfm] 1811
Baltimore Medical and Physical Recorder. ScU [mfm] 1808–9
Baltimore Medical and Surgical Journal and Review. ScU [mfm]
   1833–34
Baltimore Monthly Journal of Medicine and Surgery. ScU [mfm]
   1830–31
Baltimore Monthly Visitor. ScU [mfm] (1842)
Baltimore Philosophical Journal and Review. ScU [mfm] (1823)
Baltimore Repertory of Papers on Literary and Other Topics. . . .
   ScU [mfm] (1811)
Baltimore Weekly Magazine. ScU [mfm] 1800–1
Bankers Magazine. ScCCit 1938–43; ScU 1908–43
Bankers' Magazine [New York]. ScU [mfm] 1846–51
Banking. ScU 1935+
Banner of the Constitution. ScU 1829–31, also [mfm] 1829–32
Banner of the Cross. ScC 1839–42
Banta's Greek Exchange. ScU 1912–17
Baptist Courier. ScGF 1869+, also [mfm] 1869+; ScU (1908–47)
Baptist Education Bulletin. ScGF [mfm] 1919–24

Baptist Expositor and Southwestern Intelligencer. ScGF 1842–43
Baptist Historical Society, Transactions. ScGF 1908–21
Baptist Missionary Magazine. ScU [mfm] 1817–50
Baptist Preacher. ScGF 1829–30 (1844–59)
Baptist Quarterly. ScGF 1867–77, 1922+
Bar Examiner. ScU 1931+
Barber's Shop [Salem]. ScU [mfm] 1807–8
Bartonia. ScCleU 1908+
Bath and West and Southern Counties Societies, Journal. ScCleU 1916–23
Bay View Magazine. ScSpW 1905–13
Beach and Pool [Swimming Pool Age]. ScU (1934–55) 1956+
Beauties of the Evangelical Magazine. ScU [mfm] 1802–3
Beaux Arts Institute of Design, Bulletin. ScCleU (1925–38)
Bee Revived, or the Universal World Pamphlet. ScU [mfm] 1733–35
Bee World. ScCleU 1940+
Beilsteins Handbuch der Organischen Chemie. ScSpDm 1918+; ScU 1918+
Beitraege zur Geschichte der Deutschen Sprache und Literatur. ScU 1886–1932, 1945–48
Belfast Monthly Magazine. ScU [mfm] 1808–14
Bell Laboratories Record. ScCleU 1925+; ScU 1925+
Bell System Technical Journal. ScCleU 1922+; ScU 1922+
Bell Telephone Quarterly [Magazine]. ScCleU 1922+; ScU 1922–40, 1943+
Bell's Literary Intelligencer and New National Omnibus. ScU [mfm] (1834)
Berean, a Religious Publication [Wilmington, Del.]. ScU [mfm] 1824–28
Berean, or an Appeal to the Scriptures [Boston]. ScU [mfm] 1802–10
Berean, or Scripture—Searcher [Boston]. ScU [mfm] 1802–10
Berichte der Deutschen Chemischen Gesellschaft. ScGF 1909–14
Berichte über die Gesamte Physiologie und Experimentelle Pharmakologie. ScCM (1926–49)
Berkshire News. ScCleU 1940+
Berliner Klinik. ScCM (1888–92)
Berliner Klinische Wochenschrift. ScCM (1880–1916)
Bernard's Journal of Education. ScSpW 1855–59

Beta Club Journal. ScU 1936+

Better Crops with Better Food. ScCleU 1923+

Better Farm Equipment and Methods [Better Farming Methods]. ScCleU 1929–33, 1940+

Better Fruit. ScCleU (1924+)

Better Homes and Gardens. ScCleU 1925+; ScGBj 1932+; ScGrev 1939+; ScGrew 1933–41, 1950+; ScLaD 1928+; ScNewb 1938+; ScOran 1938+; ScOrSc 1918–30, 1962+; ScRhP 1933+; ScRhW 1937+; ScSpar 1940+; ScU 1926+

Better Roads. ScU 1931–40, 1944+

Better Vision. ScU 1940–42

Bibelot. ScU 1895–1925

Bible Student [Columbia]. ScU (1899–1902)

Biblical Archaeologist. ScGF 1939+

Biblical Recorder and Southern Watchman. ScGF 1835–37

Biblical Repertory. ScCoT 1825–68; ScDwErs–T 1829–37

Biblical Repertory, a Collection of Tracts in Biblical Literature. ScU [mfm] (1825)

Biblical Repository. ScClP 1831–38; ScCoT 1845–49; ScU [mfm] 1831–50

Biblical Review. ScGBj 1916–17

Bibliographical Society [London], Transactions. ScU (1920–49) 1952+

Bibliographical Society of America, Papers. ScU (1904+)

Bibliotheca Sacra. ScCoBi 1935+; ScCoT 1843–57; ScGBj 1844–69, 1942+; ScSpW 1831–36; ScU [mfm] 1843

Bibliothèque d'Humanisme et Renaissance. ScU 1941+

Bilderschmuck der Frühdrücke. ScU 1922–45

Bill of Rights Review. ScCCit 1940–42; ScU 1940–42

Biochemical Journal. ScCleU 1906+; ScCM 1923, 1926+; ScU 1906–21, 1946–50, 1952+

Biochemische Zeitschrift. ScCM (1906–48) 1949+

Biochemisches Centralblatt. ScCM (1902–4)

Biodynamica. ScCleU 1934+

Biological Abstracts. ScCC 1938+; ScCleU 1927+; ScCM 1927+; ScCMus 1933+; ScGF 1927+; ScOrSc 1927+; ScRhW 1927+; ScSpC 1930+; ScU 1927+

Biological Bulletin. ScCleU (1903–8) 1909+; ScCM (1902+); ScOrSc 1911+; ScU 1903–6, 1921+

Biological Photographic Association, Journal. ScCM (1932) 1944+; ScU (1932–55)

Biological Society of Washington, Proceedings. ScCleU 1923+; ScU (1880–1941)

Biological Symposia. ScCM (1941–47)

Biometricka. ScCleU 1901+

Bios. ScU (1934) 1948–52

Bird Lore [Audubon Magazine]. ScC 1906–21; ScCleU 1899–1940; ScCMus 1899–1940; ScRhW 1940; ScSpC 1934–40; ScU 1899–1940

Birmingham Philosophical Society, Proceedings. ScCMus 1889–93

Bishop Museum, Bulletin [Honolulu]. ScCMus 1922–32

Black Dwarf. ScU [mfm] 1817–24

Black Rock Forest, Bulletin. ScCleU 1930–56

Blackwood's Magazine. ScC (1817–37) 1838–75, 1876–1931 (1939–41) 1950+; ScCCit (1856–80); ScGF (1818–89); ScRhW 1817+; ScSpW 1819–21, 1844–69; ScU 1817–92 (1895–1945) 1947+

Blue Book and Catalog, Soap and Sanitary Chemicals. ScCleU (1940–52)

Blue Book of Southern Progress. ScCC (1940–55)

Blue Stocking. ScClP 1929+

Bobbin and Beaker. ScCleU 1940+

Boletim de Industria Animal. ScCleU 1938–54, 1957+

Bombay Natural History Society, Journal. ScCMus 1938–42

Book Review Digest. ScCC 1922+; ScCCit 1905+; ScDarl 1921+; ScGaLi 1927+; ScRhP 1932+; ScRhW 1905+; ScU 1905+

Booklist [and Subscription Books Bulletin]. ScCC 1938+; ScChar 1931+; ScCleU 1908–22, 1938+; ScClP 1930–47, 1957+; ScCoR 1928+; ScNewb 1931+; ScRhP 1934+; ScRhW 1908+; ScSpC 1934+; ScU 1917+

Bookman [American Review]. ScCC 1913–18; ScCCit 1924–33; ScChar (1925–26) 1931–33; ScCleU 1896–1933; ScCoR (1920–33); ScDarl 1921–32; ScFlor 1926–30; ScGF 1920–33; ScGrev 1919–33; ScGrew 1895–1901, 1921–32; ScHCok 1914–33; ScRhW 1895–1933; ScSpC 1898–1933; ScSpW 1897; ScU 1895–1933

Bookman [London]. ScRhW 1924–34

Books Abroad. ScRhW 1930+; ScSpW 1930–31, 1948+; ScU 1928+

Boston Cultivator. ScU [mfm] 1839–50

Boston Journal of Natural History. ScU 1834–1944

Boston Journal of Philosophy and the Arts. ScGF 1823–24; ScU [mfm] 1823–26

Boston Literary Magazine. ScU [mfm] 1832–33
Boston Lyceum. ScU [mfm] (1827)
Boston Magazine. ScU [mfm] 1783–86, 1802–6
Boston Masonic Mirror. ScU [mfm] 1829–34
Boston Mechanic and Journal of the Useful Arts and Sciences. ScU [mfm] 1832–36
Boston Medical and Surgical Journal. ScCM (1834–1928); ScGGh (1914–26)
Boston Medical Intelligencer. ScU [mfm] 1823–25
Boston Miscellany of Literature and Fashion. ScU [mfm] 1842–43
Boston Monthly Magazine. ScU [mfm] 1825–26
Boston Musical Gazette. ScU [mfm] 1838–39
Boston Quarterly Review. ScU [mfm] 1838–42
Boston Society of Medical Sciences, Journal. ScCM 1896–1901
Boston Society of Natural History, Bulletin. ScCMus (1915–38)
Boston Society of Natural History, Memoirs. ScCMus (1869–1912)
Boston Society of Natural History, Occasional Papers. ScCMus (1869–1931)
Boston Society of Natural History, Proceedings. ScCMus 1856–73, 1874–1940
Boston Spectator. ScU [mfm] 1814–15
Boston Weekly Magazine. ScU [mfm] (1743) 1816–19 (1824) 1838–41
Botanical Abstracts [Biological Abstracts]. ScCleU 1918–26; ScU 1918–26
Botanical Gazette. ScCleU 1875–1910, 1912+; ScHCok 1926+; ScU 1875–89, 1897+, some files on mc
Botanical Magazine. ScCMus 1793–1807; ScU 1787–1800
Botanical Review. ScCleU 1935+; ScCM 1935+; ScU 1935–44, 1950+
Botanisches Zentralblatt. ScCleU (1904–12)
Boudoir Annual [Boston]. ScU 1846
Bouquet [Charleston]. ScC 1842–43; ScU 1842–43
Bowen's Boston News-Letter and City Record. ScU [mfm] (1825)
Bower of Taste. ScC 1829
Boyce Thompson Institute, Contributions. ScCleU 1925+
Boys' Life. ScRhP 1933+
Bozart [Atlanta]. ScU 1927–30
Bragantia. ScCleU 1941+
Brain. ScCM (1896–1917) 1918+

Breeder and Dairyman. ScCleU (1934–36)

Breeders' Gazette [American Livestock Journal]. ScCleU (1883–1916) 1919+

Brick and Clay Record. ScCleU 1926+

Brigadier. ScCCit (1930–35)

British Abstracts. ScCleU (1926–52) 1953+, split into several sections in 1953, library has to date.

British and Foreign Medical Review. ScCM 1838, 1844

British and Foreign Medico-Chirurgical Review. ScCM (1848–59) 1865–77

British Apollo, or Curious Amusements for the Ingenious. ScU [mfm] 1708–11

British Association for the Advancement of Science, Report. ScC 1833–59

British Birds. ScCMus 1907–19

British Botanic Garden Record. ScCleU 1924–44

British Ceramic Society, Transactions. ScCleU 1939–45, 1947+

British Chemical Abstracts, Series A. ScCleU 1926–53; ScCM (1931–53); ScU 1926–34

British Chemical Abstracts, Series B. ScCleU 1932–53; ScCM (1931–35); ScNcWv 1926–53; ScU 1930–33

British Critic and Quarterly Theological Review. ScU [mfm] 1792–1843

British Heart Journal. ScCM 1939+

British Interplanetary Society, Journal. ScU 1934+

British Journal of Anaesthesia. ScCM (1930–50) 1951+

British Journal of Children's Diseases. ScCM (1906–17) 1920–44

British Journal of Dermatology [and Syphilis]. ScCM (1930–53) 1956+

British Journal of Educational Psychology. ScU (1933+)

British Journal of Experimental Biology. ScCleU 1923+

British Journal of Experimental Pathology. ScCM 1920–33, 1948+

British Journal of Ophthalmology. ScCM (1929–42) 1945+

British Journal of Psychology. ScU (1920–45) 1948+

British Journal of Radiology. ScCM (1925–35) 1936+

British Journal of Surgery. ScCM 1913+; ScGGh (1924–27)

British Journal of Urology. ScCM (1930) 1932+

British Magazine and Monthly Register of Religious and Ecclesiastical Information. ScU [mfm] 1832–49

British Magazine, or Monthly Repository for Gentlemen and Ladies. ScU [mfm] 1760–67

British Medical Journal. ScCM (1875+); ScCoHo 1930+; ScGGh (1914–42) 1943+

British Mycological Society, Transactions. ScCleU 1896–1921, 1923+; ScU 1896–1959, 1963+

British Quarterly Review [London]. ScU 1845–54 (1861–62)

British Quarterly Review [New York]. ScU (1871–86)

British Review. ScSpW 1811–25; ScU [mfm] 1811–25

Briton. ScU [mfm] 1762–63

Broadway Journal. ScU [mfm] 1845–46

Brooklyn Entomological Society, Bulletin. ScCleU 1878–1947, 1951+; ScU 1881–1924, 1933–52

Brooklyn Hospital Journal. ScCM 1939+

Brooklyn Institute Museum News [Quarterly]. ScCMus 1905–36

Brooklyn Institute of Arts and Sciences, Bontanical Garden, Record [Plants and Garden]. ScCleU 1924+

Brooklyn Law Review. ScU 1932+

Broom. ScU (1921–23)

Brother Jonathan. ScU [mfm] 1842–43

Browne and Munson's Phonographic Monthly. ScClP (1876–89)

Brownson's Quarterly Review [Boston]. ScU [mfm] 1844–52

Bruns Beitraege zur Klinischen Chirurgie. ScCM (1906–50)

Bryologist. ScCleU 1894+; ScU 1898+

Buffalo Society of Natural History, Bulletin. ScCMus (1874+)

Builder and Woodworker. ScC (1881–86)

Bulletin des Sciences Mathematiques Astronomiques. ScCleU 1824–31

Bulletin des Sciences Technologiques. ScCleU 1824–31

Bulletin of Basic Science Research. ScCM 1931–33

Bulletin of Bibliography. ScCleU 1902+; ScU 1899+

Bulletin of Entomological Reseach. ScCleU 1910+

Bulletin of Hygiene. ScCM (1931–50)

Bulletin of Pharmacy. ScU (1905–28)

Bulletin of Spanish Studies [Hispanic Studies]. ScU (1941–48) 1949+

Bulletin of the History of Medicine. ScCM (1933–37) 1938+

Bulletin of War Medicine [London]. ScCM 1940–46

Bulwark, or Reformation Journal. ScSpW 1851–52

Bunker Hill Monument Association, Proceedings. ScC (1889–1911)

Bureau of Standards, Journal of Research. ScClP 1929–42
Burlington Magazine. ScGBj 1906–28 (1933–53) 1954+
Burr McIntosh Monthly. ScU (1903–10)
Burrough's Clearing House. ScCleU 1933+
Burton's Gentleman's Magazine and American Monthly Review. ScU [mfm] 1837–40
Business Education World. ScGBj (1933) 1936+; ScGwLa 1941+; ScRhW 1933+; ScU 1938+
Business History Review. ScCleU 1926–53, 1955+; ScU [mfm] 1926+
Business Week. ScCCit 1932+; ScCleU 1929+; ScGBj 1937+; ScGF 1938+; ScNewb 1941+; ScOrSc 1936+; ScRhW 1940+; ScSpC 1939+; ScU (1932) 1934+
Busy Body, or Men and Manners. ScU [mfm] 1759
Butler University Botanical Studies. ScCleU 1929+
Byloe. ScU (1907–18)
Byzantion. ScU 1924+

C

Cabinet, a Repository of Polite Literature. ScU [mfm] (1811)
Caduceus. ScCM (1932–41)
Calcutta Mathematical Society, Bulletin. ScU (1910–54)
Calcutta Review. ScU [mfm] 1844–1902
California Academy of Medicine, Proceedings. ScCM 1930–32
California Academy of Sciences, Occasional Papers. ScCMus (1890+)
California Academy of Sciences, Proceedings. ScCMus 1888+
California and Western Medicine. ScCM 1907+; ScGGh (1939–43)
California Cultivator and Livestock and Dairy Journal [California Farmer]. ScCleU 1925–26, 1948+
California Fish and Game. ScCleU 1917+
California Journal of Secondary Education. ScGBj 1938+; ScGF 1926+; ScU 1925+
California Law Review. ScU 1919+
California [University], Giannini Foundations, Contributions. ScCleU (1930+)
California [University], Publications in Agricultural Sciences. ScCleU 1912–34
California [University], Publications in Botany. ScCleU (1935+)

California [University], Publications in Engineering. ScCleU (1940+)

California [University], Publications in Entomology. ScCleU (1906+)

California [University], Publications in Physiology. ScCleU 1910–15

California [University], Publications in Zoology. ScCleU (1902+); ScCMus 1910+

Calvinistic Magazine. ScSpW 1827–30

Cambrian and Caledonian Quarterly Magazine and Celtic Repertory. ScU [mfm] 1829–33

Cambridge Law Journal. ScU 1921+

Cambridge Philosophical Society, Proceedings. ScCleU (1926–53) 1955+; ScU 1920+

Cambridge University Magazine. ScU [mfm] 1840–43

Cambridge University, School of Agriculture, Memoirs. ScCleU 1928+

Campbell's Foreign Semi-Monthly Magazine. ScU [mfm] 1842–44

Camping Magazine. ScU 1935+

Canada, Department of Agriculture, Report of the Minister of Agriculture. ScCleU (1924+)

Canadian Aquaria. ScU 1933–36

Canadian Bar Review. ScU 1923+

Canadian Ceramic Society, Journal. ScCleU (1936–54) 1955+

Canadian Chemical Processing. ScCleU 1919–45, 1947–58

Canadian Engineer [Roads and Bridges]. ScCleU (1928–39)

Canadian Entomologist. ScCleU 1868+; ScCMus 1868–1934

Canadian Historical Review. ScGF (1923–32); ScU 1920+

Canadian Journal of Economics and Political Science. ScU 1935+

Canadian Journal of Medical Technology. ScCM (1940+)

Canadian Journal of Medicine and Surgery. ScCoHo 1931–32

Canadian Journal of Public Health. ScCM (1928+)

Canadian Journal of Research. ScCleU 1929–50; ScCM (1929–50); ScU 1929–35. NOTE: *Journal* split into several sections in 1951; ScCleU and ScU have to date.

Canadian Medical Association, Journal. ScCM 1912+

Canadian Methodist Review. ScSpW 1895

Canadian Naturalist and Geologist. ScCMus 1857–63

Canadian Pharmaceutical Journal. ScU 1940+

Canadian Textile Journal. ScCleU (1920–26) 1929+

Cancer Research. ScCleU 1941+; ScCM 1941+

Candid Examiner [Montrose, Pa.]. ScU [mfm] 1826–27

Canning Age. ScCleU 1930–33

Canning Trade. ScCleU 1934+

Carnegie Corporation of New York, Annual Report. ScCleU (1931+)

Carnegie Endowment, Division of Economics and History, Annual Report. ScCleU (1925–39)

Carnegie Endowment, Division of Education, Annual Report. ScCleU (1923–46)

Carnegie Endowment for International Peace, Yearbook. ScCleU (1911–41)

Carnegie Foundation for the Advancement of Teaching, Annual Report. ScCleU 1906+

Carnegie Foundation for the Advancement of Teaching, Bulletin. ScCleU 1907–40, 1953+; ScRhW 1906+

Carnegie Hero Fund Commission, Annual Report. ScCleU 1914–59

Carnegie Institution of Washington, Contributions to Embryology. ScCM 1915–57

Carnegie Institution of Washington, News Service Bulletin. ScCleU 1930–38

Carnegie Institution of Washington, Yearbook. ScCleU 1903+

Carnegie Museum, Annals. ScCMus (1901+)

Carolina Alumnus. ScU 1920–21

Carolina Baptist. ScGF 1845–46; ScU (1845–46)

Carolina Club Boy. ScCleU 1922–32, 1935–55

Carolina Farmer and Stockman. ScU (1919–21)

Carolina Journal of Medicine, Science, and Agriculture [Charleston]. ScCM 1825; ScU (1825), also [mfm] (1825–26)

Carolina Journal of Pharmacy. ScU 1941+

Carolina Law Journal. ScSpar 1830–31; ScU 1830–31, also [mfm] 1830–31

Carolina Law Repository. ScU [mfm] 1813–16

Carolina Medical Journal. ScCM 1899–1904

Carolina Teacher. ScU (1885–86)

Carolina Teacher's Journal. ScU (1889–1904)

Carolinian. ScU 1883–1940

Case and Comment. ScU (1905) 1947+

Casket [Cincinnati]. ScU [mfm] (1846)

Casket [Hudson, N. Y.]. ScU [mfm] 1811–12

Casket, or Flowers of Literature [Graham's Magazine]. ScGF (1837–39); ScU [mfm] (1829–30)
Catholic Historical Review. ScU (1933–57) 1960+
Catholic World. ScCleU 1940+; ScU 1922+
Cattleman. ScCleU (1935+)
Ce-Be-Cean. ScCoBi 1932+
Cellulose-Chemie. ScNcWv 1922–36
Censor [Boston]. ScU [mfm] 1771–72
Censor [London]. ScU [mfm] 1715–17, 1828–29
Century Club of Charleston, Publications. ScC (1904–52)
Century Illustrated Monthly. ScGrev 1918–29
Century Magazine. ScC (1883–93) 1894–1930; ScCCit (1899–1929); ScChar (1883–1922); ScCleU 1881–1929; ScClP 1884–95; ScCoCo 1883–1929; ScCoR (1919–25); ScDarl (1891–1929); ScFlor (1882–99); ScGaLi (1882–1930); ScGBj (1917–23); ScGF 1879–1930; ScGrew 1891–1900, 1923–25; ScHCok 1899–1930; ScLaD 1915–28; ScRhW 1881–1930; ScSpC 1881–1930; ScU 1881–1930; ScYork (1882–1906)
Ceramic Abstracts. ScCleU 1922+
Ceramic Age. ScCleU (1927–48) 1949+
Ceramic Industry. ScCleU (1923–47) 1948+
Ceramic Society [British Ceramic Society], Transactions. ScCleU 1917+
Ceramist [Ceramic Age]. ScCleU 1923–26
Cereal Chemistry. ScCleU 1924+
Ceres. ScCleU (1939+)
Certified Milk. ScCleU (1929–48) 1949+
Chamber's Edinburgh Journal. ScC (1832–48); ScSpW 1844
Chamber's Journal. ScU (1885–91)
Champion. ScU [mfm] 1739–40
Character and Personality [Journal of Personality]. ScCleU 1932+; ScU 1932+
Charaka Club, Proceedings. ScCM 1903–48
Charities [and the Commons, Survey]. ScU 1902–9
Charleston County Tuberculosis Association, Annual Report. ScCM (1933–40)
Charleston Department of Health, Annual Report. ScCM (1877–1935)
Charleston Gospel Messenger and Protestant Episcopal Register. ScU [mfm] 1824–53

Charleston Medical Journal and Review. ScC 1846–59, 1873–77; ScCM 1846–60, 1873–77; ScClP 1846–59; ScU 1846–60, 1873–77

Charleston Medical Register for the Year 1802. ScCM [mfm] 1802

Charleston Museum, Bulletin. ScCleU 1905–22; ScCM 1915–21; ScCMus 1905–22; ScU (1905–22)

Charleston Museum, Contributions. ScCC (1923+); ScCM 1923–36; ScCMus 1913–37

Charleston Museum, Leaflets. ScCleU 1931–52, 1956+; ScCMus 1930+

Charleston Protestant Episcopal Sunday School Society, Annual Report. ScC 1820, 1822–28

Charleston Spectator and Ladies' Literary Port Folio. ScU [mfm] (1806)

Charleston [W. Va.] General Hospital, Bulletin. ScCM 1938–41

Charlotte [N. C.] Medical Journal. ScCM (1898–1918)

Chautauquan. ScSpW 1887–92, 1895–1907; ScU 1880–1913

Cheap Repository. ScU [mfm] 1800

Chemical Abstracts. ScAikSr 1907+; ScCamDu 1913+; ScCC 1941+; ScCCit 1907+; ScCleU 1907+; ScClP 1918+; ScCM 1907+; ScGaLi 1929+; ScGF 1907+; ScNcWv 1907+; ScOrSc 1907+; ScRhW 1907+; ScSpC 1926+; ScSpDm 1912+; ScSpW 1907+; ScU 1907+; ScWinR 1907+

Chemical Age. ScCleU 1922–23, 1949+; ScU 1921–24

Chemical Age [London]. ScCleU (1924–48) 1949+

Chemical and Engineering News. ScCCit 1941+; ScCleU 1940+; ScOrSc 1925+; ScRhW 1923+; ScSpW 1940+

Chemical and Metallugical Engineering [Chemical Engineering]. ScCleU 1918+; ScNcWv 1918+; ScU 1918+

Chemical Engineer. ScU 1904–20

Chemical Industries [Chemical Week]. ScU 1937+

Chemical News. ScCleU 1908–13

Chemical Reviews. ScCCit 1941+; ScCleU 1924+; ScCM 1924–42 (1946) 1947+; ScGF 1924+; ScNcWv 1924+; ScU 1925+

Chemical Society of Japan, Bulletin. ScCleU 1926+; ScU 1926+

Chemical Society of Japan, Journal. ScU 1927+

Chemical Society of London, Annual Report. ScCleU 1904+

Chemical Society of London, Journal. ScCamDu 1921+; ScCleU 1848–1925, 1948+; ScCM 1926–56, 1958+; ScGF [mc] 1847–1950; ScU 1948+

Chemical Society of London, Proceedings. ScU 1885–1914, 1957+, included in Society's *Journal*, 1915–56

Chemical Warfare. ScU (1925–34)

Chemical Week Buyers Guide. ScU (1938–40) 1945+

Chemicals. ScU 1925–31

Chemie der Erde. ScCleU (1941–58) 1959+

Chemische Berichte. ScCleU 1868+, some files on mc; ScCM (1931–47) 1948+; ScU [mc] 1868–77

Chemische Industrie. ScCleU (1886–90)

Chemisches Zentralblatt. ScCleU 1830–1921; ScU 1890–1907, also [mc] 1865–1945

Chemist. ScCM 1938–44; ScU 1929–57

Chemist-Analyst. ScCleU 1935–59; ScCM 1937–51; ScU 1914–51

Chemist and Druggist. ScCM (1871–78); ScU (1939) 1941+

Chemistry and Industry. ScCleU 1918+

Chemistry Leaflet [Science Leaflet]. ScU 1927–36

Chester White Journal. ScCleU (1928–53)

Chicago Institute for Psychoanalysis, Report. ScCM 1932–42

Chicago Tumor Institute, Report. ScCM 1938–42

Chicago [University] Law Review. ScU 1934+

Chicora: Messenger of the South. ScU (1842)

Child [Children]. ScCleU 1936+; ScCM 1936+; ScRhW 1936+

Child Development. ScGF 1930+; ScCM 1930–38

Child Life. ScRhP 1932+

Child of Pallas. ScU [mfm] 1800–1

Child Study. ScRhW 1939–60

Child Welfare. ScU (1935–37) 1940+

Childhood Education. ScCoCo 1933+; ScGF 1934+; ScHCok 1940+; ScOrSc 1939+; ScRhW 1932+; ScU 1938+

Children's Magazine [Hartford]. ScU [mfm] (1789)

Child's Friend and Family Magazine. ScU [mfm] 1843–58

Child's Newspaper [Cincinnati]. ScU [mfm] (1834)

Chimie et Industrie. ScCleU 1918+; ScU 1939–49, 1950+

China at War [China Magazine]. ScU 1938–49

China Journal. ScU (1930–33)

China's Millions. ScCoBi 1932+

Chinese Journal of Physiology. ScCM 1941–50

Chinese Medical Journal. ScCM (1932–57) 1959+

Chinese Recorder. ScGF 1910

Christendom. ScCoT 1931–34, 1940–48, some files on mfm; ScSpC (1939–48); ScSpW 1937–46

Christian Advocate. ScSpW 1826–37, 1882–95, also mfm 1826–76; ScU [mfm] 1823–34

Christian Baptist. ScU [mfm] 1823–25

Christian Cabinet. ScU [mfm] (1802)

Christian Century. ScCCit 1936+; ScChar 1932+; ScCleU 1936+; ScClP 1940+; ScCoCo (1931–48) 1949+; ScCoR 1932+; ScCoT 1900+, some files on mc; ScDwErs 1934+; ScGaLi 1934+; ScGF 1934+; ScGrev 1928+; ScGwLa 1941+; ScNewb 1924+; ScOrSc 1931+; ScRhW 1930+; ScSpC 1924+; ScSpW 1938+; ScSumM (1934–51); ScU (1925–30) 1931+

Christian Chronical. ScU [mfm] (1818)

Christian Church. ScDwErs-T 1835+

Christian Disciple and Theological Review. ScU [mfm] 1813–23

Christian Education [Christian Scholar]. ScCoT 1930–52; ScGBj (1920–48); ScGF (1927–33) 1934+; ScU (1920–25) 1926+

Christian Examiner. ScU (1825), also mfm 1824–69

Christian Herald. ScGBj 1931+; ScRhW 1931–61

Christian Herald [Portsmouth, N. H.]. ScU [mfm] 1818–25

Christian Herald and Seamen's Magazine. ScU [mfm] 1816–24

Christian History. ScU [mfm] 1743–45

Christian Home. ScClP 1932+

Christian Instructor. ScDwErs-T 1845–57

Christian Intelligencer and Eastern Chronicle. ScU [mfm] 1821–36

Christian Journal and Literary Register. ScU [mfm] 1817–30

Christian Magazine. ScU [mfm] 1824–27

Christian Magazine of the South. Sc 1843–49; ScDwErs 1843–51; ScU 1843–49

Christian Messenger. ScU [mfm] (1815–21)

Christian Mirror. ScU [mfm] (1814)

Christian Monitor. ScU [mfm] (1806–18)

Christian Monitor and Religious Intelligencer. ScU [mfm] 1812–13

Christian Neighbor. ScSpW 1868–1900

Christian Observatory. ScU [mfm] 1847–50

Christian Observer. ScC 1802–4, 1812–15; ScU (1802–19), also [mfm] 1802–66

Christian Philanthropist. ScU [mfm] 1822–23

226

Christian Reformer, or Evangelical Miscellany. ScU [mfm] 1828–29

Christian Register [Boston]. ScU [mfm] 1821–50

Christian Register and Moral and Theological Review. ScU [mfm] 1816–17

Christian Review [Rochester, N. Y.]. ScU [mfm] 1836–63

Christian Secretary [Hartford]. ScU [mfm] 1822–49

Christian Telescope [Providence]. ScU [mfm] 1824–25

Christian Union. ScSpW 1880–93

Christian Visitant [Albany]. ScU [mfm] 1815–16

Christian Visitor [Providence]. ScU [mfm] (1823)

Christian Watchman. ScU [mfm] 1819–26

Christian Weekly. ScClP 1871–82

Christianity and Society. ScCoT [mfm] 1935–56

Christian's Magazine. ScDwErs-T 1831–38; ScU [mfm] 1806–11

Christian's Magazine, Reviewer, and Religious Intelligencer. ScU [mfm] 1805–8

Christian's Monitor [Portland, Me.]. ScU [mfm] (1799)

Christian's Scholar and Farmer's Magazine. ScU [mfm] 1789–91

Christian's Weekly Monitor. ScU [mfm] 1814–18

Chronica Botanica. ScCleU 1935–61

Chronicles of the North American Savages. ScU [mfm] (1835)

Chronique du Mois, ou les Cahiers Patriotiques. ScU [mfm] (1791–92)

Church Peace Union, Report. ScRhW (1931) 1933+

Church Record. ScU [mfm] 1822–23

Church School Promoter. ScCoBi (1939–43)

Churchman's Magazine [New Haven]. ScU 1822–23, also [mfm] (1804–27)

Churchman's Repository for the Eastern Diocese [Newburyport]. ScU [mfm] (1820)

Ciba Review. ScCleU 1937+; ScRhP 1937–54, 1963+; ScWinR 1937+

Ciba Symposia. ScCM 1939–51

Cincinnati Journal of Medicine. ScCM (1923–43) 1947+

Cincinnati Literary Gazette. ScU [mfm] 1824–25

Cincinnati [University] Law Review. ScU 1927+

Circolo Matematico [Palermo] Rendiconti. ScU 1905–33, 1956+, library also has *Supplemento* 1906–30

Circular [Wilmington, Del.]. ScU [mfm] 1821–25

Citadel Alumni News. ScCCit 1940+
City Hall Recorder [New York]. ScU [mfm] 1817–22
Civil Aeronautics Journal. ScCC (1941–52)
Civil Engineer and Architects Journal. ScU 1837–51
Civil Engineering. ScCCit 1930+; ScCleU 1930+; ScU 1930+
Classical Journal. ScCC 1941+; ScCCit 1940+; ScCoCo (1919–45); ScGF (1911–32) 1933+; ScHCok 1918–40; ScRhW 1905+; ScSpC (1908–24) 1925+; ScU 1905+
Classical Journal [London]. ScU 1810–29
Classical Museum. ScSpW 1844–49
Classical Philology. ScSpC (1909–51); ScU 1906+
Classical Review. ScU 1887+
Classical Weekly. ScU (1916–50)
Clearing House. ScGBj 1938+; ScGF 1931+; ScOrSc 1940+; ScU 1932+
Clemson University, Engineering Experiment Station Record [Engineering Division Record]. ScCleU 1932+
Clemson University, Extension Division, Annual Report. ScCleU 1935+
Clemson University, Farm and Home Week Programs. ScCleU (1929–64)
Cleveland Clinic Quarterly. ScCM 1932+
Cleveland Medical Journal. ScCM (1911–17)
Climatological Data, South Carolina, U. S. Department of Commerce. ScU 1899–1919 (1920+)
Clinical Medicine and Surgery. ScCM 1906+
Clinical Science. ScCM 1933+
Clinics. ScCM 1891–1946
Clio Medica. ScCM (1930–39)
Club-Room ScU [mfm] (1820)
Coach and Athlete [Southern Coach and Athlete]. ScU 1941+
Coast Artillery Journal. ScCCit 1929–48
Coastal Topics. ScC 1932–33; ScChar (1934–37)
Coastal Tourist. ScU (1931–34)
Cobbett's Magazine. ScU [mfm] 1833–34
Cobbett's Political Register. ScC (1802–16); ScU [mfm] 1802–35
Co-Ed [Edgefield, S. C.]. ScU (1900–9)
Coehn's Lottery Gazette and Register. ScU [mfm] 1814–15, 1817–30
Cold Spring Harbor Symposia on Quantitative Biology. ScCM (1934–36) 1939+

Collections, Historical and Miscellaneous, and Monthly Literary Journal. ScU [mfm] 1822–24

Collections of Czechoslovak Chemical Communications. ScCleU 1929+; ScU (1929–48) 1953+

College and Research Libraries. ScCC 1941+; ScCCit 1939+; ScCleU 1939+; ScGF 1939+; ScNewb 1939+; ScRhW 1939+; ScU 1939+

College Art Journal. ScCleU 1941–60; ScGF 1941–60

College English. ScCCit 1940+; ScCleU (1939+); ScCoBe 1940+; ScCoCo (1940+); ScGBj 1939+; ScGF 1939+; ScNewb 1939+; ScOrSc 1939+; ScRhW 1939+; ScSpC 1939+; ScU 1939+

College News and Views. ScGF [mfm] 1936–47

College of Charleston Magazine. ScC 1830, 1854–55, 1898–1941; ScCC (1855–1945); ScU (1854–1939)

College of Physicians of Philadelphia, Transactions. ScCM (1815–1912) 1917–30, 1937+

Collegian [Presbyterian College]. ScU (1902–24)

Collegian, or American Students' Magazine. ScU [mfm] (1819)

Colliers. ScCleU (1906–57); ScClP 1939–56; ScGrev 1936–57; ScLaD 1933–54; ScRhW 1912–57; ScU 1903–57

Colman's Rural World [St. Louis]. ScU [mfm] 1848–51

Colonization and Journal of Freedom. ScU [mfm] 1833–34

Colophon [New Graphic]. ScC (1932–35); ScChar (1935–40); ScRhW 1932–34; ScU 1930–40

Color Trade Journal. ScCleU 1918–25

Colorado Medicine. ScCM (1905–18) 1920–37

Colorado School of Mines Quarterly. ScU (1917+)

Colorado University Studies. ScCleU (1905+)

Colorado-Wyoming Academy of Science, Journal. ScCleU 1929–59

Columbia Chemical Society of Philadelphia, Memoirs. ScU [mfm] 1813

Columbia Law Review. ScU 1901+

Columbia Magazine [Hudson, N. Y.]. ScU [mfm] 1814–15

Columbia Magazine of Monthly Miscellany. ScU [mfm] 1786–90

Columbian Historian [New Richmond, Ohio]. ScU [mfm] 1824–25

Columbian Lady's and Gentleman's Magazine. ScU [mfm] 1844–49

Columbian Magazine [Danbury, Conn.]. ScU [mfm] (1806)

Columbian Museum, or Universal Asylum. ScU [mfm] 1793

Columbian Phenix and Boston Review. ScU [mfm] (1800)

Columbian Star. ScU [mfm] 1822–25

Colvin's Weekly Register. ScU [mfm] (1808)
Combustion. ScCleU 1935+
Comet. ScU [mfm] 1811–12
Commentator. ScRhW 1937–39
Commerce and Finance. ScSpW 1919–20
Commercial and Financial Chronicle. ScCCit (1918+); ScU 1917+,
also 1865–1900 on mc
Commercial Fertilizer. ScCleU (1933–61) 1962+
Commercial Fertilizer, Yearbook. ScCleU 1924–37
Common Ground. ScCleU 1940–49
Common School Advocate [Madison, Ind., and Cincinnati]. ScU
[mfm] 1837–41
Common School Journal and Educational Reformer. ScU [mfm]
1838–52
Commonhealth [Massachusetts Department of Public Health]. Sc-
CleU 1932–39
Commonweal. ScChar 1932+; ScCleU 1929+; ScGrev 1933+;
ScRhW 1937+; ScSpC 1939+; ScU 1929+
Commonwealth Fund, Annual Report. ScCM (1938–39) 1941+
Communications. ScU 1941–49
Companion and Weekly Miscellany. ScU [mfm] 1804–6
Compass [Social Work Journal]. ScU 1929–55
Compleat Library, or News for the Ingenious. ScU [mfm] 1692–94
Compleat Linguist. ScU [mfm] 1719–22
Compositio Mathematica. ScU 1934+
Compressed Air Magazine. ScCleU 1929–44, 1950+; ScU 1926+
Concept [Converse College]. ScU (1894–1932)
Concrete. ScCleU 1928–61
Concrete Paving [Highway and Public Improvements]. ScU (1919+)
Condor. ScCMus 1899+
Confederate Veteran. Sc 1893–1909; ScABBE 1894–1932; ScC 1894–
1932; ScCleU (1903–32); ScDarl 1907–20; ScFlor 1909–32; ScGF
(1897–1902) 1903–30 (1931–32); ScGrew 1895–1922; ScLaD 1929–
30; ScLaur 1926+; ScMar 1898–1928; ScRhW 1925–32; ScSpW
(1894–1916); ScU 1893–1932
Confederate War Journal. ScU 1893–95
Conference for Education in the South, Proceedings. ScCleU 1898–
1914
Conference of Presidents of Negro Land Grant Colleges, Proceedings. ScCleU (1933–54)

Confinia Neurologica. ScCM (1938–58)

Congregationalist and Herald of Gospel Liberty. ScU [mfm] 1816–50

Congress of American Physicians and Surgeons, Transactions. ScCM 1889–1938

Congressional Debates [Globe, Record]. ScABBE (1780–1920); ScCCit (1929–58) 1959+; ScClP 1888+; ScLaur (1911–27); ScRhW 1873+; ScSoH 1849–57; ScSpW (1834+)

Congressional Digest. ScCCit (1924–46) 1948+; ScChar 1933+; ScCleU 1926+; ScGBj 1938+; ScGF 1922+; ScGrev 1922+; ScNewb 1922+; ScOrSc 1941, 1951+; ScRhW 1923+; ScSpW 1926+; ScU 1921+

Congressional Review. ScDwErs-T 1869–71

Connecticut Academy of Arts and Sciences, Transactions. ScCMus (1866–1917)

Connecticut Evangelical Magazine and Religious Intelligencer. ScU [mfm] 1808–15

Connecticut Magazine. ScU [mfm] (1801)

Connecticut Republican Magazine. ScU [mfm] (1802–3)

Connecticut State Medical Journal. ScCM 1936+

Connie Maxwell [Greenwood, S. C.]. ScU (1908+)

Connoisseur. ScC 1931+; ScChar 1931+; ScCleU 1926–43; ScGBj 1938+; ScHCok (1932–33) 1939+; ScRhW 1931+; ScU 1931–56

Conservation. ScCC 1938–42

Conservator. ScSpW 1914–15

Construction. ScU 1937–53

Construction Methods. ScU 1928–37

Constructor. ScU (1927–44) 1946+

Consumer Union Reports. ScCC 1939+; ScCleU (1941–52) 1954+; ScU 1939+

Consumers' Guide. ScRhW 1934–47

Consumers' Research Bulletin [Consumer Bulletin]. ScRhW 1941; ScU (1938–56) 1957+

Contemporary Review. ScC (1873+); ScCCit (1935–55); ScCleU 1935+; ScCoCo (1922–29); ScGaLi (1901–9); ScGF 1939+; ScRhW 1866+; ScSpC 1871–73, 1946–51; ScSpW 1917–19; ScU 1866+

Contemporary Verse. ScC 1919–27

Continent. ScU [mc] 1822–84

Contractors and Engineers Monthly. ScU (1926–40) 1947+

Converted Catholic [Christian Heritage]. ScCoBi 1940–58; ScGBj (1940–45) 1946+

Cooperation [Cotton Co-Op]. ScU (1930–31)

Cooperative Digest. ScCleU 1940+

Cooperative [Marketing] **Journal.** ScCleU 1926–39

Copeia. ScCleU (1926–47) 1948+; ScCMus 1932+; ScU 1930+

Cornell Engineer. ScCleU (1935–44) 1945+

Cornell Law Quarterly. ScU 1915+

Cornell Rural School, Leaflet. ScCleU (1914–18) 1919+

Cornell University, College of Home Economics, Annual Report. ScCleU 1927+

Cornell University, New York State Veterinary College, Annual Report. ScCleU 1926+

Cornell Veterinarian. ScCleU 1932+

Cornhill Magazine. ScCleU (1882–85) 1953+; ScGF 1865–66; ScU (1860–1945) 1948+

Coronet. ScCleU 1936–61; ScCoCo (1938–61); ScCoR 1937–61; ScOrSc 1940–57; ScRhW 1948–61; ScU 1937–61

Corrector. ScU [mfm] (1804)

Correspondent. ScU [mfm] 1827–29

Corsair. ScGF 1839–40; ScU [mfm] (1839–40)

Cosmopolitan. ScClP 1886–99; ScDarl (1892–97) 1959+; ScNewb 1934+; ScSpW 1887–1908; ScU 1886–1923, also [mfm] 1886–1900

Cosmopolitan [Charleston]. ScC 1833

Cosmopolite. ScChar (1866)

Cotton [Textile Industries]. ScCleU (1926+)

Cotton [Gin] **and Cotton Oil** [Mill] **Press News.** ScCleU 1934+

Cotton Research Congress [American Cotton Congress], **Proceedings.** ScCleU 1940+

Country Gentleman [Better Farming]. ScCleU 1853–1900 (1913–49) 1949+; ScRhW 1928–55; ScU (1853–1955)

Country Home. ScCleU (1931–34) 1935–38

Country Life. ScChar 1932–42; ScCleU 1905–42; ScCMus (1903–31); ScGrev 1925–40; ScLaD 1929–40; ScRhW 1915–42; ScU 1901–42

Country Spectator. ScU [mfm] 1792–93

Courier de Boston. ScU [mfm] (1789)

Court Magazine, or Royal Chronicle. . . . ScU [mfm] 1761–65

Covenant. ScC (1842–45)

Craftsman. ScCleU (1907–16)

Creamery and Milk Plant Monthly [American Milk Review]. ScCleU
1917–30

Creamery Journal [Dairy Record]. ScCleU 1936–50

Criminal Law Magazine and Reporter. ScU 1880

Crisis. ScOrSc (1911–58) 1964+

Crisis [Richmond, Va.]. ScU [mfm] (1840)

Criterion. ScU (1923–39), also [mfm] 1922–39

Criterion [Columbia College]. ScU (1897–1950)

Critic [New York]. ScU [mfm] 1828–29

Critic [Philadelphia]. ScU [mfm] (1820)

Critic, an Illustrated Review of Literature, Art and Life. ScSpW
1896–1906; ScU [mfm] 1884–1906, also [mfm] 1881–1900

Critical Review. ScC (1760–1817); ScGF 1774–83; ScGeor 1756–
1801; ScU [mfm] 1815–17

Crops and Markets. ScRhW 1934–57

Cultivator. ScCleU 1844–50; ScU [mfm] 1834–65

Culture. ScU 1940+

Current. ScU 1884–86

Current Digest of Medical Literature. ScCM 1941–59

Current Farm Economics. ScCleU 1927+

Current Geographical Publications. ScU 1938+

Current History [and Forum]. ScC 1914–20; ScCC (1914–28) 1929–
51; ScCCit 1926+; ScChar 1930+; ScCleU 1914+; ScClP 1917+;
ScCoAl (1929–36); ScCoCo 1928+; ScCoR 1919+; ScDarl 1920–
39; ScDwErs 1918+; ScFlor (1915–30); ScGaLi 1915+; ScGBj
(1923) 1926+; ScGF (1914–18) 1922+; ScGrev 1919+; ScHCok
1914+; ScNewb 1917+; ScOrSc 1931–50, 1956, 1963+; ScRhP
1932+; ScRhW 1914+; ScSpar 1929–32 (1950) 1962+; ScSpC
1921+; ScSpW 1941+; ScSum 1935+; ScU 1916+

Current Legal Thought. ScU 1935+

Current Literature. ScU (1889–1912)

Current Opinion. ScC (1913–24); ScGrev 1919–25; ScHCok 1917–
25; ScRhW 1913–25; ScSpC 1920–25; ScU 1913–25

Curriculum Journal [Educational Leadership]. ScCCit 1927+; Sc-
GF 1937+; ScRhW 1941+; ScU 1929+

Curtis's Botanical Magazine. ScC (1793–1850); ScU 1801–4

Cyclopedic Review of Current History. ScGF 1891–1903

Cynick. ScU [mfm] (1811)

D

Daguerreotype. ScC (1847–49); ScU [mfm] 1847–49

Daily Gazetteer. ScU [mfm] (1735–48)

Dairy Farmer. ScCleU 1925–29

Dairy Science Abstracts. ScCleU 1939+

Dairy World. ScCleU 1936–53

Danske Videnskabernes Selskab [Copenhagen], Matematisk-Fysicke Meddelelser. ScU 1917+

Darby's Monthly. ScU [mfm] (1824)

Daughters of the American Revolution, Ann Pamela Cunningham Chapter Yearbook. ScU (1927–36)

Daughters of the American Revolution Magazine. ScChar 1936+; ScCleU (1913–50) 1951+; ScCMus 1922–32; ScNewb 1919+; ScMar (1927–41) 1942+

Daughters of the American Revolution, South Carolina Yearbook. ScU (1922–49)

Davenport [Iowa] Academy of Natural Sciences, Proceedings. ScCMus (1867–99)

Dawn [Wilmington, Del.]. ScU [mfm] (1822)

Dayspring [Columbia, S. C.]. ScU 1901–2

Dearborn Independent. ScCleU 1919–27

De Bow's Review. ScC 1846–58 (1859–69); ScCleU 1846–61; ScClP 1852–55; ScGF (1846–66); ScRhW (1848–60); ScSpW (1852–70); ScU 1846–64, 1866–70, also [mfm] 1846–50

Debtor's Journal. ScU [mfm] 1820–21

Defoe's Review. ScRhW 1704–13; ScU 1704–13

Delaware State Medical Journal. ScCM (1916–38) 1939+

Delineator. ScChar 1902–6, 1909–16; ScRhW 1923–37

Delphick Oracle. ScU [mfm] 1719–20

Democritus Ridens, or Comus and Momus. ScU [mfm] (1681)

Demorest's Magazine. ScClP 1880–87

Design. ScCleU (1937–44); ScHCok (1938–60)

Dessert to the True American. ScU [mfm] 1798–99

Deutsche Archiv für Klinische Medizin. ScCM (1869–1948)

Deutsche Botanische Gesellschaft. ScCleU (1883–98) 1899+

Deutsche Chemische Gessellschaft, Berlin Berichte. ScU 1868–77, 1897+, some files on mc

Deutsche Chirurgie. ScCM (1881–87)

Deutsche Medicinische Wochenschrift. ScCM (1891–1958)

Deutsche Shakespeare-Gessellschaft, Weimar Jahrbuch. ScC 1865–1915

Deutsche Texte des Mittelalters. ScU 1904–20

Deutsche Vierteljahrsschrift für Literaturwissenschaft und Geistesgeschichte. ScU 1923–33

Diadem [Philadelphia]. ScU 1848

Dial [Boston]. ScRhW 1840–44; ScU [mfm] 1840–44

Dial [New York, Chicago]. ScCleU 1906–29; ScRhW 1920–29; ScU (1880–91) 1893–1929, also [mfm] 1880–1900

Dialect Notes. ScCleU 1907–22; ScU 1896–1939

Diana and Ladies' Spectator. ScU [mfm] (1822)

Diapason. ScSpC 1936+

Digest of Ophthalmology and Otolaryngology. ScCM 1938–59

Digest of Treatment. ScGGh 1937–41

Diocese. ScCDhs 1903+; ScU (1895+)

Diplomate. ScCM 1929–53

Discovery. ScRhW 1920–40

Diseases of the Chest. ScCM 1935+

Diseases of the Nervous System. ScCM (1940–55) 1956+

Diverting Post. ScU [mfm] 1704–6

Dixie Lens. ScU 1940–41

Dixie Poultry Journal. ScCleU 1926–27

Dollar Magazine. ScGF 1848–51; ScU [mfm] (1833) 1841–42, 1848–51

Double Dealer. ScRhW 1921–25; ScU 1921–26

Drama. ScGrev 1926–30; ScU 1911–31

Drama of the Skies. ScU 1935–36

Dramatic Mirror and Literary Companion. ScU [mfm] 1841–42

Drug and Cosmetic Industry. ScU 1939+

Drug Bulletin. ScU 1928–32

Drug Standards [National Formulary Committee Bulletin]. ScU 1936–60

Drug Topics. ScU 1935–40, 1941+

Drug Trade News. ScU 1940+

Druggists' Circular. ScCM (1881–86) 1920–40

Dublin and London Magazine. ScU [mfm] 1825–28

Dublin Review [Wiseman Review]. ScU (1910+)

Dublin Royal Society, Proceedings. ScCMus 1877–1902

Dudley Herbarium, Contributions. ScCleU (1927+)

Duke Bar Journal. ScU 1933–42

Duke Endowment, Hospital Section, Annual Report. ScCleU 1925–39; ScCM 1925–39

Duke Endowment, Orphan Section, Annual Report. ScCleU 1928–39

Duke Endowment, Yearbook. ScCleU 1924–57

Duke Mathematical Journal. ScCC 1939–49; ScCCit 1938–45; ScCleU 1935–43 (1949) 1958+; ScSpW 1935–51; ScU 1935+

Duke University, School of Forestry, Bulletin. ScCleU 1935–48

Du Pont Magazine. ScCleU 1933–37, 1941–52

Dyestuffs. ScCleU 1922+

E

Earth. ScCMus (1867)

Earthquake Notes. ScU 1929+

East and West of England Society for the Encouragement of Agriculture, Arts, Manufactures and Commerce, Letters and Papers. ScC 1792–1800

East Tennessee Historical Society, Publications. ScCleU 1929+; ScU 1929+

Eastern Magazine [Bangor, Me.]. ScU [mfm] 1835–36

Echo [Furman University]. ScGF (1895–1951)

Eclectic Magazine. ScC (1844–1900); ScCCit 1879–91; ScChar 1869–77; ScGF (1846–51) 1852–84; ScSpW (1849–58) 1859–1906; ScU (1844–90), also [mfm] 1844–50

Eclectic Medical Journal [Rochester, N. Y.]. ScCM 1836–39

Eclectic Museum. ScGF 1843; ScSoH (1843–44); ScU [mfm] 1843–44

Eclectic Review. ScU [mfm] 1805–68

Ecological Monographs. ScCleU 1931+; ScU 1931+

Ecology. ScCleU 1920+; ScU 1920+

Econometrica. ScCleU 1933+; ScU 1933+

Economic Bulletin [American Economic Review]. ScCleU 1908–10

Economic Geography. ScCCit 1939+; ScCleU 1925+; ScRhW 1925+; ScU 1925+

Economic Geology. ScCCit 1939+; ScCleU 1905–6, 1918, 1925+; ScU 1906+

Economic History Review. ScCleU 1927+; ScU 1927+

Economic Journal. ScCleU 1924+; ScSpC 1930–51; ScU (1893–1932) 1937+

Economist. ScCCit [mc] 1904–12, 1960+; ScU 1923+, also 1843–1912 on mc

Ed-Clip Service [Cotton Manufacturers' Association]. ScU (1939–45)

Edinburgh Annual Register. ScU 1808–26

Edinburgh Magazine and Literary Miscellany. ScU [mfm] 1739–1826

Edinburgh Mathematical Society, Proceedings. ScU 1907+

Edinburgh Medical Journal. ScCM (1904–14) 1920–54

Edinburgh Philosophical Journal. ScC 1791–1827

Edinburgh Review. ScC (1802–1929); ScCCit 1866–70; ScCleU (1805) 1806–1924; ScGF (1809–63); ScRhW 1802+; ScSoH 1830–33; ScSpW 1802–31, 1840–57 (1870–81); ScU 1802–1929, also [mfm] (1755–56)

Education. ScCleU 1915+; ScDwErs 1928+; ScGBj (1932–38) 1939+; ScGF 1920+; ScGrev (1920+); ScHCok 1910+; ScNewb 1938+; ScOrSc 1940–49 (1956–62) 1963+; ScRhW 1932+

Education Abstracts. ScCleU 1941–43; ScRhW 1941–44; ScU 1939+

Education by Radio. ScCleU 1931–41

Education Digest. ScCleU 1939+; ScGBj 1938+; ScNewb 1938+; ScRhW 1935+; ScSpC 1935+; ScU 1935+

Educational. ScU (1902–4)

Educational Administration and Supervision. ScCleU (1920–30) 1955–60; ScGBj 1938+; ScGF 1915+; ScOrCl (1929–42) 1943–59; ScOrSc 1928–60; ScU 1919+

Educational and Psychological Measurements. ScCleU 1941+; ScGF 1941+; ScU 1941+

Educational Forum. ScOrSc 1936–45; ScRhW 1936+

Educational Method. ScCleU (1929–43); ScGBj 1938–43; ScGF (1928–43); ScOrSc 1921–43; ScRhW 1939–43; ScU 1921–43

Educational Music. ScGBj 1938–57

Educational Record. ScCC (1923–32) 1933+; ScCleU 1920+; ScCoBe 1920+; ScGF 1924+; ScHCok 1930+; ScRhW 1920+; ScU 1921+

Educational Record, Supplement. ScGF 1926–48

Educational Research Bulletin. ScOrSc 1926–28, 1933+; ScU (1923–44) 1947+

Educational Review. ScCCit 1926–28; ScCleU 1891–1928; ScGF 1907–8, 1920–28; ScHCok 1906–28; ScRhW (1891–1928); ScSpC

1894–97, 1916–24; ScSpW 1895–1918, 1919–22, 1923–28; ScU 1891+

Educational Screen [and Audio-Visual Guide]. ScCleU 1926+

Electric Journal. ScCCit (1904–13); ScCleU 1904–36

Electric Light and Power. ScCleU 1923–41

Electric Railway Journal [Transit Journal]. ScCleU (1911–19) 1920–31; ScU (1910–15)

Electric Traction [Mass Transportation]. ScU (1920–32)

Electrical Engineering [IEEE Spectrum]. ScCleU 1931+; ScU 1931+

Electrical Record. ScCleU 1915–16

Electrical Review [Factory Management and Maintenance]. ScCleU 1903–9

Electrical World. ScCCit 1933+; ScCleU 1884+; ScU (1893–98) 1910+

Electrochemical and Metallurgical Industry [Chemical Engineering]. ScCleU 1904–9; ScU 1902–9

Electrochemical Society, Transactions [Journal]. ScCleU (1931–48) 1949+; ScU 1902+

Electronic Industries. ScU 1941+

Electronics. ScCCit 1934+; ScCleU 1930+; ScSpDm 1930+; ScU 1930+

Elektrotechnische Zeitschrift. ScCleU 1890–1906; ScU 1922–56

Elementary English Review. ScGBj 1940+; ScRhW 1941–46

Elementary School Journal. ScCleU (1921–52) 1953+; ScCoBe 1917+; ScGBj 1933+; ScGF 1921+; ScGrev 1922+; ScHCok 1927+; ScNewb 1938+; ScOrCl 1926+; ScOrSc 1921+; ScRhW 1910+; ScSpC 1927–31; ScU 1902+

Elgin [Illinois] State Hospital Papers. ScCM 1939–45

Elisha Mitchell Scientific Society, Journal. ScCleU 1883+; ScCMus 1883+; ScU (1887–88) 1891+

Elks Magazine. ScRhP 1933+

Elliott Society, Proceedings. ScCMus (1853–59)

Emerald [Baltimore]. ScU [mfm] (1810–11)

Emerald and Baltimore Literary Gazette. ScU [mfm] 1828–49

Emerald, or Miscellany of Literature [Boston]. ScU [mfm] (1806–8)

Emerson's Magazine and Putnam's Monthly. ScGF (1854–57)

Empire Cotton Growing Corporation, Progress Report. ScCleU 1925+

Empire Cotton Growing Corporation, Report of Administrative Council. ScCleU (1931–62)

Empire Cotton Growing Review. ScCleU 1927+

Emporium of Arts and Sciences. ScGF (1812–14); ScU (1813–14), also [mfm] 1812–14

Endocrinology. ScCleU 1917+; ScCM 1917+; ScCoHo 1930+

Endokrinologie, Zentralblatt für das Gebiet der Inneren Sekretion und Konstitutionsforschung. ScCleU (1933–36)

Engineer. ScU (1887) 1950+

Engineering. ScU (1868) 1950+

Engineering and Mining Journal. ScCleU 1903+; ScU (1904–17) 1920+

Engineering Education. ScCleU (1897+); ScU 1912+

Engineering Foundation, Report. ScCleU 1923+

Engineering Index. ScAikSr 1919+

Engineering Magazine [Industrial Management]. ScCleU 1891–1916; ScU 1891–1916

Engineering News [Record]. ScCCit 1898+; ScCleU (1899–1917) 1918+; ScU (1903–15) 1917+

Engineering Record. ScCCit (1905–16); ScCleU 1904–17; ScU (1901–16)

Engineers Council for Professional Development, Report. ScCleU 1934–52

Englische Studien. ScC 1877–1916; ScU 1877–1909, 1910–20

English Historical Review. ScCC 1940–51; ScU (1917–18) 1923+, also 1886–1910 on mc

English Illustrated Magazine. ScU 1883–89

English Journal [College English]. ScCleU 1912–39; ScGBj (1936–39); ScGF 1928–39; ScOrSc (1928–39); ScRhW 1912–39; ScSpC 1924–39; ScSpW 1913–17 (1923–26); ScU 1912–39

English Journal [High School Edition]. ScGF 1917+; ScU 1934+

English Journal of Education. ScSpW 1847–53

English Literary History Journal. ScCleU 1936+; ScU 1934+

English Review. ScU [mfm] 1844–53

English Review of Literature, Science, Discoveries, Inventions. . . . ScSpW 1783–89; ScU [mfm] 1783–96

English Studies. ScU 1919+

Englishman's Magazine. ScU [mfm] (1831)

Entertainer. ScU [mfm] 1717–18

Entomologica Americana. ScCMus 1885–90

Entomological News. ScCleU 1890+; ScCMus 1890–1909
Entomological Society of America, Annals. ScCleU 1908+
Entomological Society of Ontario, Annual Report. ScCleU (1903+)
Entomological Society of Washington, Proceedings. ScCleU (1884–1910) 1911+
Entomologische Zeitschrift. ScCleU 1910+
Ephemeris of Materica Medica. ScCM 1882–1900
Episcopal Church Annual. ScCDhs 1910+
Episcopal Magazine. ScU [mfm] 1820–21
Epworth Orphanage Record [Columbia, S. C.]. ScU (1916–47)
Ergebnisse der Physiologie. ScCM 1902–39, 1950+
Erskinian [Erskine College]. ScU (1894–1916)
Essex Institute, Bulletin. ScCMus (1876–95)
Essex Institute, Historical Collections. ScCHis 1893+
Essex Institute, Proceedings. ScCMus 1848–71
Ethics. ScGF 1937+; ScU 1938+
Etude. ScCoBe 1906–43; ScCoR 1910–57; ScGBj 1928–52; ScGrev 1939–57; ScGrew 1936–57; ScLaD 1908–50; ScMar (1940–56); ScRhW 1938–57; ScSpC 1922–56; ScU (1923) 1933–57
European Magazine and London Review. ScC (1782–98); ScU 1782–1804, 1808, also [mfm] 1782–1826
Euterpeiad. ScU [mfm] 1820–23
Evangelical Guardian and Review. ScU [mfm] 1817–19
Evangelical Intelligencer. ScU [mfm] 1805–9
Evangelical Luminary [Schoharie, N. Y.]. ScU [mfm] 1824
Evangelical Lutheran Intelligencer [Frederick, Md.]. ScNewb 1826–27
Evangelical Monitor [Woodstock, Vt.]. ScU [mfm] 1821–24
Evangelical Quarterly. ScCoBi (1938+)
Evangelical Record [Lexington, Ky.]. ScU [mfm] 1812–13
Evangelical Recorder [Auburn and Utica, N. Y.]. ScU [mfm] 1818–21
Evangelical Repertory. ScU [mfm] 1823–24
Evangelical Repository. ScDwErs-T (1833–91); ScU [mfm] 1816
Evangelical Review. ScDwErs-T 1869–70
Evangelical Witness [Newburgh, N. Y.]. ScU [mfm] 1822–26
Evangelisches Magazin. ScU [mfm] 1811–17
Evening Fire-side, or Literary Miscellany. ScU [mfm] 1804–6
Events [Current History]. ScCleU 1937–41; ScU 1937–41
Evergreen. ScU [mfm] 1840–41

Every Youth's Gazette. ScU [mfm] 1842
Everybody's Magazine. ScC (1904–17); ScRhW 1913–22; ScU 1889–1923
Evidence, or Religious and Moral Gazette [Catskill, N. Y.]. ScU [mfm] 1807–8
Examiner [London]. ScU [mfm] 1710–14
Examiner [New York]. ScU [mfm] 1813–16
Examiner, a Weekly Paper on Politics, Literature, Music, and the Fine Arts [London]. ScU [mfm] 1808–81
Examiner and Hesperian [Pittsburgh]. ScU [mfm] 1839–40
Examiner and Journal of Political Economy. ScGF (1833–34); ScU 1834
Excavating Engineer. ScU 1937–39, 1944
Experienced Christian's Magazine. ScU [mfm] 1796–1806
Exposition [Charleston]. ScCC (1901); ScCMus 1901–2; ScRhW 1901–2; ScU 1901–2
Expositor and Universalist Review. ScU [mfm] 1830–40
Expository Times. ScCoT 1892–93, 1931–32, 1945+
Eye. ScU [mfm] 1808
Eye, Ear, Nose and Throat Monthly. ScCM 1922+

F

Factory and Industrial Management. ScCleU 1928–32; ScU 1928–32
Factory Management and Maintenance [Factory]. ScCCit 1937+; ScCleU 1933+; ScU 1933+
Falk Foundation, Annual Report. ScCleU 1937+
Family [Social Casework]. ScCleU (1933+); ScSpC (1939+); ScU (1921–22) 1924+
Family Favorite and Temperance Journal [Adrian, Mich.]. ScU [mfm] (1849–50)
Family Magazine. ScGF (1840–41); ScU [mfm] 1833–41
Far Eastern Quarterly [Journal of Asian Studies]. ScCCit 1941–56; ScU 1941+
Far Eastern Survey [Asian Survey]. ScU 1935+
Faraday Society, Transactions. ScCleU 1905+; ScGF [mc] 1905–50; ScU 1905+
Farm Economics. ScCleU 1925–60
Farm Journal [and Farmer's Wife]. ScCleU 1938+
Farm Research. ScCleU (1934+)

Farmer and Planter [Pendleton, S. C.]. ScGF (1857–60); ScU (1850–61)

Farmer's Advocate. ScCleU (1912–24) 1925+

Farmer's and Planter's Friend. ScU [mfm] (1821)

Farmer's Cabinet and American Herd-Book. ScU [mfm] 1833–42

Farmer's Digest. ScCleU (1939+)

Farmer's Register. ScCMus 1841–42; ScU [mfm] 1833–42

Farmer's Union Sun [Columbia, S. C.]. ScU (1908–9)

Farming in South Africa. ScCleU (1926–58) 1959+

Federal Council, Bulletin. ScCoT [mfm] 1918–50

Federal Reporter. ScSpDm 1880–1930

Federal Reserve Board, Annual Report. ScCleU 1914+

Federal Reserve Bulletin. ScCCit 1935+; ScCleU 1915+; ScGF 1934+; ScRhW 1931+; ScU 1915+

Fellowship News [Bob Jones University]. ScGBj (1934–59) 1960+

Female Tatler. ScU [mfm] 1709–10

Fertilizer Review [National Fertilizer Review]. ScCleU 1926+

Fibre and Fabric. ScCleU (1895–1955) 1956+

Fibre Containers [Paperboard Packaging]. ScNcWv 1940–50, 1961+

Fiction Parade and Golden Book Magazine. ScCleU 1935–38; ScU 1935–38

Field and Forest. ScCMus 1876–78

Field and Stream. ScCMus (1908–26); ScRhP 1936+

Field Illustrated. ScCleU 1922–28

Filson Club History Quarterly. ScU (1941–51) 1954+

Financial Register [U. S.] ScU 1837–38

Fire Control Notes. ScCleU 1939–61

Fish Culturalist. ScU 1921+

Flammarion. ScCleU (1914–32)

Flora, oder Allgemeine Botanische Zeitung. ScCleU 1906+

Floriad [Schenectady, N. Y.]. ScU [mfm] (1811)

Florida Academy of Sciences, Quarterly. ScU 1936+

Florida Entomologist. ScCleU 1917+

Florida Geological Survey, Bulletin. ScCleU 1930+

Florida Geological Survey, Report of Investigations. ScCleU 1934+

Florida Historical Quarterly. ScC 1932–35; ScCHis 1938+

Florida Medical Association, Journal. ScCM (1915) 1935+

Florida University, Engineering and Industrial Experiment Station, Bulletin. ScU (1933+)

Florists' Exchange and Horticultural Trade World [Exchange for the Flowery, Nursery, and Garden Center Trade]. ScCleU 1926+
Florists' Review. ScCleU (1937+)
Flour and Feed [Feed Bag]. ScCleU 1917+
Flower Grower. ScCleU 1928+; ScLaD 1940+; ScSpar 1940+
Fly, or Juvenile Miscellany. ScU [mfm] 1805–6
Flying. ScCleU (1941–52) 1953+; ScRhP 1940+; ScSpW 1941+
Foederal American Monthly [Knickerbocker]. ScU [mfm] 1833–65
Folia Haematologica. ScCM (1930–60)
Folklore Fellows, Communications. ScU 1911+
Food Industries [Food Engineering]. ScCleU 1930+; ScU 1930+
Food Research [Journal of Food Research]. ScCleU 1936+; ScCM 1936–44; ScSpC 1941–51
Fool [Salem, Mass.]. ScU [mfm] (1807)
Forbes' Magazine. ScSpar 1941+; ScU 1928–47, 1951+
Fordham Law Review. ScU (1936) 1941+
Ford's Christian Repository. ScGF (1854–57)
Foreign Affairs. ScCCit (1934–51) 1952+; ScCleU 1922+; ScClP 1926+; ScCoCo 1925+; ScGaLi 1937+; ScGBj 1938+; ScGF 1922+; ScGwLa 1941+; ScHCok 1926+; ScNewb 1941+; ScOrCl 1941+; ScOrSc 1934–45, [mfm] 1949+; ScRhW 1922+; ScSpar 1938–49, 1964+; ScSpC 1933+; ScSpW 1926+; ScU 1922+
Foreign Commerce Weekly [International Commerce]. ScCleU 1940+
Foreign Missionary. ScCoT 1928–63
Foreign Policy Association, Bulletin. ScRhW 1940–61; ScU (1928–36) 1936+
Foreign Policy Association, Report. ScCCit 1935+; ScCleU 1937–51; ScRhW 1941–51; ScU (1928–29) 1931–51
Foreign Quarterly Review. ScC (1827–46); ScSpW 1833, 1834–46; ScU 1827–39
Forerunner. ScRhW 1909–16
Forestry Abstracts. ScCleU 1939+; ScNcWv 1939+
Forestry Quarterly. ScCleU [mc] 1902–16
Forrester's Boys and Girls Magazine. ScU [mfm] 1848–57
Fortnightly Review. ScC (1887–1924); ScGF 1939–54; ScRhW 1937–54; ScU 1867–1954
Fortnightly Telephone Engineer. ScCleU 1940–44
Fortschritte auf dem Gebiete der Roentgenstrahlen. ScCM (1931+)

Fortune. ScCCit 1938+; ScChar 1930+; ScCleU 1930+; ScClP 1931+; ScCoCo 1930+; ScCoR 1934+; ScGBj 1938+; ScGF 1930+; ScGrev 1933+; ScHCok 1939+; ScNewb 1934+; ScOrSc (1940–52) 1953+; ScRhP 1934+; ScRhW 1930+; ScSpar 1930+; ScSpC 1931+; ScSpW 1939+; ScSum (1930+); ScU 1930+

Forum [and Century, Current History]. ScC (1892–1919); ScCCit (1928–40); ScChar 1930–40; ScCleU 1925–40; ScClP 1924–40; ScCoCo 1920–28; ScCoR (1926–39); ScDwErs 1925–40; ScGaLi (1928–40); ScGBj (1927–40); ScGF (1897–1912) 1924–40; ScGrev 1919–40; ScHCok 1912–40; ScRhP 1937–38; ScRhW 1925–40; ScSpC 1894–99, 1926–40; ScSpW (1886–95) 1931–40; ScU 1886–1940

Foundry. ScCleU 1926+

Four Track News [Travel]. ScU 1903–6

France Libre. ScU 1941–47

Frank Leslie's Illustrated Newspaper. ScC (1859–61); ScU (1883–84), also [mfm] 1855–1900

Franklin Institute Journal. ScCleU 1925+; ScU (1828–32) 1840+, also [mfm] 1826–51

Franklin Minerva [Chambersburg, Pa.]. ScU [mfm] 1799–1800

Free Trade Advocate. ScU 1829

Free Universal Magazine. ScU [mfm] 1793–94

Free World. ScRhW 1941–46

Freemason's Magazine and General Miscellany. ScU [mfm] 1811–12

French Review. ScCCit 1939–42; ScCoCo (1936–48) 1949+; ScGBj 1939+; ScGwLa 1941+; ScNewb 1936+; ScRhW 1935+; ScSpW 1941+; ScU 1927+

Friend [Albany, N. Y.]. ScU [mfm] 1815–16

Friend [Philadelphia]. ScU [mfm] 1827–50

Friend of Peace. ScU [mfm] 1815–22

Friendly Visitor. ScU [mfm] 1825

Friend's Review. ScU [mfm] 1847–51

Frontiers of Democrary. ScRhW 1934–43

Fuel Engineering Conference, Proceedings. ScCleU 1934–40

Fun. ScU [mfm] 1861–1901

Fundamenta Mathematica. ScSpW 1920–38; ScU 1920+

Fundamentals. ScU (1910–15)

G

Gaillard's Medical Journal. ScCM (1879–96)

Galaxy. ScSpW 1875–78; ScU (1869–77), also [mfm] 1866–78

Gamecock [University of South Carolina]. ScU 1908–56

Gamecox'n [NROTC, University of South Carolina]. ScU 1940–42

Garden and Home Builder. ScCleU 1925–27; ScGrev 1924–28; ScRhW 1925–28

Garden Club of South Carolina, Bulletin and Yearbook. ScABBE 1937–50; ScCleU (1930+); ScRhW (1938+); ScU (1932+)

Garden Magazine. ScGrev (1919–29)

Gardeners' Chronicle of America. ScCleU (1924–49)

Gardener's Monthly. ScCCit 1870–72

Garland [Auburn, N. Y.]. ScU [mfm] (1825)

Gazette des Beaux Arts. ScU (1859–1938)

Gazetter. ScU [mfm] 1824

Gegenbaurs Morphologisches Jahrbuch. ScU 1875–1923

Geistliches Magazine [Germantown, Pa.]. ScU [mfm] (1764–72)

Genealogy and History. ScRhW 1940+

General Convention of the Protestant Episcopal Church, Journal. ScCDhs 1859+

General Education Board [New York], Annual Report. ScCleU (1941+); ScCM (1921–51); ScRhW 1914–19, 1921+

General Education Board, Occasional Papers. ScCleU 1913–37

General Electric Review. ScCleU 1914–57; ScU 1903–58, some issues on mc

General Magazine and Historical Chronicle. ScU [mfm] (1741)

General Magazine and Impartial Review of Knowledge and Entertainment. ScU [mfm] (1798)

General Motors Corporation, Annual Report. ScCleU (1931+)

General Psychology Monographs. ScCleU 1940+; ScHCok 1939–58; ScU 1926+

General Repository and Review. ScU [mfm] 1812–13

General Review of British and Foreign Literature. ScU [mfm] 1806

Genesee Farmer and Gardener's Journal. ScU [mfm] 1831–39

Genetics. ScCleU (1917–22) 1923+; ScU (1923–39) 1949+

Genius of Universal Emancipation [Greeneville, Tenn.]. ScU [mfm] 1821–25

Gentleman and Lady's Town and Country Magazine. ScU [mfm] 1784–85

Gentleman's Journal of the War. ScU [mfm] 1693–96

Gentleman's Journal, or the Monthly Miscellany. ScU [mfm] 1692–94

Gentleman's Magazine and Historical Chronicle. ScABBE 1730–1824; ScC 1731–51, 1753–1815 (1816–17); ScGF 1731–1884; ScU 1731–1828

Gentlemen and Ladies' Town and Country Magazine. ScU [mfm] 1789–90

Geografiska Annaler. ScU 1919+

Geographical and Military Museum [Albany, N. Y.]. ScU [mfm] (1814)

Geographical, Historical, and Statistical Repository. ScU [mfm] (1824)

Geographical Journal. ScU 1893+

Geographical Magazine. ScU 1935+

Geographical Review. ScChar 1918–19; ScCleU (1917–39) 1941+; ScCMus 1921–44; ScRhW 1916+; ScSpC 1941+; ScU 1916+

Geographischer Anzeiger. ScU 1901–2

Geographischer Litteratur-Bericht. ScU 1886–1909

Geological Magazine. ScU 1889–92, 1917+

Geological Society of America, Bulletin. ScCleU 1888+; ScU 1890+

Geological Society of America, Proceedings. ScCleU 1933–59; ScU 1933–59

Geological Society of London, Quarterly Journal. ScU 1845+

Geological Society of London, Transactions. ScU 1811–42

Geophysics. ScCleU 1936+, some files on mc.

George Washington Law Review. ScU 1932+

Georgetown Law Journal. ScU (1937–45) 1948+

Georgia Analytical Repository. ScU [mfm] 1802–3

Georgia Bar Journal. ScU 1938+

Georgia Geological Survey, Bulletin. ScCleU (1896–1913) 1914+

Georgia Historical Quarterly. ScCHis 1917+; ScCHu 1917+; ScCleU (1917–25) 1926+; ScCoT 1928–50; ScU 1917+

Georgia Medical Association, Journal. ScCM (1911–24) 1928+

Georgia, Warm Springs Foundation, Annual Report. ScRhW (1941) 1943+

German Correspondent. ScU [mfm] 1820–21

German Quarterly. ScU 1928+

Germanic Review. ScCleU (1926–37) 1947+; ScGF 1928+; ScU 1926+

Germanistische Abhandlungen. ScU 1882–1932

Gift. ScU (1839–44)

Glasgow Medical Journal. ScCM (1920–55)

Glass. ScCleU (1940–51) 1952+

Gleanings in Bee Culture. ScCleU 1893+

Globe. ScU [mfm] (1819)

Godey's Lady's Book. ScCleU (1866–74); ScCMus (1831–69); ScCoBe (1864–66); ScCoR (1842–70); ScGF (1839–79); ScHCok (1849–57); ScLaur 1853–55; ScRhW (1856–58); ScSpar (1841–73); ScU (1848–75), also [mfm] 1830–98

Golden Book Magazine. ScCleU 1925–35; ScCoR 1925–28; ScGF 1925–31; ScU 1925–35

Good Company. ScSpW 1879

Good Housekeeping. ScChar (1886–88) 1947 (1949–59) 1960+; ScCleU 1923+; ScClP 1937–60; ScCoCo 1939+; ScFlor 1926–29; ScGBj 1931+; ScGrev 1922+; ScGrew 1931–41, 1950+; ScLaD 1927+; ScNewb 1935+; ScOran 1937+; ScOrSc (1935–50) 1963+; ScRhP 1933+; ScRhW 1912+; ScU 1916+

Good Words and Sunday Magazine. ScSpW 1867–71; ScU (1884–86)

Gospel Advocate [Boston]. ScU (1821–24), also [mfm] 1821–26

Gospel Advocate [Buffalo]. ScU [mfm] 1823–26

Gospel Herald. ScU [mfm] 1820–27

Gospel Inquirer [Little Falls, N. Y.]. ScU [mfm] 1823–24

Gospel Messenger and Southern Christian [Episcopal] Register [Charleston]. ScC (1824–50); ScCDhs 1824–29; ScU (1823–52), also [mfm] 1824–25

Gospel Palladium [Warren, R. I.]. ScU [mfm] (1823–24)

Gospel Trumpet [Dayton, Ohio]. ScU [mfm] 1822–23

Gospel Visitant. ScU [mfm] 1811–18

Grade Teacher. ScGBj 1933+; ScGF 1935+; ScGrev 1935+; ScNewb 1931+; ScRhW 1929+

Graham's [Illustrated] American Monthly Magazine. ScGF (1829–57); ScRhW 1853; ScU (1842–56), also [mfm] 1826–58

Gray's Inn Journal. ScU [mfm] 1753–54

Great Britain, Ministry of Agriculture and Fisheries, Journal [Journal of the Ministry of Agriculture]. ScCleU (1909–40)

Green Bag. ScU 1889–1914

Green Mountain Gem [Bradford, Vt.]. ScU [mfm] 1843–49

Green Mountain Repository [Burlington, Vt.]. ScU [mfm] (1832)

Greenville County Medical Society, Bulletin. ScCM 1938+; ScGGh 1938+

Greenville Medical Association, Bulletin. ScGGh 1938+
Gridiron [Dayton, Ohio]. ScU [mfm] 1822–23
Grit and Steel. ScU 1919+
Group Discussion [Audio Visual] Guide. ScU 1939+
Grub-Street Journal. ScU [mfm] 1730–37
Guardian [Albany, N. Y.]. ScU [mfm] (1807–8)
Guardian Monitor. ScU [mfm] 1819–28
Guernsey Breeders' Journal. ScCleU 1922+
Guthrie Clinic [Sayre, Pa.], Bulletin. ScCM (1932) 1936+
Guy's Hospital Reports. ScCM (1839–1921) 1927+
Gynaecological Society of Boston, Journal. ScCM 1869–72
Gynecologie et Obstetrique. ScCM 1941–48

H

Halcyon. ScU 1940–41
Halcyon Itinerary and True Millenium Messenger [Marietta, Ohio]. ScU [mfm] 1807–8
Halcyon Luminary and Theological Repository. ScU [mfm] 1812–13
Half-Yearly Abstract of Medical Sciences. ScCM (1845–74)
Harbinger. ScU [mfm] 1845–49
Harbinger of the Mississippi Valley [Frankfort, Ky.]. ScU [mfm] (1832)
Harper Hospital Bulletin. ScCM 1941+
Harper's Bazaar. ScCleU 1868–74; ScU (1933+)
Harper's Magazine. Sc 1850–1901; ScC (1850–95) 1898+; ScCC 1850+; ScCCit (1898–1943) 1944+; ScChar 1851–1911, 1918–29, 1947+; ScChes 1939+; ScCleU 1850+; ScClP 1917+; ScCoAl 1940+; ScCoCo (1873–1944) 1945+; ScCoR 1850+; ScDarl (1893–97); ScDwErs 1880–1906, 1920+; ScFlor 1925–30; ScGaLi 1850+; ScGBj 1861–62, 1883+; ScGF 1850+; ScGrev 1918+; ScGrew 1850–1902, 1908, 1921+; ScGwLa 1937+; ScHCok 1850+; ScLaD 1929–48; ScNewb 1854+; ScOrSc (1925–48), [mfm] 1949+; ScRhP 1932+; ScRhW 1850+; ScSpar 1930+; ScSpC 1850+; ScSpW 1850+; ScTiNg 1937+; ScU 1850+
Harper's Weekly Magazine. ScCCit 1860–65; ScCleU 1857–1916; ScClP 1861–65; ScRhW 1857–1916; ScSpW (1906–12); ScSpC 1861–62; ScU 1857–1916, also [mfm] 1857–1900
Harvard Business Review. ScCleU 1923+; ScOrSc (1941–49) [mfm] 1950+; ScU 1922+

248

Harvard Journal of Asiatic Studies. ScU 1936+
Harvard Law Review. ScU 1887+
Harvard Lyceum. ScU [mfm] (1810–11)
Harvard Theological Review. ScCoT [mfm] 1908–21
Harvard University, Arnold Arboretum Journal. ScCleU 1930+
Harvard University, Bussey Institution, Laboratory of Entomology, Contributions. ScCleU (1909–52)
Harvard University, Medical School Cancer Commission, Annual Report. ScCM 1932–37
Harvard University, Museum of Comparative Zoology, Bulletin. ScCMus 1869–1955
Harvard University, Museum of Comparative Zoology, Memoirs. ScCMus 1871–1938
Harvardiana. ScU [mfm] 1834–38
Harvey Society Lectures. ScCM 1905+
Hawaii Medical Society, Journal. ScCM (1941+)
Hawaiian Forester and Agriculturist. ScCleU 1925–32
Hazard's Register of Pennsylvania. ScU [mfm] 1828–35
Heart. ScCM (1909–33)
Heat Engineering. ScCleU (1928–39) 1950–56; ScU 1930–39
Heath's Book of Beauty. ScU 1836
Heating and Ventilating [Air Conditioning, Heating and Ventilating]. ScU 1935+
Heating, Piping and Air Conditioning. ScU (1930) 1932+
Hebrew Medical Journal. ScCM 1939+
Helminthological Society of Washington, Proceedings. ScCleU 1934+
Helvetica Chimica Acta. ScCleU 1918+; ScU 1918+
Helvetica Medica Acta. ScCM (1934+)
Helvetica Physica Acta. ScU 1928+
Hemisphere. ScU [mfm] 1809–11
Henry Bradshaw Society, Publications. ScCCit [mc] 1891–1950
Herald of Gospel Liberty. ScU [mfm] 1808–1930
Herald of Life and Immortality. ScU [mfm] 1819–20
Herald of Salvation [Watertown, N. Y.]. ScU [mfm] 1822–25
Herald of Truth [Cincinnati]. ScU [mfm] 1825–26, 1847–48
Herapath's Railway and Commercial Journal. ScU (1842–43)
Herbage Abstracts. ScCleU 1931+
Hereditas, Genetiskt Arkiv. ScCleU 1920+
Herpetologica. ScU 1936+

Hesperian [Cincinnati]. ScU [mfm] 1838–39

Hibbert Journal. ScC 1907+; ScCoCo (1924–55); ScRhW 1941+; ScU 1902+, some volumes on mc

Hierophant. ScU [mfm] 1842–43

High School Journal. ScGF (1930–52) 1953–61; ScU (1918–29) 1931+

High School Quarterly. ScU 1920–36

Higher Education and National Affairs. ScRhW 1941+

Highway Bulletin [Cheraw, S. C.]. ScU (1925–33)

Highway Magazine. ScU (1932–36) 1938+

Hilgardia. ScCleU 1925+; ScU (1940–46) 1948+

Hispania. ScCleU 1927+; ScRhW 1937+; ScU (1920) 1923+

Hispanic American Historical Review. ScGF (1936–42) 1943+; ScRhW 1941+; ScU 1918+

Hispanic Review. ScGwLa 1941+; ScU 1933+

Historical Magazine and Notes and Queries. ScU (1857–73)

Historical Magazine of the Protestant Episcopal Church. ScC (1933–55) 1956+; ScU (1933+)

Historical Outlook [Social Studies]. ScGF (1915–18) 1919–33; ScRhW 1927–33; ScSpC 1920–23; ScU 1925–33

Historical Register of the United States. ScC 1812–14; ScU 1812–14, also [mfm] 1812–14

Historische Zeitschrift. ScU 1935–58, 1961+

History. ScU 1916+

History of Learning. ScU [mfm] (1694)

History of Learning, or an Abstract of Several Books Lately Published. . . . ScU [mfm] (1691)

History of the Reign of Queen Anne. ScU [mfm] 1703–13

History of the Works of the Learned. ScU [mfm] 1699–1712, 1737–43

History Teacher's Magazine. ScSpC (1915–23)

Hive [Lancaster, Pa.]. ScU [mfm] (1810)

Hoard's Dairyman. ScCleU 1915+

Hobbies. ScBatL (1936–44); ScChes 1939+; ScRhP 1935+; ScU (1934–45) 1946+

Hog Breeder. ScCleU (1935–39) 1940–54

Hogg's Weekly Instructor. ScGF 1846–47

Holland's Magazine. ScGrew 1934–41; ScRhW 1930–53

Holstein-Friesian Association of America, Herd Book. ScCleU 1903–13, library also has *Yearbook* 1887–1930

Holstein-Friesian World. ScCleU (1923–32) 1933+

Home Acres [Garden Digest]. ScCleU (1928–34)
Home and Foreign Review. ScU [mfm] 1862–64
Home Aquarium Bulletin. ScU 1931–36
Home Port. ScCMus (1921)
Homiletic Review. ScSpW 1837–95
Hoosier Horticulture. ScCleU (1919–52)
Hoppe-Seyler's Beitschrift fur Physiologische Chemie. ScCM (1909–44)
Horizon. ScU 1941–45
Hormone, a Chemical Messenger. ScU 1927–43
Horn Book Magazine. ScGF 1934+; ScRhW 1938+; ScU 1941+
Hornet [Furman Paladin]. ScGF 1916+
Horseless Age. ScCleU 1905
Horticultural Register and Gardener's Magazine. ScU [mfm] 1835–38
Horticulturalist and Journal of Rural Art and Rural Taste. ScGF (1847–51); ScU [mfm] 1846–50
Horticulture. ScCleU 1926+
Horticulturist. ScCCit (1869–73); ScRhW 1849–56
Hospital for Joint Diseases, Bulletin. ScCM 1940+
Hospital Management. ScCM (1919+)
Hospital Progress. ScCM (1930+)
Hospital Social Service. ScCM 1913–33
Hospitals. ScCM (1936+)
Hound and Horn. ScU 1927–34
House and Garden. ScChar 1929+; ScCleU (1916–46) 1947+; ScFlor 1926–29; ScGrev 1927+; ScGrew 1937–42, 1950+; ScLaD 1934+; ScRhW 1924+; ScU 1921+
House Beautiful. ScCleU 1924+; ScFlor 1926–27; ScGBj 1938+; ScGrev 1919+; ScLaD 1936+; ScNewb 1938+; ScRhP 1932+; ScRhW 1926+; ScU 1921+
House of Refuge of Philadelphia, Annual Report. ScC (1832–38)
Household Words. ScC (1851–59); ScU 1850–59
Huguenot Society of London, Proceedings. ScCHu 1885+
Huguenot Society of London, Publications. ScCHu 1887+
Huguenot Society of South Carolina, Proceedings. ScC 1889+; ScCC 1941+; ScCCit 1930+; ScCHis 1889+; ScCHu 1889+; ScCleU 1889+; ScMus (1889+); ScDwErs (1906+); ScOrSc 1889+; ScSpC 1926+; ScSpW 1914+; ScU 1889+
Human Biology. ScCM 1929+; ScU 1929+

Human Fertility. ScCM 1935–48
Humming Bird [Newfield, Conn.]. ScU [mfm] 1798
Huntingdon Library Museum and Monthly Miscellany [Huntingdon, Pa.]. ScU [mfm] 1810
Huntington Library Bulletin [Quarterly]. ScCleU 1937+; ScU 1931+
Hunt's London Journal. ScU [mfm] (1844)
Hunt's Merchant's Magazine. ScCCit 1849–54; ScU 1839–49
Hygeia [Today's Health]. ScChar 1933–50; ScCleU 1927+; ScCM 1923+; ScCoBe 1923+; ScGBj 1935+; ScGF 1930+; ScGrev 1936–50; ScGrew 1931–41; ScGwLa 1935+; ScHCok 1924+; ScOrSc 1935+; ScRhP 1936+; ScRhW 1925+; ScSpC 1939+; ScU 1923+

I

Ibis. ScCMus 1859–1919
Ice Cream Field. ScCleU (1928–36) 1940+
Ice Cream Review. ScCleU (1926–37) 1938+
Ice Cream Trade Journal. ScCleU (1932–46) 1947+
Idle Man. ScU [mfm] 1821–22
Idler. ScDarl (1892–97)
Illinois Farm [Agricultural] Economics. ScCleU 1935–56, 1961+
Illinois Medical Journal. ScCM (1905–29) 1930+
Illinois Monthly Magazine. ScU [mfm] 1830–32
Illinois State Academy of Sciences, Transactions. ScCleU 1911–29
Illinois State Historical Society, Journal. ScU (1911–41) 1946+
Illuminating Engineering. ScCleU 1912–39; ScU (1915) 1940+
Illustrated London News. ScC (1849–74) 1948+; ScCCit 1939–40; ScChar 1915–16, 1960+; ScCleU (1843–82) 1940+; ScRhW 1918+; ScSpC 1922+; ScSpW (1931–32) 1935+; ScU (1843–91) 1908–13, 1914–51, 1952+
Illustrated London Times. ScSpW 1855
Illustrated World [Popular Mechanics]. ScU 1904–23
Illustration. ScRhW 1926–40; ScSpC 1923–25, 1947+; ScSpW 1926–29; ScU 1910–40
Illustration Théâtrale [Paris]. ScU 1905–13
Illustrierte Zeitung [Leipzig]. ScSpC 1936–40
Imperial Cancer Research Fund, Annual Report [London]. ScCM (1941–45) 1946+
Imperial Institute, Bulletin [London]. ScCleU 1927–48

Independent. ScCCit (1925–28); ScCleU 1914–28; ScDarl 1920–27; ScFlor 1926–29; ScGF 1898–1928; ScHCok 1900–28; ScRhW 1916–28; ScSpC 1922–28; ScSpW (1908–28); ScU 1899–1928, also [mfm] 1848–1900

Independent [National Business] Woman. ScRhP 1931+; ScRhW 1940+; ScU 1939+

Independent Reflector. ScU [mfm] 1752–53

Independent Republican [Newburyport, Mass.]. ScU [mfm] (1805)

Index. ScCleU 1925–28

Index of Patents, U. S. Patent Office. ScSpDm 1938+

Index to Dental Literature. ScCM 1886–1941, 1945+

Indian Academy of Sciences, Proceedings [Series A and B]. ScCleU 1934+

Indian Chemical Society, Journal. ScCleU 1924+; ScU (1930–48) 1951+

Indian Journal of Agricultural Science. ScCleU (1934–45) 1946+

Indian Journal of Medical Research. ScCM (1916–53)

Indian Medical Gazette. ScCM (1920–54)

Indian Medical Research Memoirs. ScCM 1927–40

Indiana Academy of Science, Proceedings. ScCleU 1924+; ScCMus 1891+

Indiana Academy of Sciences, Transactions. ScCMus 1911–29

Indiana Crops and Livestock. ScCleU 1925+

Indiana Law Journal. ScU 1932+

Indiana Magazine of History. ScCleU 1926–31

Indiana State Medical Association, Journal. ScCM 1925+

Industrial and Engineering Chemistry [various sections]. ScCamDu 1926+; ScCCit 1920+; ScCleU 1915+; ScCM 1909+; ScGF (1913+); ScHCok 1939+; ScNcWv 1910+; ScOrSc 1929+; ScRhW 1921+; ScSpC 1926+; ScSpDm 1909+; ScSpW (1918–32); ScU 1909+

Industrial Arts and Vocational Education [Industrial Arts Magazine]. ScChar 1932+; ScCleU 1918+; ScGF (1917–52) 1953+; ScGrev 1923–43; ScRhW 1940+; ScU 1914+

Industrial Development [and Manufacturer's Record]. ScU 1917+

Industrial Education Magazine. ScCleU 1922–39; ScGrev 1925–35

Industrial Engineer [Factory Management and Maintenance]. ScCleU 1926–31

Industrial Heating. ScCleU 1937–39

Industrial Management [Factory Management and Maintenance]. ScCleU 1917–27

Industrial Medicine. ScCM (1933–40) 1941+

Industry and Power. ScCleU 1937–39

Infantry Journal. ScCCit 1931–50

Inland Printer. ScCoR 1896–1930

Inquisitor. ScU [mfm] 1818–20

Institut Adrien Guébhard-Séverine, Annales Guébhard-Séverine [Institut de Géophysique et Sciences Diverses]. ScU (1926–55)

Institute for Living [Hartford], Abstracts and Translations. ScCM (1938–51)

Institute of Historical Research, Bulletin. ScCHis 1935+

Institute of Medicine of Chicago, Proceedings. ScCM (1916–53)

Institute of Metals, Journal. ScCleU (1912–38) 1958+

Institute of Paper Chemistry, Abstracts Bulletin. ScNcWv 1930+

Institute of Paper Chemistry, Research Bulletin. ScNcWv 1936+

Institute of Radio Engineers, Proceedings [IEEE]. ScCCit 1940–42; ScCleU 1927+; ScSpDm 1930+; ScU (1913) 1920+

Institute of the History of Medicine. ScCoHo 1933–34

Institution of Chemical Engineers, Transactions. ScCleU 1923+

Institution of Civil Engineers, Minutes. ScCleU (1847) 1864–1934

Institution of Civil Engineers, Proceedings. ScCleU 1847, 1864–1934, 1957+

Institution of Civil Engineers, Transactions. ScU 1836–42

Institution of Electrical Engineers, Journal. ScU (1913+), in 1941 *Journal* split into four sections, library has incomplete files to date.

Institution of Radio Engineers [Australia], Proceedings. ScU 1937–47, 1956+

Institution Quarterly. ScCM (1910–25)

Instituto Pinheiro, Anais [São Paulo]. ScCM (1938–39)

Institutum Divi Thomae, Studies [Cincinnati]. ScCM 1937–47

Instructor. ScU [mfm] (1755)

Instructor. ScDwErs 1927+; ScGBj 1936+; ScGF 1928+; ScGrev 1929+; ScRhP 1940+; ScRhW 1931+; ScU 1936+

Instruments [and Control Systems]. ScCleU (1928–42) 1943+; ScU 1928+

Insurance Law Journal. ScU 1872–1917, 1946+

Intellectual Regale, or Ladies' Tea Party. ScU [mfm] 1814–15

Inter-Allied Review [United Nations Monthly Chronicle, Review]. ScU 1941+

Inter-America. ScU 1917–26

Inter-American Quarterly. ScCleU 1940–41

Intercollegian. ScNewb 1938+

Internal Clinics. ScCoHo 1932+

International Abstracts of Surgery. ScCM 1913–18, 1919+

International Affairs. ScU 1932+

International Association of Milk Dealers [Milk Industry Foundation], Proceedings. ScCleU 1932+

International Book Review. ScRhW 1922–28

International College of Surgeons, Journal. ScCM 1938+

International Conciliation. ScCCit 1938–47, 1952+; ScCleU 1907+; ScRhW 1914+

International Conference of Agricultural Economists, Proceedings. ScCleU 1929+

International Congress of Military Medicine and Pharmacy, Report. ScCM (1923–39)

International Congress of Soil Science, Abstracts and Proceedings. ScCleU (1927–35)

International Institute of Agriculture, Bulletin. ScCleU (1914–33), library also has *Crop Reports* and *Agricultural Statistics* 1914–32 and *Documentary Leaflets* 1917–23

International Journal of Agrarian Affairs. ScCleU 1939+

International Journal of Ethics. ScCoT [mfm] 1911–48; ScSpC 1917–23; ScU (1891–1913) 1914+

International Journal of Individual Psychology. ScU 1935+

International Journal of Religious Education. ScDwErs-T 1941+; ScGF (1936) 1937+; ScNewb 1939+

International Journal of Surgery. ScCM (1888–1932)

International Labour Review. ScCleU 1933–45; ScRhW 1941+; ScU 1934+

International Medical Congress, Transactions. ScCM (1876–87)

International Medical Digest. ScCM 1921+

International Monthly. ScSpW 1900–1

International Press Correspondence [World News and Views]. ScU 1922–38

International Quarterly. ScC 1902–5; ScSpW 1904–6

International Review. ScSpW 1876; ScU 1874–82

International Review of Agricultural Economics. ScCleU 1914–26

International Review of Agriculture. ScCleU 1927–38

International Review of Missions. ScCleU 1926–28; ScCoBi 1941+; ScCoT 1924+; ScDwErs-T 1941+

International Society of Soil Sciences, Proceedings. ScCleU 1925–38

International Studio. ScC 1903–31; ScCleU (1904–31); ScCMus 1903–20; ScGrev 1924–31; ScHCok (1914–31); ScRhW 1902–31; ScU (1907–41)

International Surgical Digest. ScCM 1922+

International Yearbook of Agricultural Statistics. ScCleU (1909–46)

Interpreter [Charleston]. ScC 1844; ScGF 1844; ScU 1844

Inter-State Cotton Seed Crushers Association, Bulletin. ScU (1906–8)

Interstate Medical Journal. ScCM (1905–19)

Inventor. ScU 1855–57

Investigator and General Intelligencer [Providence, R. I.]. ScU [mfm] 1827–28

Iowa Corn Institute, Contributions. ScCleU 1935–51

Iowa Journal of History. ScCHis 1902+

Iowa Law Review. ScU 1932+

Iowa State Horticultural Society, Proceedings. ScCleU 1929–54

Iowa State Medical Society, Journal. ScCM (1918–19) 1924+, library also has *Transactions* (1890–1902)

Iowa State University, Journal of Science. ScCleU 1927+; ScU (1928–35) 1949+

Iowa State University, Studies in Engineering, Bulletin. ScCleU 1926+; ScU 1929+

Iowa [Year] Book of Agriculture. ScCleU 1901+

Iris, or Literary Messenger. ScU [mfm] 1840–41

Irish Journal of Medical Science. ScCM (1937–47) 1952+

Irish Quarterly Review. ScU [mfm] 1851–60

Iron Age. ScCCit 1940+; ScCleU 1928+

Isaqueena [Greenville, S. C.]. ScU (1906–9)

Isis. ScU (1933) 1947+

Israel's Advocate. ScU [mfm] 1823–27

Istoricheskii Viestnik, Istoriko-Literaturnyi Zhurnal. ScU (1891–1911)

Italian Studies. ScU (1937) 1952+

J

Jahrbuch für Romanische und Englische Sprache und Literatur. ScU [mc] 1859–76

Jahrbuch über die Fortschritte der Mathematik. ScU 1868–1944

Jahresbericht über die Ercheinungen auf dem Gebiete der Germanischen Philologie. ScU 1924–34

Jamaica Agricultural Society, Journal [The Farmer]. ScCleU 1928–47

Japanese Journal of Geology and Geography. ScU 1922+

Japanese Journal of Medical Sciences, Transactions: Gynecology and Tocology. ScCM (1936–41)

Japanese Journal of Medical Sciences, Transactions: Ophthalmology. ScCM (1929–40)

Japanese Journal of Medical Sciences, Transactions: Pharmacology. ScCM 1927–41

Japanese Journal of Medical Sciences, Transactions: Surgery, Orthopedy, and Odontology. ScCM 1927–36

Japanese Journal of Zoology. ScU 1922–36 (1940–41)

Jersey Bulletin [and Dairy World]. ScCleU (1910) 1922–53

Jew. ScC 1823–24; ScU [mfm] 1823–24

Jewish Exposition. ScSpW 1816–26

Jewish Intelligence. ScSpW 1835–54

Jewish Quarterly Review. ScGBj (1926–50) 1951+

John-Donkey. ScU [mfm] (1848)

John Englishman. ScU [mfm] (1755)

John F. Slater Fund, Proceedings. ScCleU (1915–36)

John Marshall Law Quarterly. ScU 1935–43

John Rylands Library, Bulletin. ScU 1903+, some files on mfm

Johns Hopkins Hospital, Bulletin. ScCM (1889+); ScCoHo (1931–45) 1946+; ScGGh (1924–53) 1954+

Johns Hopkins Hospital, Reports. ScCM (1895–1926)

Johns Hopkins University and Hospital, Researches in Urology. ScCM 1918–32

Johnsonia. ScU 1941+

Johnsonian [Winthrop College]. ScRhW 1923+

Journal de la Physiologie, de l'Homme et des Animaux. ScCM 1858–60

Journal de l'École Polytechnique. ScU 1812–45

Journal de Mathématiques Pures et Appliquées. ScU (1836+), some files on mfm

Journal de Physiologie et de Pathologie Générale. ScCM (1899+)
Journal de Physique, de Chimie, d'Histoire Naturelle, et des Arts.
ScC 1794–1802; ScU (1776–86)
Journal de Physique [Théoretique et Appliquée] et le Radium.
ScCleU 1872+
Journal des Arts, des Sciences et de la Littérature. ScU 1800–1
Journal des Dames. ScU [mfm] 1810
Journal für die Reine und Angewandte Mathematik. ScU 1826–69,
1883–93, 1941+
Journal für Praktische Chemie. ScCleU 1870+; ScU 1870–1943
Journal International de Chirurgie. ScCM 1936–53
Journal Inutile. ScU [mfm] (1825)
Journal of Abnormal and Social Psychology. ScCCit 1935+; ScCM
(1908–60) 1961+; ScGF 1930+; ScSpC 1921+; ScU 1906+, some
files on mc
Journal of Accountancy. ScCCit 1939+; ScClP 1930+; ScU (1909–
11) 1912+
Journal of Adult Education. ScCleU 1929–41; ScGF 1930–41; Sc-
RhW 1929–41; ScU 1932–41
Journal of Aeronautical [Aero/Space] Sciences. ScCleU 1940+
Journal of Aesthetics and Art Criticism. ScU 1941+
Journal of Agricultural Research. ScCleU 1913–49; ScRhW 1928–49
Journal of Agricultural Science. ScCleU 1907+
Journal of Agricultural Science and Horticulture. ScCleU 1925–36
Journal of Agriculture. ScU [mfm] 1845–48
Journal of Air Law and Commerce. ScU (1930) 1934+
Journal of Allergy. ScCM 1930+; ScCoHo 1934–52
Journal of American Folklore. ScCleU 1888+; ScRhW 1935+;
ScU 1888+
Journal of American History [New Haven]. ScC 1907–13; ScCleU
(1907–35); ScGrew (1915–20); ScU 1907–16
Journal of Anatomy [London]. ScCM (1867–81) 1886+
Journal of Animal Ecology. ScCleU 1932+
Journal of Applied Chemistry. ScOrSc 1937, 1950, 1963+
Journal of Applied Mechanics. ScU 1935+
Journal of Applied Microscopy and Laboratory Methods. ScCleU
1898–1903; ScU 1898–1903
Journal of Applied Physics. ScCleU 1937+; ScU 1937+
Journal of Applied Psychology. ScCCit 1934–42; ScGF 1934+; ScU
1917+

Journal of Applied Sociology [Sociology and Social Research]. ScU 1922–27
Journal of Aviation Medicine. ScCM 1935–58
Journal of Bacteriology. ScCleU 1916+; ScCM 1916+
Journal of Balneology and Climatology. ScCM (1898–1903)
Journal of Belle-Lettres [Lexington, Ky.]. ScU [mfm] (1819–20)
Journal of Bible and Religion. ScCoT [mfm] 1933–48, 1949+; ScDwErs-T 1939+; ScU (1936) 1940+
Journal of Biblical Literature. ScCoT (1881–1909) 1927+
Journal of Biochemistry. ScCleU 1922+
Journal of Biological Chemistry. ScCleU 1912+; ScCM 1905+; ScGaLi 1940+; ScU (1905–38) 1939+
Journal of Bone and Joint Surgery. ScCM 1919+; ScCoHo 1930+; ScGGh 1926+
Journal of Business Education. ScRhW 1930+
Journal of Calendar Reform. ScCleU 1931–55
Journal of Cancer Research. ScCM 1916–30
Journal of Cellular and Comparative Physiology. ScCM 1932+
Journal of Central European Affairs. ScU 1941–64
Journal of Chemical Education. ScCC (1925–30) 1932+; ScCCit 1934+; ScCleU 1924+; ScClP 1926+; ScCM 1924+; ScCoCo (1925–39) 1940+; ScGBj (1925–36) 1937+; ScGF 1924+; ScGwLa 1941+; ScHCok 1929+; ScNewb 1925+; ScOrSc (1924–53) 1954+; ScRhW 1928+; ScSpC 1936+; ScSpW 1937+; ScU 1924+
Journal of Chemical Physics. ScCleU 1933+; ScU 1933+
Journal of Chemistry and Physics. ScCamDu 1933+
Journal of Chemotherapy. ScCM 1926–39
Journal of Clinical Endocrinology [and Metabolism]. ScCleU 1941+; ScCM 1941+
Journal of Clinical Investigation. ScCM 1924+
Journal of Clinical Psychopathology. ScCM (1939–51)
Journal of Comparative Medicine and Veterinary Archives. ScCleU 1897–1902
Journal of Comparative Neurology. ScCM 1913, 1915+
Journal of Comparative Pathology and Therapeutics. ScCleU 1905–8
Journal of Comparative [and Physiological] Psychology. ScU 1921+
Journal of Consulting Psychology. ScU 1937+
Journal of Criminal Law, Criminology [and Police Science]. ScCleU 1938+; ScU 1910+

Journal of Cutaneous and Genito-Urinary Diseases. ScCM 1887–1902

Journal of Cutaneous and Venereal Diseases. ScCM (1883–86)

Journal of Cutaneous Diseases, Including Syphilis. ScCM 1903–19

Journal of Dairy Research. ScCleU 1929+

Journal of Dairy Science. ScCleU 1929+

Journal of Dental Research. ScCM 1919+

Journal of Documentary Reproduction. ScCC 1938–42

Journal of Ecology. ScCleU 1913+; ScU (1913–51) 1953+

Journal of Economic and Business History. ScCCit 1928–32; ScU 1928–32

Journal of Economic Entomology. ScCleU 1908+

Journal of Economic History. ScCleU 1941+; ScU 1941+

Journal of Education. ScCCit 1935+; ScCleU 1918+; ScGF (1931) 1933+; ScSpW 1931–35; ScRhW 1922+

Journal of Educational Method. ScCleU (1921–29)

Journal of Educational Psychology. ScCCit 1935+; ScCleU 1920+; ScClP 1924+; ScCoCo (1941+); ScGBj 1938+; ScGF 1910+; ScNewb 1939+; ScOrSc 1925+; ScSpC (1927–47) 1948+; ScSpW 1910–19, 1948+; ScU 1910+

Journal of Educational Research. ScCleU 1920+; ScClP 1925–56; ScOrSc 1920–34, 1938–44, 1949+; ScRhW 1920+; ScSpC 1937+; ScU 1920+

Journal of Educational Sociology. ScGBj 1938+; ScGF (1928–36) 1937+; ScRhW 1941–63; ScU 1928+

Journal of Egyptian Archaeology. ScU 1914+

Journal of Endocrinology. ScCM (1939) 1947+

Journal of Engineering Education. ScCleU 1924+; ScU 1912+

Journal of [English and] Germanic Philology. ScCleU 1897+; ScCoCo (1929–37) 1938+; ScU 1897+

Journal of Experimental Biology. ScCleU 1930+

Journal of Experimental Education. ScGBj 1938+; ScGF (1938–43) 1944+; ScRhW 1941+; ScU 1936+

Journal of Experimental Medicine. ScCleU 1896+; ScCM 1896+

Journal of Experimental Psychology. ScGF (1916–17) 1928+; ScRhW 1930+; ScU 1916+

Journal of Experimental Zoology. ScCleU 1916–32, 1941+; ScCM (1910–45) 1946+; ScOrSc 1904+; ScU (1906–12) 1915+

Journal of Farm Economics. ScCleU 1919+; ScU 1919+

Journal of Science [Food Research]. ScCleU 1936+

Journal of Foreign Medical Science and Literature. ScU [mfm] 1810–20

Journal of Forestry. ScCC 1932–47; ScCleU 1917+

Journal of General Physiology. ScCleU (1918–31) 1932+; ScCM 1918+; ScOrSc 1918–53

Journal of General Psychology. ScGBj 1940–56; ScHCok 1939+; ScRhW 1928+; ScU (1928–29) 1930+

Journal of Genetic Psychology [Pedagogical Seminary]. ScRhW 1902–24; ScU 1891–1911 (1913–24)

Journal of Genetics. ScCleU (1910–22) 1923+; ScU 1910–29, 1949+

Journal of Geography. ScCleU 1923+; ScGBj 1938+; ScRhW 1931+; ScU 1905+

Journal of Geology. ScCleU 1893+; ScNewb 1893+; ScU 1893+

Journal of Geomorphology. ScU 1938–42

Journal of Geophysical Research. ScU 1896–1959, 1961+, some files on mc

Journal of Health. ScU [mfm] 1829–33

Journal of Health, Physical Education [and Recreation]. ScCleU (1930–45) 1946+; ScDwErs 1937+; ScGBj 1938+; ScGF 1937+; ScHCok 1930+; ScOrSc (1938–51) 1952+; ScRhW 1930+; ScU 1930+

Journal of Hellenic Studies. ScU (1895–1955) 1958+

Journal of Helminthology. ScCleU 1923+

Journal of Heredity. ScCC 1937–51; ScCleU 1910+; ScCM 1940+; ScCoCo (1923–52) 1953+; ScHCok 1938+; ScRhW 1925+; ScSpC (1924–36) 1937+; ScU 1910+, some files on mc

Journal of Higher Education. ScCC 1940–50; ScCCit 1936, 1941+; ScCleU 1930+; ScClP 1939+; ScGF 1931+; ScHCok 1930+; ScOrSc 1937–45 (1947–51) 1949+; ScRhW 1930+; ScSpC 1930+; ScSpW (1931) 1941+; ScU 1930+

Journal of Home Economics. ScCleU 1931+; ScCoCo (1920–47) 1948+; ScCoR (1923–27); ScGaLi 1931+; ScGBj 1930+; ScGF 1919, 1922+; ScHCok 1917–52; ScRhW 1909+; ScU 1909+

Journal of Hygiene. ScCM (1901–33)

Journal of Immunology. ScCleU 1916+; ScCM 1916+

Journal of Industrial Hygiene and Toxology. ScCM (1919–49)

Journal of Infectious Diseases. ScCleU 1923–25, 1926+; ScCM 1904+; ScCoHo 1930–32

Journal of Investigative Dermatology. ScCM 1938+

Journal of Jurisprudence. ScU [mfm] 1821

Journal of Laboratory and Clinical Medicine. ScCM 1915+; Sc-GGh (1925–47) 1948+; ScU 1935–36, 1939–56

Journal of Land [and Public Utility] Economics. ScCleU (1925–28) 1929+

Journal of Laryngology and Otology. ScCM (1887–1949) 1951+

Journal of Mammology. ScCleU 1919+; ScU 1919+

Journal of Marine Research. ScCleU 1937+; ScU 1937+

Journal of Marketing. ScCleU 1936+; ScU 1936+

Journal of Mathematics and Physics. ScCleU 1921+; ScU 1922+

Journal of Medical Research. ScCM 1901–24

Journal of Metabolic Research. ScCM 1922–26

Journal of Milk [and Food] Technology. ScCleU 1937+

Journal of Mississippi History. ScCleU 1939+

Journal of Modern History. ScCC 1929+; ScCCit 1936+; ScHCok (1926–55) 1956+; ScNewb 1939+; ScRhW 1929+; ScSpC 1931+; ScSpW 1941+; ScU 1929+

Journal of Morphology. ScCM (1916+); ScSpC 1938–51; ScU 1916+

Journal of Musicology. ScRhW 1939–43

Journal of Musik. ScU [mfm] 1810

Journal of Mycology. ScCleU 1885–1908; ScU 1885–1908

Journal of Natural Philosophy, Chemistry and the Arts. ScC 1797–1800

Journal of Negro Education. ScCoAl 1937+; ScCoBe 1932+; ScGF 1932+; ScOrSc (1932–47) 1948+

Journal of Negro History. ScCC 1941–52; ScCleU 1916+; ScCoAl 1936+; ScCoBe 1916+; ScOrCl 1926+; ScOrSc 1916–29 (1931–54) 1955+; ScRhW 1916+; ScSpW 1916+; ScU 1916+

Journal of Nervous and Mental Disease. ScCM (1877–97) 1899+; ScCoWsh (1884–1932) 1933+

Journal of Neurology and Psychopathology. ScCM 1926–37

Journal of Neurology, Neurosurgery and Psychiatry. ScCM (1938–45) 1948+

Journal of Neurophysiology. ScCleU (1938–51) 1952+; ScCM 1938+

Journal of Nutrition. ScCleU 1928+; ScCM 1928+; ScCoCo (1931–43) 1944–54; ScGaLi (1941–52); ScGF 1928–59

Journal of Obstetrics and Gynaecology of the British Empire. ScCM (1910) 1911+

Journal of Organic Chemistry. ScCleU 1936+; ScCamDu 1936+; ScGF 1936+; ScU 1926+

Journal of Paleontology. ScCleU 1935+; ScGF [mc] 1927–56; ScU 1927+

Journal of Parasitology. ScCleU 1914+; ScCM 1915+; ScU (1924–44) 1946+

Journal of Pathology and Bacteriology. ScCM 1893+

Journal of Pediatrics. ScCM 1932+; ScCoHo 1932+; ScGGh 1932+

Journal of Pharmaceutical Sciences. ScU 1912+

Journal of Pharmacology and Experimental Therapeutics. ScCM 1909+; ScU 1938+

Journal of Philology. ScSpW 1868–72

Journal of Philosophy. ScCCit 1940+; ScSpC 1941+; ScU 1904+, some files on mc

Journal of Physical [and Colloid] Chemistry. ScCleU 1896+; ScU 1896+

Journal of Physical Education. ScNewb 1939+

Journal of Physiology. ScCM 1878–1919, 1920+

Journal of Political Economy. ScC (1893–1905) 1908–22; ScCC 1932–61; ScCCit 1936+; ScCleU 1892+, some files on mc; ScGF (1914–23) 1925+; ScRhW 1930+; ScSpC 1937+; ScSpW 1937+; ScU 1892–1904 (1907–12) 1915+, some files on mc

Journal of Politics. ScCCit (1938+); ScCleU 1937+; ScGF 1939+; ScRhW 1939+; ScSpC 1937+; ScU 1939+

Journal of Pomology and Horticultural Sciences. ScCleU (1928–48)

Journal of Preventive Medicine. ScU 1926–32

Journal of Prison Discipline and Philanthropy. ScU [mfm] 1845–55

Journal of Projective Techniques. ScU 1936+

Journal of Psychology. ScCleU 1937+; ScGBj 1940+; ScHCok 1939+; ScNewb 1939+; ScU 1936+

Journal of Radiology. ScCM 1920–25

Journal of Religion. ScCoCo (1940–44) 1945+; ScCoT 1921+, some files on mfm; ScGaLi 1941+; ScOrCl 1940+

Journal of Religious Psychology. ScU 1904–15

Journal of Research of the National Bureau of Standards [various sections]. ScCCit 1928+; ScCleU 1928+; ScRhW 1928+; ScU 1928+

Journal of Retailing. ScU 1940+

Journal of Roman Studies. ScU 1926–29, 1958+

Journal of Rural Education. ScU (1922–26)

Journal of School Health. ScU 1937+
Journal of Science and the Arts. ScU [mfm] 1817–18
Journal of Sedimentary Petrology. ScU 1931+
Journal of Social Hygiene. ScCM (1917) 1924–45, 1952; ScU 1915–54
Journal of Social Psychology. ScCleU (1930–31) 1932+; ScGBj 1940–56; ScGF (1932–38) 1939+; ScHCok 1939+; ScNewb 1939+; ScRhW 1930+; ScU 1930+
Journal of Southern History. ScA 1935+; ScC 1935+; ScCC 1935+; ScCCit 1935+; ScChar 1935+; ScCHis 1935+; ScCHu 1935+; ScCleU 1935+; ScClP 1935+; ScCoCo 1935+; ScDwErs 1935+; ScGF 1935+; ScHCok 1935+; ScNewb 1941+; ScOrSc 1935–44, 1953+; ScRhW 1935+; ScSpC 1935+; ScSpW 1935+; ScU 1935+
Journal of Speculative Philosophy. ScU 1867–93
Journal of Speech [and Hearing Disorders]. ScCoCo 1936+
Journal of Symbolic Logic. ScU (1936) 1944+
Journal of Technical Methods and Bulletin of International Association of Medical Museums. ScCM (1913–51)
Journal of the History of Ideas. ScU 1940+
Journal of the Law-School, Needham, Virginia. ScU [mfm] 1822
Journal of Theology of the American Lutheran Church. ScCoT 1936–42
Journal of Thoracic and Cardiovascular Surgery. ScCM 1931+; ScGGh (1937–44) 1945+
Journal of Tropical Medicine and Hygiene. ScCM (1909+)
Journal of Tuberculosis [Asheville, N. C.]. ScCM 1899–1901
Journal of Urology. ScCM 1917+; ScGGh (1917–35) 1936+
Journal of Wildlife Management. ScCleU 1937+
Journalism Quarterly. ScGF 1924+; ScU 1924+
Judy. ScU [mfm] (1846–47)
Julius Rosenwald Fund, Review. ScCleU (1928–46)
Junior College Journal. ScTiNg 1937+; ScU 1930+
Justus Liebig's Annalen der Chemie. ScCleU 1832+, some files on mc; ScCM (1933) 1940+; ScU 1832+, some files on mc
Juvenile Gazette [Providence, R. I.]. ScU [mfm] (1819–20)
Juvenile Magazine. ScU [mfm] 1811–13
Juvenile Magazine, or Miscellaneous Repository of Useful Information. ScU [mfm] (1802–3)
Juvenile Mirror. ScU [mfm] (1812)
Juvenile Miscellany. ScU [mfm] 1826–34

Juvenile Missionary Society [Charleston]. ScU (1833–40)
Juvenile Port-Folio and Literary Miscellany. ScU [mfm] 1812–16
Juvenile Repository. ScU [mfm] (1811)

K

Kansas Academy of Science, Transactions. ScCMus (1906–37)
Kansas Medical Society, Journal. ScCM 1928+
Kansas State Historical Society, Collection. ScCleU (1886–1925)
Kemi, Revue de Philologie et d'Archaeologie Egyptiennes et Coptes.
    ScU 1930+
Kentucky, Department of Education, Bulletin. ScCleU (1934+)
Kentucky Law Journal. ScU 1941+
Kentucky Medical Journal. ScCM (1925) 1928–49
Kenyon Review. ScCCit 1939+; ScCleU 1939+; ScCoCo (1940–42)
    1943+; ScGF 1939+; ScHCok 1940+; ScRhW 1939+; ScU 1939+
Key [Frederick Town, Md.]. ScU [mfm] (1798)
Keystone. ScC 1899–1913
Kindergarten and First Grade. ScRhW 1916–25
Kindergarten Review. ScRhW 1907–15
Kings' Business. ScCoBi 1939+; ScGBj 1938+
Klinische Wochenschrift. ScCM 1922–41, 1944+
Knickerbocker Magazine [Foederal American Monthly]. ScGF
    (1833–34) 1835–61; ScU [mfm] (1833–65)
Knight's Quarterly Magazine. ScU 1823–24, also [mfm] 1823–24
Kolloid-Zeitschrift. ScCleU 1906+, some files on mc; ScU (1915–
    19) 1922–36, 1959+, some files on mc
Korea Review. ScU 1901–6
Kunststoffe, Zeitschrift für Erzeugung und Verwendung Veredelter
    oder Chemisch Hergestellter Stoffe. ScCleU 1911+

L

Ladies Afternoon Visitor. ScU [mfm] (1806–7)
Ladies' Companion [and Literary Expositor]. ScU 1838–44
Ladies Floral Cabinet. ScU (1882–86)
Ladies' Garland [Harper's Ferry, Va.]. ScU [mfm] 1824–28
Ladies' Garland and Family Wreath. ScU [mfm] 1837–50
Ladies' Home Journal. ScChar (1927–35) 1960+; ScCleU 1935+;
    ScClP 1941–53; ScGBj 1935+; ScGrev 1919+; ScGrew 1889–1904,

1935–41, 1950+; ScLaD 1936+; ScNewb 1930+; ScOran 1941+; ScRhP 1932+; ScRhW 1923+; ScU 1886+

Ladies Literary Cabinet. ScU [mfm] 1819–22

Ladies Magazine [Providence, R. I.]. ScU [mfm] 1823–24

Ladies Magazine, or Universal Entertainer. ScU [mfm] 1749–52

Ladies' Museum [London]. ScU [mfm] (1800)

Ladies Museum [Providence, R. I.]. ScU [mfm] 1825–26

Ladies' Port Folio. ScU [mfm] (1820)

Ladies' Repository [Cincinnati]. ScHCok (1852–70); ScU 1841, also [mfm] 1841–50

Ladies' Visiter [Marietta, Pa.]. ScU [mfm] 1819–20

Ladies' Weekly Museum. ScU [mfm] 1788–1817

Lady and Gentleman's Pocket Magazine. ScU [mfm] (1796)

Lady's Magazine and Musical Repository. ScU [mfm] 1801–2

Lady's Magazine [London]. ScCMus 1780

Lady's Magazine and Repository of Entertaining Knowledge. ScU [mfm] 1792–93

Lady's Magazine, or Entertaining Companion for the Fair Sex. ScU 1786–87, 1803

Lady's Miscellany, or Weekly Visitor. ScU [mfm] 1802–12

Lady's Monitor. ScU [mfm] 1801–2

Lady's Monthly Museum. ScC (1798–1808); ScU [mfm] 1798–1832

Lady's Pearl [Lowell, Mass.]. ScU [mfm] 1840–43

Lady's Weekly Miscellany. ScU [mfm] 1802–9

Lahey Clinic, Bulletin. ScCM 1938+

Lancaster Hive [Lancaster, Pa.]. ScU [mfm] 1803–5

Lancet. ScCM 1823+; ScCoHo 1930+; ScGGh (1937–45) 1946+

Lancet by Doctor Sangrado, Junior [Newark, N. J.]. ScU [mfm] (1803)

Land We Love. Sc 1866–69; ScChes (1866–67); ScCoR 1866–69; ScGF 1866–69; ScU 1866–69

Landwirtschaftlichen Versuchs-Stationem. ScCleU (1859–77)

Language, Journal of the Linguistic Society of America. ScU 1925+, library also has *Language Dissertations* 1927+ and *Language Monographs* 1925–48

Laryngoscope. ScCM 1897+; ScCoHo 1930–32

Latin American Evangelist. ScCoBi 1939+

Latter Day Luminary. ScGF [mfm] 1818–25; ScU [mfm] 1818–25

Law and Contemporary Problems. ScCCit 1941+; ScSpC 1938+; ScU 1933+

Law and Order. ScCleU 1921–31
Law Library Journal. ScU 1908+
Law Quarterly Review. ScU 1885+
Lawn Care. ScCleU 1928+
Lawyer and Banker. ScU (1921–29)
Lawyer's and Magistrate's Magazine. ScU 1790–91
Lay-Man's Magazine [Martinsburgh, Va.]. ScU [mfm] 1815–16
Lay Monk. ScU [mfm] (1713–14)
League of Nations News. ScU 1925–31
Lederle Laboratories, Bulletin. ScCM 1935+
Leech. ScCM (1939–44)
Leghorn World. ScCleU (1925–41)
Leiden University, Communications from the Physical Laboratory.
   ScU 1909–31, library also has *Supplement* 1908–30
Leslie's Illustrated Weekly. ScRhW 1913–22
Leslie's Sunday Magazine. ScSpW 1877–79
Liberator. ScU [mfm] 1831–65
Libertarian [Greenville, S. C.]. ScChar (1925); ScGF 1924–25; Sc-
   Grev 1923–26; ScU (1923–26)
Liberty Bell. ScU [mfm] (1839–58)
Libraries. ScCleU (1926–31); ScU 1926+
Library Journal. ScC (1901–2) 1904–60; ScCCit 1926–32, 1940+;
   ScChar 1931+; ScCleU 1912+; ScCoR (1936–41); ScFlor 1925–
   29; ScGaLi 1930+; ScGBj 1938+; ScGF 1921+; ScGrev (1921+);
   ScGwLa 1941+; ScHCok 1920+; ScRhP 1935; ScRhW 1901+;
   ScSpar 1938+; ScSpC 1924+; ScSpW 1941+; ScU 1876+, some
   files on mc
Library Literature. ScCCit 1936+; ScRhW 1933+
Library Magazine. ScGF 1879; ScU 1886
Library Quarterly. ScCC 1938–48; ScCleU 1931+; ScGBj 1938+;
   ScGF 1938+; ScHCok 1931+; ScRhW 1931+; ScSpC 1931–56;
   ScU 1931+
Library World. ScU (1898–1911)
Life [Chicago]. ScCC 1936+; ScChar 1936+; ScChes 1936+; Sc-
   CleU 1936+; ScClP 1936+; ScCoBe 1937+; ScCoCo 1940+;
   ScCoR 1937+; ScDarl 1941+; ScDenV 1939+; ScGBj 1937+;
   ScGF 1936+; ScGrev 1940+; ScGrew 1936–41 (1942+); ScHCok
   (1940–41) 1942+; ScLaD 1937+; ScNewb 1936+; ScOran 1940+;
   ScRhP 1936+; ScRhW 1936+; ScSpar 1936+; ScSpC 1936+;
   ScSpW 1936+; ScU 1936+; ScWaC 1937+

Life [New York]. ScCleU (1925–29) 1930–35; ScRhW 1934–35; ScU (1884–1925)

Life and Letters Today. ScU 1939–50

Lighter. ScCleU 1940+

Limestone Star [Limestone College]. ScU (1900–16)

Lingnan Science Journal. ScCleU 1922–48

Linguistic Society of America, Bulletin. ScU (1929–42) 1945+

Linnaean Society, Transactions. ScC 1791–1827; ScU 1791–1851

Lippincott's Magazine. ScChar (1874–81); ScGF 1868; ScSpC 1871–73; ScU (1866–86), also on mc 1868–1900

Literary and Evangelical Magazine [Richmond, Va.]. ScU [mfm] 1818–28

Literary and Musical Magazine. ScU [mfm] 1817–20

Literary and Philosophical Repertory [Middlebury, Vt.]. ScU [mfm] 1812–17

Literary and Scientific Repository and Critical Review. ScC 1821–22; ScU [mfm] 1820–22

Literary Cabinet [New Haven]. ScU [mfm] 1806–7

Literary Cabinet and Western Olive Branch [St. Clairsville, Ohio]. ScU [mfm] 1833–34

Literary Chronicle and Weekly Review. ScU [mfm] 1819–28

Literary Companion. ScU [mfm] (1821)

Literary Digest. ScCCit 1914–17; ScChar (1920–26) 1931–38; Sc-CleU (1894–96) 1897–1938; ScClP 1890–1937; ScCoR 1922–37; ScDarl 1914–37; ScDwErs 1925–38; ScFlor (1924–29); ScGaLi (1923–37); ScGBj (1931–38); ScGF 1912–37; ScGrev 1914–38; ScGrew 1925–38; ScHCok 1909–37; ScLaD 1916–36; ScRhW 1891–1938; ScSpW 1922–38; ScU 1890–1938

Literary Digest and International Book Review. ScU 1922–26

Literary Examiner. ScU [mfm] (1823)

Literary Gazette [Concord, N. H.]. ScU [mfm] 1834–35

Literary Gazette [Philadelphia]. ScU [mfm] (1821)

Literary Germinae [Worcester, Mass.]. ScU [mfm] 1839–40

Literary Journal [London]. ScU [mfm] 1803–6

Literary Journal [Schenectady, N. Y.]. ScU [mfm] (1834–35)

Literary Journal and General Miscellany of Science, Art, History, Politics, Etc. ScCMus 1821; ScU [mfm] 1818–19

Literary Magazine. ScU [mfm] (1835)

Literary Magazine and American Register. ScC 1803–7; ScU [mfm] 1803–7

Literary Magazine, or the History of the Works of the Learned. ScU [mfm] (1735–36)

Literary Magazine, or Universal Review. ScU [mfm] 1756–58

Literary Magnet. ScU [mfm] 1824–25

Literary Mirror [Portsmouth, N. H.]. ScU [mfm] 1808–9

Literary Miscellany [Cambridge, Mass.]. ScU [mfm] 1805–6

Literary Miscellany [New York]. ScU [mfm] (1811)

Literary Miscellany [Philadelphia]. ScU [mfm] (1795)

Literary Museum [West-Chester, Pa.]. ScU [mfm] (1797)

Literary Pamphleteer [Paris, Ky.]. ScU [mfm] 1823

Literary Speculum. ScU [mfm] 1821–23

Literary Souvenir. ScU [mfm] 1844

Literary Table [Hanover, N. H.]. ScU [mfm] 1803–7

Literary Table [New Haven]. ScU [mfm] 1833–34

Literary World. ScGF (1847–52); ScU [mfm] 1847–53

Littell's Living Age [Living Age]. ScC (1845–1928); ScCCit (1844–1941); ScCleU (1872–84) 1926–41; ScCMus 1844–48 (1912–26); ScFlor 1926–30; ScGF (1844–1941); ScGrev 1919–41; ScHCok 1927–37; ScRhW 1844–1941; ScSpW (1879–1929); ScU 1844–1941, also [mfm] 1844–50

Little Folks. ScC (1913–20)

Little Review. ScU 1914–21

Living [Marriage and Family Living]. ScCleU 1939–40; ScU 1939–40

Living Wilderness. ScCleU 1935+

Lloydia [Lloyd Library of Botany, Bulletin]. ScCleU 1901+

London and Edinburgh Philosophical Magazine and Journal of Science. ScU (1798+)

London Magazine. ScU [mfm] 1820–29

London Magazine, or Gentleman's Monthly Intelligencer. ScU (1757), also [mfm] (1732–85)

London Mathematical Society, Journal. ScU 1936+, library also has *List of Members* (1922–50) and *Proceedings* 1866+

London Mercury. ScRhW (1935–39)

London Quarterly Review. ScCCit (1866–70); ScSpW (1840–80); ScU 1852–83

London Review. ScU [mfm] 1809+

London Spy. ScU [mfm] 1698–1700

Long Island Medical Journal. ScCM 1916–30

Look. ScU 1937–40, 1944+
Los Angeles Neurological Society, Bulletin. ScCM (1935–58)
Louisiana Historical Quarterly. ScCHis (1917+)
Louisiana Law Review. ScU 1938+
Louisville Journal of Medicine and Surgery. ScU [mfm] (1838)
Lounger. ScU [mfm] (1789)
Lowell Offering [Lowell, Mass.]. ScU [mfm] (1840–41)
Lowell Textile Institute, Bulletin. ScCleU (1932–52)
Loyola Law Review. ScU 1941+
Lubrication. ScCleU 1929+
Lutheran. ScCoT 1900+; ScNewb 1923+
Lutheran Church Visitor [Columbia, S. C.]. ScU (1904–19)
Lutheran Home. ScU (1885–90)
Lutheran Quarterly. ScCoT (1854–1927) 1928+
Lutheran Woman. ScCoT 1923+
Lyceum [Asheville, N. C.]. ScU 1890–91
Lyceum of Natural History of New York, Annals. ScCMus 1823–76
Lyre. ScU [mfm] 1824–25

M

McCall's Magazine. ScGBj 1933+; ScLaD 1933+
McClure's Magazine. ScGF (1896–1915); ScRhW 1893–1915; ScSpW
  1897–1915; ScU 1893–1920 (1922–25), also [mfm] 1893–1904
McLeod Infirmary, Bulletin [Florence, S. C.]. ScCM 1934
Machinery. ScCleU 1940+
Mademoiselle. ScGBj 1939+; ScU (1940+)
Madison Quarterly. ScU 1940–49
Magasin de Libraire. ScC 1858–59
Magazine of American History. ScCleU 1879; ScRhW 1877–93;
  ScU 1877–93
Magazine of Art. ScCC 1939–45; ScCCit 1939–53; ScChar 1937–53;
  ScCleU 1937–53; ScGaLi (1938–52); ScHCok 1939–52; ScRhW
  1937–53; ScU 1937–53
Magazine of Art [London]. ScU 1877–1904
Magnolia. ScU (1868–76)
Magnolia, or Southern Monthly. ScC 1842–43; ScFlor 1842–43
Maine Farmer [Vital Statistics Reprint]. ScU (1832–52), also [mfm]
  1833–50
Maine Medical Association, Journal. ScCM (1918–32) 1934+
Maine Monthly Magazine. ScU [mfm] 1836–37

Maintenance Engineering [Factory Management and Maintenance].
ScCleU 1931–32

Malayan Agricultural Journal. ScCleU (1912–24)

Malt Research Institution, Publications. ScCleU 1939+

Man. ScU [mfm] (1834)

Management Review. ScCleU 1914+; ScU 1914–36 (1951–56) 1959+

Manchester Guardian Weekly. ScRhW 1933+

Manchester Literary and Philosophical Society, Memoirs. ScC 1785–90

Manchester School of Economics and Social Studies. ScU 1930+

Manhattan. ScU 1883–84

Manual Training Magazine [Industrial Arts Education]. ScCleU
(1908–22); ScRhW 1905–22

Manufacturers' Record [Industrial Development and Manufacturers'
Record]. ScCCit (1924–26); ScCleU (1924–58); ScU 1917+

Manuscript. ScU [mfm] 1827–28

Market Growers' Journal. ScCleU (1920–57)

Marquette Law Review. ScU 1941+

Marquette Medical Review. ScCM 1937–48

Marriage and Family Living [Journal of Marriage and the Family].
ScGF 1941+; ScU 1939+

Maryland Agricultural Society, Report. ScCleU 1918+

Maryland Farmer. ScCCit 1870–71

Maryland Historical Magazine. ScCHis 1906+

Maryland Medical Journal. ScCM (1907–18)

Maryland University, School of Medicine, Bulletin. ScCM 1932+

Masonic Casket [Enfield, N. H.]. ScU [mfm] 1823–26

Masonic Mirror and Mechanic's Intelligencer. ScU [mfm] 1824–25

Masonic Miscellany and Ladies' Literary Magazine [Lexington, Ky.].
ScU [mfm] 1821–23

Mass Transportation. ScU (1932–50)

Massachusetts Agricultural Repository and Journal. ScU [mfm]
1798–1832

Massachusetts Baptist Missionary Magazine. ScU [mfm] 1803–16

Massachusetts Department of Mental Diseases, Bulletin. ScCM
(1918–36)

Massachusetts General Hospital, Case Records. ScCM 1920–23

Massachusetts Historical Review. ScCHis 1906–57, 1961+

Massachusetts Historical Society, Proceedings. ScCHis 1899–1957

Massachusetts Law Quarterly. ScU (1919–26) 1928+

Massachusetts Magazine. ScU [mfm] 1789–96

Massachusetts Medical Society, Medical Communications. ScU [mfm] 1790–1854

Massachusetts Missionary Magazine [Salem]. ScU [mfm] 1803–8

Massachusetts Quarterly Review. ScU [mfm] 1847–50

Massachusetts Teacher. ScU [mfm] 1818–74

Massachusetts Watchman and Periodical Journal [Palmer, Mass.]. ScU [mfm] 1809–10

Masters In Art. ScC 1900–8; ScCleU 1900–9

Matematicheskii Sbornik. ScU 1936–59, 1964+

Mathematical Correspondent. ScU [mfm] (1804–7)

Mathematical Reviews. ScCleU 1940+; ScCCit 1940+; ScGF 1940+; ScRhW 1940+; ScU 1940+

Mathematics Teacher. ScCleU (1922–25) 1929+; ScDwErs 1941+; ScGBj 1939+; ScGF (1925–26) 1927+; ScGwLa 1936+; ScHCok (1933–59); ScOrSc (1939–51) 1952+; ScRhW 1925+; ScSpC 1937+; ScU 1921+

Mathematische Annalen. ScU 1869+

Mathematische Zeitschrift. ScU [mc] 1918–44

Mayflower Descendant. ScCleU 1917–24

Mayo Clinic, Collected Papers. ScCM 1905–39; ScCleU (1905+); ScCoHo (1927–39); ScGGh (1926–59); ScOrRh (1905–49)

Mayo Clinic, Staff Meeting Proceedings. ScCM 1926+

Measure. ScC 1922–24

Mechanical Engineering. ScCleU 1923+; ScU 1922+

Mechanics Advocate [Albany, N. Y.]. ScU [mfm] 1846–48

Mechanics' Magazine. ScU 1823–28

Mechanics' Magazine and Journal of the Mechanics' Institute. ScU [mfm] 1833–37

Mediateur. ScU [mfm] (1814)

Medical and Agricultural Register. ScU [mfm] 1806–7

Medical and Physical Journal [London]. ScCM (1799–1803)

Medical and Surgical Register. ScU [mfm] 1818–20

Medical Annals of the District of Columbia. ScCM (1932–37) 1939+

Medical Bulletin of the Veterans Administration. ScCM 1926–33

Medical Classics. ScCM 1936–41

Medical Clinics of Chicago [North America]. ScCM 1915+; ScCoHo 1930+; ScCoWsh 1918+; ScGGh (1915–40) 1940+; ScOrRh 1918+

Medical Economics. ScCM (1933+)

Medical Examiner. ScCM 1839–42; ScU [mfm] 1838–56
Medical Intelligencer. ScU [mfm] 1823–25
Medical Journal and Record. ScCM 1924–33
Medical Journal of Australia. ScCM (1921–45) 1946+
Medical Library and Historical Journal. ScCM 1903–7
Medical Library Association, Bulletin. ScCM (1925) 1927+
Medical Life. ScCM (1923–38)
Medical News. ScCM (1858–59) 1866–1905; ScU 1869–72, also [mfm] 1843–50
Medical News-Paper. ScU [mfm] 1822–24
Medical Pickwick. ScCM (1915–21)
Medical Radiology and Photography. ScCM (1933+)
Medical Record. ScCM 1866–1948
Medical Reformer. ScU [mfm] (1823)
Medical Repository. ScCM (1800–21); ScU [mfm] 1797–1824
Medical Repository and Review of American Publications. ScU 1799–1801, 1804–8, 1809–11, 1813
Medical Research Council, Annual Report. ScCM (1925–55)
Medical Research Council [London], Memorandum. ScCM 1941+, library also has *Special Reports* (1931–54)
Medical Review of Reviews. ScCM 1898–1933
Medical Society of the State of New York, Transactions. ScCM (1868–1902)
Medical Society of the State of Pennsylvania, Transactions. ScCM (1889–95)
Medical Times. ScCM (1912+)
Medical Times and Gazette. ScCM (1863–83)
Medical Woman's Journal. ScCM 1941–48
Medicine. ScCleU 1922+; ScCM 1922+; ScGGh (1925–53) 1954+
Medico-Legal Journal. ScU 1907–13
Medieval and Renaissance Studies. ScCleU (1941+)
Medium Aevum. ScCleU 1932+
Medizinische Klinik [Berliner Medizinische Gesellschaft]. ScCM (1927–53), library also has *Beihefte* 1926–29
Medley, or Monthly Miscellany [Lexington, Ky.]. ScU [mfm] 1803
Medleys. ScU [mfm] (1710–12)
Melliand [Textilberichte]. ScCleU (1929–32) 1951+
Melliand Textile Monthly. ScCleU 1929–33
Memoirs of Literature. ScU [mfm] (1710–17)
Memoirs of the Ingenious. ScU [mfm] 1693

Menninger Clinic, Bulletin. ScCM 1938–46; ScU 1937+

Mental Hygiene. ScCM 1917+; ScGF (1917–26) 1927+; ScOrSc (1940–47) 1949+, some files on mfm; ScSpC 1938+

Mentor. ScCCit (1925–28); ScCleU 1913–30; ScGF 1922–30; ScRhP 1924; ScRhW 1922–30

Merchant's Magazine and Commercial Review. ScC 1839–56 (1857–60); ScGF (1839–55); ScU [mfm] 1839–70

Merck Report. ScCM 1919–56

Merck's Annual Report of Recent Advances. ScCM (1913–21)

Mercure de France. ScU (1920–24)

Merrimack Magazine and Ladies' Literary Cabinet. ScU [mfm] 1805–6 (1825)

Merry's Museum. ScGF 1854

Message. ScCoBi 1934+

Messenger of Mathematics. ScU 1927–56

Messenger of Peace [Hudson, N. Y.]. ScU [mfm] 1824–25

Metal Progress. ScCleU 1935+; ScU 1930+

Metalcraft. ScCleU 1931

Metallurgia. ScCleU 1929+

Metallurgical [and Chemical] Engineering. ScCleU 1910–18; ScNcWv 1916–18; ScU 1910–18

Metals and Alloys [Materials in Design Engineering]. ScCleU 1929+

Meteor. ScCC 1935+

Methodist. ScSpW 1872

Methodist Church South, Yearbook. ScCoT [mfm] 1924–41

Methodist Magazine [New York]. ScCoCo 1818–28; ScSpW 1818–19; ScU [mfm] 1818–25

Methodist Magazine [Philadelphia]. ScU [mfm] 1797–98

Methodist Quarterly Review. ScCoCo (1830–1930); ScSpW 1923–30

Methodist Recorder. ScU [mfm] 1824–25

Methodist Review. ScU [mfm] 1818–25

Metropolitan Magazine. ScU [mfm] 1831–50

Michigan Academy of Sciences, Papers. ScCleU 1921–36; ScCMus 1921+

Michigan Farmer and Western Horticulturist [Jackson, Mich.]. ScU [mfm] 1843–50

Michigan, Geological Survey, Bulletin. ScCleU 1909–20

Michigan Law Review. ScU 1902+

Michigan, State Board of Agriculture, Annual Report. ScCleU (1871–1957)

Michigan State Horticultural Society, Annual Report. ScCleU 1881–1926

Michigan State Medical Society, Journal. ScCM (1917) 1925+

Michigan University, Department of Engineering Research, Bulletin. ScCleU 1926+

Michigan [University] Medical Bulletin. ScCM (1936+)

Michigan University, School of Forestry and Conservation, Bulletin. ScCleU 1932–43

Microcosm. ScC (1790)

Microentomology. ScCleU 1936+; ScU 1936–58

Microscope. ScCMus 1893–1959

Microscope [Albany, N. Y.]. ScU [mfm] 1823–25

Microscope [New Haven]. ScU [mfm] (1820)

Microscope and General Advertiser [Louisville, Ky.]. ScU [mfm] 1824–25

Microscopical Journal. ScCMus (1879–98)

Midwife, or Old Woman's Magazine. ScU [mfm] 1750–53

Migrant. ScCMus 1937+

Milbank Memorial Fund, Quarterly. ScU 1924+

Milbank Quarterly Bulletin. ScCM (1924–40) 1942–52

Military Affairs. ScCCit 1941+

Military and Naval Magazine of the United States. ScU [mfm] 1833–36

Military Engineer. ScCleU 1920+; ScU (1922–29) 1941+

Military Monitor and American Register. ScU [mfm] 1812–14

Military Reporter. ScU [mfm] (1810)

Military Service Institute, Journal. ScCCit 1894–1902

Military Surgeon. ScCM (1891–1917) 1918+

Milk Dealer. ScCleU (1926–37) 1938+

Milk Plant Monthly. ScCleU (1931–57)

Milking Shorthorn Journal. ScCleU (1941–43) 1944+

Mind. ScU (1876–1919) 1921+

Mind and Body. ScU 1894–1936

Mineral Industry Statistics, Technology and Trade. ScCleU 1892–1910

Minerva. ScU [mfm] 1822–25

Minerviad. ScU [mfm] (1822)

Mining and Metallurgy. ScCleU 1925–44; ScU 1920–48

Minnesota Horticulturist. ScCleU 1928–36

Minnesota Law Review. ScU 1917+

Minnesota Medicine. ScCM 1922+

Mirror of Literature, Amusement and Instruction. ScU 1823–29, also [mfm] 1823–25

Mirror of Taste and Dramatic Censor. ScC (1810–11); ScGF 1810; ScU [mfm] 1810–11

Miscellaneous Cabinet [Schenectady, N. Y.]. ScU [mfm] (1823–24)

Miscellaneous Letters. ScU [mfm] 1694–96

Miscellaneous Magazine [Trenton, N. J.]. ScU [mfm] 1824

Miscellany [Trenton, N. J.]. ScU [mfm] (1805)

Missionary [Columbia, S. C.]. ScU (1868–76)

Missionary Herald. ScU [mfm] 1805–25

Missionary Review. ScDwErs-T (1881–1916); ScGF 1892–96

Missionary Review of the World. ScChar 1934–39; ScCoBi (1926–39); ScCoT 1899–1910; ScDwErs-T (1888–96); ScGrev 1923–39; ScRhW 1888–1939

Missions on the Border of Afghanistan. ScCoBi (1939–52)

Mississippi Academy of Science, Journal. ScU (1939+)

Mississippi Doctor. ScCM 1935–59

Mississippi Farm Research. ScCleU 1941+

Mississippi Law Journal. ScU 1928+

Mississippi Valley Historical Review [Journal of American History]. ScCC 1941+; ScCCit (1930–32) 1933+; ScCleU 1914+; ScOrSc (1914–51), [mfm] 1954+; ScRhW 1930+; ScU 1914+

Mississippi Valley Medical Journal. ScCM (1927–60)

Missouri Botanical Gardens, Annals. ScCleU 1914+

Missouri Historical Review. ScCHis 1906–57, 1961+

Missouri State Medical Association, Journal. ScCM 1915–16, 1920–52

Mistletoe [Athens, Ga.]. ScU [mfm] (1849)

Mitteilungen aus den Grenzgebieten der Medizin und Chirurgie. ScCM (1904–14)

Mitteilungen uber Allgemeine Pathologie und Pathologische Anatomie. ScCM 1919–39

Modern Concepts of Cardiovascular Disease. ScCM 1932+

Modern Drugs. ScCM (1935+)

Modern Hospital. ScCM 1913–16, 1917+; ScU (1918–49) 1951+

Modern Industry. ScCleU 1941–53; ScU 1941–53

Modern Language Association, Publications. ScCC 1923+; ScCCit 1935+; ScCleU 1884+; ScClP 1930+; ScCoAl 1938+; ScCoCo (1927–32) 1933+; ScGF 1884+; ScRhW 1884+; ScSpW 1924+; ScU 1884+

Modern Language Forum. ScU (1937) 1950–57

Modern Language Journal. ScCC (1921–51); ScCCit 1935+; ScCleU (1919) 1925+; ScCoCo (1926–47) 1948+; ScGF (1926–48) 1961+; ScGwLa 1941+; ScHCok 1940+; ScRhW 1925+; ScSpC 1925+; ScU 1916+

Modern Language Notes. ScCC 1935–51; ScCleU (1886+); ScCoCo 1927–60; ScGF 1886+; ScHCok 1939+; ScNewb 1941+; ScRhW 1886–1908, 1936+; ScSpW (1889–1912) 1913+; ScU 1886+

Modern Language Quarterly. ScCoCo 1941+; ScU 1940+

Modern Language Review. ScCleU (1905–47) 1948+; ScU (1925–46) 1950+

Modern Law Review. ScU 1937+

Modern Medicine. ScCM 1934, 1936+

Modern Music. ScRhW 1941–46; ScSpC 1928–33, 1937–46

Modern Philology. ScCC 1940–50; ScCleU 1924+; ScCoCo (1925–33) 1934+; ScGF 1903–13, 1926–33; ScSpC 1923–51, 1960+; ScU 1904+

Modern Plastics. ScCleU 1938+; ScU 1940+

Modern Publicity. ScU (1924+)

Modes Parisiennes Illustrées, Journal de la Bonne Compagnie. ScU (1868)

Monatshefte für Chemie und Verwandte Teile Anderer Wissenschaften. ScCC 1941+; ScCleU 1880+, some files on mc; ScU 1880+, some files on mc

Monatchefte für Deutschen Unterricht. ScU (1928–38) 1941+

Monatsschrift für Geburtshülfe und Gynaekologie. ScCM (1907–20)

Monatsschrift für Kinderheilkunde. ScCM (1926–37)

Monitor. ScU [mfm] 1823–24

Monthly Abstract of Medical Science. ScCM 1874–79

Monthly American Journal of Geology and Natural Science. ScU [mfm] 1831–32

Monthly Anthology and Boston Review. ScC (1803–6); ScGF (1809–10); ScU 1804–10, also [mfm] 1803–11

Monthly Chronicle. ScU [mfm] 1838–41

Monthly Cyclopaedia of Practical Medicine. ScCM (1898–1914)

Monthly Journal of Foreign Medicine. ScU [mfm] 1828–29
Monthly Journal of Medicine. ScU [mfm] 1823–25
Monthly Labor Review. ScCC 1921+; ScCCit 1935+; ScChar 1940+; ScCleU 1915+; ScOrSc 1937+; ScRhW 1916+; ScSpC 1929+; ScU 1915+
Monthly Law Reporter. ScU [mfm] 1838–66
Monthly Magazine [Lancaster, Pa.]. ScU [mfm] 1808–9
Monthly Magazine and American Review. ScC 1799–1800; ScU [mfm] 1799–1800
Monthly Magazine and British Register. ScC 1797–1809; ScU [mfm] 1796–1843
Monthly Magazine and Literary Journal [Winchester, Va.]. ScU [mfm] 1812–13
Monthly Military Repository. ScU [mfm] 1796–97
Monthly Mirror. ScC 1795–1802
Monthly Miscellany, or Vermont Magazine. ScU [mfm] (1794)
Monthly Record [Charleston, S. C.]. ScU (1871–79)
Monthly Recorder. ScU [mfm] (1813)
Monthly Register and Review of the United States [Charleston, S. C.]. ScC (1805–6); ScU [mfm] 1805–7
Monthly Repository. ScU [mfm] 1806–38
Monthly Review and Literary Miscellany of the United States [Charleston, S. C.]. ScU 1805–6, also [mfm] 1805–6
Monthly Review, or Literary Journal. ScC 1749–1820; ScU [mfm] 1749–1844
Monthly Scientific Journal. ScU [mfm] (1818)
Monthly Visitant [Alexandria, Va.]. ScU [mfm] (1816)
Monthly Visitor and Pocket Companion. ScC (1898–99)
Monthly Vital Statistics Bulletin [Report]. ScCM (1938) 1942+
Monthly Weather Review. ScCleU (1894–1902) 1903+; ScRhW 1935+
Moody Monthly. ScCoBi 1921+; ScGBj (1928–33) 1934–59
Moonshine [Baltimore]. ScU [mfm] (1807)
Moral Advocate [Mt. Pleasant, Ohio]. ScU [mfm] 1821–24
Moral and Religious Cabinet. ScU [mfm] (1808)
Moralist. ScU [mfm] (1814)
Morning Star and Catholic Messenger. ScU [mfm] 1868–69, 1870–79
Mosquito News. ScCleU 1941+
Motive. ScU 1941+
Motor Age. ScCleU 1911–21

Mount Sinai Hospital, Journal. ScCM 1934+
Mount Vernon Ladies Association, Annual Report. ScC (1898–99)
  1916+
Mount Vernon Record. ScC 1858
Muenchener Medizinische Wochenschrift. ScCM (1907–40)
Municipal and County Engineering [Municipal News and Water
  Works]. ScU (1918+)
Municipal Sanitation. ScCleU 1930–40
Munsey's Magazine. ScU 1891–1926 (1928–29)
Museum of Foreign Literature and Science [and Art]. ScC (1822–
  42); ScGF (1826–42); ScU 1826–27, 1831–33, also [mfm] 1822–25
Museum Rusticum et Commerciale. ScU 1763–66
Music and Letters. ScSpC 1939+
Music Educators' Journal. ScNewb (1940+); ScGBj (1934–37) 1938+
Musical America. ScCoCo (1927–54) 1955+; ScGBj 1940+; ScRhW
  1931+; ScSpC 1922+; ScU (1921–27) 1929+
Musical Courier. ScGBj (1934–36) 1937+; ScSpC 1924+
Musical Digest. ScSpC (1923–32)
Musical Herald. ScU (1884–86)
Musical Magazine [Cheshire, Conn.]. ScU [mfm] 1792–1801
Musical Observer. ScSpC 1925–31
Musical Quarterly. ScC 1915–51; ScChar 1934+; ScCoCo 1916+;
  ScGaLi (1929+); ScGBj (1930–36) 1938+; ScGF 1915+; ScGwLa
  (1941–57) 1958+; ScHCok 1927+; ScNewb 1932+; ScRhW
  1931+; ScSpC 1915+; ScU (1919–34) 1936+
Musical Times. ScSpC 1891–96, 1928+
Musician. ScGrev (1923–45); ScRhW 1930–48
Muslim World. ScCoBi 1938+; ScCoT [mfm] 1911–48
Mutual Rights of Ministers and Members of the Methodist Episco-
  pal Church. ScU [mfm] 1824–25
Mycologia. ScCleU 1909+; ScHCok 1939–56; ScU 1909+
Mycopathologia et Mycologia Applicata. ScCM 1938+
Mysore Agricultural [and Experimental Union] Journal. ScCleU
  1926+

N

Nation. ScC (1890–96) 1898+; ScChar 1931+; ScCCit (1925–32),
  [mfm] 1943+; ScCleU 1887+; ScCoCo (1923–43) 1944+; ScCoR
  1934+; ScDwErs 1925+; ScFlor (1926–29); ScGaLi (1941–50);
  ScGBj 1938+; ScGF (1865–66) 1867+; ScGrev 1921+; ScHCok

(1926–27) 1939+; ScOrSc 1935+; ScRhW 1868+; ScSpar (1938–49) 1950+; ScSpC 1883+; ScSpW (1897–1907) 1908+; ScU 1865+, some files on mc

National Academy of Sciences, Biographical Memoirs. ScCleU (1886–1901) 1902+

National Academy of Sciences, Memoirs. ScCleU 1891–1941

National Academy of Sciences, Proceedings. ScCleU 1915+; ScU 1915+

National Academy of Sciences, Report. ScCleU 1917+

National Association for Study and Prevention of Tuberculosis, Transactions. ScCM (1905–21)

National Association of Boards of Pharmacy, Proceedings. ScCM (1918–50)

National Association of Cotton Manufacturers, Transactions. ScCleU 1894–1908

National Association of Cotton Manufacturers, Yearbook. ScCleU 1920–24

National Association of Mutual Insurance Companies, Proceedings. ScCleU 1936–40

National Association of Referees in Bankruptcy, Journal. ScU (1934–42) 1946+

National Association of Retail Druggists, Journal. ScU 1929–52

National Association of Secondary School Principals, Bulletin. ScRhW 1940+; ScU 1937+

National Association of State Universities, Transactions. ScCleU 1941+

National Board of Health, Bulletin. ScCM 1879–82

National Board of Health, Report. ScCM (1879–83)

National Business Education Quarterly. ScU 1937+

National Butter and Cheese Journal. ScCleU (1933–49)

National Cancer Institute, Journal. ScCleU 1940+; ScCM 1940+; ScRhW 1940+

National Cleaner [and Dyer]. ScCleU 1931+

National Commercial Gas Association, Proceedings. ScCleU 1911+

National Council for the Social Studies, Publications. ScCC (1921–45)

National Council for the Social Studies, Yearbook. ScCleU (1936–48) 1954+; ScRhW (1931+)

National Council of Farm Cooperatives, Blue Book. ScCleU 1939+

National Council of State Boards of Engineers, Proceedings. Sc-CleU (1932+)

National Council of State Garden Clubs, Bulletin [National Gardener]. ScCleU 1941+

National Council of Teachers of Mathematics, Yearbook. ScCleU 1928–45, 1957+

National Education Association, Department of Elementary School Principals, Yearbook. ScCleU (1938+); ScRhW 1911+; ScU (1938+)

National Education Association, Journal. ScCC 1940+; ScCCit (1926–38), [mfm] 1959+; ScCleU 1921+; ScDwErs 1929+; ScGaLi 1938+; ScGBj 1939+; ScGF 1913; ScGrev 1924+; ScHCok 1922+; ScNewb 1939+; ScOrSc 1922+; ScRhW 1921+; ScU 1922+

National Education Association, Proceedings. ScCleU 1873+; ScRhW (1872–1952) 1953+; ScU (1873+)

National Education Association, Research Bulletin. ScCC 1933+; ScCleU 1923+; ScGF 1925–62; ScHCok (1923–52); ScRhW 1923+; ScSpW 1926+; ScU 1922+

National Education Association, Rural Education Department, Yearbook. ScCleU 1933–59

National Education Association, Yearbook. ScCleU 1903–19

National Electric Lamp Association, Engineering Department Bulletin. ScCleU 1907–15

National Electric Light Association, Bulletin. ScCleU 1912–13, 1915, 1928–32

National Electric Light Association, Proceedings. ScCleU (1891–1932)

National Formulary Committee, Bulletin [Drug Standards]. ScCM 1938–50; ScU 1936–60

National Foundation for Infantile Paralysis, Annual Report. ScCleU 1938–50

National 4-H News. ScCleU 1941+

National Geographic. ScABBE 1908+; ScBatL (1927+); ScBenM 1917+; ScCC 1909+; ScCCit 1931+; ScCenW 1915+; ScChar 1911, 1914+; ScChes 1930+; ScCleU 1906+; ScClP 1911+; ScCMus 1904+; ScCoAl 1926+; ScCoBi 1938+; ScCoCo 1920+; ScConH (1913–32) 1933+; ScCoR 1906+; ScDarl 1918+; ScDwErs 1923+; ScFlor (1922–56); ScGaLi 1924+; ScGBj (1910–11) 1912+; ScGeor 1915+; ScGF 1912+; ScGrev 1915+; ScGrew

(1915–27) 1928+; ScGwLa (1916–20) 1921+; ScHart 1932+; ScHCok 1910+; ScKing 1939+; ScLaD 1915+; ScLanc 1926+; ScLaur 1926+; ScMar 1920+; ScMoB 1912+; ScMyB 1925–36; ScNewb 1906+; ScOran 1906+; ScOrSc 1922+; ScRhP 1922+; ScRhW 1896+; ScSpar (1909) 1910+; ScSpC 1914+; ScSpJr 1916+; ScSpW 1911+; ScStM 1927+; ScTiNg 1914+; ScU 1899+; ScWaC 1915+; ScWinF 1918+; ScWs 1926+

National Government Journal. ScU [mfm] 1823–25

National Grange Monthly. ScCleU 1930–62

National Historical Magazine. ScCleU 1938–46; ScRhW 1938–45

National Horticultural Magazine [American Horticultural Magazine]. ScCleU 1927+

National Institute for Research in Dairying, Annual Report. ScCleU 1937–56

National Joint Committee on Fertilizer Application, Proceedings. ScCleU 1940+

National Lawyers Guild, Quarterly. ScU 1937–40

National Livestock Producer. ScCleU 1936+

National Lumber Manufacturers' Association, Annual Report. ScCleU 1910–12

National Magazine [London]. ScSpW 1856–57; ScU [mfm] 1856–64

National Magazine [Richmond, Va.]. ScU [mfm] 1799–1800

National Magazine [Washington, D. C.]. ScU [mfm] (1801–2)

National Mathematics Magazine. ScSpW (1936–43)

National Medical Association, Journal. ScCM 1911–12, 1946+

National Municipal [Civic] Review. ScCCit 1935–52, 1954+; ScCleU 1940+; ScGF 1936–58; ScU 1912+

National Museum and Weekly Gazette. ScU [mfm] 1813–14

National Nurseryman [American Nurseryman]. ScCleU 1925+

National Nut Grocers' [Pecan] Association, Proceedings. ScCleU (1913–33)

National Observer and British Review of Politics. ScU [mfm] 1888–97

National Parent Teacher. ScU (1938+)

National Proctologic Association, Journal. ScCM (1940–49)

National Republic. ScRhW 1930–47

National Research Council, Highway Research Board, Proceedings. ScCleU (1922+)

National Research Council of Canada, Report. ScCleU 1922+

National Research Council, Report. ScCleU 1929–31
National Society for the Study of Education, Yearbook. ScCleU 1902+
National Society for Vocational Education, Bulletin. ScCleU (1907–23)
National Tax Association, Bulletin [National Tax Journal]. ScCCit (1936–47); ScCleU 1916+; ScGF 1931+; ScU 1915–47
National Tax Association, Proceedings. ScCleU (1913+)
National Tuberculosis Association, Annual Report. ScCM (1943–54)
National Tuberculosis Association, Bulletin. ScCM (1936–52) 1953+
National Wholesale Druggists' Association, Proceedings. ScCM (1925–38)
Nation's Agriculture. ScCleU 1936+
Nation's Business. ScCleU 1925+; ScGBj 1931+; ScGF 1935+; ScNewb 1924+; ScRhW 1933+; ScSpar 1930–32, 1939–49, 1961+; ScSpW (1940–57); ScU 1925+
Nation's Health. ScCM (1919–27)
Nation's Schools. ScGBj 1938+; ScGF (1928–43) 1944+; ScNewb 1930+; ScOrSc (1932–40) 1941+; ScRhW 1941+; ScSpC 1937+; ScU 1929+
Natural History. ScCleU 1920+; ScGrev 1940+; ScRhW 1934+; ScSpar 1935+; ScU 1914+
Naturalist. ScC (1931–32)
Naturaliste Canadien. ScU 1939+
Naturalist's Miscellany. ScU (1789–1807)
Nature. ScCleU 1869+; ScCM (1869+); ScHCok 1869–1912; ScU 1869+
Nature Magazine. ScCC 1940+; ScCCit 1939–59; ScChar 1933–59; ScChes 1941+; ScCleU 1923–59; ScCMus 1923–59; ScDarl 1925–52; ScDwErs 1923+; ScGF (1935–53); ScGrev (1925–59); ScGwLa 1941+; ScHCok 1935+; ScOrSc 1935+; ScRhP 1933+; ScRhW 1923–59; ScTiNg 1937+; ScU 1923+
Naturwissenschaftliche Zeitschrift für Forst- und Landwirtschaft. ScCleU 1903–16
Naturwissenschaften. ScCleU 1913+; ScCM (1930+); ScU [mc] 1913–27
Naunyn-Schmiedeberg's Archiv für Experimentelle Pathologie und Pharmakologie. ScCM (1908–32) 1933+
Nautilus. ScCMus 1889+
Naval Chronicle. ScU (1799–1806)

Nebraska Law Review. ScU (1928) 1953+

Nebraska State Medical Journal. ScCM 1927+

Negro History Bulletin. ScOrSc (1940–62) 1963+

Nervous and Mental Disease Monographs. ScCM (1912–48)

Nervous Child. ScU 1941–56

Neurological Institute of New York, Bulletin. ScCM 1931–38

New American Magazine [Woodbridge, N. J.]. ScU [mfm] 1758–60

New Eclectic. ScSpW 1868

New England Cotton Manufacturers' Association, Transactions. ScCleU 1894–1905

New England Farmer. ScU [mfm] 1822–25

New England Farmer and Horticultural Journal. ScU 1832

New England Galaxy. ScU [mfm] 1817–25

New England Historical and Genealogical Register. ScCHis 1847+; ScCHu 1890+; ScU 1847+

New England Journal of Medicine. ScCM 1928+; ScGGh 1937+; ScU 1958+, also [mfm] 1828–51

New England Journal of Medicine and Surgery. ScU [mfm] 1812–26

New England Literary Herald. ScU [mfm] (1809–10)

New England Magazine of Knowledge and Pleasure. ScU [mfm] (1758–59)

New England Missionary Intelligencer and General Repository [Concord, N. H.]. ScU [mfm] (1819)

New England Missionary Magazine [Concord, N. H.]. ScU [mfm] 1815–16

New England Quarterly. ScCleU 1928+; ScGF 1928–37

New England Quarterly Magazine. ScU [mfm] (1802)

New Englander. ScSpW 1878–79; ScU 1868

New Englander and Yale Review. ScU [mfm] 1843–50

New Hampshire and Vermont Magazine and General Repository [Haverhill, N. H.]. ScU [mfm] (1797)

New Hampshire Magazine [Concord, N. H.]. ScU [mfm] (1793)

New Hampshire New Jerusalem Magazine [Portsmouth, N. H.]. ScU [mfm] (1805)

New Haven Gazette and Connecticut Magazine. ScU [mfm] 1786–89

New Jersey Agriculture. ScCleU 1919+

New Jersey and Pennsylvania Agricultural Monthly Intelligencer and Farmer's Magazine [Camden, N. J.]. ScU [mfm] (1825)

New Jersey Genealogical Magazine. ScCHis 1929+

New Jersey Historical Society, Proceedings. ScCHis 1900+

New Jersey Journal of Pharmacy. ScU (1933–36) 1938–52

New Jersey Magazine and Monthly Advertiser [New Brunswick]. ScU [mfm] (1786–87)

New Jersey Medical Society, Journal. ScCM (1907–22) 1924+

New Jersey Monthly Magazine. ScU [mfm] (1825)

New Jersey State Horticultural Society News. ScCleU 1940+

New Jerusalem Church Repository. ScU [mfm] 1817–18

New Jerusalem Missionary and Intellectual Repository. ScU [mfm] 1823–24

New Jerusalem Record. ScU [mfm] (1820)

New Memoirs of Literature. ScU [mfm] 1725–27

New Mirror. ScGF 1843–44; ScU 1843–44

New Monthly Magazine and Literary Journal. ScC (1821–24); ScCMus 1822; ScU [mfm] 1814–84, library also has American edition [mfm] 1821–25

New Music Review. ScSpC 1913–33

New Orleans Medical and Surgical Journal. ScCoHo (1932–40); ScCM (1846–1911) 1916–52

New Orleans Monthly Review. ScGF (1874–76)

New Phytologist. ScCleU 1902+

New Princeton Review. ScU 1886–88

New Republic. ScC 1915+; ScChar 1931+; ScCleU 1914+; ScClP 1917+; ScCoR 1938+; ScGaLi 1934+; ScGBj 1938+; ScGF (1917–23) 1924+; ScGrev 1928+; ScHCok (1916–37) 1938+; ScOrSc 1934+; ScRhP 1938+; ScRhW 1917+; ScSpC 1920+; ScSpW 1940+; ScU 1914+

New Star [Concord, N. H.]. ScU [mfm] (1797)

New Star [Hartford]. ScU [mfm] (1796)

New Statesman [and Nation]. ScCleU [mfm] 1931+; ScRhW 1925+; ScU 1938–40, 1948+

New York Academy of Medicine, Bulletin. ScCM 1925+

New York Academy of Sciences, Annals. ScCleU 1887+; ScCMus 1877–1917

New York Academy of Sciences, Transactions. ScCMus 1881–97

New York Botanical Club, Bulletin. ScCMus 1896–1926

New York Botanical Garden, Bulletin. ScCleU 1925–32

New York Botanical Garden, Journal [Garden Journal of the New York Botanical Garden]. ScCleU 1900+

New York City Hall Recorder. ScU [mfm] 1816–22

New York Entomological Society, Journal. ScCleU 1893+; ScCMus 1893–1905

New York Farm Research. ScCleU (1934+)

New York Genealogical and Biographical Register. ScCHis 1897+

New York Herald Tribune Books [Lively Arts]. ScRhW 1929+

New York Historical Quarterly. ScCHis 1917+

New York Journal of Medicine. ScCM 1851–52; ScU [mfm] 1843–60

New York Journal of Romance, General Literature, Science and Art. ScGF 1855–56

New York Literary Journal and Belles-Lettres Repository. ScU [mfm] 1819–21

New York Magazine and General Repository of Useful Knowledge. ScU [mfm] (1814)

New York Magazine, or Literary Repository. ScU [mfm] 1790–97

New York Medical and Philosophical Journal and Review. ScU 1810, also [mfm] 1809–11

New York Medical and Physical Journal. ScU [mfm] 1822–25

New York Medical College, Bulletin. ScCM 1938–56

New York Medical Journal. ScCM 1874–1923

New York Medical Magazine. ScU [mfm] 1814–15

New York Mirror and Ladies' Literary Gazette. ScU [mfm] 1823–25

New York Missionary Magazine. ScU [mfm] 1800–3

New York Monthly Chronicle of Medicine and Surgery. ScU [mfm] 1824–25

New York Monthly Magazine. ScU [mfm] (1824)

New York Produce and American Creamery. ScCleU 1927–30

New York Public Library, Bulletin. ScC (1931+); ScU 1897+

New York Religious Chronicle. ScU [mfm] 1824–25

New York Review. ScC 1837–42; ScGF (1838–41); ScSoH 1838–42; ScU 1838–39

New York Review and Atheneum Magazine. ScU [mfm] 1825–26

New York State Bar Association, Bulletin. ScU 1939+

New York State College of Forestry, Technical Publications. ScCleU 1914+

New York State Historical Association, Publications. ScGF (1925–40)
New York State Hospital Commission, Annual Report. ScCM 1918–26
New York State Journal of Medicine. ScCM (1901) 1906+; ScGGh 1937–45
New York State Medical Association, Transactions. ScCM 1884–99
New York State Museum, Annual Report. ScCMus 1865–1917
New York State Museum, Bulletin. ScCleU (1888+); ScCMus (1899+)
New York State Museum, Circulars. ScCleU 1928–56
New York State University, Education Department, Annual Report. ScCleU 1905+
New York Theatre Critics' Reviews. ScGF (1940+)
New York Times Book Review. ScCCit 1935+; ScRhW 1922+
New York Times Current History of the European War. ScU 1914–16
New York Times Magazine. ScOran 1938+; ScRhW 1934, 1936+
New York Tract Magazine and Christian Miscellany. ScU [mfm] (1824)
New York University Law Review. ScU 1924+
New York Weekly Magazine. ScU [mfm] 1795–97
New York Zoological Society, Bulletin [Animal Kingdom.]. ScCleU 1918+
New Yorker. ScClP 1937+; ScRhW 1941+; ScU 1929–34, 1935+
New Zealand Journal of Agriculture. ScCleU 1925+
New Zealand Journal of Science [and Technology]. ScCleU 1938+, divided into several sections in 1957, library has to date
News and Review, South Carolina Unemployment Compensation Commission. ScU (1938–43)
News Letter, Woman's Work Department, Works Progress Administration of South Carolina. ScU (1935–36)
Newsweek. ScCCit 1936+; ScCleU 1937+; ScClP 1941+; ScCoCo (1940–44) 1945+; ScDwErs 1940+; ScGwLa 1940+; ScLaD 1938+; ScNewb 1941+; ScOrSc 1941+; ScRhP 1934+; ScRhW 1933+; ScSpW 1939+; ScU 1936+
Nicholson's Journal. ScU 1798–1801
Nightingale. ScU [mfm] (1796)
Niles' National [Weekly] Register. ScC (1811–49); ScCleU (1812–49); ScGBj 1812–13, 1825–28; ScGF 1811–39; ScRhW 1811–48; ScU 1811–49, also [mfm] 1811–49

Periodical Files

Nineteenth Century [and After, Twentieth Century]. ScC (1878–91) 1892–1960; ScCCit 1926–32; ScChar 1934–41; ScCleU 1877+; ScCoCo (1921–41); ScGaLi (1902–5); ScGF (1869–70) 1939+; ScHCok (1918–50); ScRhW (1869–70) 1877+; ScSpW 1897–99, 1915–20; ScU 1877+

Nippon, Zeitschrift für Japanologie. ScU 1940–42

Norges Landbrukshoiskole [Oslo], Meldinger. ScCleU 1925+

Normal Instructor and Primary Plans. ScRhW 1917–31

North American Flora. ScCleU 1907+

North American Miscellany. ScGF 1851

North American Review. ScC (1877–1939); ScCCit 1925–40; ScChar (1887–1939); ScCleU 1815–1940, 1964+; ScClP 1888, 1922–33; ScCoCo (1911–37); ScCoR (1934–35); ScDarl 1920–37; ScGaLi 1884–1939); ScGF (1815–87) 1888–1940; ScGrev 1929–40; ScHCok 1899–1940; ScRhW 1815–1939, 1964+; ScSoH 1822–29; ScSpC 1891–1940; ScSpW 1856–57; ScU 1815–1940, 1964+, also [mfm] 1815–50

North American Veterinarian [Modern Veterinary Practice]. ScCleU 1933, 1936+

North British Review. ScC (1846–68); ScCCit (1866–70); ScU 1849–55 (1856–66) 1869–71

North Carolina Booklet. ScC 1905–23

North Carolina Department of Archives and History, Report. ScCleU 1906+

North Carolina Geological and Economic Survey [Division of Mineral Resources], Bulletin. ScCleU 1891+

North Carolina Geological Survey, Report. ScCleU 1858, 1875

North Carolina Historical and Genealogical Register. ScLanc 1900–3; ScRhW 1900–3

North Carolina Historical Review. ScA 1927+; ScCHis 1924+; ScCleU 1924+; ScClP 1925+; ScCoT 1924+; ScGF 1924+; ScHCok (1937–53); ScRhW 1924+; ScSpC 1924+; ScSpW 1924+; ScU 1924+; ScU-Lanc 1924+

North Carolina Law Journal. ScU 1900–2

North Carolina Law Review. ScU 1922+

North Carolina Magazine [New Bern]. ScU [mfm] (1764–65)

North Carolina Magazine; Political, Historical and Miscellaneous. ScU [mfm] (1813)

North Carolina Medical Journal. ScCM (1878–99) 1940+

North Carolina University Magazine. ScSpW 1852–53

North Central Association, Quarterly. ScGF 1928+; ScRhW 1938–39, 1943+; ScU 1926+

North Dakota State Laboratories Department, Bulletin. ScCleU 1923+

North Staffordshire Field Club, Reports and Transactions. ScCMus 1890–1914

Northern Nut Growers Association, Report. ScCleU 1910+

Northampton Miscellany, or Monthly Amusement. ScU [mfm] (1721)

Northwest Medicine. ScCM (1910) 1912+

Northwest Science. ScU 1927+

Northwestern Druggist. ScU 1929+

Northwestern University Law Review [Illinois Law Review]. ScU 1906+

Northwestern University Medical School, Bulletin. ScCM (1931–42)

Northwestern University Medical School, Division of Surgery, Publications. ScCM 1934–38

Northwestern University Medical School, Quarterly Bulletin. ScCM 1940+

Notes and Queries. ScC 1849–1909, 1916–19; ScCleU 1849+; ScCoCo (1937–61) 1962+; ScGF 1849–84 (1909–15); ScU 1910–16, 1947+

Notulae Naturae. ScU 1939+

Nova Scotian Institute of Science, Proceedings and Transactions. ScCMus 1886+

Nutrition Abstracts and Reviews. ScCleU 1931+; ScCM (1931–44)

O

Observator. ScU [mfm] 1702–12

Observer [Baltimore]. ScU [mfm] 1806–7

Observer [New York]. ScU [mfm] (1809)

Obstetrical Journal of Great Britain and Ireland. ScCM 1873–80

Obstetrical Society of London, Transactions. ScCM 1866–84

Occasional Reverberator. ScU [mfm] (1753)

Occupations [Personnel and Guidance Journal]. ScCleU 1939+; ScGBj 1939+; ScOrSc 1939+; ScRhW 1937+; ScSpC 1940–52; ScU 1941+

Oceanography. ScCleU 1927+

Octagon [American Institute of Architects, Journal]. ScCleU 1935+; ScU 1921–28, 1944+

Odd Fellows Magazine. ScU [mfm] (1825–26)

Office Internationale d'Hygiene Publique, Bulletin. ScCM (1919–46)

Oficina Sanatoria Panamericana, Boletim. ScCM 1939+; ScU 1939+
Ohio Biological Survey, Bulletin. ScCleU 1914+
Ohio Farmer. ScCleU 1925–27
Ohio Journal of Science. ScCleU 1900+; ScCMus 1915+
Ohio Miscellaneous Museum [Lebanon, Ohio]. ScU [mfm] (1822)
Ohio State Medical Journal. ScCM (1923) 1925+
Ohio State [University] Law Journal. ScU 1937+
Oil and Soap [American Oil Chemists Society, Journal]. ScCleU 1940+
Okajimas Folia Anatomica Japonica. ScCM (1923–33)
Oklahoma Geological Survey, Bulletin. ScCleU (1908–29)
Oklahoma State Medical Association, Journal. ScCM (1921–23) 1925+
Old Guard. ScGF (1863–68)
Old-Time New England. ScCleU (1938–57)
Olio. ScU [mfm] 1813–14
Olive Plant and Ladies Temperance Advocate. ScGF (1841–43)
Omnium Botherum, or Strictures on the Omnium Gatherum. ScU [mfm] (1821)
Omnium Gatherum. ScU [mfm] 1809–10
Onde Electrique. ScU 1922+
Onderstepoort Journal of Veterinary [Science and Animal Husbandry] Research. ScCleU 1933+
One Act Plays Magazine. ScGF 1937–38
Ontario Agricultural College and Experimental Farm, Report. ScCleU 1909–50
Ontario Department of Agriculture, Report. ScCleU 1885–1955
Ontario Department of Agriculture, Report of the Minister. ScCleU (1910–18) 1920+
Ontario Hydro-Electric Power Commission, Report. ScCleU 1908–11
Oologist. ScCMus 1886–1926
Opera News. ScGBj (1941–54) 1955+; ScSpC 1939+
Ophthalmic Literature. ScCM 1920–22
Ophthalmic Record. ScCM (1893–1904) 1905–17
Ophthalmic Yearbook. ScCM (1911–27)
Ophthalmology. ScCM (1904–17)
Ophthalmoscope. ScCM (1904–16)
Opportunity. ScOrSc (1930–46)

Optical Society of America, Journal. ScCCit (1936+); ScCleU 1917+;
ScU 1924+
Ordeal. ScGF 1809; ScU [mfm] (1809)
Oregon Law Review. ScU 1937+
Oregon [University] Medical School, Reprints. ScCM 1923–26
Organic Syntheses. ScCM 1921–61
Original Session Magazine [Edinburgh]. ScDwErs-T 1852–70
Orion [Penfield, Ga.]. ScC (1842–44); ScFlor 1844; ScGF (1842–43)
Orphan Work [Clinton, S. C.]. ScU 1937–45
Orphanage Notes [Greenville, S. C.]. ScU 1901–8
Osiris. ScU 1936–39
Osprey. ScCMus 1896–1902
Ottawa Naturalist. ScCMus 1880–1916
Our Animal Friends. ScCMus 1892–1906
Our Dumb Animals. ScC 1892–93
Our Monthly [Farm and Garden, Clinton, S. C.]. ScClP 1867–1916;
ScU (1880–1942)
Outdoor Life. ScCMus (1908–17)
Outing. ScC 1904–20; ScCMus 1908–12; ScSpW 1906–23; ScU 1882–
1922
Outlook. ScC 1904–31; ScCCit (1925–35); ScCleU 1901–35; ScCoR
(1928–35); ScDarl 1920–35; ScFlor 1929; ScGF (1897–1907) 1908–
35; ScGrev 1920–35; ScGrew 1922–31; ScHCok 1901–34; ScLaD
1915–31; ScRhW 1897–1935; ScSpC (1922–30); ScSpW 1895–
1935; ScU 1870–1935, some files on mfm
Overland Monthly [and Out West Magazine]. ScCleU 1912–25;
ScU (1892–1933), also [mfm] 1868–1900

P

Pacific Affairs. ScU 1929+
Pacific Coast Journal of Nursing. ScCM (1934–39)
Pacific Drug Review [Western Pharmacy]. ScU 1929+
Pacific Historical Review. ScU 1932+
Pall Mall Magazine. ScDarl 1893–97
Palladium [Presbyterian College]. ScU (1895–96)
Palmetto [Columbia, S. C.]. ScU (1901–15)
Palmetto Leaves Bulletin. ScU (1941–48)
Palmetto School Journal. ScU 1890–91
Pan American Geologist. ScU 1922–42

Pan American Union, Bulletin. ScCC 1933–48; ScCCit 1938–48; ScChar 1934–48; ScClP 1931–42; ScGF 1940–47; ScGrev 1921–48; ScRhW 1913–48

Panopolist. ScC 1806–12

Pan-Pacific Entomologist. ScCleU 1924+

Paper Trade Journal. ScNcWv 1924+

Papier-Fabrikant. ScNcWv 1922–39

Parasitology. ScCleU 1908+; ScCM 1929–33

Parents Magazine. ScCoCo (1935–63); ScGBj (1941) 1945+; ScGrev 1928+; ScLaD 1934–47, 1953–60; ScOrSc (1941–48) 1949+; ScRhP 1935+; ScRhW 1931+

Paris, Ecole Nationale Supérieure des Beaux-Arts: Concours d'Architecture de l'Année Scolaire. ScCleU 1906–14, 1917–25

Paris, Ecole Nationale Supérieure des Beaux-Arts: Grands Prix de Rome d'Architecture. ScCleU 1850–1925, 1930

Paris, Ecole Nationale Supérieure des Beaux-Arts: Médailles des Concours d'Architecture. ScCleU 1902–13

Paris, Ecole Polytechnique Journal ou Bulletin du Travail. ScU 1812–45

Paris Medical. ScCM (1919–37)

Parley's Magazine. ScGF 1833–43; ScU [mfm] 1833–44

Parlour Companion. ScU [mfm] 1817–19

Parterre. ScU [mfm] 1816–17

Partisan Review. ScU 1934+

Pastime [Albany, N. Y.]. ScU [mfm] 1807–8

Pathfinder. ScC (1906–11)

Patriot [Stonington-Port, Conn.]. ScU [mfm] 1801–2

Patrons of Husbandry, Journal of Proceedings. ScCleU (1875–1901)

Peabody Journal of Education. ScCleU (1923–28) 1949+; ScGBj 1939+; ScOrSc 1939+; ScRhW 1923+; ScU 1923+

Peanut Journal and Nut World. ScCleU (1926–47) 1948+

Pedagogical Seminary [and Journal of Genetic Psychology]. ScCleU 1940+; ScGBj 1940+; ScRhW 1924–53; ScU 1924+

Pediatria. ScCM 1908–14

Pediatrics. ScCM (1898–1901)

Pen and Pencil. ScChar 1853–55

Pencil Points [Progressive Architecture]. ScCleU 1922+

Peninsula Horticultural Society, Transactions. ScCleU (1907+)

Pennsylvania Journal of Prison Discipline and Philanthropy. ScU [mfm] 1845–55

Pennsylvania Magazine. ScU 1877–1924
Pennsylvania Magazine of History and Biography. ScCHis 1877+;
  ScCHu 1899+
Pennsylvania Magazine, or American Monthly Museum. ScU [mfm]
  1775–76
Pennsylvania State College, Abstracts of Doctoral Dissertations. Sc-
  CleU 1938–55
Pennsylvania State College, Annual Report. ScCleU 1869–1917
Pennsylvania State Medical Journal. ScCM (1914) 1930+
Pennsylvania [University] Law Review. ScU 1900+
Penny Magazine. ScC (1841–45); ScChar 1833; ScCMus 1832–38;
  ScU 1832–38
Penny Post. ScU [mfm] (1769)
Pentagon. ScU 1941+
People. ScCMus (1932); ScU (1931–34)
People's Magazine of Useful Information. ScU 1833–35
Percy Society, Publications. ScCCit [mc] 1840–52
Periodical Sketches. ScU [mfm] (1820)
Personalist. ScU 1921+
Personnel. ScU 1919–46, 1963+
Personnel Journal [Personnel Research]. ScU 1924+
Petermanns Geographische Mitteilungen. ScU 1855–96, 1900–14
Peterson's Magazine. ScCMus 1861
Petit Censeur. ScU [mfm] (1805)
Petit Courrier des Dames. ScCMus (1828)
Petite Illustration. ScRhW 1926–34; ScSpW 1928–30; ScU (1913–39)
Petroleum Technology. ScU 1938–46
Pflueger's Archiv für die Gesamte Physiologie des Menschen und
  der Tiere. ScCM (1936–44) 1947+
Phalanx. ScU [mfm] 1843–45
Pharmaceutica Acta Helvetiae. ScU 1926+
Pharmaceutical Abstracts. ScCM 1935–47
Pharmaceutical Archives. ScCM 1898–1942; ScU 1936–48
Pharmaceutical Era. ScU (1913–30)
Pharmaceutical Journal. ScU (1842–1930) 1934+
Phi Beta Kappa Key. ScU 1910–31
Philadelphia Academy of Natural Sciences, Proceedings. ScCMus
  1852+
Philadelphia Journal of Medical and Physical Sciences. ScCM
  (1822–24); ScU [mfm] 1820–27

Philadelphia Journal of Science. ScCM (1920–34)

Philadelphia Magazine and Review. ScU [mfm] (1799)

Philadelphia Magazine, or Weekly Repository of Polite Literature. ScU [mfm] (1818)

Philadelphia Medical and Physical Journal. ScU [mfm] 1804–8

Philadelphia Medical Journal. ScCM 1898–1903

Philadelphia Medical Museum. ScU (1804–11), also [mfm] 1804–11

Philadelphia Medical Times. ScCM (1873–76)

Philadelphia Minerva. ScU [mfm] 1795–98

Philadelphia Monthly Magazine. ScU [mfm] (1798)

Philadelphia Museum. ScU [mfm] (1824)

Philadelphia Repertory. ScU [mfm] 1810–12

Philadelphia Society for Promoting Agriculture, Memoirs. ScC 1808–14

Philadelphia Universalist Magazine and Christian Messenger. ScU [mfm] 1821–23

Philadelphisches Magazin. ScU [mfm] (1798)

Philanthropist [Mount Pleasant, Ohio]. ScU [mfm] (1817) 1818–22

Philippine Agricultural Review [Journal of Agriculture]. ScCleU 1908–41

Philippine Agriculturalist. ScCleU 1929+

Philippine Medical Association, Journal. ScCM 1939+

Philips Technical Review. ScCleU 1936+

Philological Quarterly. ScCleU 1922+; ScCoCo (1937–44) 1945+; ScSpW 1926–54; ScU 1922+

Philosophic Abstracts. ScCC 1940–51; ScCleU 1939–54; ScGF 1939–54; ScU 1940–54

Philosophical Magazine. ScC (1798–1860); ScCleU 1901+; ScU (1798+)

Philosophical Review. ScCC 1938–40; ScCCit 1940+; ScGF 1909–13, 1935+; ScU (1892–1901) 1907+

Philosophy. ScU 1931+

Philosophy and Phenomenological Research. ScU 1940+

Philosophy of Science. ScCC 1940–49; ScU 1934+

Phonetic Journal. ScClP 1892–96

Photo Technique. ScCleU 1940–41

Phrenological Journal and Miscellany. ScU 1823–27

Phylon. ScOrCl 1940+; ScOrSc 1940+; ScU 1940+

Physica. ScCleU 1933+

Physical Abstracts. ScCCit 1919+

Physical Education. ScU 1957+, also 1893–96 on mc

Physical Educator. ScU 1940+

Physical Review. ScCCit 1920+; ScCleU 1913+; ScGF 1930–43, 1945+; ScOrSc 1913+; ScU 1893+

Physical Society of London, Proceedings. ScCleU 1934+; ScU (1919+)

Physical Society of London, Reports on Progress in Physics. ScCleU 1934+

Physician's Bulletin. ScCM 1937–62

Physics [Journal of Applied Physics]. ScCleU 1931–36; ScU 1931–36

Physics Abstracts. ScCleU 1941+; ScGF 1930+

Physikalisch-Chemisches Centralblatt. ScU 1903–9

Physikalische Zeitschrift. ScU 1899–1945

Physiological Abstracts. ScCM (1918–35)

Physiological Reviews. ScCC 1941–55; ScCleU 1921, some files on mc; ScCM 1921+; ScU 1921+

Physiological Zoology. ScCM 1928–33; ScU 1928+

Phytopathologische Zeitschrift. ScCleU (1929+)

Phytopathology. ScCleU 1911+, some files on mc

Pictorial Review. ScGrev 1934–39; ScRhW 1922–39

Piedmont Churchman. ScU 1929+

Piedmont Hospital [Atlanta, Ga.], Bulletin. ScCM (1926–39)

Pilgrim, or Monthly Visitor [New Haven]. ScU [mfm] 1822–23

Pilot [New Haven]. ScU [mfm] 1821–24

Pine Institute of America, Abstracts, Chemical Section. ScU 1927–31

Pioneer [Boston]. ScGF (1843)

Pioneer [Pittsburgh]. ScU [mfm] (1812)

Piscataqua Evangelical Magazine [Portsmouth, N. H.]. ScU [mfm] 1805–8

Pitman's Shorthand Weekly. ScClP 1892–1901

Pittsburgh Recorder. ScU [mfm] 1822–27

Pittsburgh [University] Law Review. ScU 1935+

Plain Dealer. ScU [mfm] 1724–25

Planning and Civic Comment. ScU 1935+

Plant Breeding Abstracts. ScCleU 1936+

Plant Disease Reporter. ScCleU 1917+, also has *Supplement* 1919–59

Plant Physiology. ScCleU 1926+

Plant World. ScCleU 1903–10

Planta. ScCleU 1925+, some files on mc

Players Magazine. ScGBj 1933+; ScRhW 1941+; ScU 1935–48, 1953+

Playground [Recreation]. ScCMus 1908–18; ScU 1907–30

Plough Boy [Albany, N. Y.]. ScU [mfm] 1819–23

Plough, Loom and Anvil. ScCMus 1849

Plymouth Rock Monthly. ScCleU (1929–38)

Poet Lore. ScC 1913–21; ScU (1889–1908) 1913–30

Poetry. ScC 1921–44 (1945–46); ScCC 1940–50; ScCCit (1937–64); ScChar 1920, 1931+; ScCleU 1927+; ScDwErs 1938+; ScGBj (1932–37) 1938+; ScGF 1922+; ScHCok 1924+; ScNewb 1939+; ScRhP 1940+; ScRhW 1923+; ScSpC 1926+; ScSpW 1940–43, 1955+; ScU 1912+

Poetry Society of South Carolina, Yearbook. ScCMus 1921–33

Political Censor. ScU [mfm] (1796–97)

Political Economist. ScU [mfm] (1824)

Political Magazine and Miscellaneous Repository [Ballston, N. Y.]. ScU [mfm] (1800)

Political Magazine and Parliamentary, Naval, Military and Literary Journal. ScC (1780–83)

Political Quarterly. ScU 1940+

Political Register. ScU 1832–35

Political Science Quarterly. ScCC 1941–52; ScCCit 1930+; ScCleU (1886–1920) 1921+; ScGF 1929+; ScGrev 1924–36; ScNewb 1939+; ScRhW 1886+; ScSpW 1903+; ScU 1886+

Political State of Europe. ScC 1794–95

Polyanthos. ScGF 1814; ScU [mfm] (1805–14)

Pomological Magazine. ScU 1827–30

Popular Astronomy. ScRhW 1936–51; ScU 1925–51

Popular Aviation. ScCleU 1938–40

Popular Educator [Grade Teacher]. ScRhW 1908–26

Popular Mechanics. ScCCit (1935) 1937+; ScCleU (1916–38) 1939+; ScCoR 1936+; ScGBj 1933+; ScGrev 1924+; ScOran 1939+; ScOrSc (1941–46) 1952+; ScRhP 1933+; ScSpW 1912–17, 1946+; ScU (1917–18) 1923+

Popular Science Monthly. ScC 1872–86 (1887) 1888–1915; ScCleU (1873–1959) 1960+, some files on mc; ScCMus (1890–1930); ScCoR 1941+; ScDwErs 1927+; ScGBj (1873–74) 1938+; ScHCok 1910–15; ScOran 1940+; ScRhP 1933+; ScRhW 1872–1915, 1935+;

ScSpW 1872–75, 1894+; ScU 1872–1915, 1927+, some files on mfm

Porcupine's Political Censor. ScU [mfm] (1796–97)

Port Folio. ScC (1801–25); ScCMus 1813; ScGF (1806–20); ScU (1809–12) 1816–24, also [mfm] 1801–27

Portico. ScU [mfm] 1816–18

Portland Magazine [Portland, Me.]. ScU [mfm] (1805)

Portsmouth Weekly Magazine [Portsmouth, N. H.]. ScU [mfm] 1824–25

Possett's Textile Journal. ScCleU (1911–23)

Postgraduate Medical Journal. ScCM 1941+

Poultry Item. ScCleU (1925–40)

Poultry Science. ScCleU 1923+

Poultry Science Association, Proceedings. ScCleU 1908–10

Poultry Tribune. ScCleU (1927+)

Power. ScCleU 1902+; ScU 1931+

Power Plant Engineering. ScCleU (1926–35) 1936+; ScU 1935+

Practical Farmer. ScCleU (1893–99)

Practical Home Economics. ScDwErs 1938+; ScGF 1929–44; ScOrSc 1939+

Practical Mechanic and Engineer's Magazine. ScU 1841–47

Practical Mechanic's Journal. ScU (1848–56)

Practitioner. ScCM 1869–85 (1896–1904) 1906+

Prater. ScU [mfm] (1756)

Preacher and Homiletic Monthly. ScSpW 1879–82

Presbyterian and Reformed Review. ScDwErs-T 1894–96

Presbyterian Historical Society, Journal. ScCoT 1901–29, 1941+

Presbyterian Magazine. ScGF 1851; ScU [mfm] 1821–22

Presbyterian Quarterly. ScClP 1887–1904

Presbyterian Review. ScGBj (1882–90)

Present State of the Republick of Letters. ScU [mfm] 1728–36

Press Medicale. ScCM (1904+)

Primary Education [Grade Teacher]. ScRhW 1907–29

Princeton Review. ScClP 1837–60; ScCoBe (1844–64); ScDwErs-T 1837–81; ScGBj (1841–65); ScSpW 1878–83; ScU [mfm] 1825–50

Princeton University Library Chronicle. ScU 1939+

Printers' Ink Monthly. ScCCit 1925–26, 1932–41

Printers' Ink Weekly. ScCCit 1925–27, 1932+; ScU (1921–35) 1946+

Printing Art. ScCoR (1921–24)

Professional Engineer. ScU 1920–26 (1936–37) 1939+

Progressive Education. ScGF 1927–57; ScRhW 1924–57; ScU 1929+
Progressive Farmer. ScCleU (1924–38) 1939+
Progressive Medicine. ScCM (1899–1931)
Prompter. ScU [mfm] 1734–36
Prospect, or View of the Moral World. ScU [mfm] 1803–5
Protestant Episcopal Society for the Advancement of Christianity in South Carolina, Annual Report. ScC (1816–81)
Providence Theological Magazine. ScU [mfm] (1821)
Psyche. ScCleU (1874–1914) 1928+
Psychiatric Quarterly. ScCM 1928+; ScU 1939+
Psychiatry. ScCM 1938+; ScCoWsh 1938+; ScU 1938+
Psychoanalytic Review. ScCM (1925–47)
Psychological Abstracts. ScCleU 1927+; ScCM (1930–61); ScGF 1927+; ScRhW 1927+; ScSpC 1927+; ScU 1927+
Psychological Bulletin. ScCleU 1922–29; ScGF (1935–38) 1939+; ScRhW 1930+; ScSpC 1923+; ScU 1904+
Psychological Clinic. ScRhW 1907–18
Psychological Review. ScCC 1941–50; ScCleU 1924–29; ScGF (1929–45); ScHCok (1932–33) 1941+; ScSpC 1934+; ScSpW 1937–43, 1960+; ScU 1894+
Psychometrika. ScU 1936+
Psychosomatic Medicine. ScCM 1939+; ScU 1939–54
Public Administration. ScU 1930+
Public Administration Review. ScCCit 1941+; ScGF 1940+; ScU 1940+
Public Affairs Pamphlets. ScRhW 1936+
Public Health Nursing [Nursing Outlook]. ScCM 1919–52; ScCoHo (1938–47) 1948+; ScGGh-N 1931–52; ScU (1922–24) 1928–52
Public Health Reports. ScRhW 1912+
Public Libraries [Libraries]. ScCleU (1906–25); ScU 1896–1925
Public Management. ScCleU 1940+; ScU 1928+
Public Opinion. ScC (1874–75); ScU 1888–1906
Public Opinion Quarterly. ScCCit 1937+; ScCleU 1937+; ScU 1937+
Public Personnel Review. ScU 1940+
Public Roads. ScCleU (1920–32) 1936+
Public Utilities Fortnightly. ScCleU 1934–45; ScU (1929) 1930–42
Public Utilities Reports [Annual Digest]. ScCleU 1915–45
Public Works. ScU (1928–61)

Publishers' Weekly. ScCC 1938–50; ScCleU 1939+; ScNewb 1941+; ScRhP 1937+; ScRhW 1930+; ScSpC 1937+; ScU 1940+
Puerto Rico Health Bulletin. ScCM 1939–40
Puerto Rico Journal of Public Health and Tropical Medicine. ScCM 1927–50
Puerto Rico University, Journal of Agriculture. ScCleU 1919+
Pulp and Paper Magazine of Canada. ScNcWv 1940+
Punch. ScC (1853–65); ScChar (1846–1930); ScGF 1841–1938; ScRhW 1936–46, 1964+; ScU 1841–95 (1897–58) 1959+
Purdue Agriculturalist. ScCleU (1924–35)
Puritan. ScU 1897
Putnam's [Monthly] Magazine. ScChar (1853); ScGF (1853–1909); ScSpW 1906–19; ScU 1853–54, 1870, also [mfm] 1853–57, 1868–70

Q

QST, a Magazine Devoted Exclusively to the Wireless Amateur. ScCleU 1931+; ScGrev 1937+; ScU 1924+
Quarterly Christian Spectator [New Haven]. ScU [mfm] 1819–38
Quarterly Cumulative Index to Current Medical Literature [Index Medicus]. ScCleU (1925+); ScCM (1879+); ScCoHo 1930+; ScGGh 1941+; ScOrRh 1916–56, 1960+
Quarterly Journal of Economics. ScCleU 1940+; ScGF 1886+; ScRhW 1939+; ScU 1887+
Quarterly Journal of Experimental Physiology. ScCM 1908–33, 1937+
Quarterly Journal of Mathematics [Oxford Series]. ScU 1930+
Quarterly Journal of Medicine. ScCM 1907–11, 1917+
Quarterly Journal of Microscopical Science. ScCM (1888–1948)
Quarterly Journal of Pharmacy and Pharmacology. ScCM 1928–48
Quarterly Journal of Science, Literature and Art. ScU 1820–23, 1825–26
Quarterly Journal of Speech. ScCCit 1939+; ScCleU 1938+; ScGBj 1923+; ScGF (1929–34) 1935+; ScHCok 1939+; ScOrSc 1940+; ScRhW 1940+; ScSpC 1927+; ScU 1928+
Quarterly Journal of Studies on Alcohol. ScCM 1940+; ScU 1940+
Quarterly Review. ScC 1809–37 (1838–1914) 1915+; ScCM 1824–25; ScCMus (1809–96); ScGF (1809–18); ScHCok 1932–36; ScRhW 1809+; ScSoH (1826–36); ScSpW 1809–37; ScU (1809+)
Quarterly Review of Biology. ScCC 1941+; ScCleU 1926+; ScCM (1926–41) 1947+; ScNewb 1941+; ScU 1926+

Periodical Files

Quarterly Review of Higher Education Among Negroes. ScOrSc
1934+
Quarterly Sunday-School Magazine. ScU [mfm] 1824–32
Quebec Society for the Protection of Plants, Report. ScCleU 1936+
Queensland Agricultural Journal. ScCleU (1924–42) 1943+
Quick Frozen Foods [and the Locker Plant]. ScCleU (1940–42)
1943+
Quiver [Charleston, S. C.]. ScU (1807), also [mfm] (1807)

R

Radical. ScU [mfm] 1821
Radio [and TV] News. ScCCit (1939–58); ScCleU (1923–48) 1949–
59; ScGrev 1937–59
Radio [Audio Engineering, Audio]. ScU 1938+
Radio Corporation of America Review. ScCleU 1936+; ScU 1936+
Radiography. ScCM (1935–60)
Radiology. ScCM 1923+; ScCoHo (1930) 1960+; ScGGh 1929+
Radium. ScCM (1915–25)
Railway Age Weekly. ScCCit 1938+; ScFlor 1906–13; ScU 1916–32,
1941+
Railway and Corporation Law Journal. ScU 1887–92
Railway Mechanical Engineer [Railway Mechanical and Electrical
Engineer, Railway Locomotives and Cars]. ScU (1887–1963)
Railway Review. ScU 1923–26
Railway Signaling. ScCleU 1936–39
Railway Surgical Journal. ScU 1906–16
Rambler [Charleston, S. C.]. ScC 1843–44; ScU [mfm] 1848–62
Rambler's Magazine and New York Theatrical Register. ScU [mfm]
1809–10
Rayon [Modern Textiles]. ScCleU 1929+
Rayon Organon. ScCleU 1937+
Reactions. ScU (1908–20)
Reader. ScU [mfm] 1863–67
Reader's Digest. ScCC 1936+; ScCCit 1936+; ScChar 1937+; Sc-
Ches 1939+; ScCleU 1930+; ScClP 1936+; ScCoBe 1930+; Sc-
CoCo (1927–33) 1934+; ScCoR 1935+; ScDarl 1934+; ScDwErs
1929+; ScGaLi 1934+; ScGBj 1928+; ScGeor 1934+; ScGF
1932+; ScGrev 1930+; ScGrew 1932+; ScGwLa 1938+; ScHart
1939+; ScHCok 1934+; ScLaD 1933+; ScNewb 1928+; ScOran
1936+; ScOrSc 1932+; ScRhP 1934+; ScRhW 1937+; ScSpar

1928+; ScSpC 1932+; ScSpW 1928+; ScSum 1940+; ScTiNg 1934+; ScU 1926+

Reclamation Era. ScRhW 1921+

Record of Chemical Progress. ScU 1939+

Recorder [Columbia, S. C.]. ScCM 1937+; ScU 1937+

Records of Mining. ScU 1829

Records of the Past. ScC 1902–14

Recreation. ScCC 1940–51; ScCleU 1937+; ScDwErs 1935+; ScGF 1936+; ScHCok 1931+; ScRhW 1930+; ScU 1930+

Recreations in Agriculture, Natural History, Arts and Miscellaneous Literature. ScC 1799–1801

Recreative Magazine. ScU [mfm] (1822)

Recueil des Historiens des Croisades, Documents Armeniens. ScU [mfm] 1869–1906

Recueil des Historiens des Croisades, Historiens Grecs. ScU [mfm] 1875–81

Recueil des Historiens des Croisades, Historiens Occidentaux. ScU [mfm] 1844–95

Recueil des Historiens des Croisades, Historiens Orientaux. ScU [mfm] 1872–1906

Recueil des Historiens des Croisades, Lois, Assises de Jerusalem. ScU [mfm] 1842–43

Recueil de Travaux Chimiques des Pays-Bas et de la Belgique. ScCleU 1882+; ScU 1882+

Reference Shelf. ScU 1922+

Reflector. ScU [mfm] (1821)

Reformed Church Review. ScCoT [mfm] 1849–1926; ScU [mfm] 1849–50

Reformer. ScU [mfm] 1820–25

Refrigerating Engineering. ScCleU 1937+; ScU 1937+

Register of the Times and Literary Review. ScC (1794–96); ScU (1795)

Registered Nurse. ScCoHo 1939–47; ScU 1937–39, 1944+

Reliable Poultry Journal. ScCleU 1930–32

Religion in Life. ScCoT 1933+, some files on mc; ScNewb 1935+

Religious and Literary Repository [Annapolis, Md.]. ScU [mfm] (1820)

Religious Education. ScCoCo (1921+); ScCoT 1926+; ScDwErs-T 1915+; ScGBj 1941+; ScGF (1911–35) 1936+; ScHCok 1918–20, 1929+; ScNewb 1939+; ScSpC 1925+; ScU 1906+

Religious Enquirer [Cooperstown, N. Y.]. ScU [mfm] (1811)

Religious Informer [Enfield, N. H.]. ScU [mfm] 1819–25

Religious Inquirer [Hartford, Conn.]. ScU [mfm] 1821–25

Religious Instructor [Carlisle, Pa.]. ScU [mfm] (1810–11)

Religious Intelligencer [New Haven, Conn.]. ScU [mfm] 1816–30

Religious Magazine [Kennebunk, Me.]. ScU [mfm] 1811–22

Religious Miscellany [Carlisle, Pa.]. ScU [mfm] 1823–24

Religious Monitor. ScDwErs-T 1803–18

Religious Monitor and Evangelical Repository. ScU [mfm] 1824–42

Religious Monitor, or Theological Scales [Danbury, Conn.]. ScU [mfm] 1798

Religious Museum [Milton, Pa.]. ScU [mfm] 1818–19

Religious Outlook [Columbia, S. C.]. ScU 1897–98

Religious Repository [Concord, N. H.]. ScU [mfm] 1807–9

Reliquary. ScU 1861–86

Remembrancer for Lord's Day Evenings [Exeter, N. H.]. ScU [mfm] (1797)

Remembrancer, or Debtors Prison Recorder. ScU [mfm] (1820)

Remembrancer, or Impartial Repository of Public Events. ScC 1776–82; ScU (1776–79)

Reminder [York, S. C.]. ScU (1926+)

Repertoire Bibliographique. ScU 1940–59

Repertory of Arts and Manufacturers. ScC 1794–1820

Reporter's Journal. ScClP 1886–1901

Repository and Ladies' Weekly Museum. ScU [mfm] 1800–6

Repository of Knowledge. ScU [mfm] 1801–2

Republic of Letters. ScU 1834

Republican Magazine [Fairhaven, Vt.]. ScU [mfm] (1798)

Republican Rush-Light. ScU [mfm] (1800)

Research Quarterly. ScCCit 1938+; ScDwErs 1936+; ScGF (1941–44) 1945+; ScHCok 1930+; ScU 1930+

Resorts Life [Aiken, S. C.]. ScU 1930–31

Retrospective Review. ScC (1820–25); ScU 1820–26

Retrospective Review and Historical and Antiquarian Magazine. ScU 1827–28

Review of American Chemical Research. ScCM (1898–1906); ScU 1895–1906

Review of Applied Entomology [Series A and B]. ScCleU 1913+

Review of Applied Mycology. ScCleU 1929+, some files on mfm

Review of Economic [Economics and] Statistics. ScCleU 1928+; ScU 1919+

Review of Economic Studies. ScCleU 1933+; ScU 1933+

Review of Educational Research. ScCCit 1935+; ScCleU 1931–64; ScGF 1931+; ScOrSc 1931+; ScRhW 1931+; ScSpW (1931–49) 1950+; ScU 1931+

Review of English Studies. ScCleU 1925+; ScU 1939–41, 1952+

Review of Gastroenterology. ScCM 1934–53

Review of Politics. ScU 1939+

Review of Reviews and World's Work. ScCCit (1924–36); ScChar 1891, 1893, 1932–37; ScCoCo 1907–24; ScCleU 1893–97, 1929–37; ScCoR (1929–37); ScDarl 1920–37; ScDwErs 1931–36; ScFlor 1926–29; ScGaLi (1919–37); ScGF 1893–1937; ScGrev 1914–37; ScHCok 1899–1937; ScRhW 1890–37; ScSpC 1894–1937; ScSpW 1891–1937; ScU 1890–1937

Review of Scientific Instruments. ScCCit 1933+; ScCleU 1930+; ScCM 1933+; ScOrSc (1930–60); ScSpDm 1936+; ScU 1930+

Review of Tumor Therapy. ScCM 1937+

Reviewer. ScC (1923–25)

Reviews of Modern Physics. ScCleU 1929+; ScOrSc 1930+; ScU 1929+

Revista Chilena de Higiene y Medicina Preventiva. ScCM (1938–53)

Revista de Archivos, Bibliotecas y Museos. ScU (1903+)

Revista de Filologia Española. ScU 1926+

Revista de Historia de América. ScU 1938+

Revista Hispánica Moderna. ScU 1934+

Revista Iberoamericana. ScU 1939+

Revista Médico-Cirurgica do Brazil. ScCM 1931–35

Revista Sud-Americana de Endocrinologia, Inmunologica y Quimioterapia. ScCM 1931–38

Revue Archéologique. ScU 1844–48 (1938) 1947+

Revue Belge des Sciences Médicales. ScCM 1937–38

Revue d'Artillerie. ScC 1872–94 (1895–96)

Revue d'Historie Littéraire de la France. ScU 1923–27, 1930–34, 1952+

Revue d'Immunologie. ScCM (1935–55)

Revue d'Oka [Institut Agricole d'Oka, Université de Montréal]. ScCleU 1926–62

Revue de Droit International des Sciences Diplomatiques et Politiques. ScU 1926–39, 1947+
Revue de Géologie et des Sciences Connexes. ScU 1920–36, 1938–40
Revue de Littérature Comparée. ScU 1921+
Revue de Médicine. ScCM 1927–32
Revue de Philologie, de Littérature et d'Histoire Anciennes. ScU 1904–10
Revue de Phonétique. ScU 1928–30
Revue de Seizieme Siecle. ScU 1913–31
Revue des Deux Mondes. ScC (1878–1930); ScGF 1939–40; ScRhW 1929–41; ScU (1868–1909) 1911–30, 1931–42
Revue des Etudes Slaves. ScU 1921+
Revue des Livres Anciens. ScU 1913–14
Revue Française d'Entomologie. ScCleU 1935+
Revue Française de Gynécologie et d'Obstétrique. ScCM (1938) 1950+
Revue Hispanique. ScU 1894–1915 (1925–30)
Revue Neurologique. ScCM (1939–61)
Revue Universelle des Mines, de la Métallurgie, des Travaux Publics, des Sciences et des Arts Appliqués à l'Industrie. ScU 1857–59
Rheinisches Museum für Jurisprudenz. ScU 1827–29
Rheinisches Museum für Philologie. ScU 1827–29
Rhode Island Baptist. ScU [mfm] 1822–24
Rhode Island Institute of Instruction, Journal. ScU [mfm] 1845–48
Rhode Island Literary Repository. ScU [mfm] 1814–15
Rhode Island Medical Journal. ScCM 1917–61
Rhode Island Red Journal. ScCleU 1929–32
Rhodora. ScCC (1912–42); ScCleU 1899+; ScCMus 1899–1918; ScU 1899+
Richmond [Va.]. Academy of Sciences, Bulletin. ScCM 1933–41
Richmond [Va.] Medical Journal. ScCM 1866
Rivista di Parassitologia. ScCleU 1937+; ScU 1937–40, 1947+
Roads and Bridges [Roads and Engineering Construction]. ScCleU 1940+
Roads and Streets. ScCleU (1933–43) 1944+; ScU (1931) 1932+
Roanoke Religious Correspondent [Danville, Va.]. ScU [mfm] 1821–23
Robinson's Magazine. ScU [mfm] 1818–19

Roche Review. ScCM (1939–48)

Rochester Magazine and Theological Review [Rochester, N. Y.]. ScU [mfm] 1824

Rochester Telephone Corporation, Bulletin. ScCleU 1922–30

Rock Hill Magazine [Rock Hill, S. C.]. ScRhW (1915–18); ScU (1915–18)

Rockefeller Foundation, Annual Report. ScCleU (1913+); ScCM 1913–60; ScRhW 1913–19, 1923, 1928+

Rockefeller Foundation, Division of Medical Education, Annual Report. ScCM 1924–32

Rockefeller Foundation, International Health Division, Annual Report. ScCleU 1917–49; ScCM 1913–25, 1934–50; ScRhW 1936–51

Rockefeller Foundation, President's Review. ScCleU (1917+); ScCM (1917–36)

Rockefeller Foundation, Publications. ScCM 1919–22

Rockefeller Institute for Medical Research, Monographs. ScCM (1919–30)

Rockefeller Institute for Medical Research, Studies. ScCM (1907–42)

Rocks and Minerals. ScCleU 1926–40

Rocky Mountain Medical Journal. ScCM 1938+

Romania. ScU (1872+)

Romanic Review. ScCC 1941+; ScCleU 1910–29, 1947+; ScRhW 1928+; ScU 1910+

Roosevelt Wildlife Annals. ScCleU 1926–34, library also has *Bulletin* 1921–50

Roper Hospital [Charleston, S. C.], Annual Report. ScCM 1921, 1926–51

Rorschach Research Exchange [Journal of Preventive Techniques and Personality Assessment]. ScU 1936+

Rose Bud [Southern Rose]. ScC 1832–39; ScU 1832–35, also [mfm] 1832–39

Rotarian. ScCCit 1932+; ScCleU (1924–34) 1935+; ScFlor 1926–32; ScGBj (1933–48) 1949+; ScLaD 1934+; ScRhP (1939+); ScRhW 1935, 1937+; ScSpC 1938+; ScU 1921–26, 1937+

Rothamsted Memoirs on Agricultural Science. ScCleU 1886+

Round Table. ScCleU (1914–27); ScU 1918–23, 1924–35, 1938+

Rover. ScGF (1843)

Royal Academy of Medicine in Ireland, Transactions. ScCM 1910–14

Royal Agricultural Society of England, Journal. ScCleU 1839+; ScU 1840–51

Royal American Magazine. ScU [mfm] 1774–75

Royal Army Medical Corps, Journal. ScCM (1915–20) 1944–58

Royal Astronomical Society of London, Memoirs. ScU 1822–60

Royal Entomological Society of London, Transactions. ScCleU 1920+; ScU 1836–49, 1850–58

Royal Geographical Society of London, Journal. ScU 1843–51, 1868–80

Royal Horticultural Society, Journal. ScCleU 1901+

Royal Horticultural Society of London, Transactions. ScU 1812–30

Royal Irish Academy, Proceedings. ScCMus 1891+

Royal Irish Academy, Transactions. ScCMus 1891–1906

Royal Microscopical Society, Journal. ScCleU (1903–4) 1945+; ScU (1922+)

Royal Society of Arts, Journal. ScU (1857–63) 1864+

Royal Society of Edinburgh, Proceedings B [Biology]. ScCleU 1941+

Royal Society of London, Proceedings. ScCleU (1830–1904) 1905+, some files on mc; ScCM 1914–19, 1922+; ScCMus 1859–1921; ScU 1800+

Royal Society of London, Transactions. ScC 1665–1854, 1858; ScCM (1876–1941); ScU (1719–50)

Royal Society of Medicine, Proceedings. ScCM 1908+

Royal Society of Tropical Medicine and Hygiene, Transactions. ScCM (1927–39) 1940+

Royal Spiritual Magazine. ScU [mfm] 1771

Royal Statistical Society of London, Journal. ScU 1931–40, 1943, 1946+, library also has *Supplement* (1934–47)

Rubber Chemistry and Technology. ScNcWv 1928+

Ruffin's Farmers Register. ScU 1834

Rural Alabamian. ScCCit 1872–73

Rural America. ScCleU 1928–41

Rural Carolinian. Sc 1870–73; ScC 1869–76; ScChes (1873); ScGF (1869–76); ScRhW 1870–74; ScU 1869–76

Rural Casket [Poughkeepsie, N. Y.]. ScU [mfm] (1798)

Rural Magazine [Newark, N. J.]. ScU [mfm] 1789–99

Rural Magazine and Farmer's Monthly Museum [Hartford, Conn.]. ScU [mfm] (1819)

Rural Magazine and Literary Evening Fireside. ScU [mfm] (1820)

Rural Magazine, or Vermont Repository [Rutland]. ScU [mfm] 1795–96
Rural Manhood. ScU 1911–20
Rural New Yorker [Penn-Jersey Farming]. ScCleU (1894+)
Rural Repository Devoted to Polite Literature [Hudson, N. Y.]. ScU [mfm] 1824–51
Rural Sociology. ScCleU 1936+; ScGF 1937+; ScU 1936+
Rush-Light. ScU [mfm] (1800)
Russell's Magazine. Sc 1857–60; ScC 1857–60; ScCMus (1857–59); ScFlor 1857; ScGF (1857–59); ScRhW 1857–60; ScU 1857–60
Russian Review. ScCleU 1941+; ScGF 1941–46; ScRhW 1941+; ScU 1941+
Russkaia Starina. ScU [microprint] 1870–1918
Ruskii Arkiv—Istoriko-Literaturnyi Sbornik. ScU [microprint] 1863–1917

S

Sabbath School Repository and Teacher's Assistant [New Haven, Conn.]. ScU [mfm] 1823
Safety Education. ScU 1938+
St. Bartholomew's Hospital [London], Report. ScCM (1866–1939)
St. John's Law Review. ScU (1926–40) 1948+
St. Louise [Mo.] Botanical Garden, Annual Report. ScCleU 1890+
St. Nicholas. ScC (1890–96) 1898–1931; ScCoR (1887–1932); ScRhW 1880–81, 1907–29; ScU (1878–94), also [mfm] 1873–1900
St. Paul's Magazine. ScSpC 1872–73
St. Tammany's Magazine. ScU [mfm] (1821)
Salamagundi. ScU [mfm] 1807–8
Sales Management. ScCCit 1939+
San Diego Society of Natural History, Bulletin. ScCMus 1924+
San Diego Society of Natural History, Transactions. ScCMus 1924+
Sanitoria São Lucas, Boletim. ScCM (1939+)
Santee Cooper Safety News. ScU (1930–49)
Sartain's Union Magazine of Literature and Art. ScGF (1847–52); ScU [mfm] 1847–52
Satirist. ScU [mfm] (1812)
Satirist, or Monthly Meteor. ScU [mfm] 1807–14
Saturday Analyst and Leader. ScU [mfm] 1850–60
Saturday Evening Post. ScCleU (1920–33) 1934+; ScClP 1938+; ScCoCo (1937–48) 1949+; ScGBj 1932+; ScGrev 1935+; ScLaD

1923+; ScNewb 1937+; ScNgTi 1941+; ScRhP 1932+; ScRhW 1922+; ScU 1927+, also [mfm] 1821–25

Saturday Magazine. ScU [mfm] 1819–22

Saturday Review [London]. ScC (1881–1920)

Saturday Review of Literature. ScCC 1928+; ScCCit 1935+; ScChar 1930+; ScCleU 1924+, some files on mfm; ScClP 1929+; ScDarl 1940+; ScDwErs 1937+; ScFlor 1926–29; ScGaLi 1930+; ScGBj 1935+; ScGF (1928–35) 1936+; ScGrev 1925+; ScGrew 1938–41, 1949+; ScGwLa 1936+; ScHCok (1930–34) 1935+; ScLaD 1939+; ScNewb 1939+; ScOrSc 1939+; ScRhP 1937+; ScRhW 1924+, some files on mfm; ScSpC 1915+; ScU 1925+

Schimmel Briefs. ScU 1935+

Scholastic [Senior Scholastic]. ScGBj 1932+; ScGwLa 1938–51; ScRhW 1938+; ScU (1929–63)

School Activities. ScRhW 1938+; ScU (1933) 1935+

School and Society. ScCC 1937–51; ScCCit 1928+; ScChar 1934+; ScCleU 1915+; ScClP 1928+; ScCoCo (1940–47) 1948+; ScDwErs 1922+; ScGaLi 1935+; ScGBj 1939+; ScGF (1917–40) 1941+; ScGrev 1919+; ScGrew 1940–42; ScGwLa 1939+; ScHCok 1923+; ScNewb 1919+; ScOrCl 1940+; ScOrSc 1927+; ScRhW 1922+; ScSpC 1915+; ScU 1915+

School Arts. ScOrSc 1940+; ScRhW 1923+

School Executive. ScRhW 1928+; ScU 1930+

School Life. ScCC 1921+; ScCleU 1918–64; ScClP 1935–40; ScGBj 1936+ ScGF 1932–40, 1949+; ScGrev 1924+; ScHCok 1925+; ScNewb (1925+); ScOrSc 1929+; ScRhW 1922+; ScSpC (1937–52); ScU 1918+

School of Education [University of South Carolina] Gazette. ScU (1931–42)

School Review. ScCCit 1935–46; ScCleU (1920+); ScCoCo (1940–54) 1955+; ScGBj 1938+; ScGF 1903–8, 1910+; ScGrev 1926+; ScHCok 1925+; ScOrCl 1928+; ScOrSc 1928+; ScRhW 1897+; ScU 1893+

School Science and Mathematics. ScCCit (1920+), some files on mfm; ScCleU 1912+; ScCoBe 1906+; ScCoCo (1940–43) 1944+; ScDwErs 1927+; ScGF (1912–23) 1924+; ScHCok (1932–59); ScOrCl 1928+; ScOrSc 1936+; ScRhW 1922+; ScSpC 1932+

Schoolfellow [Charleston, S. C.]. ScC (1849); ScU (1850–55)

Schweizerische Medizinische Wochenschrift [Basel]. ScCM (1931–45) 1946+

Schweizerische Naturforschende Gesellschaft, Denkschriften. ScU (1829–42)

Science. ScCC 1940+; ScCCit 1934+; ScCleU 1895+, some files on mc; ScClP 1921+; ScCM (1885–95) 1901+; ScCoCo (1925–48) 1949+; ScDwErs 1924+; ScGaLi 1936+; ScGBj 1931+; ScGF 1926+; ScHCok (1925) 1936+; ScNewb (1936+); ScOrCl 1923+; ScOrSc 1935+; ScRhW 1932+; ScSpW 1931+; ScU 1883+

Science Abstracts, Section A: Physics [Physics Abstracts]. ScCleU 1898–1902, 1921+; ScU (1904–11) 1913+

Science Abstracts, Section B: Electrical Engineering. ScCleU 1898–1902, 1910+; ScU 1903+

Science and Society. ScU 1936+

Science Digest. ScCleU 1939+, some files on mfm; ScGBj 1938+; ScSpC 1940+; ScU 1937+

Science Education. ScCleU 1939+; ScDwErs 1941–52; ScGF (1930–53) 1954+; ScOrSc 1937+

Science News Letter. ScCC 1930–58; ScCCit 1933+; ScChar (1937–44) 1953+; ScCleU 1926+, some files on mfm; ScCM (1938–53); ScCoBe 1931–52; ScCoCo 1951+; ScDwErs 1937+; ScGBj 1930+; ScGwLa 1935+; ScHCok 1935+; ScNewb 1936+; ScOrCl 1933+; ScOrSc 1936+; ScSpW 1941+; ScU 1926+

Science Progress. ScCM (1921–33)

Scientia. ScCM 1928–33

Scientific Agriculture [Canadian Journal of Science]. ScCleU 1923+

Scientific American. Sc 1846–58 (1896–1905) 1907–24; ScCCit 1927–34, 1936+; ScChar 1931+; ScCleU 1850+, some files on mfm; ScClP 1929–41; ScCoR 1919+; ScDwErs 1927+; ScGBj (1929–38) 1939+; ScGF (1846–1920) 1921+; ScGrev 1923+; ScGrew 1935–42, 1950+; ScHCok (1922–27) 1928+; ScNewb 1910+; ScOrSc 1935+; ScRhP 1932+; ScRhW 1923+; ScSpC 1895+; ScSpW 1847–58, 1909+; ScSum 1941+; ScU 1859+, also [mfm] 1845–59, 1866, library has *Supplement* 1876–1919

Scientific American Monthly. ScCleU 1920–21

Scientific Journal. ScU [mfm] 1818–20

Scientific Memoirs [London]. ScCMus 1837–53

Scientific Monthly. ScC 1915–53; ScCC 1941–53; ScCCit 1924–57; ScChar (1934–46); ScCleU 1915–57; ScCM (1919) 1921–57; ScCMus 1916–57; ScGBj (1930–32) 1938–57; ScGF 1922–57; ScHCok 1926–57; ScOrCl 1918+; ScOrSc 1935+; ScRhW 1915–57; ScSpC 1915–57; ScSpW 1915–57; ScU 1915–57

Scope. ScCM 1941–57
Scottish [Journal of] Agriculture. ScCleU 1920+
Scottish Geographical Magazine. ScU 1885+
Scottish Historical Review. ScU 1912–15
Scourge. ScU [mfm] (1811)
Scourge and Satirist. ScU [mfm] 1811–16
Scrap Book. ScCleU (1906–11); ScU 1906–9
Scribner's Commentator. ScCleU 1940–41; ScRhW 1939–41
Scribner's Magazine. ScC (1887–95) 1897–1931; ScCC 1898–1903; ScCCit (1887–1938); ScChar (1891–1929); ScCleU 1887–1939; ScClP (1887–99) 1917–31; ScCoCo (1910–39); ScCoR 1919–38; ScDarl 1892–97; ScFlor 1926–29; ScGaLi (1887–1933); ScGBj 1921, 1932–38; ScGF 1887–1939; ScGrev 1919–39; ScGrew 1924–39; ScHCok 1900–39; ScLaD (1927); ScRhW 1887–1939; ScSpC 1887–1939; ScSpW 1887–94, 1896–1939; ScU 1887–1939
Scribner's Monthly [Century]. ScC (1870–81); ScCCit (1875–81); ScChar (1871–81); ScCleU 1870–81; ScClP (1870–81); ScCoCo 1870–81; ScCoR 1872–75; ScGaLi 1872–81; ScGBj (1870–71); ScGrew 1870–81; ScRhW 1870–81; ScSpC 1870–81; ScSpW 1870–81; ScU 1870–81
Scripta Mathematica. ScCoCo (1939–61); ScRhW 1941+; ScU 1932+
Scrutiny. ScCleU 1932–53; ScSpC 1932–53; ScU 1932–53
Sea Island Report. ScCMus 1890–1920
Sea Side Thoughts [Charleston, S. C.]. ScC 1892–93
Sea View Hospital, Quarterly Bulletin. ScCM 1935–60
Secondary Education. ScGBj 1938–50
Seed World. ScCleU 1927–29, 1948+
Seismological Society of America, Bulletin. ScU 1911+
Selden Society, Yearbook. ScU 1937–48
Select Journal of Foreign Periodicals. ScGF 1833–34
Select Reviews of Literature. ScC 1809–11; ScU [mfm] 1809–12
Senator, or Clarendon's Parlimentary Chronicle. ScU 1791–92
Sentimental and Literary Magazine. ScU [mfm] (1797)
Seven Arts. ScSpW 1916–17; ScU 1916–17
Sewage Works Engineering [Wastes Engineering]. ScCleU 1941+
Sewage Works Journal [Sewage and Industrial Wastes]. ScCleU 1940+; ScU 1941+
Sewanee Review. ScC 1892–1960; ScCCit 1929+; ScChar 1934+; ScCleU 1893+; ScCoCo (1927–29) 1930+; ScGF (1912–21) 1922+;

ScHCok 1939+; ScNewb 1907+; ScRhW 1913+; ScSpC 1892+; ScSpW 1892+; ScU 1892+

Shakespeare Association of America, Bulletin. ScGBj 1935–46; ScU (1930–48)

Shako [Citadel]. ScCCit 1921+; ScU (1934–53)

Sheep Breeder [and Sheepman]. ScCleU 1938, 1940+

Shirley Institute, Bulletin. ScSpDm 1928+

Shorthorn World. ScCleU 1928+

Sight Saving Review. ScCM (1940–58)

Silliman's Journal of Science [American Journal of Science and Arts]. ScU (1818+)

Skandinavisches Archiv für Physiologie. ScCM (1891–1936)

Sky [and Telescope]. ScRhW 1937+; ScU 1936+

Slapstick. ScCleU 1941+

Slavonic and East European Review. ScU (1924) 1932–44

Smith and Barrow's Monthly Magazine. ScU 1864

Snappy Stories. ScU 1913–15, 1916–17

Soap and Sanitary Chemicals [Specialties]. ScCleU 1935+

So Ca San Piper. ScRhW 1935+; ScStpSan 1926+; ScU 1929–59

Social Education. ScCC 1937–44; ScDwErs 1937+; ScRhW 1937+; ScSpC 1940+; ScU (1937+)

Social Forces. ScCCit 1939+; ScCleU 1922+; ScGF 1925+; ScOrSc 1939+; ScRhW 1923+; ScSpC (1929–35) 1936+; ScSpW 1923+; ScU 1922+

Social Frontier. ScRhW 1934–39

Social Research. ScU (1934–60) 1962+

Social Science Abstracts. ScCCit 1929–32; ScRhW 1929–32; ScSpC 1929–32; ScU 1929–32

Social Science Research Council, Annual Report. ScCleU 1923+

Social Security Bulletin. ScCleU 1938+; ScRhW 1938–59

Social Service Review. ScRhW 1927+; ScU 1929+

Social Studies. ScCC 1934–50; ScGF 1934+; ScRhW 1934+; ScU 1934+

Sociedad Mexicana de Historia Natural, Mexico, Revista. ScU 1939–48

Société Astronomique de France, Bulletin. ScCleU 1930–32

Société Chimique de France, Bulletin. ScU 1898–1906, 1946+, library also has *Conferences* 1893–1900, *Documentation* 1934–41, and *Mémoires* 1934–45

Société de Biologie, Comptes Rendus Hebdomadaires des Séances et Mémoires. ScCleU 1849+; ScCM 1849+

Société de l'Histoire du Protestantisme Français. ScCHu (1852+)

Société des Antiquaires du Normandie, Mémoires. ScABBE 1824–36

Société des Naturalistes de Moscou [Moskovskoe Obshchestvo Ispytatelei Prirody]. ScU 1829–48

Société Entomologique de Belgique, Annales. ScCMus (1878–1902)

Société Entomologique de France, Annales. ScCMus 1836–1903

Société Entomologique de France, Bulletin. ScCleU 1896+

Société Géologique de France, Bulletin. ScU 1913+

Société Mathématique de France, Bulletin. ScU 1921+

Société Médicale des Hôpitaux de Paris, Bulletin et Mémoires. ScCM (1914–46)

Society for Experimental Biology and Medicine, Proceedings. ScCleU 1903+, some files on mc; ScCM (1906) 1908+; ScU 1932–33, 1948+

Society for the Advancement of Management, Journal [Advanced Management]. ScCleU 1936–39

Society for the Encouragement of Arts, Manufactures and Commerce, Transactions. ScC 1785–1813

Society for the Promotion of Agricultural Science, Proceedings. ScCleU 1883+

Society for the Promotion of Engineering Education, Proceedings. ScCleU 1897+; ScU 1912+

Society of American Foresters, Proceedings. ScCleU 1905+, some files on mc

Society of Arts, Journal. ScC 1863–86, 1887–94, 1895–1902

Society of Automotive Engineers, Transactions. ScCleU (1915+)

Society of Chemical Industry [London], Journal. ScCleU 1882+; ScNcWv 1904–50; ScU 1911–41, 1949–50

Society of Chemical Industry, Journal [Chemical and Industrial Review]. ScNcWv 1918–44

Society of Dilettanti [London]. Antiquities of Ionia. ScU 1769

Society of Dyers and Colourists, Journal. ScCleU 1884+

Society of Glass Technology, Journal. ScCleU 1917+

Society of Physicians in London, Medical Observations and Inquiries. ScCM 1757–58

Sociology and Social Research. ScCleU (1927–28) 1940+; ScU 1927+

Sociometry. ScU 1937+

Soil Conservation. ScRhW 1935+

Soil Research. ScCleU (1928–41)

Soil Science. ScCleU 1916+

Soil Science in Florida, Proceedings [Soil and Crop Society of Florida]. ScCleU 1940+

Soil Science Society of America, Proceedings. ScCleU 1936+

Solemn Review of the Custom of War. . . . ScU [mfm] (1817)

Something. ScU [mfm] 1809–10

Sons of the American Revolution Magazine. ScCCit 1931–41; ScU (1935–50)

Sound Currency. ScU 1895, 1897–1905

South Africa, Department of Agriculture, Entomology Memoirs. ScCleU 1940–56

South Africa, Department of Agriculture, Journal. ScCleU 1920–26, library also has this Department's *Bulletin* (1927+) and its *Science Bulletin* (1916+)

South African Journal of Medical Sciences. ScCM 1936–61

South African Medical Journal. ScCM (1927–36) 1941+

South and World Affairs. ScCC (1941–46); ScCleU 1939–43; ScU 1941–48

South-Atlantic [Wilmington, N. C.]. ScU (1878)

South Atlantic Bulletin. ScCC 1938+; ScCleU 1935+; ScGF (1937–43) 1944–60; ScNewb (1940+); ScRhW 1935+; ScU 1935+

South Atlantic Quarterly. ScC 1921+; ScCCit 1929–47, 1949+; ScCHis 1931+; ScCleU 1902+; ScCoCo (1940–47) 1948+; ScGF 1911+; ScHCok 1940+; ScRhW 1910+; ScSpC 1902+; ScSpW 1904+; ScU 1902+

South Australia, Department of Agriculture, Journal. ScCleU 1920+

South Carolina Academy of Sciences, Bulletin. ScCC 1935+; ScCleU 1935+; ScCM 1935+; ScCMus 1935+; ScRhW 1935+; ScU 1935+

South Carolina Agriculturalist. Sc 1829–46; ScU (1856)

South Carolina Board of Charities and Corrections, Bulletin. ScC 1916–19; ScCM 1915–19

South Carolina Board of Health, Annual Report. ScCM 1880–1913 (1915–19) 1922+

South Carolina Board of Medical Examiners, Proceedings. ScCM (1899–1917)

South Carolina Board of Public Welfare, Quarterly Bulletin. ScC 1920–25; ScCM (1920–26), library also has *Annual Report* (1920–26); ScU (1915–41)

South Carolina Commission of Forestry, Report. ScCleU 1928+

South Carolina Education. ScCleU (1919+); ScRhW 1919–45; ScU 1919–45

South Carolina Highway Department, Bulletin. ScU (1922–39)

South Carolina Historical [and Genealogical] Magazine. ScA 1900+; ScAHJ 1900+; ScC 1900+; ScCC 1939+; ScCCit 1900+; ScChar 1900+; ScChes 1900+; ScCHis 1900+; ScCHu 1900+; ScCleU 1900+; ScClP 1900+; ScCMus 1900+; ScCoCo 1900+; ScCoR 1900+; ScCoT 1900+; ScDarl 1900+; ScDwErs 1900+; ScGF 1900+; ScGrew 1900+; ScGwLa 1900+; ScLanc 1900+; ScMar 1900+; ScNewb 1941+; ScRhP 1900+; ScRhW 1900+; ScSpC 1900+; ScSpW 1900+; ScU 1900+; ScWaC 1900+

South Carolina Historical Association, Proceedings. ScA 1931+; ScCCit 1935+; ScCleU 1931+; ScCoCo 1931+; ScDwErs 1931+; ScGBj 1931+; ScRhW 1931+; ScSpC 1931+; ScSpW 1931+; ScU 1931+

South Carolina Historical Commission, Bulletin. ScCleU 1915–32

South Carolina Lutheran. ScCoT (1928) 1932+; ScNewb 1936+

South Carolina Magazine. ScCC 1938+; ScCCit (1941+); ScChar 1937+; ScChes 1937+; ScCleU 1937+; ScConH 1939+; ScDarl 1937+; ScDwErs 1937+; ScGaLi 1937+; ScGF 1937+; ScHCok 1937+; ScLanc 1937+; ScNewb 1940+; ScOran 1937+; ScRhP 1937+; ScRhW 1936+; ScSpW 1937+; ScU 1937+; ScU-Lanc 1937+

South Carolina Market Bulletin. ScU (1926+)

South Carolina Masonic Journal. ScU (1911–14)

South Carolina Medical Association, Journal. ScCM 1905+; ScCoHo (1925–48) 1949+; ScGGh (1927–39) 1940+; ScU (1907–55)

South Carolina Newsview. ScChar (1936); ScRhW (1936); ScU (1936)

South Carolina Odd Fellow. ScU 1909–25

South Carolina Pharmaceutical Association, Proceedings. ScCM (1926–51)

South Carolina Planning Board, Publications. ScCC (1941–44)

South Carolina Public Welfare Statistics. ScCC 1937+; ScCleU 1938+; ScU (1938+)

South Carolina Publications on Phosphates. ScCMus 1859–82

South Carolina Reporter. ScCCit (1899–1904) 1949+

South Carolina Speech Association, Bulletin. ScU 1939–42
South Carolina Temperance News. ScSpW 1938–46; ScU 1938–46
South Carolina Tuberculosis Association, Yearbook and Report. ScCM (1918–52)
South Carolina [University] Alumni News. ScU 1940+
South Carolina University, Bulletin. ScCleU 1905–35; ScCMus (1906–27); ScU 1905–35
South Carolina [University] Weekly News. ScU 1920–27
South Carolina Weekly Museum. ScU 1797, also [mfm] 1797–98
South Carolina Works Progress Administration, Publications. ScCC (1936–41)
South Seas Society, Journal. ScU 1940+
Southeastern Drug Journal. ScCM (1928) 1937+; ScU (1928–56) 1957+
Southeastern Library Association, Proceedings. ScCleU 1928–48
Southeastern Pecan Growers Association, Proceedings. ScCleU (1938–49) 1950+
Southern Agriculturalist [Charleston, Louisville, Nashville, etc.]. ScCleU (1838–49); ScGF (1832–54); ScU (1828–71)
Southern and Western Masonic Miscellany. ScC 1847–52
Southern and Western Monthly Magazine and Review. ScC (1845); ScU 1845
Southern Architect and Building News. ScCleU (1927–31); ScU 1928–31
Southern Association of Colleges and Secondary Schools, Proceedings. ScCC 1938+; ScCleU 1933+
Southern Association of Colleges for Women, Proceedings. ScRhW (1931+)
Southern Association Quarterly. ScCCit 1937–48; ScCleU 1937–48; ScGF 1937–48; ScGwLa 1941–48; ScHCok 1937–48; ScRhW 1937–48; ScSpC 1937+; ScSpW 1927–48; ScU 1937–48
Southern Baptist. ScCoT [mfm] 1847–60
Southern Baptist and General Intelligencer. ScCoT [mfm] 1835–38; ScU (1835)
Southern Baptist Educator. ScGF 1941–61
Southern Baptist Review and Eclectic Monthly. ScCoT [mfm] 1855–61
Southern Bell Telephone and Telegraph, Annual Report. ScCleU 1935+

Southern Bivouac. ScGF 1885–86; ScU 1885–87

Southern Botanic Journal. ScU (1837–40)

Southern Cabinet. ScU 1841

Southern California Academy of Sciences, Bulletin. ScCleU 1940+

Southern California Law Review. ScU (1931) 1937+

Southern Christian Advocate [South Carolina Methodist Advocate]. ScCoCo (1879–1917) 1919+; ScSpW 1837–59, 1879+; ScU 1837+

Southern City. ScU 1940–47

Southern Cultivator. ScCCit (1861–73); ScU (1847–75)

Southern Dairy Products Journal. ScCleU (1930–34) 1935+

Southern Eclectic. ScGF (1853–54)

Southern Economic Journal. ScCCit 1936+; ScChar 1936+; ScCleU 1933+; ScCoCo (1940–48) 1949+; ScGF 1935+; ScNewb (1940+); ScRhW 1933+; ScSpW 1937+; ScU 1934+

Southern Education Association, Proceedings. ScCleU 1899+

Southern Episcopalian. ScC 1854–61; ScCDhs 1854–61; ScCMus (1859–61); ScU 1851–61

Southern Evangelical Intelligencer. ScU (1819–21)

Southern Farm Magazine. ScCleU 1903–4

Southern Florist and Nurseryman. ScCleU (1925–56) 1957+

Southern Folklore Quarterly. ScCleU 1937+; ScRhW 1937+; ScU 1937+

Southern Forestry Congress, Proceedings. ScCleU 1916–29

Southern Good Roads. ScU (1911–15)

Southern History Association, Publications. ScC (1897–1907); ScGF 1901–5; ScGrew 1897–1907; ScU (1897–1903)

Southern Home [Columbia, S. C.]. ScU (1904)

Southern Journal of Medicine and Pharmacy. ScU 1846

Southern Light [Edgefield, S. C.]. ScGF (1856); ScU 1856

Southern Literary Gazette [Athens, Ga.]. ScU (1848–49), library also has *Supplement* 1852

Southern Literary Journal and Magazine of Arts [Charleston, S. C.]. ScC 1835–37; ScGF (1835–38); ScSpW (1836); ScU (1835–38), also [mfm] 1835–38

Southern Literary Magazine. ScGF 1923–24; ScRhW 1923–24; ScU 1923–24

Southern Literary Messenger. ScC (1835–61); ScCleU (1837–43); ScGF (1834–64); ScRhW [mc] 1836–64; ScSpar 1834–41; ScSpW 1838–44, 1846; ScU (1842–64), also [mfm] 1834–64

Southern Literary Messenger, Devoted to Every Department of Literature and the Fine Arts. ScCleU 1939–43; ScRhW 1939–45; ScU 1939–44

Southern Literary Register [Columbia, S. C.]. ScU (1820)

Southern Lutheran. ScCoT [mfm] 1862–64

Southern Magazine [Baltimore, Md.]. ScU 1871–75

Southern Magazine [Manassas, Va.]. ScU 1899

Southern Medical [and Surgical] Journal. ScCM (1836–58) 1908+; ScCoHo (1932–41); ScGGh 1931+; ScU (1851)

Southern Medicine and Surgery. ScCM 1920–53; ScCoHo 1930–32; ScGGh 1940+

Southern Monthly. ScGF (1861–62)

Southern Pasture and Forage Crops. ScCleU (1940–60) 1961+

Southern Pharmaceutical Journal. ScU 1929–31, 1938+

Southern Philatelist. ScU (1889–96)

Southern Planter and Farmer [Richmond, Va.]. ScCCit 1869–71; ScCleU 1940+

Southern Political Science Association, Proceedings [Journal of Politics]. ScCleU 1933–37; ScSpC 1930–37

Southern Power Journal [Southern Power and Industry]. ScCleU (1926+); ScU 1935+

Southern Practitioner. ScCM (1879–1906)

Southern Presbyterian. ScClP 1898–1904

Southern Presbyterian Review. ScClP 1847–85; ScDwErs 1847–72; ScGF (1849–54); ScU 1847–63 (1864–85)

Southern Quarterly Review. ScC 1842–57; ScChar (1851–53); Sc-CleU (1845–54); ScGF (1842–57); ScNewb 1842–48; ScRhW 1842–50; ScSpW 1842–48, 1851; ScU (1842–57), also [mfm] 1842–57

Southern Review [Baton Rouge, La.]. ScCleU 1939–42, 1965+; ScGF 1935–42; ScRhW 1935–42, 1965+; ScSpC 1937–42; ScU 1935–42, 1965+

Southern Review [Charleston, S. C.]. Sc 1828–32; ScC 1828–32; ScCCit (1828–32); ScCM 1828; ScFlor 1829; ScGF 1828–32; Sc-RhW 1828–32; ScU 1828–32, also [mfm] 1828–32

Southern Review [Methodist Episcopal Church, South]. ScC (1867–75); ScSpW 1867–78; ScU 1867–71, also [mfm] 1867–71, 1879

Southern School News [Columbia, S. C.]. ScRhW 1908–17; ScSpC 1909–17; ScU 1909–17

Southern Seedsman [Seed and Garden Merchandising]. ScCleU 1938–60

Southern Sentinel. ScU (1863)

Southern Speech Bulletin [Journal]. ScGBj (1937–39) 1940+; ScGF (1938) 1939+; ScU 1935+

Southern Surgeon. ScCM 1933–50

Southern Surgical Association, Transactions. ScCM 1888–1957, 1959+

Southern Telephone News. ScCleU 1935–54

Southern Textile Bulletin [Textile Bulletin]. ScCleU (1911–33)

Southern Unitarian. ScU 1893–95

Southern University Conference, Proceedings. ScCC 1935–58; ScCleU 1938+; ScRhW 1935+

Southern Workman. ScRhW 1937–39

Southwest Review. ScRhW 1924+; ScSpC 1937+; ScU (1916–17) 1924+

Southwestern Historical Quarterly. ScU 1897+

Southwestern Medicine. ScCM (1927–43)

Southwestern [Political and] Social Science Quarterly. ScU (1924–45) 1946+

Souvenir. ScU 1829–30

Sovremennyia Zapiski. ScU 1920–40

Spartanburg [S. C.] Department of Public Health, Bulletin. ScCM (1914–15)

Special Libraries. ScU 1914–18 (1921–34) 1938+

Spectacles. ScU [mfm] (1807)

Spectator. ScC 1901–20; ScRhW 1931+; ScU 1937+

Spectrochimica Acta. ScCleU 1939+; ScU 1939–44, 1952+

Speculum. ScCleU 1926+; ScU 1926+

Speech Bulletin. ScU 1929–31

Speech Magazine. ScGBj (1938–42)

Sperryscope. ScCleU 1929+

Spice Mill [Coffee and Tea Industries]. ScCleU 1941+

Spirit of the Forum and Hudson Remarker [Hudson, N. Y.]. ScU [mfm] (1817)

Spirit of the Public Journals. ScU [mfm] 1806

Spirit of the Times: A Chronicle of the Turf, Agriculture, Field Sports, Literature and the Stage. ScU [mfm] 1831–61

Spirit of the Times and the New York Sportsman. ScU [mfm] 1859–1902

Spiritual Magazine, or Gospel Treasury. ScU [mfm] 1813–14

Squibb Abstract Bulletin. ScU 1930–38

Stain Technology. ScCleU 1926+; ScCM (1926–35) 1937–62; ScU 1926+

Stahl und Eisen. ScU (1940) 1960+

Stand, by a Society of Young Men [Hartford, Conn.]. ScU [mfm] 1818–20

Stanford University Food Research Institute, Wheat Studies. ScCleU 1924–44

Star and Lamp of Pi Kappa Phi. ScCC 1937+

State Government. ScCleU 1940+; ScGF (1936–41) 1942+; ScU 1931+

State News Letter [South Carolina Federation of Business and Professional Women's Clubs]. ScU (1938–42)

Staten Island Association of Arts and Sciences, Bulletin. ScCMus (1889+), library also has *News* (1889+) and *Transactions* (1889+)

State Sanitary Engineers, Transactions. ScCM (1919–23)

Statistical Bulletin [Metropolitan Life Insurance Company]. ScCM 1921+

Stethescope [Medical Society of Virginia]. ScCM 1853–54

Story. ScCleU 1939+

Story Parade. ScCoBe 1936–46

Strand Magazine. ScDarl 1893–97

Strukturbericht. ScCleU 1913–39

Stryker's American Register and Magazine. ScGF 1848–51; ScU [mfm] 1848–51

Stuart Circle Hospital [Richmond, Va.], Bulletin. ScCM 1931–40

Student World. ScCoT 1908+; ScRhW 1930–61

Studies in Philology. ScCC 1941–60; ScCleU 1906+; ScCoCo (1927–42) 1943+; ScGF 1922+; ScU 1906+, some files on mc

Studio. ScU (1893–1930) 1952+

Stylops [Royal Entomological Society of London, Proceedings]. ScCleU 1932+

Stylus [Newberry College]. ScNewb 1900–30; ScU (1884–1929)

Subscription Books Bulletin. ScCC 1938–56; ScChar 1930–56; ScCleU 1930–56; ScCoR 1930–56; ScGF 1936–56; ScRhW 1930–56; ScU 1930–56

Subterranean. ScU [mfm] 1845–47

Successful Farming. ScCleU (1924–44) 1945+

Summerville [S. C.] Infirmary, Yearbook. ScCM 1932

Sunday Magazine. ScSpC 1871–73; ScSpW 1897–1905; ScU 1884–86

Sunday School Repository. ScU [mfm] 1816–19
Sunday School Times. ScCoBi 1918+; ScRhW 1937–61
Sunday Visitant [Charleston, S. C.]. ScGF 1818–19; ScU (1818–19), also [mfm] 1818–19
Surgery. ScCM 1937+; ScCoHo 1938+; ScGGh (1941) 1947+
Surgery, Gynecology and Obstetrics. ScCM 1905+; ScCoHo 1930+; ScGGh (1917–18) 1949+
Surgical Clinics of Chicago [North America]. ScCM 1917+; ScCoHo 1930+; ScGGh (1928–40) 1941+; ScOrRh 1921+
Surgical Clinics of John B. Murphy. ScCM 1912–16
Survey [Midmonthly]. ScC 1913–31; ScCCit (1923–52); ScChar 1931–52; ScCleU 1924–52; ScCoBe 1909–48; ScGaLi (1931–51); ScGF 1909–52; ScGrev 1917–52; ScGrew 1935–41; ScRhW 1913–52; ScSpC 1939–48; ScU 1902–52
Survey Graphic. ScCCit 1936–48; ScCleU (1924–48); ScCoR (1940–51); ScGaLi (1933–48); ScGBj 1938–51; ScGF 1933–48; ScGrev 1933–48; ScGrew 1935–41; ScGwLa 1936–48; ScHCok 1915–46; ScRhW 1933–48; ScSpC 1939–48; ScU 1933–48
Survey of Current Business. ScCleU (1924–30) 1931+; ScRhW 1932+
Swine World. ScCleU 1926–28
Symposium. ScU 1930–33

T

Tablet. ScU [mfm] (1795)
Tait's Edinburgh Magazine. ScU [mfm] 1832–61
Talisman. ScU [mfm] 1828–30
Tamassee Sun-Dial. ScU (1940–54)
Tatler. ScU [mfm] 1830–32
Taxes. ScCCit 1940–47, 1949+; ScCleU 1939+
Teachers College Record. ScCleU 1916+; ScGBj 1938+; ScOrSc 1925+; ScRhW 1900+; ScU 1911+
Technical Association Papers. ScNcWv 1926–48
Technical Book Review Index. ScCleU 1935+
Technical World [Illustrated World] Magazine. ScU 1904–5
Technology Quarterly and Proceedings of the Society of Arts. ScU 1895–96
Technology Review. ScCCit 1937+; ScU 1935+
Telefunken-Zeitung. ScU 1920–39, 1950+
Telegraph and Telephone Age. ScCleU (1924–34)

Telegrapher. ScCleU 1864–65
Telephone Engineer. ScCleU 1909–44
Telephone Magazine. ScCleU (1899–1902)
Telephony. ScCleU (1927–37)
Tele-Tech [Electronic Industries and Tele-Tech]. ScU 1941+
Temple Bar. ScU 1886–91
Tennessee Division of Geology, Bulletin. ScCleU (1911+)
Tennessee Folklore Society, Bulletin. ScU (1935+)
Tennessee Historical Quarterly. ScCHis 1915+
Tennessee Law Review. ScU 1934+
Tennessee Speech Journal. ScGBj 1936–47
Tennessee State Medical Association, Journal. ScCM (1926–27) 1931+
Tennessee University, Rural Research Monographs. ScCleU (1935+)
Terrestial Magnetism and Atmospheric Electricity [Journal of Geophysical Research]. ScCleU 1896+, some files on mc
Teutsche Merkur. ScU (1773–1810)
Texas Law Review. ScU 1922+
Texas Medical Journal. ScCM (1910–16)
Texas State Journal of Medicine. ScCM (1926–32) 1933+
Texas Studies in English. ScCleU (1925–43) 1944+
Textile American. ScCleU 1904–11
Textile Bulletin. ScCleU (1933–46) 1947+
Textile Colorist [American Dyestuff Reporter]. ScCleU 1892+
Textile Industries. ScCleU 1939+
Textile Industries Journal [and Abstracts]. ScCleU 1910+
Textile Industry of Canada, Manual. ScCleU 1934+
Textile Institute Journal. ScCleSl 1925+; ScCleU 1932+; ScGrev 1927–41; ScSpDm 1910+; ScWinR 1910+
Textile Manufacturer [Charlotte, N. C.]. ScCleU 1910–11
Textile Manufacturer [Manchester]. ScCleU 1903+
Textile Manufacturer, Yearbook. ScCleU 1921–39
Textile Manufacturer's Journal [Textile World]. ScCleU 1901–15
Textile Recorder. ScCleU (1930–55) 1956+
Textile Recorder Annual. ScCleU 1933+
Textile Research Journal. ScCleU 1932+; ScRhCel 1932+; ScWinR 1932+
Textile World [and Industrial] Record. ScCCit 1939+; ScCleU 1899+
Theatre, a Monthly Review and Magazine. ScChar 1878–82

Theatre Arts. ScCCit 1938–53, 1955–64; ScChar 1931–64; ScCleU 1916–64; ScCoCo (1916–64); ScCoR 1936–64; ScDwErs 1933–64; ScGaLi (1933–64); ScGBj 1929–64; ScGF 1928–64; ScGrev 1927–64; ScNewb 1939–64; ScOrCl 1937–64; ScRhP 1937–64; ScRhW 1925–64; ScSpC 1929–64; ScU 1920–64

Theatre Magazine. ScU 1911–17

Theatrical Censor. ScU [mfm] (1805–6)

Theatrical Inquisitor. ScU [mfm] 1812–20

Theatrical Recorder. ScU [mfm] 1805–6

Theological and Literary Journal. ScClP 1848–61

Theological Magazine. ScU [mfm] (1798–99)

Theological Quarterly. ScCoT 1897–1901

Theological Repertory and Churchman's Guide. ScU [mfm] (1827)

Theological Review and General Repository of Religious and Moral Information. ScU [mfm] 1822

Theophilanthropist. ScU [mfm] 1810

Therapeutic Notes. ScCM (1925+); ScU 1935–39

Thespian Mirror. ScU [mfm] (1805–6)

Thespian Monitor. ScU [mfm] (1809)

Thespian Oracle. ScU [mfm] (1798)

This Way [Batesburg, S. C.]. ScU (1896–97)

Thistle. ScU [mfm] (1807)

Thornwell Messenger. ScClP 1910–16

Through the Ages. ScU 1923–32

Tickler. ScU [mfm] 1807–13

Tidings from the Temple [South Carolina Masonic Lodge]. ScU (1923–26)

Tile and Till. ScU 1930–51

Time. ScCC 1934+; ScCCit 1939–42, 1954+; ScChar 1935+; ScChes 1941+; ScCleU 1924+; ScClP 1933+; ScCoBe 1931+; ScCoCo (1931–41) 1942+; ScCoR 1928+; ScDarl 1935+; ScDwErs 1926+; ScGaLi 1935+; ScGBj (1928–33) 1934+; ScGF 1928+; ScGrev 1935+; ScGrew 1933+; ScGwLa 1938+; ScHCok 1926+; ScLaD 1937+; ScNewb 1935+; ScOran 1941+; ScOrSc 1937+; ScRhP 1932+; ScRhW 1930+; ScSpar 1926+; ScSpC 1936+; ScSpW 1931+; ScU 1924–26, 1928+

Time [London]. ScU [mfm] 1879–91

Time Piece. ScU [mfm] 1797–98

Times [London] Literary Supplement. ScRhW 1925+

Tobacco. ScCleU (1925–29)

Toilet [Charleston, S. C.]. ScU (1801)
Torch Bearers of South Carolina. ScU (1922–28)
Toronto [University] Law Journal. ScU 1935+
Toronto [University] Quarterly. ScU (1933–46) 1953+
Torrey Botanical Club, Bulletin. ScCleU 1870+; ScHCok 1937–56;
    ScU (1870+), library also has *Memoirs* (1889+)
Torreya. ScCleU 1902–45; ScU (1906–43)
Tory Tatler. ScU [mfm] (1710–11)
Touchstone. ScCleU 1917–21
Town. ScU [mfm] (1807)
Town Development. ScGeor 1910–12
Tractor Field Book [Farm Equipment Red Book]. ScCleU 1941+
Trained Nurse and Hospital Review. ScCM (1932–38) 1939–50;
    ScCoHo 1939–57; ScGGh-N 1930–50; ScU 1920–60
Transatlantic Review. ScU (1924)
Travel. ScCCit (1930–35) 1936+; ScChar 1938+; ScCleU 1908+;
    ScGrev 1926+; ScRhP 1936+; ScRhW 1928+; ScU 1906+
Tri-State Medical Association, Transactions. ScCM (1900–19)
Tri-State Medical Journal. ScCM (1929–38)
Tropical Agriculture. ScCleU 1924+
Tropical Disease Bulletin. ScCleU 1922+; ScCM (1912–56)
Tropical Woods. ScCleU (1925–60)
Trudeau Sanatorium, Annual Report. ScCM 1931–44
True Baptist. ScGF 1853
True Catholic. ScU (1844–47)
Truth. ScU [mfm] (1819)
Tufts Medical Journal. ScCM (1939–54)
Tulane Law Review. ScU (1929–31) 1933+
Tyler's Historical and Genealogical Quarterly. ScU 1919–52

U

Ueber Land und Meer. ScCMus 1874–76; ScU (1867–85) 1889–90
Um Die Welt. ScU (1884)
Unauthorized Practice News. ScU 1934+
Union Internationale Contre la Tuberculose, Bulletin. ScCM (1929–
    53)
Union Panamericano, Boletim. ScU (1913–23)
Union Seminary Review. ScSpC (1936–61)
Unitarian Defendant [Charleston, S. C.]. ScU [mfm] (1822)
Unitarian Miscellany and Christian Monitor. ScU [mfm] 1821–24

United Daughters of the Confederacy [Bulletin] Magazine. ScCleU (1938–43) 1944+

United Session Magazine [Edinburgh]. ScDwErs-T 1833–46

United States Army Corps of Engineers, Professional Memoirs. ScCleU 1913–19

United States Artillery Journal. ScC 1892–94

United States Bureau of Census, Mortality Statistics. ScCM (1908–35), library also has *Vital Statistics* (1934+)

United States Bureau of Labor, Statistics. ScGF 1930+

United States Bureau of Livestock, Sanitary Association, Proceedings. ScCleU (1897+)

United States Catholic Magazine. ScU [mfm] 1842–49

United States Catholic Miscellany. ScC 1824; ScU (1824–31)

United States Christian Magazine. ScU [mfm] (1796)

United States Commissioner of Education, Report. ScCM (1872–1903)

United States Democratic Review. ScGF 1837–59; ScU 1838–51, also [mfm] 1837–59

United States Department of State, Bulletin. ScCleU 1939+; ScRhW 1939+; ScU 1939+

United States Eggs and Poultry Magazine [Poultry Processing and Marketing]. ScCleU 1933+

United States Federal Reserve System, Annual Report. ScCleU 1914–62

United States Law Review [New York Law Review]. ScU 1929–32

United States Literary Gazette. ScC 1824–25; ScU 1824–25, also [mfm] 1824–26

United States Magazine, a Repository of History, Politics and Literature. ScU [mfm] (1779)

United States Magazine and Literary and Political Repository. ScU [mfm] (1823)

United States Magazine, or General Repository of Useful Instruction and Rational Amusement. ScU [mfm] (1794)

United States Marine Hospital Service, Annual Report. ScCM (1878–1911)

United States Military Philosophical Society, Minutes. ScU [mfm] (1806–9)

United States Monthly Law Magazine. ScU 1850

United States Nautical Magazine and Naval Journal. ScCleU 1854–58

United States Naval Chronicle. ScU [mfm] (1824)
United States Naval Institute, Proceedings. ScU (1930–42) 1944+
United States Naval Medical Bulletin. ScCM (1913–18) 1920–49
United States News [and World Report]. ScCleU 1940+; ScGF
   1940+; ScHCok 1940+; ScNewb 1940+; ScOrSc [mfm] 1940+;
   ScRhW 1934+; ScSpW (1941–43) 1949+; ScU 1940+
United States Patents Quarterly [Weekly, Official Gazette]. Sc-
   CleSl 1939+; ScDuCy 1929+; ScSpDm 1929+; ScWinR 1936+
United States Public Health Service, Report. ScCM (1898–1909)
   1910+
United States Public Health Service, Venereal Disease Information.
   ScCM 1923–51
United States Steel Corporation, Annual Report. ScCleU 1941–61
United States Steel News. ScCleU 1937+
Universal Asylum and Columbian Magazine. ScU [mfm] 1786–92
Universal Magazine of Knowledge and Pleasure. ScU 1779
Universalist Magazine. ScU [mfm] 1818–26
Universalist Quarterly and General Review. ScU [mfm] 1844–50
University Administration Quarterly. ScRhW 1941–43; ScU 1941–43
University Hospital [Atlanta, Ga.], Bulletin. ScCM (1939–45)
University Quarterly. ScGF 1860
University Review [University of Kansas City]. ScU 1934+
Unpartizan [Unpopular] Review. ScC 1914–20; ScU 1914–20
Urological and Cutaneous Review. ScCM (1913–52); ScCoHo 1930–
   52
Useful Cabinet. ScU [mfm] (1808)
Utah Farm and Home Science. ScCleU 1940+
Utica Christian Magazine [Repository]. ScU [mfm] 1813–16, 1822–
   26

V

Vaccine Inquirer. ScU [mfm] 1822–24
Valley Farmer [St. Louis, Mo.]. ScU [mfm] (1849–51)
Valve World. ScU (1920–32)
Vancoram Review. ScU 1929–51
Van Nostrand's Eclectic Engineering Magazine. ScU 1869–77, 1885
Vegetable Growers Association of America, Annual Report. ScCleU
   1935+
Verein Deutscher Ingenieure, Zeitschrift. ScCleU 1901–19
Verfahren der Anorganisch-Chemischen Industrie. ScCleU 1934–35

Vermont Baptist Missionary Magazine. ScU [mfm] 1811–12
Vermont State Medical Society, Quarterly Bulletin. ScCM (1923–26)
Veterinary Medicine [Small Animal Clinician]. ScCleU 1940+
Victoria [Australia] Department of Agriculture, Journal. ScCleU (1908–11) 1912+
Vigil [Charleston, S. C.]. ScU [mfm] (1798)
Village Museum [Cortland Village, N. Y.]. ScU [mfm] (1820)
Villager [Greenwich Village, N. Y.]. ScU [mfm] (1819)
Virchows Archiv für Pathologische Anatomie und Physiologie und Klinische Medizin. ScCM (1875+)
Virginia Baptist Preacher. ScGF 1842–43
Virginia, Division of Mineral Resources, Bulletin. ScCleU (1905+)
Virginia Law Register. ScU (1895–1919)
Virginia Law Review. ScU 1913+
Virgina Magazine of History and Biography. ScCHis 1893+; ScCleU 1929+; ScGF (1915–59); ScU 1893+
Virginia Medical Monthly. ScCM (1874–1933) 1934+
Virginia Quarterly Review. ScCCit 1926+; ScChar 1931+; ScCleU 1925+; ScCoCo (1926–43) 1944+; ScDwErs 1930+; ScGBj 1940+; ScGF 1925+; ScGrev 1937+; ScHCok 1930+; ScNewb 1940+; ScRhW 1925+; ScSpC 1925+; ScSpW 1925+; ScU 1925+
Virginia Religious Magazine [Lexington, Va.]. ScU [mfm] 1804–7
Visitor [Richmond, Va.]. ScU [mfm] 1809–10
Visual Education. ScCleU 1920–24
Vital Speeches of the Day. ScCC 1941–50; ScCCit 1937+; ScChar 1938+; ScCleU 1934+, some files on mfm; ScDwErs 1940+; ScGBj 1934+; ScGrev 1937+; ScNewb 1934+; ScOrSc 1940+; ScRhP 1940+; ScRhW 1936+; ScSpar (1938–44) 1945+; ScSpC 1937+; ScU 1934+, some files on mfm
Vocational Education Magazine. ScCleU 1922–24
Vocational Guidance Digest. ScU 1936–42
Vocational Trends. ScU 1939–47
Vogue. ScCoCo (1938+); ScRhP 1936+; ScU (1892–1900) 1938+
Volcano Letter. ScU 1925–40 (1947–55)

W

Wadsworth Gas Attack and Rio Grande Rattler. ScSpW (1917–18)
Wagner Free Institute of Science of Philadelphia, Bulletin. ScCleU 1926–35

Waldie's Select Circulating Library. ScGF 1833–35

Walker's Hibernian Magazine. ScU [mfm] 1771–1811

Wallace's Farmer. ScCleU 1925, 1945+

Wall's Etched Monthly. ScCleU 1921

Walpole Society Note Book. ScCMus 1937–55

War Medicine. ScCM 1941–45

Washington Academy of Sciences, [Proceedings] Journal. ScCleU (1921–27) 1930+; ScCMus 1899–1913; ScU 1899+

Washington and Lee Law Review. Sc-SC 1939+

Washington Law Review [and State Bar Journal]. ScU 1938+

Washington Quarterly Magazine of Arts, Sciences, and Literature. ScU [mfm] 1823–24

Washington State College, Research Studies. ScCleU 1929+

Washington Theological Repertory and Churchman's Guide. ScU [mfm] 1819–26

Washington University Medical Alumni Quarterly. ScCM 1941–51

Wasp [Hudson, N. Y.]. ScU [mfm] (1802–3)

Watchman [New Haven, Conn.]. ScU [mfm] (1819)

Watchman-Examiner [Worcester and Boston, Mass.]. ScU [mfm] 1819–26

Water and Sewage Works [Municipal Utilities]. ScCleU (1930+); ScU (1930+)

Water-Cure Journal. ScU [mfm] 1845–62

Water Pollution Control Federation, Journal. ScU 1941+

Water Works [and Wastes Engineering]. ScCleU (1935+); ScU (1930+)

Watson's Magazine [Atlanta, Ga.]. ScU 1907–10, 1911–17

Watson's Magazine [New York]. ScU 1905–6

Wee Wisdom. ScRhP 1940+

Weekly Magazine of Original Essays, Fugitive Pieces, and Interesting Intelligence. ScU [mfm] 1798–99

Weekly Magazine, or Edinburgh Amusement. ScU [mfm] 1768–84

Weekly Monitor. ScU [mfm] (1804)

Weekly Monitor, Entertaining and Instructive. . . . ScU [mfm] (1817)

Weekly Museum. ScU [mfm] (1797)

Weekly Recorder [Chillicothe, Ohio]. ScU [mfm] 1814–21

Weekly Visitant [Salem, Mass.]. ScU [mfm] 1806

Weekly Visitor. ScU [mfm] 1810–11

Wellcome Tropical Research Laboratories, Report. ScCM 1904–11

Wesleyan Journal. ScNewb 1825–26
Wesleyan Methodist. ScCenW 1910+
Wesleyan Missionary. ScCenW 1927+
Wesleyan Repository. ScU [mfm] 1821–24
Wesleyan Young People's Journal. ScCenW 1936+
West American Scientist. ScCMus 1887–93
West China Union University, College of Medicine and Dentistry, Reprints. ScCM 1938–45
West Coast Druggist [and Western Pharmacy]. ScU (1929–31) 1940+
West Virginia Academy of Science, Proceedings. ScCleU (1934–55) 1956+
West Virginia Law Quarterly and the Bar [West Virginia Law Review]. ScU 1939+
West Virginia Medical Journal. ScCM (1915–28) 1930+
Western Academician and Journal of Education and Science [Cincinnati, Ohio]. ScU [mfm] 1837–38
Western Architect. ScCleU (1927–30)
Western Australia, Department of Agriculture, Journal. ScCleU 1924+
Western Christian Monitor [Chillicothe, Ohio]. ScU [mfm] 1816
Western Examiner [St. Louis, Mo.]. ScU [mfm] 1834–35
Western Farm Economics Association, Proceedings. ScCleU 1927+
Western Farmer and Gardener [Cincinnati, Ohio]. ScU [mfm] 1839–45
Western Gleaner [Pittsburgh, Pa.]. ScU [mfm] 1813–14
Western Journal and Civilian [St. Louis, Mo.]. ScU [mfm] 1848–56
Western Journal of Medical and Physical Sciences [Cincinnati, Ohio]. ScU [mfm] 1827–38
Western Journal of Medicine and Surgery [Louisville, Ky.]. ScU [mfm] 1840–55
Western Journal of Surgery, Obstetrics and Gynecology. ScCM (1930+)
Western Ladies' Casket [Connersville, Ind.]. ScU [mfm] (1824)
Western Law Journal [Cincinnati, Ohio]. ScU [mfm] 1843–53
Western Literary Journal and Monthly Review [Cincinnati, Ohio]. ScU [mfm] (1836–45)
Western Medical Times. ScCM (1919–31)
Western Messenger [Cincinnati, Ohio]. ScU [mfm] 1835–41

Western Minerva [Lexington, Ky.]. ScGF [mfm] (1820); ScU [mfm] (1820)

Western Missionary Magazine [Washington, Pa.]. ScU [mfm] 1803–5

Western Monthly Magazine and Literary Journal [Cincinnati, Ohio]. ScU [mfm] 1833–37

Western Monthly Review [Cincinnati, Ohio]. ScU [mfm] 1827–30

Western New York Baptist Magazine [Morrisville, N. Y.]. ScU [mfm] 1814–25

Western Ontario [University] Medical Journal. ScCM (1930+)

Western Quarterly Review [Cincinnati, Ohio]. ScU [mfm] (1849)

Western Reserve University School of Medicine, Clinical Bulletin. ScCM (1939–46)

Western Review [Columbus, Ohio]. ScU [mfm] (1846)

Western Review and Miscellaneous Magazine [Lexington, Ky.]. ScU [mfm] 1819–21

Western Society of Engineers, Journal. ScCleU (1929–44)

Western Society of Engineers [Chicago], Proceedings. ScCleU 1879–80

Westinghouse Engineer. ScCleU 1941–61; ScU 1941–61

Westminster Review. ScC (1824–85); ScCCit 1860–69; ScRhW 1824–1914; ScU (1824–1913)

Wheatsheaf. ScCleU (1929–36)

Whim. ScU [mfm] (1814)

Whitaker's [Southern] Magazine. ScGF (1850–52); ScU (1850–52)

Whitin Review. ScCleU (1933–55)

Wiener Klinische Wochenschrift. ScCM (1903–47)

Wildlife Abstracts. ScCleU 1935+

Wildlife Review. ScCleU 1935+

William and Mary Quarterly. ScCHis 1924+; ScU 1892+

Wilson Library Bulletin. ScCC 1929+; ScCCit 1926+; ScChar 1930+; ScCleU (1914–29) 1930+; ScClP 1929+; ScCMus 1896+; ScCoBe 1929+; ScCoR 1931–42; ScGaLi 1932+; ScGBj (1929–33) 1934+; ScGF (1919–26) 1927+; ScGrev 1934+; ScHCok (1918–25) 1926+; ScNewb 1935+; ScRhP 1935+; ScRhW 1929+; ScSpC 1932+; ScSpW 1929+; ScU 1929+

Winthrop College Alumnae News [Winthrop Alumnae Magazine]. ScRhW 1926+

Winthrop College Journal. ScRhW 1902–60; ScU (1902–45)

Winthrop Weekly News. ScRhW 1915–22

Wisconsin Academy of Sciences, Arts and Letters, Transactions. ScCMus 1870+

Wisconsin Bar Bulletin. ScU 1938+

Wisconsin Engineer. ScCleU (1928–50) 1951+

Wisconsin Law Review. Sc-SC 1926+; ScU 1930+

Wisconsin Medical Journal. ScCM (1919–25) 1926+

Wisconsin Natural History Society, Bulletin. ScCMus 1900–15

Witness. ScU [mfm] (1809)

Wofford College Journal. ScSpW 1889+; ScU (1893–1952)

Woman's Home Companion. ScLaD 1926–57; ScRhW 1922–57

Wonderful Magazine and Extraordinary Museum [Carlisle, Pa.]. ScU [mfm] 1808

Wood: Forestry, Marketing, Application [London]. ScCleU [mc] 1936–49

Wood Preserving News. ScCleU 1924+; ScU 1923+

Woods Schools, Child Research Clinic, Proceedings. ScCM (1937–59)

Wool and Cotton Reporter [American Wool and Cotton Reporter]. ScCleU 1906–8

Worcester Magazine. ScU [mfm] 1786–88

Words. ScU 1937–41

Workingman's Advocate. ScU [mfm] 1829–36, 1844–49

Works of the Learned or an Historical Account . . . of Books Newly Printed. ScU [mfm] 1691–92

World Dominion and the World Today. ScCoBi 1929–57; ScCoT 1941–57

World News and Views. ScU 1938–53

World Tomorrow. ScHCok 1927, 1929; ScRhW 1929–34

World Unity. ScSpC (1932–35)

World Youth Review. ScU [mfm] 1939

World's Work. ScCCit (1925–31); ScCleU (1903–32); ScClP 1913–32; ScCoR (1924–32); ScDarl 1920–31; ScFlor 1924–29; ScGaLi (1906–32); ScGF 1902–32; ScGrev 1916–32; ScGrew 1921–31; ScHCok 1900–32; ScLaD (1915) 1929; ScRhW 1900–32; ScSpC 1900–31; ScSpW 1903–32; ScU 1900–32

Writer. ScGF (1926–37) 1938+

Wyoming University, Publications. ScCleU 1922–59

X

X-Ray Technician. ScCM (1929–44) 1945+

Y

Yale Journal of Biology and Medicine. ScCM (1933) 1940+
Yale Law Review. ScU 1891+
Yale Literary Magazine. ScU [mfm] 1836–51
Yale Review. ScCC (1918–23) 1927+; ScCCit 1924–45, 1947+;
ScChar 1933+; ScCleU 1911+; ScClP 1926+; ScCoCo (1925+);
ScCoR 1933+; ScGaLi 1930+; ScGBj 1938+; ScGF 1911+; Sc-
Grev 1919+; ScHCok 1917+; ScNewb 1914+; ScOrSc 1934+;
ScRhW 1911+; ScSpC 1911+; ScSpW 1913+; ScU 1911+
Yale University, School of Forestry, Bulletin. ScCleU 1912+
Yankee and Boston Literary Gazette. ScGF (1829)
Yellow Book. ScCMus (1896–97); ScU 1894–97
Your Health. ScU (1939–40) 1947–59
Your Life. ScU (1939–40) 1943–45, 1947+
Youth's Cabinet [Utica, N. Y.]. ScU [mfm] (1815)
Youth's Repository of Christian Knowledge. ScU [mfm] (1813)
Y's Bird [University of South Carolina YMCA]. ScU (1928–42)

Z

Zeitschrift für Analytische Chemie. ScCleU 1912+
Zeitschrift für Angewandte Chemie [Angewandte Chemie]. ScU
1932–38, 1950+
Zeitschrift für Angewandte Mathematik und Mechanik. ScCleU
1921+
Zeitschrift für Anorganische und Allgemeine Chemie. ScCleU
1892+, some files on mc; ScU 1922–32, 1959+
Zeitschrift für Kotanik. ScCleU 1909+
Zeitschrift für Deutsches Altertum und Deutsche Litteratur. ScU
(1867+)
Zeitschrift für Diatetische und Physikalische Therapie. ScCM 1898–
1904
Zeitschrift für die Alttestamentliche Wissenschaft. ScCoT 1881+
Zeitschrift für Elektrochemie und Angewandte Physikalische
Chemie. ScU (1912–38) 1945+
Zeitschrift für Französische Sprache und Litteratur. ScU 1879+
Zeitschrift für Geburtschülfe und Gynäkologie. ScCM (1893–1900)
Zeitschrift für Kirchengeschichte. ScCoT 1924+
Zeitschrift für Pflanzenkrankheiten. ScCleU (1900+)
Zeitschrift für Physik. ScCleU 1940+; ScU 1920+

Zeitschrift für Physikalische Chemie [Leipzig]. ScCleU [mc] 1887+;
  ScU (1887+)

Zeitschrift für Romanische Philologie. ScU 1877+, library also has
  Bibliographie 1909–55, *Register* 1910–32, and *Supplement* 1878–
  1908

**Zeitschrift für Vergleichende Sprachforschung auf dem Gebiete des
  Deutschen, Griechischen und Lateinischen [der Indogermani-
  schen Sprachen].** ScU (1853–83)

Zeitschrift für Völkerpsychologie und Sprachwissenschaft. ScU 1860

Zeitschriften-Dienst. ScU 1840–44

**Zentralblatt für Kakteriologie, Parasitenkunde und Infektionskrank-
  heiten.** ScCleU (1900–4) 1941–45

Zentralblatt für Chirurgie. ScCM (1887–1937)

Zentralblatt für Gynäkologie. ScCM (1910–40)

Zentralblatt für Innere Medizin. ScCM (1882–1913)

Zentralblatt für Mathematik und Ihre Grenzbebiete. ScCleU 1931+;
  ScU 1931–48

Zentralblatt für Physiologie. ScCM (1903–19)

Zoe, a Biological Journal. ScCMus 1890–1900

Zoologica. ScCleU 1907+

Zoological Journal. ScCMus 1824–29

Zoological Miscellany. ScU 1814–17

Zoological Record. ScCleU 1864+; ScGF 1929–34, 1948–60; ScU
  1864+

Zoological Society, Proceedings. ScCMus 1833–1919, library also
  has the society's *Record* 1864–1916

Zwischen den Zeiten [Evangelische Theologie]. ScCoT [mfm] 1931–
  47

INDEX

The main (bold-face) entry for any given institution or organization that incorporates the name of a town in its title is not indexed here, for it can readily be found under the town's name in Part One. However all citations of such an institution or organization in places other than the main entry are indexed here. Extensive manuscript collections, e.g., those of the South Carolina Historical Society and the South Caroliniana Library, are handled in the same way: the entry for a given manuscript under these libraries is not indexed, but mentions of it elsewhere are. Subject areas (agriculture, music, etc.) and important data included in the descriptions under individual entries are always indexed. Random newspapers and some periodicals (especially files begun since 1941) are indexed here, but one should also look at the page references given below under "newspaper collections" and at the periodical listings in Part Two.

Caldwell family 110
Calhoun County 67, 170-1
Calhoun family 110
Calhoun, John C. 14, 84, 102; monument 73; *Papers* 65
Calhoun Times 170, 171
California 21, 83, 90, 101
Camden 67, 68, 73, 74, 78, 79, 81, 83, 84, 87, 91, 94, 95, 97, 99, 104, 106, 107, 111, 112, 116, 121, 136, 137
Camden Chronicle 87
Camden District 44, 111
Camden Journal 77
Camellia Journal 33
Camellian 33
Campbell, James B. 25
canals 25, 26, 80, 88
Cancer Wise 33
Cantey & Henry 12
Cantey, E. B. 116
Cantey family 106
Capers, Ellison 17
Carleton, Sir Guy 48
Carlisle, James H. 174
Carnegie Library [Sumter] 175; [Union] 176
Carolina Camellia Bulletin 168
Carolina Camellias 168
Carolina Christian 154
Carolina Cockpit 33
Carolina Confidential 34
Carolina Cooperator 180
Carolina Cotton Grower 180
Carolina Economist 153
Carolina Highways 34, 50
Carolina Kiwanian 180
Carolina Materials Project 52, 55-61
Carolina Museum 160
Carolina Messenger of Truth 153
Carolina Rifle Club 14, 25
Carolina Spartan 172, 173
Carolina Sportsman 145
Cash, William E. B. 81, 119
Castchen, Thomas 99
Catawba Indians 169; language 102
Catesby, Mark 16
Catholic Banner 14
Caughman 93
Ce-Be-Cean 34
Cedar Springs 73, 115
Cedar Springs Institute 91
Celanese Fibers Company 168
Central America 91
census returns 10, 27, 28, 43, 47, 169, 170
Ceramic Abstracts 165
Chandler, J. J. 104
Chapin Library 163
Chaplin family 87
Charleston 12, 47, 66, 67, 68, 69, 72,

73, 74, 76, 77, 79, 80, 81, 83, 84, 85, 86, 87, 88, 89, 90, 91, 92, 93, 94, 95, 96, 97, 98, 99, 100, 101, 102, 103, 104, 105, 106, 107, 108, 109, 110, 112, 113, 114, 115, 118, 119, 120, 121, 122, 123, 124, 125, 127, 128, 129, 130, 131, 133, 134, 135, 36, 137; Board of Police 174; *City Directories* 22; *Yearbooks* 51
Charleston Air Force Base 165
Charleston County 105, 124
Charleston Courier 43, 172
Charleston Naval Base 165
Charleston Southern Intelligencer 28
Charleston, W. Va. 135
Charlotte, N. C. 76; *Observer* 168
Charlottesville, Va. 69, 125
Chattanooga, Tenn. 92
Chaucer, Geoffrey 63
Checklist of South Carolina State Publications 34
Chemical Abstracts 13, 34, 165, 168, 175
Chemical Reviews 34
Chemische Berichte 165
Chemstrand 157; *Chemstrand-Greenwood* 31
Cheraw 81, 91, 94, 105, 108, 110, 118, 133
Cherokee County 151
Cherry Hill 104
Chesnut family 135
Chester 86, 90, 95, 97, 99, 103, 118, 121, 122, 134, 137
Chester Bulletin 140
Chester County [District] 68, 86, 88, 112, 126
Chester Reporter 160
Chesterfield 118, 133
Chesterfield County 99, 113, 119
Chestertown, Md. 120
Childs, Arney R. 93
Christian Action Council 35
Christian Church 79
Church of Christ 153
Citadel 17, 93, 135; *Alumni News* 13; *Brigadier* 14; *Monographs* 17; *Shako* 20
Civic Club [USC] 132
Civil War 17, 21, 23, 24, 25, 26, 27, 41, 42, 44, 45, 47, 51, 63, 67, 68, 69, 72, 73, 74, 76, 77, 78, 79, 81, 82, 84, 85, 86, 87, 88, 89, 90, 91, 92, 93, 94, 95, 98, 99, 100, 101, 102, 103, 104, 105, 106, 107, 109, 110, 112, 114, 118, 119, 120, 121, 122, 123, 124, 125, 126, 127, 128, 129, 130, 131, 133, 134, 135, 136, 137, 149, 158, 160, 163, 171
Civilian Defense 125